AFRICAN FRONTIERS

The Ashgate Plus Series in International Relations and Politics

The Ashgate Plus Series in International Relations and Politics is designed to provide a more intensive examination of a subject area. These longer more in-depth studies, containing original essays on innovative and emerging topics, allow authors to fully explore a research area and provides readers with a more inclusive treatment of the current research.

African Frontiers

Insurgency, Governance and Peacebuilding in Postcolonial States

Edited by

JOHN IDRISS LAHAI
TANYA LYONS
Flinders University, Australia

ASHGATE

Published by
Ashgate Publishing Limited
Wey Court East
Union Road
Farnham
Surrey, GU9 7PT
England

Ashgate Publishing Company
110 Cherry Street
Suite 3-1
Burlington, VT 05401-3818
USA

www.ashgate.com

British Library Cataloguing in Publication Data
A catalogue record for this book is available from the British Library.

Library of Congress Cataloging-in-Publication Data
African frontiers : insurgency, governance and peacebuilding in postcolonial states /
[edited] by John Idriss Lahai and Tanya Lyons.
    pages cm. – (Ashgate plus series in international relations and politics)
    Includes bibliographical references and index.
    ISBN 978-1-4724-6008-0 (hardback) – ISBN 978-1-4724-6009-7 (ebook) – ISBN 978-1-4724-6010-3 (epub)
    1. Conflict management--Africa. 2. Peace-building--Africa. 3. Insurgency--Africa. 4. Postcolonialism--Africa.
5. Nation-building--Africa. 6. Africa--Politics and government--1960– I. Lahai, John Idriss. II. Lyons,
Tanya.
    JZ5584.A35A365 2015
    303.6'6096–dc23
                                                                                    2015018449

ISBN: 9781472460080 (hbk)
ISBN: 9781472460097 (ebk – PDF)
ISBN: 9781472460103 (ebk – ePUB)

Printed in the United Kingdom by Henry Ling Limited,
at the Dorset Press, Dorchester, DT1 1HD

This book is dedicated to the mother of Dr John Idriss Lahai,
Chief Madam Fatou Yaya Kargbo (nee Konko-Kamara) (1954–2014),
and to all those who, like her, endure conflict and work for peace in Africa.

Contents

PART I: INSURGENCY AND GOVERNANCE

PART II: PEACEBUILDING

List of Tables and Boxes

Notes on Contributors

Daniel Egiegba Agbiboa is a doctoral candidate at the University of Oxford, Department of International Development. He holds an MPhil in Development Studies from the University of Cambridge, UK, and an MA in International Relations from the University of KwaZulu-Natal, South Africa. His research includes conflict transformation, security and development in sub-Saharan Africa. His works have appeared in several internationally refereed journals.

Mamadou Diouma Bah is a visiting research fellow in the Political Science and Public Policy Programme, the University of Waikato, New Zealand. He holds a PhD in Political Science from the University of Waikato. His research interests include mineral resource policy, identity politics, resilient peace, conflict transformation, regional security, and civil-military relations in transitional societies. Bah's recent publications on related issues have appeared in the *Australasian Review of African Studies* (2012), *Review of African Political Economy* (2014) and *Armed Forces & Society* (2015).

David John Duriesmith is a scholar of International Relations who focuses on critical security studies, intra-state conflict and masculinities. David completed his PhD at the University of Melbourne, Australia, focusing on new war, masculinity and patriarchy. In particular his research explores the issues of masculinity, age, class and ethnicity in civil conflict from a pro-feminist perspective. He has worked with the United Nations multi-programme agency Partners for Prevention on masculinities in Aceh Indonesia. David's work has been published in the *International Feminist Journal of Politics* and the *Australasian Review of African Studies*.

Isabelle Duyvesteyn is Special Chair in Strategic Studies at Leiden University and senior lecturer-researcher at the Department of History of International Relations, Utrecht University in the Netherlands. She completed her PhD at the Department of War Studies at King's College in London. Previously she has worked at the Royal Military Academy in the Netherlands and the Netherlands Institute for International Relations. Her recent publications include "The Determinants of the Continuation of Civil War," in Edward Newman and Karl DeRouen (eds), *The Routledge Handbook of Civil Wars* (London: Routledge 2014); and with Esther Visser, "The Irrelevance of the Security Dilemma for Civil Wars," *Civil Wars*, 16 (1), 2014: 65–85.

Georg Frerks holds a Chair in Conflict Prevention and Conflict Management at Utrecht University and a Chair in International Security Studies at the Netherlands Defence Academy. He held the chair of Disaster Studies at Wageningen University, the Netherlands until mid-2014. Frerks served for nearly 20 years in the Dutch Foreign Service both at headquarters and abroad. He also was head of the Conflict Research Unit of the Netherlands Institute of International Relations 'Clingendael.' Frerks focuses on conflict and disaster-induced vulnerabilities and local responses as well as on international and national policies and interventions. He also works on the topic of gender and conflict. Frerks has co-authored or co-edited 15 academic books, over 60 journal articles and book chapters, and 70 policy reports and monographs on conflict and disaster-related topics. He has published extensively on the tsunami and conflict in Sri Lanka.

Boukje Kistemaker is a researcher at the Centre for Conflict Studies at Utrecht University. Boukje graduated from the MA Conflict Studies and Human Rights at Utrecht University, in which she focused on the conflict transformative qualities of urban destruction. Her research interests include private- and non-state actor governance, conflict urbanism, and risk management in complex emergencies. Her publications include *All Quiet on the Bahraini Front?* (July 2013) and *Palestinians as 'Strategic' Refugees* (October 2013) for the European Union Institute of Security Studies; and *Dealing with Culture and Education in Emergencies* (March 2013) for the Institute of Developing Economies of the Japan External Trade Organization.

John Idriss Lahai is a Visiting Research Scholar at Flinders University, South Australia. He was awarded his PhD at the University of New England, Australia. Much of Dr Lahai's research and applied work has investigated the experiences of vulnerable groups on the margins of society; the impact of armed conflicts on governance and peacebuilding; and, insurgent groups and the political economy of war, seeking to integrate perspectives from political science, international relations, strategic studies, peace and conflict studies, anthropology, African studies, gender studies, international law and human rights.

Tanya Lyons is the President of the African Studies Association of Australasia and the Pacific, the Editor of the *Australasian Review of African Studies*, and a Senior Lecturer who specializes in teaching African Political History at Flinders University. She has co-edited the books *New Engagement: Contemporary Australian Foreign Policy Toward Africa* (with David Mickler, Melbourne University Press, 2013); *South Sudanese Diaspora in Australia and New Zealand: Reconciling the Past with the Present* (with Jay Marlowe and Anne Harris, Cambridge Scholars Press, 2013), and *Africa on a Global Stage* (with Gerry Pye, Africa World Press, 2006). Tanya Lyons has also written chapters on "Australian Foreign Policy Toward Africa" (Oxford University Press, 2012) and "The State of African Studies in Australia" (with Elizabeth Dimock, CODESRIA, 2007). She is the author of *Guns and Guerrilla Girls: Women in the Zimbabwean Liberation Struggle* (Africa World Press, 2004).

Mbekezeli Comfort Mkhize is a Researcher at the Centre for Military Studies, Faculty of Military Science, University of Stellenbosch, South Africa. He is also currently a PhD candidate at the University of KwaZulu-Natal, and holds two Masters Degrees in political science, and community development studies. Mkhize has been both a Research Assistant and Field Supervisor, and has participated in international and national conferences. His research interests include social movements; service delivery protests; conflicts in Africa; politics of transitional governments; and police brutality.

Paul Munro is a Lecturer in Environmental Humanities at the University of New South Wales in Australia. His research is situated within the fields of political ecology, environmental history and human geography, with a particular interest in society-environmental relations and how they change through time. He has carried out extensive field research on environment and development issues in Africa, with funding from the European Union, the United Nations Food and Agricultural Organization, USAID and the United Kingdom's Department for International Development. Outside of Africa, he has also been involved in research projects on mining conflicts (in Australia) and water governance (in Mexico).

Oscar Gakuo Mwangi is Associate Professor of Political Science at the Department of Political and Administrative Studies, National University of Lesotho, Roma, Lesotho, and holds a PhD from Rhodes University, Grahamstown, South Africa. He has several published book chapters as well as articles in internationally refereed journals. He has also taught in the Department of Political Science and Public Administration, University of Nairobi and Department of Social Sciences, Catholic University of Eastern Africa, and the National Defence College and Defence Staff College in Kenya. Mwangi has also served as a research consultant for the International Institute for Democracy and Electoral Assistance and the United Nations Development Programme.

Kialee Nyiayaana is a Lecturer in the Department of History and Diplomatic Studies, University of Port Harcourt, Nigeria, and he is currently an African Leadership Centre's Fellow at the Centre of Criminology, University of Cape Town, South Africa. Nyiayaana was a 2008/2009 Junior Fulbright Scholar at the Department of Conflict Analysis and Resolution, Graduate School of Humanities and Social Sciences, Nova Southeastern University, Florida. He has published in the journal *African Security* and his area of specialization includes small arms proliferation, conflict resolution, security, leadership and peacebuilding.

Saira Bano Orakzai is currently a Research Fellow and Adjunct Lecturer at the Asia Pacific Centre, and completed her PhD, in 2013, at the University of New England, Australia. Saira was and Australia Award Scholar between 2009–2013, and a Charles Wallace Trust fellow 2014–2015 at the School of Advanced

Studies, University of London. She was also an Initiative of Change—Caux Scholar in 2010. Her research focusses on conflict transformation and resolution techniques; approaches to peacebuilding in various conflict zones; peacebuilding and conflict transformation in Islam; and fragile states and religious-cultural approaches to peacebuilding.

Nora Stel is a Research Fellow at Maastricht School of Management and a PhD candidate at Utrecht University's Centre for Conflict Studies. She is an affiliated scholar at the American University of Beirut's Issam Fares Institute for Public Policy and Foreign Affairs. Nora holds a BA in Political History and a *cum laude* MA in Conflict Studies and Human Rights. Her PhD research explores the interaction between Palestinian and Lebanese authorities in informal Palestinian settlements in South Lebanon. Nora has published in *Mediterranean Politics, Middle East Policy, Africa Spectrum, European Journal of Development Research, Journal of Developmental Entrepreneurship* and *Contemporary Readings of Law and Social Justice*.

Niels Terpstra is a researcher at the Centre for Conflict Studies at Utrecht University and Research Fellow at the Cooperation for Peace and Unity in Kabul. He graduated *cum laude* from the MA Conflict Studies and Human Rights at Utrecht University. His research interests include the nature of state and non-state governance in the developing world as well as policies of peace- and state-building at the national and international level. His publications include *The Dynamics of Justice Provision in the Context of Irregular Warfare and Legal Pluralism* (September 2013) and *What the New Deal can Learn from the Human Security Approach* (May 2014).

Noel Twagiramungu holds a PhD from The Fletcher School at Tufts University and an LLM from Utrecht University. A former fellow at Harvard University, Noel is a Visiting Assistant Professor of International Relations at the University of Massachusetts Lowell, and a post-doctorate Research Fellow at the World Peace Foundation. He previously taught at the University of Dar es Salaam and Smith College. A contributor to Oxford bibliographies online; a peer-reviewer for several scholarly journals; and winner of the 2011 African Studies Association's Best Graduate Paper Prize; his publications include a dissertation on variation in the transition from genocidal violence to rebel governance in Rwanda and Burundi, and two co-edited books, *Supporting the Post-conflict Transition in Rwanda: The Role of the International Community*, and *Cyiza Un Homme Libre au Rwanda*. His forthcoming works include a project on the endgame of mass atrocities, a Historical Dictionary of Burundi, and a co-edited volume on liberation movements in power in Africa.

Greg van der Horst is completing his PhD in Resource Management and Geography at the University of Melbourne, Australia. Greg's research is informed by a wide range of influences including Ecology, Political Ecology, Political Geography, Anthropology and Science and Technology Studies. Broadly speaking, his research focuses on the dynamics and evolution of human-environmental relationships and practices, as well as the (frequent) tensions between environmental narratives and ecological theory and data. Working predominantly in the field, he has conducted a variety of studies across sub-Saharan Africa on topics ranging from urbanization and fuelwood use in Botswana to satellite image analysis of land-cover change in Sierra Leone.

Foreword
The Urgency of Peace, The Insurgency of Hope, and the Potency of Knowledge

Toyin Falola

Drs John Idriss Lahai and Tanya Lyons have combined to edit a powerful book on the intersections of peace, conflict, conflict mediation, and governance. The muscularity of war and the patriarchy of violence are exposed in the agonizing brutal practices of insurgencies, complicated by the failure of governance and weak peace-building institutions. At once a study on war and leadership, *African Frontiers* is a study from above; but it is also a study of the consequences of war on the poor, women, and the marginalized, thus making it a study from below. *African Frontiers'* coverage is expansive, including but not limited to political and security issues, economic and environmental dimensions, and national and international politics.

That the subjects of war and peace are important cannot be overstated. Africa has seen wars between nations, civil wars, domestic insurgencies, riots, conflicts, and serious violence, all within the context of leadership crises. Colonial wars had seen invasions by outsiders, while Africans were drafted to serve both in the First and Second World Wars. All regions have been affected, and most countries have experienced one form of war or another. An entire intellectual industry has also been devoted to analyzing the causes of these various violent conflicts, usually blamed on ethnicity, religious divisions, poverty, struggles over strategic minerals, and/or the failure of democratic institutions. *African Frontiers* reviews these factors and their ideological underpinnings.

Critical chapters in *African Frontiers* focus on the hot spots—Uganda, Rwanda, Darfur, Somalia, Nigeria, Guinea, Sierra Leone, Libya, South Sudan, and the Congo. Well-written chapters also examine a number of core themes: peace mediation, governance, principles of reconciliation, war-avoidance strategies, state responses, along with the responsibilities and actions of international agencies and networks. As well, there are compelling ideas in this highly readable book around theories and practices of peace and war, activities of war leaders, economic underpinnings, historical legacies, and future scenarios.

The reality presented in the book is sometimes depressing: some states had previously collapsed; some had engaged in long wars; and many continue to witness conflicts of an ethnic and religious nature. Details of many of these conflicts and wars are offered in *African Frontiers*. However, more important are the details around human survival, dignity, and adjustments. The book narrates the struggles to overcome wars and to rebuild communities.

The tension and transition between crises and hope, conflicts and peace, give rise to the notion of a *frontier*, not in terms of geographic space and movement that have traditionally defined this concept in the literature, but by challenges posed by contemporary problems. Thus, the editors redefine the meaning of a *frontier* within the trajectories of impediments and hope.

This *frontier of problems* requires an explanation, which the editors carefully undertake in their competent introduction, with cogent emphasis on the colonial origins and postcolonial mismanagement of nation states and their resources. Similarly, a review of previous positions by different writers supplies an intellectual foundation for the contributors to *African Frontiers* both to build upon and to query.

In breaking down the elements in the *frontier* there is the trajectory of *warscapes*, with several essays on armed insurgencies and specific case studies. At the roots of the conflicts are the propelling insurgent forces of religious and ethnic identities, opportunistic calculations, and ambitions for resource control. The consequences of wars and conflicts are substantial, and the volume calls attention to sexual and gender-based violence among other forms that have been ignored.

There is the second trajectory of *peacescapes*, the policies that are always crafted to ensure peace, via economic development, and political stability via the agency of democracy. The book examines the role of peace-centric organizations such as the African Union, the United Nations, as well as development-oriented policies to minimize conflicts.

All in all, there are two planks of elaboration in *African Frontiers*. The first is that the book succeeds in analyzing the origins and consequences of wars. The second is to plug the narratives of conflicts into the epistemology of wars, thereby fusing realities with theories. In this careful fusion, local events become connected with global forces; and international actors impact local characters, as conflicts become embedded in their geographic context, geo-political realities, and knowledge formation.

African Frontiers offers significant answers to a variety of questions on the causes, courses, and consequences of postcolonial wars, the role of peacebuilding institutions, the knowledge about conflicts, and the role of local and global actors. Our knowledge is extended and enriched on such issues as insurgent formations and groups, warlords and rebel governance, terrorism, arms, and the military.

The humanistic thread in *African Frontiers* is one of ensuring peace and stability in Africa. The ideas in the book preach rationality, and they vehemently oppose beliefs and ideas that are counter-intuitive and counter-productive. Indeed, the emphasis, as the editors argue, should be on how people in troubled areas respond to war memories, rebuild their lives and communities, and generate collective responsibilities to live in peace and envision new possibilities.

For reassuring us that we all can live in peace, *African Frontiers* merits our praise. For seeking measures to enhance good living, the book attracts our commendation. In the years ahead, we can hope that as democratic forces are consolidated; as various groups learn to engage in political bargaining; as the economy becomes more and more diversified; as the scale of corruption reduces; and as opportunities expand for entrepreneurial initiatives, the forces of division will decrease, dialogue will take over from violence, and peace will become the core value that all political actors will be committed to promoting. Warriors will hopefully become sharecroppers, and the definitive marker of the African frontier will be that of *Africa Rising*.
Peace!

Toyin Falola
President, African Studies Association,
Jacob and Frances Sanger Mossiker Chair in the Humanities, and
University Distinguished Teaching Professor, The University of Texas at Austin

Acknowledgements

The editors would like to acknowledge the enthusiasm and support from contributing authors; and the African Studies Association of Australasia and the Pacific—AFSAAP—which hosted a workshop for some of the authors and their chapters published here. We thank Flinders University for hosting Dr John Idriss Lahai as a Visiting Research Fellow in the School of International Studies. Dr John Idriss Lahai would like to thank his immediate family members and Reverend Kaye Collier, for their selfless sacrifices and encouragement that has enabled him to continue his research activities. Dr Tanya Lyons would like to thank Rob, Harry and Tom for their ongoing support for her research in African Studies.

List of Abbreviations

AFDL	Alliance of Democratic Forces for the Liberation of Congo – *Alliance des Forces Démocratiques pour la Libération du Congo*
AFRC	Armed Forces Revolutionary Council
AFRICOM	United States Africa Command
AL	Arab League
AMIS	African Union Mission in Sudan
AMISOM	African Union Mission in Somalia
ANPP	All Nigeria Peoples Party
APC	All Peoples' Congress
AQIM	Al-Qaeda in the Islamic Maghreb
ASWJ	*Ahlu Sunna Wal Jama'a*
AU	African Union
BBC	British Broadcasting Corporation
CANS	Civil Authority of the New Sudan
CAR	Central African Republic
CSM	Chain Saw Milling
DDR	Disarmament, Demobilization and Reintegration
DRC	Democratic Republic of Congo
ECOMOG	Economic Community of West African States Military Observer Group
ECOWAS	Economic Community of West African States
EITI	Extractive Industries Transparency Initiative
EO	Executive Outcomes
EU	European Union
EWRRC	Early Warning and Rapid Response Cell
FAO	UN Food and Agricultural Organization
FARDC	Armed Forces of the Democratic Republic of Congo
FDLR	Rwandan *Democratic Forces for the Liberation of Rwanda*
FGS	Federal Government of Somalia
FIB	Force Intervention Brigade
FIC	Forest Industries Corporation Sierra Leone
FLEGT	Forest Law Enforcement, Governance and Trade
FRELIMO	Frente de Liberatacao de Mozambique
FRONASA	Front for National Salvation
GFG	Global Forest Governance
GMR	Great Man-Made River
GNC	General National Congress
GoS	Government of Sudan
HIV/AIDS	Human Immunodeficiency Virus/Acquired Immune Deficiency Syndrome
HRW	Human Rights Watch
ICC	International Criminal Court
ICD	Inter-Congolese Dialogue
ICID	International Commission of Inquiry on Darfur
ICJ	International Court of Justice
ICLGR	International Conference on the Great Lakes Region
ICTRP	International Coalition for the Responsibility to Protect

IDP	Internally Displaced People
IGAD	Intergovernmental Authority on Development
IMF	International Monetary Fund
INEC	Nigerian Independent Electoral Commission
IRIN	Integrated Regional Information Networks
JCET	Joint Combined Exchange Training Program
JEM	Justice and Equality Movement
JMC	Joint Military Commission
JTF	Joint Military Task Force
JTORO	Joint Task Operation Restore Order
KDF	Kenya Defence Forces
LGTB	Lesbian, Gay, Trans-gender and Bisexual
LNA	Libyan National Army LNA
LPNM	Libyan Popular National movement
LRA	Lord's Resistance Army
LURD	Liberians United for Reconciliation and Democracy
M23	March 23 Movement
MENA	Middle East and North Africa
MEND	Movement for the Emancipation of the Niger Delta
MODEL	Movement for Democracy in Liberia
MONUC	The United Nations Mission in the Democratic Republic of Congo—*Mission de l'Organisation des Nations Unies en Republique Democratique du Congo*
MONUSCO	The United Nations Stabilisation Mission in the Democratic Republic of the Congo —*Mission de l'Organisation des Nations unies pour la stabilisation en République démocratique du Congo*
MOSOP	Movement for the Survival of the Ogoni People
MPLA	Marxist Popular Movement for the Liberation of Angola
MSF	*Medicine San Frontiers*/Doctors without Borders
NATO	North Atlantic Treaty Organization
NESG	Nigerian Economic Summit Group
NGO	Non-governmental organization
NIF	National Islamic Front
NNDC	Niger Delta Development Commission
NPFL	National Patriotic Front of Liberia
NPRC	National Provisional Ruling Council
NRA	National Resistance Army
NRM	National Resistance Movement
NSAG	Non-State Armed Group
NSS	National Stabilisation Strategy
NTC	National Transitional Council
OECD	Organisation for Economic Development and Cooperation
ONLF	Ogaden National Liberation Front
OPC	O'odua People's Congress
PAGE	Promoting Agriculture, Governance and the Environment
PLO	Palestinian Liberation Organization
PRP	*Party du Renouveau et Progrès*
PUP	*Parti de l'Unité et du Progrès*
RCD	Congolese Rally for Democracy
RPF	Rwandan Patriotic Front
RPG	*Rassemblement du Peuple de Guinee*
RtoP	Responsibility to Protect
RUF	Revolutionary United Front

RUF-SL	Revolutionary United Front of Sierra Leone
SC	Security Council
SCS	Supreme Council of State
SCSL	Special Court of Sierra Leone
SILETI	Sierra Leone Timber Industries
SLA	Sudan Liberation Army
SLF	Sudan Liberation Front
SLPP	Sierra Leone Peoples Party
SLTRC	Sierra Leone Truth and Reconciliation Commission
SNA	Somali National Army
SoFA	Status of Forces Agreements
SPLA	Sudan People's Liberation Army
SPLM	Sudan People's Liberation Movement
SPLM/A	Sudan People's Liberation Movement/Army
SSHRC	Social Sciences and Humanities Research Council
SSR	Security Sector Reform
START	Study of Terrorism and Responses to Terrorism
TFG	Transitional Federal Government
UAE	United Arab Emirates
UASF	University African Students' Front
UIC	Union of Islamic Courts
UN	United Nations
UNAMID	African Union–United Nations Hybrid Operation in Darfur
UNDP	United Nations Development Programme
UNHCR	United Nations High Commissioner for Refugees
UNITA	National Union for the Total Independence of Angola
UNITAF	Unified Task Force
UNOSOM	United Nations Operation in Somalia
UNPBF	United Nations Peacebuilding Fund
UNPP	United National People's Party
UNR	*Union pour la Nouvelle République*
UN-REDD+	United Nations' Reducing Emissions from Deforestation and Forest Degradation
UNSC	United Nation's Security Council
UPDF	Uganda People's Defence Force
US	United States [of America]
USSR	Union of Soviet Socialist Republics
WSB	West Side Boys

PART I
Insurgency and Governance

Chapter 1
Understanding Postcolonial African Frontiers: History, Theory, Policy and Practice

John Idriss Lahai and Tanya Lyons

Introduction

Not by natural selection, but through human endeavors, Africa is a continent where states have collapsed (Zartman 1995), internecine wars have been fought (see Nhema and Zeleza 2008a; Zack-Williams, Frost and Thomson 2002; Kaplan 1994), inter-generational and inter-community/country relationships have broken, people's dignities and identities have, and are still being violated through politically motivated and culturally induced violence in peace and in wartimes (Turshen and Twagiramariya 1998; Meintjes et al. 2001). However, it has been people's individual and collective desires for peace and progress that have enabled them to endeavor to rebuild their lives, amid the depravity that surrounds them (Doyle and Sambanis 2006). In the processes of rebuilding their lives and communities, and depending on their collective or individual circumstances, people have had to give up some of their beliefs and practices that were a priori aiding them to politically and socially navigate the continent's perilous environment. Traditions have to be compromised, social and political systems modified for the assimilation of new thought processes, even if they run contrary to their long-held beliefs (Mudimbe 1994; Mudimbe 1988); and people's national identities have to be adjusted to give meaning to the concepts of westernization and modernization, and the corresponding geo-political processes that always accompany the international community's conflict management and post-conflict national reconstruction and recovery policies in Africa (Nhema and Zeleza 2008b).

What is interesting amid all of these complex internal changes is the fact that in postcolonial Africa destitution has led to desperation, and desperation has contributed to the blending of hitherto contending social and political systems, complex beliefs and competing societal values. One example is the fluid assimilation of competing micro/meso political ideologies and cultural value systems and economic doctrines to understand not just the people, for/against whom wars are being fought, and by whom peacebuilding intervention measures are adopted, but the very nature and processes surrounding the problems affecting the continent. The positioning of Africa within the international political economy and human rights architecture reveals that the continent is still a frontier with many problems, as well as the potentials for peace and development.

Unfortunately, the festering attempts by competing schools of thoughts to understand issues of insurgency, governance and peacebuilding within their theoretical boundaries—amid epistemological possibilities in proffering a lasting solution—have led to instances where the less known methods of peace activism have been relegated to the backburner. To the Eurocentric schools of thought, the persistency of war and underdevelopment are as a result of the lack of political will to accept the legitimating values of political (neo-) liberalism (see Hirshleifer 1991; Taylor and Williams 2004). For their part, Pan-Africanist scholars believe that Africa is merely a frontier whose problems have created the space necessary for the experimentation of the political, cultural and economic ideals and ideas of Western liberal states—whose true intentions for peace in the continent are somewhat shrouded in self-serving political and economic interests (Mudimbe 1994). As such, Africa's political institutions and social systems, which have been the mainstay for the resolution of the continent's problems, have been rendered ineffective. Interestingly, however, while some have come to accept this political order, others have not. Wars, for many of the insurgents and rebel groups that transverse the continent, are a form of political critique of this liberal order, as both Agbiboa's and Duyvesteyn et al.'s contributions to this volume attest to. It is this resistance that has created the dais for the emergence of a constituent power-base for the penetration of political narratives into what should be mediated by morality, and guided by the apolitical convictions that peace is a permanent human condition.

Throughout the social histories of the countless communities across the African continent, there is an overriding order of knowledge over Africa's country-specific internal problems. In practice however, these epistemologies, developed mostly within a Eurocentric theoretical praxis, have made it difficult to comprehend these realities. Thus, rather than relying on essentialist theoretical framing, it is important that, when writing about the implications of insurgencies (i.e. both historical and new wars) on governance and (grassroots) peacebuilding activities, the focus of analysis should be on whether the transition from wars to peace, and from fragility to development creates opportunities for the emergence of an intermediate space for people to collectivize their individualized memories of war, and transform their social circumstances into agentive possibilities for the accentuation of an African alternative to the future of the continent.

The Postcolonial States: Towards an Anthropocentric Intellectual History

After most African countries achieved political independence in the 1960s and 1970s, several attempts were made, from both policy and epistemological cycles, to understand and provide lasting solutions to the endemic insurgent-related challenges. One of the earliest theoretical attempts to understand these postcolonial states is Robert D. Kaplan's (1994) seminal work *The Coming Anarchy*. In this work, he uncomfortably fuses together Martin van Creveld's (1991) thesis about the nature of the post-Cold War conflicts that are instigated by state actors and fought by non-state actors: guerrilla armies, terrorists, and mercenaries with different goals, and through either the most primitive or sophisticated weapons; Thomas Homer-Dixon's (1991) pessimistic analysis of how the terrestrial, atmospheric, and aquatic environmental pressures: such as global warming, o-zone depletion, and loss of tropical forest and marine life, have shaped the nature of low and high intensity conflicts after the Cold War; Samuel P. Huntington's (1993) thesis on the pending violent clash of cultures, and the western media's interpretation of questions of ethnic rivalry, to describe the "uncivil" nature of civil wars that are being fought in Africa, with the potential of not only destroying the social fabric of society, but also in taking Africans back to their Hobbesian state of nature—characterized by corporeal barbarity, innate cruelty and utter cannibalistic trepidation (also see Kaplan 2001).

To better understand the controversial nuances in Kaplan's understanding of the postcolonial states and the people found within them—that is, understanding that until recently, they guided the processes of the international community's engagement in the troubled spots of the continent, we must veer into the idea of the African "political man [*sic*]," herein referred to as the African "political person" with the corresponding effect of "place" (the community and society) on the psychology, sociology, politics, and economics on them. According to this idea, as noted in many paleontological studies (see Condemi and Weniger 2011), this "political person" was born in Sub-Saharan Africa, then their antediluvian generation migrated north of the Sahara and into what become the ancient Pharaohnic Egyptian empire in the Nile, and through the Gaza Strip into the Middle East, and then into Europe, Asia and the Americas. However, or course, some never left, and after the sacking of the Pharaohnic Egyptian Empire, some returned and resettled in Sub-Saharan Africa. Those who never left, and those who returned to the protective ambits of the dense tropical rainforest communities of Sub-Saharan Africa, were morphed into being hunter-gathers. The abundance of "nature's own" in the forest meant that tropical food could easily be gathered—at least before civil wars and the chaotic demographic shifts that ensured due to conflicts, the engendering of communal relationships, deforestation, famine and drought. The relatively stable climate, with almost no recorded extremes of floods and hurricanes meant that people would need not plan ahead for the next season. No need to store food for the winter season, as in the temperate and cold climates of Europe and North America.

Then came European colonialism into these vast territories, and soon afterwards, the people of Africa were pushed into the whirlpool of western modernity (Palmberg 2001), not on their own terms but on those set and regulated by the core states in the West (Pakenham 1991; Wai 2012; Duffield and Hewitt 2009; Mehta 1999). New thoughts, within the vastly expanded science and technology fields, spurred by the industrial revolution, soon emerged (Hobsbawm 1999). Then, after independence in the 1960s and 1970s, equipped with standardized western formal education and modern existentialist thoughts, the African political person—usually a man—took over the reins of government in their newly independent countries. At first, it appears independence would bring peace and security, and the building of a governance structure that would emphasize the equitable distribution of the economic goods, and political power. However, soon after independence, the blame-game (against colonial rule and against the internal political others, such as the opposition) started and the path of progress was replaced by a bush path to the destruction of the continent.

Of course, colonial rule is not without its own criticism, beyond the political narratives that link the origins of war and bad governance with colonial rule (see Mamdani 1996; Wai 2012), there are also many other socio-poetic commentaries on the forced conversion and subjugation of the political will of the Africans to the grand imperial project of the West. David Diop (1967, quoted in Okunoye 2007: 125) argued that prior to the 1950s:

> civilization (colonial rule) kicked [Africans on] the face ... and holy water (Christianity) slapped [their] cringing brows. [The colonial governments] built in the shadow of their talons the blood stained monument of tutelage. [...] there was painful laughter on the metallic hell of the road. And the monotonous rhythm of the paternoster drowned the howling on the plantations (where Africans were working as slaves). O!! The bitter memories of extorted kisses; of a promise broken at the point of a gun. Of foreigners who did not seem human; who know all the books but did not know love. But [the Africans] whose hands fertilize the womb of the earth in spite of your songs of pride. In spite of the dissolute villages of torn Africa, hope was preserved in us as in a fortress; And from the Mines of Swaziland to the factories of Europe, spring [hope] will be reborn under [their] bright steps.

David Diop was motivated by the question of what good the colonizers, and their talk of liberating Africa was, if the so-called liberated people of Africa do not have ownership of the reins of government. The elegiac message that he hoped will be accepted by the people in these postcolonial states, has as its foci the intrusive ills of European domination of Africa and its resultant effect, neo-liberal political interventions in the postcolonial states. It tells of how a people, doomed by western colonialism, are hopeful that one day they will be free.

Indeed that dream came to an end in the 1990s for much of Sub-Saharan Africa. However, despite the remodeling of the pre-colonial institutions that led to the systematic demystification of traditional authorities, who controlled grassroots war and peace activism (see Mamdani 1996), colonial rule had its own positive impacts, not least in bringing the continent into the international community of states; a community whose agenda is to promote international peace and security through the liberal political ideas and ideals. As such, whilst Diop's poetic narrative offers a sense of literal optimism, the incidences of insurgent wars in the continent show that independence offers at best a charade of a dream long lost, and at worst exposes the unpreparedness of the political person to govern their postcolonial state in ways that would prevent war and promote peace.

After many decades of political independence many of the states in Sub-Saharan Africa keep stumbling, which leads the international community to realize that the confidence in the post-independent politicians that would have spurred them to provide an all-rounded leadership for their independent states has, so far, being an illusion.

The essence of being independent was not only lost, what emerged afterwards in these so-called postcolonial African states is a predatory style of governance regulated by a political and military elite class that is good at using what Jean Francois Bayart (2009) has referred to as the "politics of the belly" (*la politique du ventre*) to create a state of exotic aberration in which a postcolonial political patronage system of governance, which enables the patrons (the [un]-elected governors) to subject their clientele (the masses) to political oppression in ways that made them subservient to the political leadership, and to beg for what should be their entitlement, food. Thus, while at the helm of politics as both Lahai and Lyons, and Twagiramungu describe in this volume, these predatory political and/or military elites, and their machine gun wielding supporters and foot soldiers (see Boas and Dunn 2007) are more inclined to prey on the state with wonton abandon. Despite their supposedly enlightened first-hand knowledge about the colonial struggles, they would take a chance on that which is cynical and what they can prey on: i.e. the public and private sector goods in an already dysfunctional political and economic system (Zack-Williams, Frost and Thomson 2002). The political elites appear to be recklessly despoiling the continent for their people, who have been caught in the web of *the Politics of the Belly*.

This is not to say that the postcolonial states have not made efforts to turn their situations around. After the 1970s, efforts were made to build what Crawford Young (2012: 55) referred to as an *integral state* system.

This system, he argues, was spurred by the intellectual belief that economic centralization, fiscal control and intervention and direct government authority would help mitigate Africa's economic miseries. However, a lack of pluralism within the postcolonial political structures led to political disorder and economic stagnation (see also Chrétien 2003). By the end of the 1970s, this integral model of governance was no longer working. As a result of over-population, demographic shift and greed, the level of consumption increased to unsustainable levels. In Wodemariam's (2013) purview, the problems that resulted out of these postcolonial efforts were exacerbated by the neo-patrimonial logic of governance. In line with this logic, governance is not about fulfilling the aspirations of their people, but their neo-patrimonial connections with external interests. As market distortions and corruption increased, the suppression of dissenting opinions became the adhesive that glued the governing elites to their network of financiers (originating from either the Middle East for example Lebanon and Syria; Eastern European for example Russia; and the western democracies. As a consequence, growth rates plunged, state institutions began to disintegrate, and political turmoil engulfed the continent. By the 1980s, the African crunch was in full swing, and no externally induced economic reform would succeed in removing the continent out of this quagmire—a situation that led to the emergence of junta governments and insurgent movements (see Howe 2001).

These aforementioned problems, compounded with the persistent violent ethnic relations and state sanctioned gender-based violence for example, shows why all attempts to promote development and political stability in much of postcolonial Africa has proven to be elusive (Bayart, Ellis and Hibou 1999). Therefore, in Eurocentric terms (understood within the theoretical limits of Kaplan's *Coming Anarchy*), the inability of the political person to prevent the incidences of politically motivated violence and underdevelopment have not only led to a permanent state of dependency, but it has also led to the acceptance of the imperfections of inequalities as a permanent identifier of the postcolonial states in the continent. Despite the criticisms, the nature of the modern forms of inter-state relations within the continent; and between individual African countries and the international community, have also led to instances of instability. The re-ordering of the global political and economic systems, have also contributed to the non-recognition of some of the continent's internal processes to political maturation, and in turn it has also reinforced the marginal otherness of African states.

To prevent a situation where this otherness would compromise their political relevance, African countries created for themselves several security-centric integrated bloc systems, such as the 2002 reformation of the Organization of African Unity (OAU) into the African Union (AU), as well as East Africa's Intergovernmental Authority Development (IGAD), West Africa's Economic Community of West African States (ECOWAS), and Southern Africa's Development Community (SADC). Their resolve to provide political and economic alternatives to peace, security and economic development will, however, only prove to be insufficient if they cannot rise above the challenges faced on their African frontiers (see de Waal 2002).

What can the so-called neo-liberal future do for the postcolonial states of Africa? Should the international community be responsible for all of the investments in time, resources and energy into all of the relevant sectors (public and private) in ways that would project a sense of hope into a future of uncertainties? Is a new Africa possible?

The Warscapes: Typologies of Armed Insurgencies and their Internal Dynamics

The spread of civil wars across independent African states has left millions dead, many more injured, and even more displaced internally or forced to flee as refugees. Francis (2006) has referred to this as the "continent's new menace." The implication of this menace has been the persistent underdevelopment of the continent. Wars, no matter the typology, do not create the level of stability needed to promote political and economic development (Nitzen and Bichler 2004), let alone allow space for the mitigation of environmental problems (Homer-Dixon 1999). Despite the reduction in the number of countries in civil wars since the 2000s (see Elbadawi and Sambanis 2002; Collier and Sambanis 2005), the internal political and cultural dynamics of Africa's countries in transition, are indicative that there remains a greater possibility for wars to re-emerge within two decades after political peace deals have been reached between factions—even where they received the legal and political backing of the international community (Francis 2008).

Based upon qualitative data that show variations and similarities in the contextual conditions of Africa's conflicts, the chapters on insurgency by Lahai and Lyons, Lahai, Mwangi, and Agbiboa, presented in this volume identify and discuss the nature and character of wars and how the internal dynamics of rebel groups (understood broadly to include former rebel groups that have been transformed into political parties and have since formed part of government) have affected the post-war governance framework and peacebuilding trajectories. Chapters by Duyvesteyn et al., Orakzai, and Dureismith, in particular provide this analysis.

In this volume the authors' framing of insurgency, conflict and war (used interchangeably) in their case studies are informed by the *intensity threshold* set by the Collier-Hoeffler model on the framing of the definition of armed conflicts (see Collier and Sambanis 2005). That is, where a high intensity armed violence has occurred, and the fighting involves the armed forces of the de-facto state government (with a centralized command and control), and at least one organized contending rebel force, and during the fighting at least one thousand battle-related deaths are reported, then it can be described as a *war*, and thus, in Collier and Sambanis' view, this is what differentiates low and high-intensity insurgencies. These conflicts or insurgent movements may not necessarily be protracted ones to be considered within the analyses contained in this volume.

The proceeding chapters are written around the internal dynamics of four insurgent typologies: opportunistic resource-driven, religious ideological, ethnic and secessionist insurgencies. Through the available qualitative data the contributors Part I on Insurgency and Governance in this volume interpret the internal character of war and the patterns of combatant interactions with others, and between them and the state. The main empirical innovation has been to demonstrate how insurgent wars shape the internal dynamics of governance and the politics of peacebuilding. Motivated by "insurgent typology" as the theoretical framework, the authors here position both the observed and unobserved factors such as the prevailing pre-war internal cultures, the wartime economic regimes and the war ideologies of the rebel forces to determine not only the character of wars, but also how they affect the efficaciousness of international peacebuilding and intervention approaches created to end them. Although we recognize the role of power asymmetry in shaping the outcome of conflicts (see for example Abrahamsen and Williams 2007), peacemaking, peacekeeping and peacebuilding activities also hinge upon the aspirations of the international actors towards the country-specific countries in the continent (see Rotberg 2000; Taylor and Williams 2004; Olonisakin 2000).

The framing of peacebuilding interventions in resource-driven wars is more intense and coercive than other forms of wars. Coercion is informed by the impact of these wars on the highs and lows of the international political economy and the balance of trade of the major economies. In the secessionist war that culminated in the creation of Africa's newest state, South Sudan, for instance, the questions of the (in)divisibility of the state, the political legitimacy of the secessionist forces, as well as the political interests of the external actors, including the contributing countries to the peacekeeping troops, are a determinant of the level of the intensity of peacekeeping (the creation of a buffer between the belligerents) and peacebuilding (see Duriesmith in this volume; Berman and Sams 2000; Clapham 2002). In ethnic conflicts such as the conflict in Darfur, Sudan, in which Lahai analyses in this volume (also see Gompert, et al. 2005), external intervention is at best non-intensive and at worst non-existent. In most instances, not wanting to see itself in a position where it will be peremptory to impose an intervention force, the meta-narratives of denial to downgrade the intensity of the violence so as to prevent a situation whereby the use of an international reactionary force, as it occurred in the resource-driven wars such as in West Africa, and the ideological insurgencies such as in Somalia, become necessary.

In religious ideological wars such as those being fought in Northern Nigeria and Somalia, the international community's approach to peace are anchored in a politically-infused reactionary liberal peace agenda (see Mwangi, and Agbiboa's chapters in this volume). In these wars, it should be noted that the tensions are mostly between contending ideals and ideas. As a result, the attempt to resist the supremacist tendencies of the dominant faction (mostly those wanting to institute a western-styled political liberal state) to impress on the contending factions (mostly those intending to institute a non-liberal, and mostly theocratic systems of governance) have led to the internationalization of low intensity insurgent uprisings.

However, there are exceptions. In that, unlike the Somali conflict, in Northern Nigeria it is very difficult for the international community to impose its political will in the determination of the outcome of the war, for two reasons: first, since the International Community does not want to see the destabilization of an already polarized warzone, amid the unfeasibility of having a multiplex approach to peace that might compromise the policy priorities of both the state and federal governments, support for the federal government has been in the form of technical (political and military) and financial assistance; second, and perhaps the most politically viable reason, is found in the argument surrounding the existence of a strong and legitimate government, with greater control over the country's territorial borders and a well-structured civilian-led security architecture.

Despite these differences, the generic characteristic features shared by these wars and the countries affected by them are: Firstly, these are wars that resulted from a violent pre-war politics of patronage. Secondly, the armed insurgent groups and factions within these warscapes are led by a factionalized pseudo-political elite class whose relationships with one another is at best based on mistrust and violence (Rotberg 2000), and as such, they are able to attract local support through the use of illiberal ethno-religious and nationalistic narratives, patron-clientele (i.e. the relationship between the warlords, their combatants and the external actors doing business with them, and personal relationships) incentives and the systematic use of sexual and gender based violence as a weapon of war (see Turshen 1998; Meintjes et al. 2001); Third, beyond the challenges of not knowing post-war disarmament, demobilization and integration would lead to the demilitarization of the mindsets of people (see Kingma 2002), the peace deals negotiated between the belligerents offer, at their best, a lull in the fighting, and in the aftermath, conflicts do not re-emerge, but peace remains largely politically elusive; Finally, during the post-war national reconstruction, the elements of liberal peacebuilding such as the promotion of democracy, the rule of law, a free market economy, and good governance are emphasized because it is believed they offer the best possible outcomes.

The Processes of Creating a Peacebuilding Framework: Policy Directions and Pitfalls

In 2012, the Obama Administration issued a New US Strategy towards Sub-Saharan Africa. This policy, while it is different, on principles, from the assertive bilateral (i.e. the joint US/UN Security Council) approach of Presidents George Herbert Bush and George Walker Bush, and in line with the assertive multilateral (i.e. the joint state, non-state, and international community) approach of the Clinton Administration (see Franke 2007), seeks to strengthen democratic institutions, spur economic growth and trade investment, as well as promote opportunities, as strategies to contain conflicts and promote peace and security in the continent. However, such transformative diplomacy, inasmuch as it appeases the vexed American businesses wanting to do business in Africa, in the face of China's economic expansion within African economies, is unfeasible. The reasons being, this policy directive, like those before it, for example the role of the pre-Obama US government's counter-terrorism approach through its Africa standby force, Africa Command (also known as AFRICOM) (see Mills and Herbst 2007), is blind to the internal dynamics within these postcolonial African states, where political instability and conflicts, not trade barriers, continue to prevent political stability, and compromise the promotion of human security (Mulikita 2000) and economic growth in the continent (see Deng and Zartman 2002).

What then could be the way out of this challenge? In the 1990s the idea of an *Agenda for Peace*—developed by Boutros-Ghali (1995)—was Africa's preferred path to peace and development. However, the lack of sustained international support (financial and technical) led to mixed results. These failures had played a major role for a return to the past. The political constructions of *self* as a template for measuring the progress that has been made in peacebuilding would at least create the enabling environment for the emergence of political egalitarianism. However, this will be hard to achieve, especially where, after several decades of experimenting with a series of externally framed panaceas, a new elixir called "liberal democratic governance" is being foisted (sometimes through force) as the best possible solution to Africa's internecine problems.

In this volume we are not contending the fact that political liberalism cannot solve some of the longstanding challenges affecting the continent. After all, with democracy being *practiced* in several African countries there has been a stimulating breath of fresh air—although this is sometimes achieved through force (see O'Hanlon 2002)—people are being granted their basic human rights. Through democracy, the largely marginal political and racial minorities have come to the realization that political power should be in the hands of the masses, irrespective of the racial, sex, class and social statuses. The emergence of democracy has also led to the creation of the space in which the ubiquities of the print and electronic media are no longer confined and under the control of the government. The media outlets have been empowered enough to act as the "fiduciaries" of the continent, and where possible, to oversee the activities of the legislative, executive and judicial arms of government within their state political boundaries. With democracy, it should be noted, Africans have come to understand that politics is about the competition of ideas in the political arena, and the creation and sustenance of the ethos of socio-economic egalitarianism, as well as increases in the standards of living of the people (due, in part, to the possibilities that with democracy foreign investment is encouraged and jobs will be available to ordinary people).

Unfortunately, despite the increasing trends of pro-democratic protests, spurred, in part, by President Obama's fiery speeches in Cairo and Accra, in 2009, it appears as if African governments will continue to place the cart before the horse. The democracy that permeates in much of Africa is spurious democracy. Perchance, it is the Chinese experience of striving for accelerated economic growth before aiming for democracy that is teaching African governments and political leaders, especially those calling for stronger ties with China (see Moyo 2010), that there should first be a relentless drive for economic development before a considerable degree of political egalitarianism and human rights are achieved. However, will the experimentation with a free-wheeling democracy ever be possible; and if so, is democracy what Africa needs, or perhaps just a level playing field with the west?

Nonetheless, if it is the resolve of the international community to bring democracy into the troubled spots of postcolonial Africa, rather than insisting on bringing about democratic changes immediately after wars end, there should be a gradualist approach. It is only through this, that these African states will create the enabling space for their people to begin the processes of memorializing their political past, and to evaluate the impact of that past on their present situational circumstances. From a practical point of view, where the post-conflict peacebuilding processes are decentralized, the processes of memorialization would also contribute to the creation of the space for people to realize that they have a hand in the development of the democratic institutions, and inculcating the spirit of liberal political socialization and culture (see Broch-Due 2005).

The point we are trying to make here is that, for many Africanist commentators, since western governments have insisted that Africans should make a bold leap into the direction of western democracy, they should equally be ready to accept the fact that economic liberalization and political freedoms are processes that may not always lead to conventional outcomes of, say, developmentally-oriented progressive thinking that solves the problems of wars (including ethnic tensions), bad governance (including corruption: i.e. bribery, embezzlement and misuse of power) and un-sustained peace activism.

At the same time, it has long being hoped that African states should create the institutions that will make it possible for them to start from the beginning and later end up at the graduating point of democracy, liberal utopia (which is a human condition described in Hannah Arendt's [1958] Heideggerian hermeneutic philosophy, as a process that is also full of continuities and discontinuities). Moreover, African states should also start by raising the living standards of their people, transform and expand their lumpen middle class elite groups into a self-reliant middle class.

However, to make this middle class more akin to the liberalizing values of western democracy, the educational sectors have been subjected to the regulation and austerity measures of international financial and developmental institutions such as the International Monetary Fund (IMF) and the World Bank. Regrettably, these austerity measures, unlike the gradualist approach with which they were implemented in Western Europe immediately after the end of the Cold War, were in Africa implemented in badly, through the conditioning of countries' national budgets on welfare and security spending, amid the lack of effective policies that would create the enabling environment for the private sector to step in and help in promoting sustainable development (see Duffield 2001; Moyo 2010).

It is against this backdrop that many have argued that, the postcolonial African state remains a frontier where the policy directions of the west have led to a series of unforeseen outcomes. However, these considerations are absent in most internationally framed intervention measures in some of these troubled spots on the continent. What is being promoted to justify western intervention measures in the warscapes of Africa is the inability of African governments to prioritize liberal peace over other non-liberal approaches to peace. For Hardt and Negri (2001) this situation is best understood when explained with reference to the historical understanding of Empire (i.e. the post-Cold War re-engineered economic and political supra-national empire) as a universal order that has legitimated (not forgetting that such legitimating order is not always grounded on the tenets of the UN Charter—Human Rights, Peace and Security) what they referred to as new hybrid forms of racism, new conceptions of identity (of same and difference), new social networks of communication, new clandestine means of control, and new trails of migration that accepts no overriding order that would regulate its expansion (and defects, thereof) in the new frontiers, including Africa.

Ultimately, after the 2003 World Summit that culminated in the formulation of the Responsibility to Protect (R2P), the AU (Makinda and Okumu 2007; de Waal 2002) and its multilateral/bilateral peace, security and development partners, have called for liberal integration of the African economies, and the creation of a loose form of a political union in the continent. Such integration, from a theoretical point of view, is a process through which political actors in several distinct national settings are persuaded to shift their loyalties, expectations and political activities towards a new and larger center, whose institutional processes demand jurisdiction over the pre-existing national states.

However, the current patterns of integration in Africa cannot proffer solutions to the complex political emergences affecting the continent (see Francis 2006). The reason being that, there has been a pseudo-functionalist reengineering (i.e. the imposed restrictions in the regulation of transnationalism and the international peace and security architecture aimed at building 'peace by pieces') of statism, which has contributed to the amalgamation of the political structures within these countries, and not the will of the people, for whom and by whom peace processes are being cultivated (Callaghy, Kassimir and Latham 2001). Curiously, those, especially pan-African scholars who have remained critical of the relevance of the geo-political and economic transformative role that regional integration plays, have been labeled as "spoilers of peace" (see Makinda 2006).

As such, the processes of integration have failed, in some instances, to take into consideration the aspirations and desires of the people in the postcolonial state. The emergence of transnational organizations, do not necessarily promote the relevance of postcolonial African states, although some scholars have argued that the actions of these organizations are aimed at the sharing of sovereignty rather than the ultimate abolition of the state system in contemporary Africa. However, integration has played a major role in the resolution of conflicts in the continent (see Leatherwood 2002; Francis 2006; Murithi 2005).

Understanding Postcolonial African Frontiers

Enquiries into the wars and "peacescapes" of postcolonial Africa has increased significantly in recent decades due, in part, to the internationalization of efforts aimed at addressing the sometimes intractable, yet complex political emergencies affecting postcolonial states. Spearheading these global efforts is the United Nations and other peace and security-centric regional organizations such as the African Union (AU) (see Murithi 2005, 2008), the international financial institutions (IFIs), and a plethora of multilateral and bilateral agencies and international non-governmental organizations (INGOs) (see Okumu 2003). These efforts have resulted in the domestication of two main global processes: the Millennium Development Goals (MDGs) and the Responsibility to Protect Doctrine. The implications of these "glocal" (global and local) (see Robertson 1994) processes is the expansion and mainstreaming of disaster risk reduction methodologies; early warning mechanisms within Africa's security and human rights architecture, and, investing in the institutional capacities of African created and led institutions working towards peace and security governance issues.

However, the persistency of low (and sometimes high) intensity civil wars, the spatial implications of sexual and gender-based violence, poverty and under-development, and their corresponding implications on peace processes, among others, are a demonstration of the fact that there is the need for further research on what we have referred to as "The African Frontiers." We are interested in understanding not just the origins, character and implications of wars on people, but also their impact on the epistemological framing of the local realities in the postcolonial states. Whilst many perspectives have been presented within the ambits of their theoretical limitations, this volume will reveal that while the external processes shaping the discursive representation of insurgency in Africa are, of course, important to the resolution of the immediate and long term crises affecting the continent, to omit the relevance of the intersectional issues that are addressed here in this volume, has led to these issues being less understood or under-theorized.

We acknowledge the profound gains that the global security and peacebuilding architecture have achieved in Africa over the past two decades, seen from the increasing numbers of countries in transition from war to peace; and even from elusive peace to nation building and economic development. This volume of *African Frontiers* sheds light on the origins, nature and character of the historically relevant, intractable and emergent conflicts and unconventional peace strategies. This volume puts a premium on the varying forms of armed conflicts and the global implications they have on Africa and beyond. It presents an in-depth analysis of the constructive engagement of actors (and their motivations) with a variety of country-specific, national, communal and grassroots conditions.

Through a multidisciplinary approach, *African Frontiers* aims to counter the superficial, Eurocentric and gender insensitive dominant discursive representations of Africa within the discourse of war and conflict management; security and peace/nation-building. This volume historicizes and theorizes the realities of the postcolonial African states, and the ramifications it has on the future of the continent. It situates the study of *African Frontiers* within the context of the prevailing cultural and geo-political realities. Against this backdrop, the following chapters illustrate the complex ways in which events and processes are experienced at the local level; and how these local realities in turn impact and shape the patterns of political and military engagement in Africa and beyond.

African Frontiers offers a comprehensive analysis of the multifaceted dimensions of insurgency, governance and peacebuilding in Africa, attending especially to the relationships between the local (country-specific; and continental) and regional/continental forces. This volume addresses the important and less important, but consequential issues of relevance to our understanding of the nature and impact of insurgent activism in the postcolonial states in Africa, and offers an up-to-date and comprehensive analysis of how political and security sensitive events and processes are framed, and the factors responsible for such framing. This volume also discusses the prevalence of discourses on insurgency and policy practices, and the on-the-ground interventions they guide, to demonstrate how they are inspired by ideologies that increasingly reflect glocal understandings.

African Frontiers balances attention to the local conditions that frame the social, familial and cultural contexts of populations facing political crises, with a concern for the broader geo-political issues of securitization, global governance, poverty, (under)development, armed conflicts, and displacement, as found in current approaches to humanitarian action within and beyond African borders. *African Frontiers* contributes to the growing body of literature on the incidences of war and peacebuilding activities, and the representation of actors, as well as the vulnerable populations in a variety of contemporary contexts.

There are many scholarly publications on the postcolonial wars and peacescapes of Africa, that focus on the political and security arena, the economic arena, the environmental, and the institutional, that are available: for example, Williams (2011), Mengisteab (2013), Abrahamsen (2013), Keller (2014), and Araoye (2014). These volumes have broadened our understanding of the epistemologies and on-the-ground implementation of the internationally-framed peacebuilding policies in Africa.

Yet the thematic issues that draw on the often less theorized issues, especially where they are concerned with the new wars and grassroots war/peace activism in the continent, or their post-war implications on people's everyday lives, state governance and the future directions of/for these postcolonial states, however, remains insufficiently explored. That said, *African Frontiers* makes a unique contribution, because it presents the latest research on insurgency, wartime governance and peacebuilding in Africa in a wide variety of circumstances that draws a binary relationship between the local realities and global processes with a view of offering a comprehensive examination of the relevant issues of pan-African relevance. It is this explicit examination of these locally and globally relevant issues by the scholars contributing to this volume, with firsthand knowledge about Africa, that unifies the various themes that are analyzed here. This will therefore be of a great interest to all scholars analyzing cross-cutting themes on insurgency and peace in Africa, and in general.

The questions that will be addressed in this volume include: How has the discursive framing of subjects of liberation historically affected conflicts and what can that tell us about the current patterns of insurgency in Africa? What are the determinants of war in the postcolonial states in Africa; and in what ways have the populations and countries for whom peacebuilding measures are framed and implemented reacted to some of the new forms of insurgent wars and the unconventional ways conflicts are being mediated and peacebuilding framed? How are the local realities—the socio-cultural, political, security and environmental changes impacting the neo-liberal approach to armed intervention in Africa? How do the incidences of war and peace, actors and motivations spur a change in the global institutional and ideological approach to peace in the continent? In what ways have the local responses to these complex political emergencies in the postcolonial states of Africa differed from conventional means and what are the possible ways they can achieve their intended motives? What challenges and opportunities do marginal groups have in relation to their efforts in changing the ways how we understand "agency" in the theorization of the *African Frontiers*? Are glocal efforts to promote peace and security in Africa constrained by the framing of and the use of the neo-liberal peace agenda, that seeks to promote the global interests of the western democratic states, rather than the needs and interests of the populations for whom and by whom these peacebuilding agendas are framed? What is the contribution of the African security architecture in the promotion of an "African future" in the new millennium? How can these contributions be strengthened? What lessons have been learnt so far? And what are the implications for future research and practice?

The volume is organized along two major themes: Part I: Insurgency and Governance, and Part II: Peacebuilding. The topics that are covered include: rebel and insurgent formations such as the National Patriotic Front of Liberia (NPFL), the Revolutionary United Front (RUF), the Lord's Resistance Army (LRA) and Boko Haram, and the various warlords from East to West Africa; state governance and corruption; the political marketplace, terrorism, security and counter terrorism; grassroots activity and women's actions for peace and security; non-violent actions and peacebuilding; and a particular focus on the tensions and challenges facing the newest nation-state on the continent, South Sudan.

In Part I: Insurgency and Governance, John Idriss Lahai and Tanya Lyons (Chapter 2), examine the character of insurgent opportunism, rebel governance and the political constructions of peace in West Africa, with a special focus on Liberia and Sierra Leone. Using the Charles Taylor-led National Patriotic Front of Liberia (NPFL) and the Revolutionary United Front (RUF) of Sierra Leone, they analyze the pseudo-liberal governance framework of these rebel factions, and explain why the NPFL had a relative success in governance, and the RUF failed. To this end, attempts made by insurgents to use a neo-liberal path towards governance, have been both tumultuous and controversial. Setting the analytical context for the further chapters Duyvesteyn et al. (Chapter 3) argue for the re-focusing of scholarly attention to rebel groups and their leadership in governance. By studying the political dynamics and complexities surrounding rebel governance, through case studies: the SPLM/A in South Sudan, the NRA in Uganda and the UIC in Somalia, they shed light on policy debates on insurgency, peacebuilding and development in contexts of state fragility in the African borderlands. Noel Twagiramungu (Chapter 4) focuses on the leadership styles of Museveni in Uganda and Kagame in Rwanda to empirically explain the real politics behind the acceptance of neo-liberalism by neo-Marxist revolutionaries. Twagiramungu finds that, by manipulating the economics of Marxist-Capitalist ideologies, these revolutionaries succeeded in hijacking the donor-driven enterprise of democratic peace, which would have created a balance between the promises of democratic change and economic development, and recreate their countries into a political marketplace with entrenched networks that promotes militarism. John Idriss Lahai (Chapter 5), uses the conflict in Darfur, Sudan to show how political considerations in the conflict, as well as the competing individual interests of (external and internal) actors, have led to tensions with regards to the question of genocide, Sudan's sovereignty and peacekeeping in the region. Oscar Gakuo Mwangi (Chapter 6) analyzes the conditions that perpetrate state collapse and recommend ways promoting peacebuilding and good governance in Somalia. Daniel Agbiboa (Chapter 7) explores the rise of Boko Haram in Northern Nigeria and asks the questions, who are they; why do they rebel; and importantly how has the Nigerian state responded to their extremism? Agbiboa argues that inasmuch as Boko Haram have used the religious, ethnic and regional fault-lines to challenge the political, security and socio-economic aspects of governance in Nigeria, Boko Haram's growing connection to transnational terrorist groups like al-Qaeda and al-Shabaab pose further challenges to the state and prospects for human security.

In Part II: Peacebuilding, the analysis begins with Mamadou Diouma Bah's (Chapter 8) intriguing analysis of the Republic of Guinea and its *avoidance* of civil war, in a neighborhood riddled with conflict. He asks why Guinea was spared from civil war, despite being surrounded by two countries—Liberia and Sierra Leone—that were destabilized by catastrophic, decade-long civil wars; and despite having experienced some of the pre-war problems such as ethnic rivalry, politicized military, poverty and inequitable distribution of wealth, the spill-over effect that contributed to conflicts in the sub-region. He presents a convincing argument on how the political establishment in Guinea was able to stabilize the internal triggers for conflict on one hand, and on the other, by framing stability in ways that provided an opportunity for the government to attract international military and humanitarian assistance as a preventive measure against the domino-effect of war in the region. The turn of the millennia, however, also witness attempts to break with the past from resource-drive wars. Paul Munro and Greg van der Horst (Chapter 9) explain how the re-evolution of forest socioecologies in Sierra Leone shaped the country's movement away from conflict and displacement, and, in tandem, promoted the idea of *resettlement* as a socioecological pathway to peace and development. However, the internal structures of *local communities*, attending especially to their affinities to armed groups during the warring era for most African countries, also has a role to play not just in distorting the distinction between conflict zones and post-conflict settings, but also in the making of identities, actors' motivations for war and peace, and the community-driven paths to peacebuilding. This is an issue that Kialee Nyiayaana (Chapter 10) examines in relation to the arming of vigilante groups in the Niger Delta, and thus the proliferation of the militarization of these communities, a clear problem for the sustenance of peace in the region. Saira Bano Orakzai (Chapter 11) examines the post-2011 insurgency in Libya and the prospect for neo-liberal peacebuilding and national reconciliation. Orakzai argues that ethnic tensions were polarized in the subsequent civil war over territorial spaces, and that both local and international interventions and understandings of peace and peacebuilding are required to bring the civil war to an end. Taking the discursive representation of peacebuilding further David Duriesmith (Chapter 12) argues that the theorizing of the processes involved in building peace with warlords should be sensitive to the gendered structures of peacebuilding. Using South Sudan as a case study, he contends that peacebuilding efforts should be considered *failed attempts* where disorder is a normalcy, and where peacebuilding does not empower the already marginal groups, the non-militarized men, women, and non-violent forms of conflict resolution. In Chapter 13 Mbekezeli Mkhize explores the enabling environment for a peace process in the Democratic Republic of Congo (DRC). Mkhize argues that the DRC's many bordering countries and neighbors have "created an unfavorable climate" to the detriment of sustainable peace and development within the DRC—in what Bah in this volume has analyzed as the "bad neighborhood effect." From the proceeding analysis of the various attempted peace agreements, Mkhize demonstrates that success will rely upon a locally driven and "context-specific" response to address the causes and cessation of conflict. John Idriss Lahai and Tanya Lyons (Chapter 14) re-evaluate the ways in which theory and policy directions have (re)positioned the African continent, and suggest that the ways in which the incidences of insurgency, the structures of governance and the attempts at peacebuilding, all remain a challenge, not just for the ordinary men and women for whom and by whom the continent is understood, imagined and theorized, but for the very relevance of the study of African politics and international relations, and the external engagement of African countries with the rest of the world.

References

Abrahamsen, R. (2013). *Conflict and Security in Africa*. Oxford: James Currey.
Abrahamsen, R. and Williams, M. (2007). Introduction: The Privatisation and Globalisation of Security in Africa. *International Relations*, 21(2): 131–41 doi:10.1177/0047117807076998.
Araoye, A. (2014). *Sources of Conflict in the Postcolonial African State*. New York/Asmara: Africa World Press.
Arendt, H. (1958) *The Human Condition*. Chicago, IL: University of Chicago Press (English Translation 1998 reprint).
Bayart, J.F., Ellis, S., and Hibou, B. (1999). *Criminalisation of the State in Africa*. International African Institute: Oxford.
Berman, E.G. and Sams, K.E. (2000). *Peacekeeping in Africa*. Geneva: United Nations Institute for Disarmament Research.
Boas, M. and Dunn, K. (2007). *African Guerrillas: Raging Against the Machine*. Boulder, CO: Lynne Rienner.
Boutros-Ghali, B. (1995). *An Agenda for Peace*. New York: United Nations.
Broch-Due, V. (2005). *Violence and Belonging: The Quest for Identity in Post-colonial Africa*. New York: Routledge.
Callaghy, T., Kassimir, R., and Latham, R. (eds) (2001). *Intervention and Transnationalism in Africa*. Cambridge: Cambridge University Press.

Chrétien, J.P. (2003). *The Great Lakes of Africa: Two Thousand Years of History*. New York: Zone Books.

Clapham, C. (2002). Problems of Peace Enforcement: Lessons to Be Drawn from Multinational Peacekeeping Operations in Ongoing Conflicts in Africa. In T. Zack-Williams, D. Frost, and A. Thomson (eds), *Africa in Crisis: New Challenges and Possibilities* (pp. 196–215), Sterling, VA: Pluto Press.

Collier, P. and Sambanis, N. (2005). *Understanding Civil War: Evidence and Analysis*, Volume 1. Washington DC: World Bank.

Condemi, S. and Weniger G.C. (eds) (2011). *Continuity and Discontinuity in the Peopling of Europe*. Dordrecht: Springer.

De Waal, A. (ed.) (2002). *Demilitarizing the Mind: African Agendas for Peace and Security*. Trenton: Africa World Press.

Deng, F.M. and Zartman, W. (2002). *A Strategic Vision for Africa: The Kampala Movement*. Washington DC: Brookings Institution Press.

Doyle, M. and Sambanis, N. (2006). *Making War and Building Peace*. Princeton, NJ: Princeton University Press.

Duffield, M. (2001). *Global Governance and the New Wars: The Merging of Development and Security*. London: Zed Books.

Duffield, M. and Hewitt, V. (eds) (2009). *Empire, Development and Colonialism: The Past in the Present*. Oxford: James Currey.

Elbadawi, I. and Sambanis, N. (2009). How Much Civil War Will We See? Explaining the Prevalence of Civil War. *Journal of Conflict Resolution*, 46(3): 307–34.

Francis, D.J. (2006). *Uniting Africa: Building Regional Peace and Security Systems*. Aldershot: Ashgate.

Francis, D.J. (ed.) (2008). *Peace and Conflict in Africa*. London: Zed Books.

Franke, B. (2007). Enabling a Continent to Help Itself: U.S. Military Capacity Building and Africa's Emerging Security Structure. *Strategic Insights*, 6(1) January, http://www.operationspaix.net/DATA/DOCUMENT/5480~v~Enabling_a_Continent_to_Help_Itself__U_S__Military_Capacity_Building_and_Africa_s_Emerging_Security_Architecture.pdf.

Gompert, D.C., Richardson, C., Kugler, R.L., and Bernard, C.H. (2005). *Learning from Darfur: Building a Net-capable African Force to Stop Mass Killings*. National Defense University Center for Technology and National Security Policy, July. http://oai.dtic.mil/oai/oai?verb=getRecord&metadataPrefix=html&identifier=ADA450148.

Goodhand, J. and Hulme, D. (1999). From Wars to Complex Political Emergencies: Understanding Conflict and Peace-Building in the New World Disorder. *Third World Quarterly*, 20(1): 13–26.

Hirshleifer, J. (1991). The Paradox of Power. *Economics and Politics*, 3(3): 177–200.

Hobsbawm, E. (1999). *Industry and Empire: The Birth of the Industrial Revolution*. New York: New Press.

Homer-Dixon, T. (1991). On the Threshold: Environmental Changes as Causes of Acute Conflict. *International Security*, 16(2): 76–116.

Howe, H. (2001). *Ambiguous Order: Military Forces in African States*. Boulder: Lynne Rienner.

Huntington, S.P. (1993). The Clash of Civilizations? *Foreign Affairs*, 72(3): 22–49.

Kaplan, R.D. (1994). The Coming of Anarchy. *Atlantic Monthly*, February 1, http://www.theatlantic.com/magazine/archive/1994/02/the-coming-anarchy/304670/.

Kaplan, R.D. (2002). *The Coming Anarchy: Shattering the Dream of the Post Cold War*, New York: Knopf Doubleday Publishing Group.

Keller, E. (2014). *Identity, Citizenship, and Political Conflict in Africa*, Bloomington: Indiana University Press.

Kingma, K. (2002). Demobilization, Reintegration and Peacebuilding in Africa. *International Peacekeeping*, 9 (Summer):181–201.

Leatherwood, D.G. (2002). Peacekeeping in West Africa. *Joint Force Quarterly*, 29 (Autumn-Winter): 76–81.

Makinda, S. (2006) African Thinkers and the Global Security Agenda. In M. Mwagiru and O. Oculli (eds), *Rethinking Global Security: An African Perspective?* Nairobi: Heinrich Böll Foundation, 21–37.

Makinda, S. and Okumu, W. (2007). *The African Union: Challenges of Globalization, Security and Governance*. London: Routledge.

Mamdani, M. (1996). *Citizen and Subject: Contemporary Africa and the Legacy of Late Colonialism*. Princeton, NJ: Princeton University Press.

Mehta, U.S. (1999). *Liberalism and Empire: A Study in 19th Century British Liberal Thought*. Chicago, IL: University of Chicago Press.

Meintjes, S., Pillay, A., and Turshen, M. (eds) (2001). *The Aftermath: Women in Post-conflict Tranformation*. London: Zed Books.

Mengisteab, K. (2013). *The Horn of Africa*, Cambridge: Polity Press.

Mills, G. and Herbst, J. (2007). *Africa, Terrorism and AFRICOM. Royal United Services Institute for Defence and Security Studies Research*, 152(2): 40–44.

Moyo, D. (2009). *How the West Was Lost: Fifty Years of Economic Folly—and the Stark Choices Ahead*. London: Allen Lane.

Moyo, D. (2010). *Dead Aid: Why Aid is Not Working and How There is a better Way for Africa*. New York: Farrar, Straus and Giroux.

Mudimbe, V.Y. (1988). *The Invention of Africa: Gnosis, Philosophy, and the Order of Knowledge*, London: James Currey.

Mudimbe, V.Y. (1994). *The Idea of Africa*, London: James Currey.

Mulikita, N.M. (2000). Enhancing Human Security in Africa: What Role for the International Community? *Peacekeeping & International Relations*, 29(12): 13–18.

Murithi, T. (2005). *The African Union: Pan-Africanism, Peacebuilding and Development*. Aldershot : Ashgate.

Murithi, T. (2008). The African Union's Evolving Role in Peace Operations. *African Security Review*, 17(1): 70–82.

Nhema, A. and Zeleza, P.T. (2008a). *The Roots of African Conflicts: The Causes and Costs*. Oxford: James Currey.

Nhema, A. and Zeleza, P.T. (2008b). *The Resolution of African Conflicts: The Management of Conflict Resolution & Post- Conflict Reconstruction*. London: James Currey.

Nitzen, J. and Bichler, S. (2004). Dominant Capital and the New Wars. *Journal of World Systems Research*, 10(2): 255–327.

O'Hanlon, M.E. (2002). Saving Lives with Force: An Agenda for Expanding the ACRI. *Journal of International Affairs*, 55(2): 289–300.

Okumu, W. (2003). Humanitarian International NGOs and African Conflicts. *International Peacekeeping*. 10(1): 120–37.

Okunoye, O. (2007). Postcoloniality, Modern African Poetry, and Counter-Discourse. In T.R. Klein et al. (eds), *Texts, Tasks, and Theories: Versions and Subversions in African Literatures* (3rd edn). Amsterdam; New York: Rodopim, 111–32.

Olonisakin, F. (2000). *Reinventing Peacekeeping in Africa*. Boston: Kluwer Law International.

Pakenham, T. (1991). *The Scramble for Africa: 1876–1912*. London: Abacus.

Palmberg, M. (2001), *Encounter Images in the Meetings Between Africa and Europe*. Uppsala: Nordic Africa Institute.

Robertson, R. (1994) Globalisation or Glocalisation? *Journal of International Communication*, 1(1): 33–52.

Rotberg, R. (2000). *Peacekeeping and Peace Enforcement in Africa: Methods of Conflict Prevention*. World Peace Foundation.

Taylor, I. and Williams, P. (eds) (2004). *Africa in International Politics: External Involvement on the Continent*. Abingdon: Routledge.

Turshen, M. and Twagiramariya, C. (eds) (1998). *What Women Do in War Time: Gender and Conflict in Africa*. London: Zed Books.

van Creveld, M. (1991). *The Transformation of War*, New York: The Free Press.

Wai, Z. (2012). *Epistemologies of African Conflicts Violence, Evolutionism, and the War in Sierra Leone*. Basingstoke: Palgrave Macmillan.

Willliams, P. (2011). *War and Conflict in Africa*, Cambridge: Polity Press.

Zack-Williams, T., Frost, D., and Thompson, A. (eds) (2002). *Africa in Crisis*. London: Pluto Press.

Zartman, W. (ed.) (1995). *Collapsed States*. Boulder, CO: Lynne Rienner.

Chapter 2

The West African Warscapes: Rebel Factions, Insurgent Opportunism and State Governance

John Idriss Lahai and Tanya Lyons

Abstract

This chapter examines the character of insurgent opportunism, rebel governance and the political constructions of building peace and seeking justice in West Africa, with a special focus on Liberia and Sierra Leone, to explain the opportunistic origins, the nature and character of rebel governance, and its associated impact on the political economy of war. It also examines the reasons for the successes and the failures of two warring factions: The National Patriotic Front of Liberia (NPFL) and the Revolutionary United Front (RUF) of Sierra Leone, to institute an alternative governance infrastructure in their areas of political and economic control in these countries during the 1990s. Despite the differences in terms of these rebel groups' strategic governance frameworks within their overall war aims, it was the political and economic considerations around the question of state governance that made it difficult for peace deals to be reached. Until there is a balance between the political need for peace and people's desire for justice on their own terms, and not by the interest-driven approach of the international community, peace will remain elusive.

Introduction

Why do some rebel groups succeed in governance and others do not? What role do rebel groups play in the creation of an alternative wartime governance framework within the embattled political economies of West Africa during the 1990s? Using Ledow's theory on rebel governance, which examines the political and economic conditions that contribute to the successes and/or failures of warring factions, this chapter focuses on two case studies: Liberia: The Charles Taylor-led National Patriotic Front of Liberia (NPFL) (between 1989 and 1997); and Sierra Leone: The Revolutionary United Front (RUF) (between 1991 and 2000), to explain the opportunistic origins of these factions, and the nature and character of rebel governance, and its associated impact on the political economy of war. It also examines the reasons for the successes of the NPFL in Liberia, and the failures of the RUF in Sierra Leone, to institute an alternative governance infrastructure in their respective areas of political and economic control during the 1990s. Despite the differences in terms of their strategic governance frameworks within their overall war aims, we contend that, it was the political and economic considerations around the question of state governance that made it difficult for peace deals to be reached in both countries. The chapter concludes with the suggestion that, until there is a balance between the political need for peace and people's desire for justice (in their own terms, and not by the interest-driven approach of the international community), peace in both countries will remain elusive.

One of the earliest interpretations of the wars in the West African sub-region was Richards' (1996) analysis of the role of "forest-economic relation" in shaping the opportunistic and violent nature of the war in Sierra Leone (also see Ellis 2007; Reno 1995). Though Richards' analysis has been contested by Sierra Leonean scholars (such as Abdullah 1998; Abdullah and Muana 1998; Bangura 1997; Gberie 2005; Lahai 2010a; 2010b), he does position the role of the "forest" in shaping the psychology, politics and economics of the resource-rich, albeit war-torn and violent prone, postcolonial Sierra Leone, and the psyche of its people.

However, what made these resource-drive wars hard to resolve was the political economy behind the conflict, and the role that such economy plays in state governance. Central to the economic activities of the warring factions, and their associated political roles, is the forest. The dense tropical rainforest performed two main functions in the warscapes of Liberia and Sierra Leone. First, it offered protection for the human predators: the combatants, and the external actors doing business with them—i.e. exchanging raw products for guns. The international peacekeeping forces were unable to move into such treacherous and intimidating environments, the jungle to fight against a lumpenproletariat rag tag army or rebels in these opportunistic resource-driven wars. The peacekeepers, who were coming from non-forested and grassland regions, were certainly awestruck by the huge forests: with their lurking dangers of frighteningly carnivorous mammals, reptiles and amphibians—not forgetting how many people who were also fleeing from the warring factions were killed when afflicted by innumerable disease-causing micro-organisms as they ventured into the protective ambits of these dense forests.

Secondly, the forest also offered the resources that were needed to keep the weapons active. In other words, the rain forest played a central role in the sustenance of these wars because it provided the natural resources that were sold to finance the wars of these armed insurgent groups. For example, Gberie (2005: 183–4) informs us that between 1994 and 1999, illicit diamonds, from the territory controlled by the Charles Taylor-led National Patriotic Front of Liberia (NPFL), that were for sale in the Belgian (Antwerp) diamond market was estimated at $2 billion USD. Whereas those mined by its Sierra Leonean supported group, the Revolutionary United Front (RUF) accounted for about 15 percent of the World's total diamond trade around that time. Moreover, during the protracted conflict in Angola, the two active warring factions: the Marxist Popular Movement for the Liberation of Angola (MPLA) and the anti-Marxist National Union for the Total Independence of Angola (UNITA) used illicit diamonds and oil to finance their war efforts (Lahai 2010a). In the Congo, the persistency of war, especially in the diamond rich Kivu region, was attributed to the role that illicit diamonds in keeping weapons in the hands of the fighters. It is within this dual usage of the rain forest in these resource-driven wars, that we situate our analysis of the internal dynamics of war, rebel factions, insurgent opportunism and state governance in the West African warscapes, with a focus on Sierra Leone and Liberia.

Despite their initial intractability, the civil wars in Liberia and Sierra Leone came to an end through the fusion of political incentives and economic overtures. Within these wars, the nature and character of armed intervention was pursued from two main angles. The first, and politically viable, approach was the use of an international armed force. Arguably, the level of intensity of the intervention, and coercive nature of the peacekeeping force in keeping the peace, were formulated to read, at least for starters, that its main aim was to protect civilians. However, beyond this "do-good" narrative lay the liberal economic agenda. The international political economy of core states (the developed economies of the West), despite their comparative advantages within the global and world economies, depended on the availability of raw products from the rain forest economies of Africa, as they would in other regions, Asia and Latin America. Although we recognized the fact that in real terms the liberal economic regimes were designed to thrive best when poorer economies are in chaos, we contend here that it was the fear of the possibility that these "shadow" economies of wars would create an alternative economic structure that led to the heightened levels of intervention in West Africa in the 1990s. True to the fact that during the wars in Liberia and Sierra Leone, it was the "mercenary" economies of Eastern Europe that benefited the most from the economic activities of the rebels (see Smillie et al. 2000). Sensing the impact that this shadow economy would have on the international balance of trade deficits, already accrued by these Western economies, with no hope of using the international financial institutions of the West to invest or sell economic incentives to these war-torn countries that remained outside of the liberal path to peace, resulted in the intensification, and even the perfection of neo-liberal peacebuilding.

The second approach, which is a relatively new strategy, was the use of economic and financial incentives to dissuade the factions from engaging in these opportunist resource-driven armed conflicts. At the height of these conflicts, peace deals were reached—with the rebel leaders agreeing to the terms—through the provision of economic concessions, such as the control of natural resource sectors, to the rebel leaders. This approach, pursued mainly by Western food aid agencies, deployed simultaneously with the peacekeeping forces, sought to create other economic opportunities and alternatives through the provision of food aid, farm tools, as well as educational opportunities to divert the attention of the combatants, most of whom enter into the war in search for economic means of survival (Richards 2010). An in the end combatants become disinterested in the pseudo-ideologies of their respective warring factions, trade their weapons with the monies and food aid from these humanitarian aid agencies, and cooperate, though with unmet grievances, in the peacebuilding processes. A case in point is Sierra Leone.

Despite these economic outcomes, the motivations for war and structure of rebel factions and governance, also contributed to the adoption of unsuitable peace deals—such as the Lome Peace Agreement (that ended the civil war in Sierra Leone) and the Accra Comprehensive Peace Plan (that ended the Liberian civil war)—which contributed to ongoing violence, political turmoil and few options for organic peacebuilding to be nurtured by international intervention or local construction.

That said, section one traces the origins and character of the civil wars, as they violently unfolded first in Liberia in 1989 and later spread to Sierra Leone. Section two will analyze the wartime governance framework of the Charles Taylor-led NPFL and the RUF of Sierra Leone. Since the armed opportunistic activities of the RUF cannot be discussed in isolation to the National Provisional Ruling Council (NPRC) junta government, the discussion of their relationships with the RUF is also presented to provide a clearer picture of armed opportunism in Liberia and Sierra Leone.

Civil Conflicts in Liberia and Sierra Leone

The war that started in Liberia on December 24, 1989 was essentially a war that was shrouded in ethno-centricism (Ellis 2007) and patronage induced narratives and counter-narratives of economic opportunism (Sawyer 2004; Reno 1995) that were to eventually destabilize not just Liberia and neighboring Sierra Leone, but the whole of the West African sub-region (see Sawyer 2004). Charles Taylor had invaded Liberia with about 250 combatants from the heartland of Nimba County, Northern Liberia (Hubbard 1998), home to the ethnic groups that hated then Liberian President Doe's Krahn ethnic group and their Mandingo protégé (Ellis 2007). Doe initially unleashed his troops on the indigenous ethnic groups in Nimba (Sawyer 2004; Lahai 2012a; 2012c). The soldiers of the Armed Forces of Liberia, who had been marginalized, and lived in terror of being secretly murdered by Doe's intelligence units, were naturally not ready to fight Doe's War (Ellis 2007: 55, 62–3, 65). In any case, most of them had been disarmed.

The marginalization of the national army was perpetrated in two main ways: First, by distorting the civil processes of civil-military relationships. The civilianization of the military structures and procedures for recruitment and operation would have led to the infusion of public opinion and the media on military strategy and modes of operation. From a social theory perspective, the effectiveness of the armed forces, including its rational modes of operation, were determined by its hierarchical structures that emphasize discipline and a commitment to the collective values of their people (Ellis and Haar 2004). They are expected to act as an embodiment of state sovereignty-including the willingness of the civilian populations to understand this purpose; and for the leaders of the armed forces to understand that their claims to the monopoly on the use of force, within their country's national boundaries, are for the purpose of satisfying not just the perceived/actual sense of safety of the people. It also goes to tell so much about the symbolic role of representing the national identity of the country. Many were of the view that, by marginalizing them, the army would have toppled Doe's regime (see Ellis 2007). This did not happen because Doe's second tool, which further perpetrated the marginalization of the top officials (specifically, those that were from other ethnic groups), was the use of the ethnic identifier. As ethnic identification with the promotion or demotion within the army increases; and individual rights and universal military ethical standards deceases, those who would have challenged his leadership either resigned (or where executed). Amid these horrific incidences, ethnic connections to the presidency began to be rated higher than those that would have promoted the civilianization of the relationships between the military and the state; and the state (which was being governed by an army Major-General, Samuel Doe) and the people.

In any case, the implication of this politically perpetrated marginalization of the army meant the empowerment of President Doe's Special Forces. In conjunction with the rise in the powers of these special group of armed men and women, was the gradual decrease in public confidence in President Doe's regime. The government became less important in Liberian public perception-a phenomenon which further reinforces the marginalization of ethical armed forces culture within the country. Doe's elite forces were equipped to kill with automatic weapons and martial arts skills. Many had expected that Doe's attempt at military reform and the induction of modernized methods of warfare would have at least enabled his so-called special forces to conduct themselves within the rules that govern armed engagement during their first attempt to purge Liberia of the rebels in the north of the country. But that did not happen. These elite forces were not only undisciplined and ruthless in their torture tactics of suspected NPFL supporters; they were also firm believers in the unholy creed that war offered the best opportunity to get rich or die trying (Sesay 1996).

In retrospect, these elite forces were experienced enough in command and control to fight in the treacherous dense tropical rainforest regions, which were largely populated by rebels from tribes hostile to them. However, they retreated from this jungle war front, and Charles Taylor's equally ruthless but drug-crazed youth/child army advanced speedily and easily, and reached the gates of the capital city Monrovia within six months of the start of the war (Youboty 1993: 6). It was in street-to-street battle in the capital city that Doe's elite army, insensitive to the high toll in civilian lives this could mean (Omonijo 1990), but aware of the available loot that awaited them, hoped to lure Charles Taylor's army to fight (Schuster 1994).

In the early months of the war, peri-urban and rural areas with high concentrations of people were systematically attacked and people killed on the basis of their wealth, ethnicity, social class, sex and political affiliations. Even before Doe's troops reached the counties that separated Nimba from Montserrado County, news of the massacre of the innocent civilians raged in the capital city, Monrovia; and Charles Taylor's army burgeoned with coerced children and volunteer youth joining its ranks, some to avenge the killing of their loved ones by Doe's troops (Ellis 2007: 78). Recalling the trend of voluntary recruitments as he was advancing on the Capital, Taylor was quoted as saying, "we didn't even have to act. People came to us and said: 'Give me a gun. How can I kill the man who killed my mother?'" (Berkeley 1992: 129). Charles Taylor's mantra of either you fight for him or be killed (by him or other factions, thereof) meant that the choice for these northern tribes was not a difficult one. Fighting for Taylor, and against Doe, also meant responding to an opportunistic war in Liberia (Sawyer 2004). This war was fought by child soldiers and rebels (boys and girls) under the influence of drugs and motivated not only by the ritual beliefs that their charms and amulets were protecting them (Hubbard 1998; Ellis 2001), but by the desire for loot (Reno 1995).

Soon after this first fight for Monrovia in 1990/1991, many ethnic-affiliated warring factions and splinter groups emerged. Some joined Charles Taylor's army of child-soldiers, while others fought against it and other rival factions, but all in search of wealth (Ellis 2007); and the prized political trophy, the Executive Mansion- the seat of power of the Liberian presidency, and the sole aim for Taylor's opportunistic war.

This war in Liberia soon spilled over into neighboring Sierra Leone. The regional peacekeeping force, the Economic Community of West African States Military Observer Group (ECOMOG) had used Sierra Leone as their base from which they ferried troops, planes, and boats into Liberia. By July of 1990, only two miles and these ECOMOG troops stood between Taylor the Executive Mansion. Frustrated by their presence Charles Taylor promised that Sierra Leone would also taste the bitterness of war, for allowing ECOMOG to be based there (Gberie 2005). However, the internal instability in Sierra Leone, informed largely by the ineptitude of the one party dictatorship of the All Peoples' Congress (APC), makes it safe to conclude that Taylor's utterance was merely a coincidence, because there was talk of war among the lumpen and mal-educated youth against the APC government that had ruled the country along despotic lines since 1968 (Abdullah 1998).

Things fell apart when the Foday Sankoh led RUF of Sierra Leone mobilized men and resources from Liberia and attacked the country in 1991. It was no secret that Charles Taylor actively and strategically supported Sankoh. Charles Taylor had wanted to use Sierra Leone as a launching pad for his invasion of Liberia in 1989. But, when he visited Sierra Leone to do surveillance, he was arrested by Sierra Leone's intelligence services. From the time of that strategic rebuff, Taylor bore a strong grudge against the government in Sierra Leone (Sierra Leone Truth and Reconciliation Commission [SLTRC] 2004). This was intensified when the Nigerian-led ECOMOG forces checkmated his inexorable march through the Liberian rainforest into the capital city, Monrovia.

From the on-set, it was evident that the Sankoh's RUF was attempting to replicate the strategies of Charles Taylor, in Sierra Leone. Charles Taylor had made potent use of international media to disseminate his propaganda in Liberia, especially the British Broadcasting Corporation (BBC). So, on entering Gbanga, where Taylor had formed his parallel government (which operated as a counter to the national transitional government in Monrovia; and from where the NPFL engineered the destabilization of the sub-region), Foday Sankoh called BBC's Focus on Africa Programme and ordered the then Sierra Leone President, General Joseph Saidu Momoh to resign from office. The Momoh government dismissed Sankoh as a lunatic (Gberie 2005). When Sankoh entered Bomaru, Kailahun District, which had always been fanatically supportive of the dormant opposition party, the Sierra Leone Peoples Party (SLPP), and thus passionately opposed to the APC, Sankoh claimed that he was fighting to end the APC's rule. A few youth joined his ranks voluntarily, but some of those who did not join him were killed instead, to impress upon the populace that he was serious (see Gberie 2005). It was soon after this violent display in Bomaru that Sankoh's war for liberation turned into an opportunistic war. Countless innocent civilians became its victims- but many, though temporarily, also benefited from it by accessing lootable goods from rebel controlled towns and being enabled to mine for diamonds in the forest areas with rebel support (see Richards 1996; Zack-Williams 1994; Smillie et al. 2000; Reno 1993).

These invasions—of the NPFL in Liberia and the RUF in Sierra Leone, resulted in the tragic destabilization of both countries. They also exposed the lack of preparedness on the side of the governments. Sierra Leone's APC government of General Joseph Saidu Momoh, like President Doe's in Liberia, could not understand the guerrilla war started by the rebels. Both governments had been in power for decades, and were perhaps too comfortable with the compliance of the people, or as Kandeh (1996; also see Abraham 2004; Ellis 2007) have pointed out they were too familiar with their coercive tactics of ferreting out perceived enemies, going through a charade of trials, and executing them anyway (Kandeh 1999; Abraham 2004; Ellis 2007).

In Sierra Leone and Liberia, there were clear problems of command and control among the older generation of military officers, who had become too political, and less strategically minded. The formal armies were quite unused not only to going to the war front, but, their military schools apparently did not prepare them for the guerrilla warfare tactics of the rebels. They were being outmaneuvered and killed by the guerrillas. In Sierra Leone, frustrated by their battle-related deaths, they staged a violent coup that saw the toppling of the APC by a group of malcontent young army officers on April 27, 1992. The coup leaders immediately suspended the 1991 Constitution and formed the Supreme Council of State (SCS) to run the junta government, which they dubbed NPRC. According to Jimmy Kandeh (1996; also see Riley 2007; Allen 1995) despite its "militariat" character and populist rhetoric of liberation, the willingness of the junta to court the support of the youths, and not the older section of the masses, shows that the NPRC was also trying to sway support from the rebels to itself, and to also break from the traditional structure of patron-client ties, which had dogged pre-war Sierra Leone.

The NPRC junta maintained relations with the sub-regional organization Economic Community of West African States (ECOWAS) and it also strengthened its support for the Sierra Leone-based ECOMOG troops, who were struggling to keep the peace in Liberia. But within two years of stimulating dramatic developmental changes in the capital city Freetown, the NPRC governing council members relapsed into APC mode. They started engaging in flagrant and rampant corruption, with Ray Ban sunglasses becoming one of their trademarks. The NPRC proved to be as ineffectual as the Momoh-led APC government in repelling Sankoh's RUF. More and more of the country fell to RUF fighters, and by 1995, they held much of the diamond-rich Eastern Province. It became clear that the soldiers sent to the war front were wary of risking their lives by fighting against the rebels, whilst the lumpen elite in the junta were seen to be clearly living it up in the capital. As a result of this, the army battalions sent out to fight a war against the RUF enemy started collaborating with the RUF enemy to loot towns and villages in the provinces; and in illicitly engaging in artisanal diamond mining, not only in their controlled territories, but also in rebel held areas (see Gberie 2005; Keen 2005; Richards 2006).

Not making much headway with the war using their own military, the NPRC hired several hundred mercenaries from the South African-based private security firm Executive Outcomes (EO). Within a month, the Executive Outcomes had driven RUF fighters back to enclaves along Sierra Leone's border with Liberia, and cleared the RUF from the Kono diamond producing areas of Sierra Leone (see Richards 2006). The price for this military feat was that they would henceforth control the diamond fields through a company set up to do the mining. Once in control of the diamond fields, EO was unwilling to take risks fighting in the rest of the country. With the alluvial diamond pits under the firm control of EO, the rebels and their soldier-collaborators, turned to the livestock of the villagers in the peri-urban areas (Gberie 2005). With that depleted, they turned their attention to humanitarian aid convoys and the Sierra Leonean internally displaced and Liberian refugee camps (Richards 2010: 141). These convoys and camps were constantly targeted for food. The constancy of the RUF attacks against food aid convoys was interpreted by the Junta, which felt it had isolated the rebels after the pits were taken from them, as a strategic setback. Not wanting to know about the lack of security and the dangerous terrain that these foreign aid workers were subjected to, the NPRC accused most of them of providing supplies and possibly information about military movements, to the rebels. Therefore, the junta took a more punitive measure of stopping aid from reaching the thousands of civilians behind enemy lines as a way of cutting off the food supplies to the RUF. Agencies such as Médicins San Frontiers (MSF) and the International Red Cross that insisted on the rights of the vulnerable civilians to medical assistance were labeled pro-RUF and were marshaled out of the country by 1994.

With the military proving itself increasingly incapable of checkmating the RUF, the rural populace began to mobilize themselves into the defense of their communities. A civil defense force gained momentum, but this led to instances of mistrust between the soldiers and the civilian community (Abdullah and Muana 1998). The rebels increased their insurgent activities against civilian communities, and a cycle of retaliatory violence ensued as ordinary farmers, fishermen, herbalists, students, teachers, academics and traders, continued to join these anti-RUF/NPFL militias (Hoffman 2003, 2005, 2007; Wlodarczyk 2009).

By late 1995, civil society had become restive, fearing that the NPRC was trying to mutate into a civilian regime—like many other military juntas had done in Africa. A series of national consultative meetings (otherwise known as the Bintumani I and II conferences) were held in Freetown and politically active youth defied the soldiers who sought to harass them, and/or beat them in public. In January 1996, after nearly four years in power, Captain V.E.M Strasser was ousted in a bloodless palace coup led by his NPRC deputy, Brigadier General Julius Maada Bio, who was more committed to the idea of reconfiguring the military's role in line with its democratic constitutional functions and powers in a democratic Sierra Leone (Abdullah and Muana 1998; Clapham 1996; Conteh-Morgan and Dixon-Fyle 1999). Elections were held in 1996 and Ahmad Tejan Kabbah, a former senior executive in the United Nations, an ethnic Mandingo and the candidate of the SLPP, won 59 percent, while John Karefa-Smart, the candidate of the United National People's Party (UNPP), won 41 percent of the votes cast. Bio, still under 30 years of age, fulfilled his promise of a return to civilian rule, and handed power to newly elected President Tejan Kabbah, whose party had also won a majority of the seats in Parliament.

However, within a year of being in power, on May 25, 1997, Tejan Kabbah's government was also overthrown by the military, which included Kabbah's Chief of Army Staff and Chief of Defence Staff. The military formed the Armed Forces Revolutionary Council (AFRC), and in another bizarre twist of the Sierra Leone rebel war, the AFRC invited the RUF "to come from the bush," and join them in governing the country. Their motto—Peace done kam! De War done done! (Peace is here; the war is over)—was chanted by this AFRC/RUF alliance as they entered Freetown. This unprecedented political twist shocked the international community, which had hoped the presidency of Tejan Kabbah would usher in a lasting peace. For David Keen (2005) it is a demonstration of the opportunistic nature of the war-where factions collided, and sometimes, collaborated in their search for natural resources and wealth.

There was widespread rejection of the AFRC/RUF even as Tejan Kabbah and his government fled into exile in neighboring Guinea. Not a single international body or government, recognized the AFRC/RUF junta. The Kamajors in the south eastern region of Sierra Leone kept the AFRC/RUF rebels from taking control of their diamond mining areas. In February of 1998, the Nigerian-led ECOMOG forces moved on the junta in Freetown and sent them scampering to the Northern Province. As the junta tried to escape from the ECOMOG forces, some of them started indiscriminately shooting missiles into the city—hoping that this would be blamed on the ECOMOG forces. They also abducted thousands of young male youth, women and children to be used as combatants, and sex slaves, respectively, as they fled (SLTRC 2004: 35, 65).[1]

The Nigerian-led ECOMOG forces pursued these retreating AFRC/RUF fighters whom along with the junta that had formed the AFRC government moved into the bush to form a new joint rebel force—a rare instance of a formal army reverting to become a rebel force. The transformation of the army, or at least some of its commanders, to the status of rebels offered them an opportunity to modernize the rebel's command

---

1   For more on the legal implications of these abductions, see the documents of the postwar war crimes tribunal, the Special Court for Sierra Leone (SCSL): *Prosecutor v Alex Tamba Brima, Brima Bazzy Kamara, & Santigie Borbor Kanu*, Case No. SCSL 2004-16-PT; *Prosecutor v Brima*, SCSL-2003-06-1: Indictment, (March 7, 2003); *Prosecutor v Brima*, SCSL-2003-1: Decision Approving the Indictment and ORDER FOR Non-disclosure (March 7, 2003); *Prosecutor v Kamara*, SCSL-2003-10-1: Indictment (May 26, 2003).

and control structure. While the rebel leaders, such as Issa Sesay, Samuel "Mosquito" Bokarie and Eldred Collins had the economic and ruthless incentives to maintain order in the territories they controlled, the AFRC introduced strategic planning and command to their ranks. It was this strategic thinking at their disposal that contributed to their successful and devastating reentry into the capital on January 6, 1999.

Contrary to some scholarly opinion (such as Bøås 2001; Bangura 2000; Reno 2001; and Williams 2001), the ECOMOG peacekeepers led by a General Felix Mojukpero were incapable of defeating the RUF, whose supply line of weapons was strong, in part due to the extraction and sale of alluvial diamonds (see Smillie et al. 2000). Furthermore, Mojukpero was constrained by then civilian President Kabbah who would not allow ECOMOG to bomb the rebels' positions prior to their advance into the capital. Thus, only 6 months after they were expelled from the capital the AFRC/RUF operation code-named "No Living Thing" resulted in the worst violence and death toll in the history of Sierra Leone's civil war. Over 5,000 people were brutally killed, and thousands were raped, during the three weeks siege of Freetown. But in the end the AFRC/RUF rebels were dislodged from the capital and were forced back into the rain forests of the provincial areas.

In his economic characterization of these wars-which is also very relevant to, but have not been fully understood by proponents of the Clausewitzian ideas of war, Bangura (1997: 117; see also Collier et al. 2004) contends that it was the available economic incentives and opportunity that led to the prolongation of fighting, as the combatants gradually accepted, as sacrosanct, the nuanced unholy war narrative that the conflict offered an opportunity for them to get rich or die trying. As such, rebel forces collided with government forces in their illicit economic activities in the rain forests under their control (see Gberie 2005; Ellis 2007; Sawyer 2004).

Governance Architecture of the Rebel Factions—Successes and Failures

After his failed attempts to capture the capital in 1993, Taylor retreated northwesterly and instituted a parallel government in Gbarnga, Bong County-which became the political and economic capital of Greater Liberia. From here Taylor was able to effectively run his warlord economic empire. Reno (1995) has given us a graphic picture of how Taylor's war was financed by Liberia's (as well as Sierra Leone's) natural resources. Taylor dominated the political scene in Liberia, and according to Ellis (2007) even the peacekeepers found themselves in a position where they had no alternative but to accept his nominal political control over other factions and the peace processes. There are several factors that have been presented to explain Taylor's successes as a military commander (and the lead role of the NPFL in forming a relatively successful parallel government in Gbangha). First amongst these was Taylor's ability to use both armed violence and access to resources to his advantage. In spite of the chaotic theory espoused by Robert Kaplan (1994) which argued that the Liberian warscapes were an example of a violent war perpetrated by primitive Africans, Nicholi Lidow (2010), argues that, although the faction leaders used violence to sustain order, the internal dynamics of rebel governance architecture should be understood beyond the simplistic analysis that situates military organizations (and civilian life) as an outcome of state failure. According to Lidow, Taylor succeeded because he was able to impose an economic regime and a system of governance that operated in parallel to the dysfunctional formal economy and, by doing so, he was able to gain a comparative economic and political advantage over his rivals. From his headquarters in Gbarnga, Charles Taylor ordered his troops to protect civilians and encourage market activity. Taylor often gave stern speeches to his commanders and warned against harassing civilians (Lidow 2010: 16). Civilians held the key not only to NPFL's food supply, but also to Taylor's legitimacy as a political leader and businessman. In fact, according to Ellis (2007: 141–2):

> The immediate aim of each faction (especially Taylor's NPFL) was simple: it was to take and defend a core territory from which economic resources could be extracted, and where possible to extend this area, while the faction's political bosses turned this strength on the ground into political capital … Factions, and the people who lived under their yoke, were ingenious in finding new sources of livelihood or profit. A particular innovation was the collection of buried rubber waste from the Firestone plantation which, it was discovered, could be sold for reprocessing at US$50 per tonne. This led to the world's first known example of runner being mined. It was known to the diggers as *bouncing diamonds*. Fighters took food from villagers as a form of direct tribute, but they also supervised or took levies from gold and diamond mining, rubber-tapping and palm oil

manufacture all of these processes being carried out using artisanal methods by civilians who then had to pay at least a part of the proceeds to the fighters who ruled them.

Foreign firms were able to justify their business with Taylor because he was able to maintain the appearance of a responsible leader (Reno 1998: 102). In Ellis's (2007: 142) purview, "where foreign firms were operating with heavy equipment, factions would simply tax them for the right to export rubber or logs." In the end, the peacekeepers were forced to accept his pseudo-democratic political legitimacy following his election to the presidency in 1997.

Beyond the economic explanation lies other factors for Taylor's success, there are other factors that explain these successes. Factors such as the educational attainment of the NPFL leadership (which the RUF leadership in Sierra Leone lacked), Taylor's regional/international connections and Taylor's ability to use ethnicity and identity politics narratives to his advantage played an equally important role in the successes of the NPFL in Liberia (Ellis 2007: 138–40). However, the political structure of the NPFL faction contributed more in creating the enabling environment for Taylor's NPFL faction to succeed both economically and politically. This is because, like the other factions in Liberia the NPFL was no more than a political party in arms "and the ultimate of the main leaders was to take state power. Rank-and-file fighters, and their habitual victims, were also the voters in democratic elections. The most eloquent illustration of this was that the July 1997 presidential election produced a landslide victory for Charles Taylor, the greatest warlord or them all"; and furthermore, other faction leaders also "affected to be called 'Mr President' in anticipation of the day that they would govern the whole country" (Ellis 2007: 140–41).

Closely related to this political factor is the use of divide-and-rule tactics. In that, as Ellis further tells us,

> Charles Taylor was particularly adept in playing off his commanders against each other. In the important Harbel sector, which for most of the war faced the Ecomog (the West African peacekeeping force) front line, Taylor would appoint his best officers to forward commands but would make sure that two commanders who disliked each other held neighbouring districts, minimizing the risk that they would combine against him. (Ellis 2007: 141)

In Sierra Leone, unlike the Charles Taylor-led NPFL rule in Greater Liberia, while the RUF leadership was a collection of illiterate, albeit pseudo-revolutionaries (Abdullah 1998), their joining forces with the mutinied soldiers to form the joint AFRC/RUF government (or as they called themselves—The Peoples' Army) did not help them get better. Besides, their union led to the total destabilization of the country. They were unable to maintain order in their areas of control. The economic incentive, through tax concessions to foreign firm doing business with them; and the imposition of a tax-for-security on an already war weary people (a system that was working well for its counterparts in Liberia, the NPFL (see Ellis 2007: 143) were far less to the huge sums of money it was making from its loot: in livestock and alluvial diamonds—which by 1999 accounted for at least 70 percent of RUF's funding (see Smillie et al. 2000). In the end, the people did not matter much to the AFRC/RUF rebel government. From its formation (as a government in 1997) to its ultimate final battle for control of the capital, the ARFC/RUF lunched a series of attacks on the civilian populations: Operation No Living Soul; Operation burn-se (Operation Burning of Houses); Operation cut-han (Operation Cutting of Hands/limbs/feet); Operation fen you yon woman (Operation Find Your Woman [to rape]), are all examples of the kind of relationship they had with the people.

However, it would be unfair to dismiss the AFRC as junta without any economic governance capacity. In fact, Major Koroma initially wanted to institute stringent economic policies, but instead of taxing the people, his aim was to use the diamonds to finance his government programs. This, as expected, did not go down well with Charles Taylor, who had relied on the diamonds (for guns) program run by the RUF, to govern his country, hence the nativity of their sour relationship.

In reaction to what he saw as an attempt by Taylor to compromise his legitimacy as junta leader, Johnny Paul Koroma arrested a number of his close aides, including Tamba Gborie, whom he suspect were working closely with the Liberian leadership to undermine "'the revenue-generating capacity' of the Ministry of Mines and Mineral Resources" (Gberie 2005: 115). Moreover, from our estimation and recollection of the nature of the AFRC/RUF rule, Major Koroma initially attempted to create for himself a local support base when he set up several phone-help lines to enable the people to report incidences of RUF's ruthlessness and looting activities, as well as through the imposition of a military decree which placed a dusk 'til dawn curfew (Riley 2007: 290), thus restricting the movement of the RUF rebels who were not part of his governing council. However, it proved a futile response to control the countless numbers of armed and often drug-crazed RUF rebels (Gberie 2005). Since he was unable to feed them, Koroma had no option but to allow them to continue doing *jah-jah* (the RUF word for the use of violence to hunt for lootables and food) in the capital (Lahai 2012b: 50).

Moreover, since the RUF grows out of the violent and drug prone peri-urban slums, and its leadership is peopled by mal-educated and illiterate young men from disadvantaged backgrounds (Richards 1996: 25; Rashid 2004: 66; Bangura 2004; Zack-Williams 1999) who had ended up in the *pote*—peri-urban drug infested shanty settlements for the poor, a home to violent youth (Abdullah 1998; 2004)—, the nature of the RUF's relationship with the more structured AFRC was chaotic. Any attempt to checkmate their perpetration of violence against civilians was interpreted as an attempt to hijack the movement from them.

Despite the fact that Taylor was somewhat sympathetic to the cause of Major Johnny Paul Koroma in Sierra Leone, (Gberie 2005), it would later emerge that he did not trust the soldiers, whose economic policies were diametrically opposed to Taylor's. This however does not mean the AFRC junta soldiers were not trying to enter into a political courtship with the maverick Liberian warlord-president. In fact, they were in a fierce competition with the RUF for his attention. But, since he did not believe their promises of maintaining the constant flow of Sierra Leone's alluvial diamonds, Taylor opted to support the RUF.

With the leadership structure of the RUF on the verge of changing hands, which would have meant a distortion in its patron-client relationship with its benefactor Taylor, it was alleged, in the local media houses in Sierra Leone, that he handpicked Issa Sesay as tentative commander of the RUF in 1999. He insisted that the mutinied soldiers, while they should retain the chairmanship of the Junta, they should accept Issa Sesay as the interim nominal leader of the RUF, and thus become the vice president of the junta government (if they hoped to be under Taylor's protective political backing and military assistance). At first this structural arrangement appeared to work, for example, both sub-groups were collaborating in some of their attacks and in their secret meetings with their Liberian patron, Taylor.

After their disastrous attempt to retake the capital in 1999, the RUF and AFRC split because of differences over strategies (Williams 2001). While the mutinied soldiers wanted to continue the siege of the capital Freetown, the RUF insisted that they pull back to their pre-1997 positions in the diamond areas-in Koidu and its out Eastern fringes on the Sierra Leone-Liberian border townships, where they believed they would be able to regroup and rearm before attempting to venture into the western axis of the country's capital city, Freetown.[2]

The soldiers ended up forming the West Side Boys (WSB) and remained in the capital until they were defeated by a team of British commandos. According to Utas and Jörgel (2008), despite societal constructs that they were a group of renegade and anarchistic bandits, the WSB had a well devised military structure. Indeed, because of their skills "military commanders and politicians employed the WSB as a tactical instrument in a larger map of military and political strategies" (Utas and Jörgel 2008: 488).

Negotiating Peace and Seeking Justice

The US government in conjunction with ECOMOG, persuaded President Tejan Kabbah to capitulate to the AFRC/RUF demands resulting in the 1999 Lome Peace Agreement. This gave the RUF four cabinet positions in Kabbah's government in a power-sharing agreement, and conceded them access to the natural resources sector-which led to a series of post-Lome Accord protests by university students and market women, and other sectors of the civil society who saw this political concession as a betrayal (Gberie 2005: 135).

The peace deal also included the clause that dictated that Foday Sankoh should be (and was indeed) given the political status equivalent to that of the country's vice president. He was also appointed Chairperson of

---

2 Comments by Sierra Leonean Political Commentator Oswald Hanciles, interviewed by John Idriss Lahai, July 20, 2014.

the Strategic Minerals Commission, which had power to control, monitor, and market all precious minerals (see, Hirsh 2001; Smillie et al. 2000).[3] He also had the power to determine how proceeds from the sales of these precious minerals would be disbursed. In effect, it made Foday Sankoh, at least by the pecuniary powers granted him, more powerful than the elected President, Tejan Kabbah (see Gberie 2005).

The Lome Peace Agreement allowed Foday Sankoh to become ensconced in the capital. Following his return from exile to pick up his political appointment, Sankoh was cruising around the capital city in a motorcade with dispatch riders; and until his arrest by the people, he lived comfortably in the affluent Spur Road suburb of Freetown (Rashid 2000). In May 2000, rumors abounded that Foday Sankoh was plotting a coup against Tejan Kabbah's government. According to Ofuatey-Kodjoe,

> Foday Sankoh announced publicly that UNAMSIL (the United Nations Armed Mission to Sierra Leone) On May 8, 2000, over 100,000 civilians (mainly of women and university students) was a threat to the security of the people of Sierra Leone. Following this declaration, the AFRC/RUF forces proceeded to reignite the conflict. In the eastern part of the country, rebel forces attacked UNAMSIL forces, and there were almost daily reports of outbreaks of violence. (Ofuatey-Kodjoe 2003: 136)

With the lack of progress, despite the UN Security Council's decision (through Resolution 1289, of February 7, 2000) to double the size of the peacekeeping force to 11, 100, including the 260 international observers already deployed, the people—women's groups and university students—marched on his residence in a show of defiance to avoid plunging the country back into civil war (Ofuatey-Kodjoe 2003: 136). Foday Sankoh's bodyguards opened fire on the crowds—killing eight (Onishi 2000: 1–6). Sankoh fled, but was later captured by the enraged crowd. He was handed over to the Kabbah government, thus putting an end to the charade of the Lome Peace Agreement (Ofuatey-Kodjoe 2003: 136–7).

It was not until 2002 when an economic and political compromise was reached that ended the conflict in Sierra Leone. The United Nations established the Special Court of Sierra Leone (SCSL), which put Foday Sankoh and several of the RUF leaders on trial, including Chief Hinga Norman, a Kamajor leader who was arrested while he was the Minister of Internal Affairs in Tejan Kabbah's SLPP government. Both Sankoh and Norman died while being prosecuted by the Special Court, before justice could be served for their war-crimes.

In Liberia, in order to achieve peace for the country, Charles Taylor was under the impression he would retire in peace, somewhere in Nigeria with the continued financial support and gratuity pension from ECOWAS (Tejan-Cole 2009). Spurred by these promises, Taylor agreed to negotiate with the rebels in 2002. In 2003, during peace talks in Accra, Ghana between Taylor and the leaders of the rebel groups—Sekou Conneh of the Liberians United for Reconciliation an Democracy (LURD), and Thomas Nimerly of the Movement for Democracy in Liberia (MODEL)—Taylor accepted the economic and political overtures of ECOWAS and went into exile in Calaba State, Nigeria. However, in 2005 he was arrested and handed over to the Special Court of Sierra Leone which found him guilty of aiding and abetting the criminal activities of the RUF. He was sentenced in June 2012 to 50 years' imprisonment, which he is currently serving in a jail in England. Ironically, England has also played host to many of the Sierra Leoneans migrants and refugees affected by the wars, and this diaspora is now faced with the fact that their taxes are being used to fund his prison sentence.

Conclusion

One of the most prevalent types of armed conflict in West Africa is the opportunistic resource driven wars. Inasmuch as other factors contributed to their emergence in the 1990s, the economic considerations played an important part in determining the nature of violence, and in the prolongation of the fighting. Prior to the eruption of these kinds of wars in the sub-region, the political economy was largely infested with political patrimonialism and corruption: abuse of office, bribery and embezzlement. Moreover, it was the ineptitude of the political elites that led to the emergence of a shadow economy, a "parallel state economy" controlled by a class of pseudo-entrepreneurs, mostly of Middle Eastern origins (the Syrians and Lebanese business

---

3   See Article VII Lome Peace Accord, http://www.sierra-leone.org/lomeaccord.html.

men) (Reno 1998), on whom the governments relied upon to provide the basic necessities for the populace in exchange for a hold of the country's natural resources. Within such a situation, the informal economy dwarfed the weak formal economic sector.

To salvage this situation, international financial institutions, such as the International Monetary Fund (IMF) and World Bank, had entered the scene with economic conditionality that could not be met because of the level of corruption. These internal workings of bad governance contributed to state failure, amid the inability of the governments to monopolize the use of force. Politically motivated violence becomes the order, and political measures to control them, the exception; where inter-generational tensions (between the largely marginalized youth and the octogenarian political elites) became the norm that guided people's socialization processes; where the legitimacy of the government disappeared and in its place emerged competing violence-prone centers of power controlled by young men (and sometimes women—as the leaders, dubbed Mammie Queens, from the women's wing of the governing political party, APC) (Lahai 2010b: 32), as they gradually moved from their peri-urban drug infested slums into the jungles to start fighting against the predatory central government peopled largely by octogenarian political elites (Abdullah 1998; Ellis 2007; Gberie 2005). In the jungles, these fighters lost sense of their initial intentions, of overthrowing the system and replacing it with a better one. What emerged thereafter were rogue systems in which these young men and women engaged in the economic exploitation of the country's natural resources (Richards 2006). They targeted and killed the very people they were supposed to protect. In this situation, the targeting of innocent civilians was a way of making their point: to get the recognition they needed from the international community. Indeed, it is true that the idea of wanting to replace the government remained for most of these countries. At least in all the peace negotiations in Liberia and Sierra Leone between 1991 and 1999 the rebel factions had insisted on their right to control government. For scholars such as Gberie (2005), Smillie et al. (2000) and Sawyer (2004), among others, the rebel groups' desires to control government was to give them the space and legitimacy in their dealings with the international community and as well as with the rogue international economic regimes interested in doing business with them. That notwithstanding, the overall aim of war was to continue fighting for natural resources and resources for guns (Collier et al. 2004).

We have seen how in his characterization of these wars, Bangura (1997: 117; also see Collier et al. 2004) has talked about how the available economic incentives and associated economic opportunities had helped prolong these wars, as the combatants gradually accept, as sacrosanct, the nuanced unholy war narrative that conflict offered an opportunity for them (men and women) to get rich or die trying. In these warscapes, rebel forces collided with government forces in their illicit economic activities (see Gberie 2005; Sawyer 2004).

As such, economic incentives were an effective tool to entice combatants to stop fighting. From a neo-Durkheimian analytical perspective, Richards (2010) gave us an illustration of how feeding the collective created social loyalties, as well as in helping to save the lives of civilians in the warzones. Of course during the fighting farms were raided and the food in refugee and IDP camps had depleted. As a result, many entered the warscapes in search for food; to kill for it, even if it is not necessary. Understanding this opportunistic nature of the war, the intervening agro-based humanitarian agencies created a *seed security approach to peace* in central Sierra Leone (what he referred to as Northern Jungle). To avert the possibility where the ex-fighters would return to the bush (which actually occurred on several occasions), Richards informed us that, the project, which was being implement by a non-governmental organization had two major components: "a seed exchange programme; and an annual 'peace and rights day' consultation, during which ritual elements were brought to bear on local tensions and grievances resulting from disputes over relief distribution" (Richards 2010: 141). Apart from preventing the ex-fighters from returning to their opportunistic adventures, this agro-based economic incentive, Richards contends, also mitigated tensions between "returnees" (those returning to their communities after the fighting) and the "stayees" (those that stayed behind and lived among the rebel forces in their war communities). It was a common occurrence during the last stages of the conflicts in both countries, for the "stayees" to engage in violent clashes with the "returnees." Whereas, the former were accusing the latter of abandonment, and were insisting that they should not benefit from the food aid that NGOs were delivering in former rebel controlled areas. The returnees were accusing the "stayees" of collaborating with the rebels and therefore should not be seen as people in need of food assistance. They premised their grievance on the belief that those that stayed behind participated in the destruction of their communities and in pillaging their rice farms. Despite these threats, the wars came to an end, and peace, no matter how elusive, had offered the people in these countries with the opportunities to memorialize their wartime past and begin the processes of post-conflict nation-building.

References

Abdullah, I. (1998). Bush Path to Destruction: The Origin and Character of the Revolutionary United Front/Sierra Leone. *Journal of Modern African Studies*, 36(2): 203–35. DOI:10.1017/S0022278X98002766.

Abdullah, I. (ed.) (2004). *Between Democracy and Terror: The Sierra Leone Civil War*. Dakar: Council for the Development of Social Science Research in Africa.

Abdullah, I. and Muana, P.K. (1998). The Revolutionary United Front of Sierra Leone. A Revolt of the Lumpenproletariat. In Clapham, Christopher (ed.), *African Guerrillas*. Oxford: James Currey, 45–76.

Abraham, A. (2004). The Elusive Quest for Peace: From Abidjan to Lome. In Ibrahim Abdullai (ed.), *Between Democracy and Terror: The Sierra Leone Civil War*. Dakar: Council for the Development of Social Science Research in Africa, 199–219.

Allen, C. (1995). *Understanding African Politics. Review of African Political Economy*, 22(65): 301–20.

Bangura, Y. (2004). The Political and Cultural Dynamics of the Sierra Leone War: A Critique of Paul Richards. In I. Abdullah (ed.), *Between Democracy and Terror: The Sierra Leone Civil War*. Dakar: Council for the Development of Social Science Research in Africa.

Bangura, Y. (1997). Understanding the Political and Cultural Dynamics of the Sierra Leone War: A Critique of Paul Richard's "Fighting for the Rain Forest." *Africa Development*, 22(3/4): 117–48.

Bangura, Y. (2000). Strategic Policy Failure and Governance in Sierra Leone. *The Journal of Modern African Studies*, 38(4): 551–77.

Bøås, M. (2001). Liberia and Sierra Leone-Dead Ringers? The Logic of Neopatrimonial Rule. *Third World Quarterly*, 22(5): 697–723.

Clapham, C. (1996). *Africa and the International System: The Politics of State Survival*. Cambridge: Cambridge University Press.

Collier, P., Hoeffler, A., and Söderbom, M. (2004). On the Duration of Civil War. *Journal of Peace Research*, 41(3): 253–73.

Conteh-Morgan, E. and Dixon-Fyle, M. (1999). *Sierra Leone at the End of the Twentieth Century: History, Politics, and Society*. New York: Peter Lang Publishing.

Ellis, S. (2001). Mystic Weapons: Some Evidence from the Liberia War. *Journal of Religion in Africa*, 31(2): 222–36.

Ellis, S. (2007). *The Mask of Anarchy: The Destruction of Liberia and the Religious Dimension of an African Civil War*. New York: New York University Press.

Ellis, S. and Haar, G.T. (2004). *Worlds of Power: Religious Thoughts and Political Practice in Africa*. London: Hurst and Company.

Gberie, L. (2005). *A Dirty War in West Africa: The RUF and the Destruction of Sierra Leone*. Bloomington: Indiana University Press.

Hoffman, D. (2003). Like Beasts in the Bush. *Postcolonial Studies*, 6(3): 295–308.

Hoffman, D. (2005). Violent Events as Narratives Blocs: The Disarmament at Bo, Sierra Leone. *Anthropological Quarterly*, 78(2): 329–54.

Hoffman, D. (2007). The Meaning of a Militia: Understanding the Civil Defence Forces of Sierra Leone. *African Affairs*, 106(425): 639–62.

Hubbard, M. (1998), *The Liberian Civil War*. London: Frank Cass.

Kandeh, J. (1996). What does the "Militariat" Do When it Rules? Military Regimes in The Gambia, Sierra Leone and Liberia. *Review of African Political Economy*, 23(69): 387–404.

Kandeh, J. (1999). Ransoming the State: Elite Origins of Subaltern Terror in Sierra Leone. *Review of African Political Economy*, 26(81): 349–66.

Kaplan, R. (1994 [1996]). *The Ends of the Earth: A Journey to the Frontiers of Anarchy*, New York: Vintage Books.

Keen, D. (2005). *Conflict and Collusion in Sierra Leone*. New York: Palgrave Macmillan.

Lahai, J.I. (2010a). Gendered Battlefields: A Contextual and Comparative Analysis of Women's Participation in Armed Conflicts in Africa. *Peace and Conflict Review*, 4(2): 1–15. http://www.review.upeace.org/pdf.cfm?articulo=98&ejemplar=19.

Lahai, J.I. (2010b). Sexing the State: The Gendered Origins of the Civil War in Sierra Leone. *Minerva Journal of Women and War*, 4(2): 26–45.

Lahai, J.I. (2012a). Women and the Gendered Frontiers of Conflict and Post-conflict Transformation in Sierra Leone and Liberia (PhD Thesis), University of New England, Australia.

Lahai, J.I. (2012b). Youth Agency and Survival Strategies in Sierra Leone's Post War Informal Economy. In Marisa O. Ensor (ed.), *African Childhoods: Survival, Education and Peace-Building in the Youngest Continent*. New York: Palgrave Macmillan Press, 65–85.

Lahai, J.I. (2012c). Fused in Combat: Unsettling the Gendered Hierarchy and Women's Roles in the Fighting Forces during the Sierra Leone Civil War. *Australasian Review of African Studies*, 33(1): 34–55.

Lidow, N. (2010). *Rebel Governance and Civilian Abuse: Comparing Liberia's Rebels Using Satellite Data.* Paper prepared for WGAPA, Berkeley, California (December 17–18). http://www.sscnet.ucla.edu/polisci/wgape/papers/19_Lidow.pdf.

Ofuatey-Kodjoe, W. (2003). Sierra Leone. In Jane Boulden (ed.), *Dealing with Conflict in Africa: The United Nations and Regional Organisations*. New York: Palgrave Macmillan, 127–52.

Omonijo, M. (1990). *Doe: The Liberian Tragedy*. Ikeja, Nigeria: Sahel Publishing.

Onishi, N. (2000). Fighting Resumes near the Capital of Sierra Leone. *New York Times*, May 8, A1, A10.

Rashid, I. (2000). The Lomé Peace Negotiations. In David Lord (ed.), *Accord: Paying the Price: The Sierra Leone Peace Process*, Accord: 9. London: Conciliation Resources.

Rashid, I. (2004). Student Radicals, Lumpen Youth, and the Origins of Revolutionary Groups in Sierra Leone, 1977–1996. In Ibrahim Abdullah (ed.), *Between Democracy and Terror: The Sierra Leone Civil War*. Dakar: Council for the Development of Social Science Research in Africa, 238–54.

Reno, W. (1993). Foreign Firms and the Financing of Charles Taylor's NPFL. *Liberian Studies Journal*, 18(2): 175–87.

Reno, W. (1995). The Reinvention of an African Patrimonial State: Charles Taylor's Liberia. *Third World Quarterly*, 16(1): 109–20.

Reno, W. (1998). Sierra Leone's Transition to Warlord Politics. In William Reno (ed.), *Warlord Politics in African States*. Boulder, CO: Lynne Rienner Publishers, 113–45.

Reno, W. (2001). The Failure of Peacekeeping in Sierra Leone. *Current History*, 100(646): 219–25.

Richards, P. (1996). *Fighting in the Rain Forest: War, Youth and Resources in Sierra Leone*. Oxford: James Currey.

Richards, P. (2006). An Accidental Sect: How War Made Belief in Sierra Leone. *Review of African Political Economy*, 33(110): 651–63.

Richards, P. (2010). Ritual Dynamics in Humanitarian Assistance. *Disasters*, 34(2): 138–46.

Riley, S. (2007). Sierra Leone: The Militariat Strikes Again. *Review of African Political Economy*, 24(72): 287–92.

Sawyer, Amos. (2004). Violent Conflict and Governance Challenges in West Africa: The Case of the Mano River Basin Area. *The Journal of Modern African Studies*, 42(3): 437–63.

Schuster, L. (1994). The Final Days of Dr. Doe. *Granta*, 48 (Summer): 39–95.

Sierra Leone Truth and Reconciliation Commission (SLTRC). (2004). *Final Report: Witness to the Truth*. Freetown, Sierra Leone: SLTRC.

Smillie, I., Gberie, L., and Hazleton, R. (2000). *The Heart of the Matter, Sierra Leone, Diamonds and Human Security*. Ottawa: Partnership Africa-Canada.

Tejan-Cole, A. (2009). A Big Man in a Small Cell: Charles Taylor and the Special Court for Sierra Leone. In Ellen L. Lutz and Caitlin Reiger (eds), *Prosecuting Heads of State*. Cambridge: Cambridge University Press, 205–32.

Utas, M. and Jörgel, M. (2008). The West Side Boys: Military Navigation in the Sierra Leone Civil War. *Journal of Modern African Studies*, 46(3): 487–511.

Williams, P. (2001). Fighting for Freetown: British Military Intervention in Sierra Leone. *Contemporary Security Policy*, 22(3): 140–68.

Wlodarczyk, N. (2009). *Magic and Warfare: Appearance and Reality in Contemporary African Conflict and Beyond.* New York: Palgrave Macmillan.

Youboty, J. (1993). *Liberian Civil War: A Graphic Account.* Philadelphia, PA: Parkside Impressions Enterprises.

Zack-Williams, A.B. (1999). Sierra Leone: The Political Economy of Civil War, 1991–98. *Third World Quarterly*, 20(1): 143–62.

Zack-Williams, Alfred B. (1994). *Tributors, Supporters and Merchant Capital: Mining and Underdevelopment in Sierra Leone.* Aldershot: Ashgate.

Chapter 3
Reconsidering Rebel Governance

Isabelle Duyvesteyn, Georg Frerks, Boukje Kistemaker, Nora Stel and Niels Terpstra[1]

Abstract

In debates on governance in weak or fragile states, non-state actors are often overlooked. A particularly under-recognized governance actor is the rebel group. Rebel groups have substantive involvement in several governance domains, and as such acquire authority and legitimacy among their constituents. While previous research shows that non-state governance cannot be seen as the sole result of state weakness or as opposition to the state necessarily, this chapter addresses the complexity, multiplicity and (practical) dynamics of rebel governance. International actors, such as states and non-governmental organizations (NGOs), struggle to decide on whether or how to engage with rebel groups. Studying the dynamics of rebel governance will shed new light on policy debates on insurgency, peacebuilding and development in contexts of state fragility in the African borderlands. The cases of the Sudan People's Liberation Movement/Army (SPLM/A) in South Sudan, the National Resistance Army (NRA) in Uganda and the Union of Islamic Courts (UIC) in Somalia will serve as examples of rebel governance in the African context.

Introduction

Traditionally, governance was viewed as a synonym for government, as the acts and processes by which the state attempts to maintain public order (Mampilly 2007; Stoker 1998). Increasingly, however, social and political science recognize that providing security, welfare and political representation is not, and never has been, a prerogative of the state (Clements et al. 2007; Milliken and Krause 2002; Kalyvas et al. 2009; Krasner 2004). While the state may still be regarded as a dominant actor in the provision of public goods, non-state actors—including those in direct contention with the state—have proven to possess the means (i.e. armed forces, administrative system and taxation) and ambition to provide a constituency with security (through regulating the internal use of force and offering protection from external threats), welfare (by means of offering social and utility services) and political representation (through institutions for consultation and normative regulation)—often in a relatively demarcated territory (Mampilly 2007; Hagmann and Péclard 2010; Lund 2006). Governance, therefore, should not be viewed through a state-centric lens, but more broadly, as the "whole set of practices and norms that govern daily life in a specific territory" (Mampilly 2007: 61; see also Raeymakers et al. 2008; Stoker 1998). Hence, there is a need to move away from a focus on sovereignty and an assumed state exclusivity, towards a more comprehensive and agnostic study of political hybridity (Boege et al. 2009a; 2009b) and state-society interaction (Migdal 2001).

Particularly relevant in this discussion are common notions of "failed" or "failing" states which assume that weakness or absence of the state would lead to Hobbesian anarchy, supposedly also undermining (inter) national security and development (Krasner 2004; Mampilly 2007; Boege et al. 2009a; 2009b). Many developing states indeed lack the capacity to uphold the Weberian monopoly of force over their territory,

---

1 The secondary research underlying this chapter was made possible thanks to a grant by the Gerda Henkel Stiftung for the research project *Rebel Governance* by Utrecht University. This chapter was partly written on the basis of the unpublished working paper *Rebel Governance: Post-Conflict Life Under Non-State Rule*, written by Georg Frerks, Isabelle Duyvesteyn, Matthew Lower and Thijs Jeursen which was presented at the Rebel Governance Seminar, December 6, 2013, at Utrecht University. The authors of this chapter would like to acknowledge the inputs of Thijs Jeursen and Matthew Lower.

and whilst these states possess *de jure* sovereignty, including international recognition, they do not possess *de facto* sovereign control (Krasner 2004; 2005). Presence of non-state authorities, it is argued, would then represent an absence of not only the state, but of any governance at all—as the words of "failed states"; "weak states" (Rice and Patrick 2008); "quasi states" (Jackson 1990); or "fragile states" (Naudé et al. 2011; McIouglin 2010) suggest.

Tellingly, analyses of state fragility are often accompanied by ideas on "ungoverned spaces" and "institutional voids" (Rabasa et al. 2008). Yet, these arguments are made without analysis or recognition of non-state governance. This discussion is particularly of relevance to the study of postcolonial African states, as many of those are labelled as fragile, weak, or failed states.[2]

Rebel Groups

A particularly under-recognized governance actor within the debates on state fragility is the rebel group. Rebel groups frequently have substantive involvement in most or even all governance domains, often without the state's permission (Mampilly 2007; Hagmann and Péclard 2010; Weinstein 2007; Reno 2009). These groups can also represent legitimate and popular grievances within the status quo. Toft shows rebel groups may even produce improvements in "good governance," compared to state performance (2010: 25).

Indeed, where traditional perspectives on these groups focus on warlords, looting, human rights abuses, and their role as "spoilers" in development and democratization, in practice, the activities of rebel groups vary. Mampilly defines them as "armed factions that use violence to challenge the state" (2007: 2), distinguished from "militias" which includes all non-state armed groups, even those working alongside government forces (Mampilly 2007: 2). Podder (2013) employs the broader term of Non-State Armed Groups (NSAGs), which incorporates groups which are armed, use violence for political goals, are independent from state control and seek some level of control over a territory. Toft focuses on groups vying for control over governance tasks in a given territory (2010: 12). Our own definition does not necessarily equate rebel governance with opposition to the state, nor does it necessitate territorial control, but includes: armed non-state groups, independent from state control, who possess the capacity to contest other actors' hegemony over governance tasks. Contesting control over geographical areas may naturally extend from a group's efforts to fulfil their objectives, but it is not always central to its activities. By not necessitating that relevant armed non-state groups be in violent opposition to the state, our focus is not exclusively on anti-state governance.

The discussion on the potential legitimacy of rebel groups is of clear relevance to policy and academic debates on international engagement in African borderlands. A growing body of literature demonstrates a primary problem with development and state-building discourses that lack engagement with non-state actors, and particularly rebel groups (Mampilly 2007; Branch and Mampilly 2005; Toft 2010; Podder 2012; Autesserre 2009). Where the state is unfamiliar, distant and often irrelevant, several authors argue that non-state actors are instrumental in fulfilling the social contract demanded by a local population (Arjona 2010; Podder 2013; also see Kialee Nyiayaana in this volume).

Despite extensive research on rebel recruitment and self-financing (Mampilly 2007), there is a lack of recognition and a lack of broader understanding of the role of rebel groups in governance tasks. This has arguably led to a disconnect between counter-terrorism and development discourses on the one hand and realities on the ground on the other (Podder 2013; Hagmann and Péclard 2010; Reno 2009; Boege et al. 2009a; 2009b). David Chandler demonstrates that human rights discourses have become characterized by a simplistic "good versus evil" narrative (2006), with a commensurate vilification of rebel groups, condemned not to be negotiated with, nor properly understood (Reno 2009; Raeymakers et al. 2008; Podder 2013).

For donors, non-governmental organizations (NGOs) and transnational actors the existence of armed non-state actors and the way to deal with these actors provide clear dilemmas (Harvey et al. 2007; Department for International Development 2010; Podder 2012). Obviously, it would be problematic to assume that a majority of rebel groups are appropriate development partners, however, the variety and multiplicity of actions that

---

2   Countries such as Somalia, the Democratic Republic of the Congo, Sudan, South Sudan are often ranking "high" in state fragility indexes. This, however, naturally depends on the parameters used to establish such outcomes.

rebel groups perform signifies the necessity of understanding the wider context of rebel governance, beyond pre-determined or simplistic narratives misinterpreting realities on the ground.

The Organisation for Economic Co-operation and Development (2008) asserts that the resilience of a social contract should determine state-building strategies, but views the social contract only in a state-centric context. The "resilience" of a non-state actor's social contract with a constituency is also relevant, particularly if such a relationship will reduce violence and instability in the region under that actor's hegemony (United Nations Development Programme 2012). These actors may carry varying levels of legitimacy, and some may indeed be "spoilers," but others require engagement, and may be potential partners in state-building (Podder 2012; Boege et al. 2009a; 2009b).

Hence, in denouncing the "good versus evil" narrative, we advocate a more fine-grained understanding and reconsideration of a number of issues within the conception of rebel governance. Primarily, this chapter seeks to address the lack of understanding regarding the practical dynamics of rebel governance, and, consequently, the otherwise unrecognized legitimacy these groups may acquire. What type of governance tasks do rebel groups perform? How do they interact with other relevant governance actors? How and to what extent do they acquire, possess and project legitimacy? And, ultimately, should our perception of rebel groups, otherwise regarded as "spoilers" and detrimental to development and governance, be fundamentally reconsidered?

In an attempt to answer these questions, the multiplicities of third-world governance—distinct from pro-state, traditional or transnational governance within the state, and from exclusively *anti*-state governance—and the relevance of non-state actors performing such tasks will be highlighted. We shall refer to African examples, including the cases of the Sudan People's Liberation Movement/Army (SPLM/A), the National Resistance Army (NRA) and the Union of Islamic Courts (UIC).

Performing Governance

Rebel groups engage in governance practices and provide services to their constituents in three major domains: security, welfare, and political representation (Milliken and Krause 2002; Weinstein 2007). More specifically, rebel groups may provide health care, education, a legal system, a financial system, a police force, as well as institutions and administrations that deal with a variety of civilian concerns. Depending on their sources of income, rebel groups have developed complex bureaucratic structures for the collection of taxes and the distribution of public goods (Mampilly 2007; Podder 2014).

The division of labor and dynamics involved in the provision of governance services may differ in each political context. Tasks may partly be delivered by international organizations active in rebel-controlled territory, or still by the state itself. The SPLM/A in Sudan, for example, focused its resources mainly on its security and justice system. For the provision of public goods, such as education and health care, the population relied on the involvement of transnational aid organizations that proliferated in rebel controlled territory (Mampilly 2011: 6; see Box 3.1). The Congolese Rally for Democracy (RCD) in the Democratic Republic of Congo (DRC) developed a civil administration with specific departments of education, health care, social affairs, whereas at the same time several other public services continued to be delivered by the central government (Autessere 2006; Mampilly 2011).

Interactions with Other Relevant Governance Actors

As the example of the SPLM/A illustrates, non-state governance often involves overlapping "networks" with the state, other non-state actors and international actors. Rebel groups may contest other actors, but they may also cooperate (Gates 2002; Hagmann and Péclard 2010: 554).

As observed by Hagmann and Péclard (2010) a primary source of conflict is the provision of security, based on the state's limited ability to cater for the security of its citizens. Yet, in many cases the state remains a key stakeholder in this context (if more in theory than practice) primarily because the state is elevated above all other entities as the only actor potentially capable of providing long-term security (Migdal 2001: 18). Secondly, rebel groups and state institutions compete to control the institutional structure of governance

---

Box 3.1   Performing governance: Sudan People's Liberation Movement/Army

In 1994, the Civil Authority of the New Sudan (CANS) was established to change the governance of "individual rebel administrators" into more formalized political structures that were distinct from the military command (Mampilly 2011; Podder 2014). Yet, Johnson (1998) points out that all CANS officials were ex-rebels, which led to the intermingling of civilian and military culture in the supposedly civil apparatus. Nevertheless, the basic objective was to decentralize power to a hierarchy of local (civil) authorities, delegating governance tasks to local level leadership, particularly in order to avoid internal ethnic tensions and to keep support from the different southern ethnic groups (Mampilly 2011: 145–8). As a strategy, the establishment of the civil administration served to maintain popular appeal domestically, and to consolidate international legitimacy with the large number of foreign (aid) actors that also became involved in rebel controlled territories (Mampilly 2011; Podder 2014).

The SPLM/A introduced a military code of conduct to deal with complaints against rebel soldiers, and co-opted traditional authorities and customary legal mechanisms into a comprehensive judicial system for civilians. By formalizing customary law and using traditional courts, in combination with a military-based justice mechanism, the legal system served to regulate daily life for rebel cadres and the civilian population (Mampilly 2011: 156–8). To serve educational and health care needs, the SPLM/A resorted to the co-optation and/or manipulation of foreign International Organizations and NGOs (Podder 2014). While the security and justice system could be seen as relatively functional, the functioning of the health and educational system varied widely from one locality to another (Mampilly 2011).

---

provision. This predominantly relates to the decentralization of the state apparatus, which revolves around "the balance of power between the 'center' of the state and its 'peripheries'" (Hagmann and Péclard 2010: 553).

Finally, identity and the politics of inclusion and exclusion are commonly an area of contestation. "Processes of state (de-) construction in Africa have been shaped by dynamics of inclusion and exclusion: the question of defining who belongs and who does not belong to the nation (state), who is indigenous and who is foreign" (Hagmann and Péclard 2010: 554).

The distinction between contestation and cooperation, however, is not always as clear-cut as it may seem. A pertinent question here is how to conceptualize rebel governance in relation to the state, particularly in situations where the performance of extensive governance tasks occurs in parallel with predatory behavior. There is a tendency in the literature to equate non-state actor governance with anti-state governance. Within approaches focusing on anti-state sovereignty, rebel groups are perceived as rejecting ineffective, abused and transplanted "state" institutions which cannot fulfil the basic requirements of a sovereign system (Mampilly 2007: 4). However, this perspective may not suit every instance of rebel governance. For instance, Hagmann and Péclard (2010) question whether the existence of rebel groups necessarily erodes or contends the power of the state. Scholars have discussed and documented the various interactions, partnerships and alliances between rebel groups and state institutions (Duffield 1998; Hibou 2012; Siniawer 2012; Stel 2015), and conceptualized this phenomena in various models, namely: "mediated states" (Menkhaus 2007), "limited states" (Migdal 2001), "hybrid political orders" (Boege et al. 2009a, 2009b), and "twilight institutions" (Lund 2006).

Subsequently, on-going interactions between state and rebel groups are linked to transformations of the state itself (Tull 2003; Müller 2012). For example, Müller (2012) shows how rebel leaders became Ministers in the state apparatus of Eritrea, and Tull (2003) explains in what way local strongmen became part of the Mobutist state in the DRC. Podder (2014) shows how rebel governance and post-conflict legitimacy are connected in the case of the SPLM/A.

The question is whether parallel governing institutions accurately reflect these varying models. Goodfellow and Lindemann (2013) argue that a lack of synthesis of these different institutions means they can be better conceptualized as (a part of) institutional multiplicity, "providing distinct and different normative frameworks and incentive structures in which [political and economic actors] act" (Hesselbein et al. 2006: in Goodfellow and Lindemann 2013: 7). Moreover, Duffield's notion of reflexive modernity comes to mind (2002). In addition, many theoretical and empirical studies refer to the diversity of political environments in which non-state/rebel actors attempt to govern (Müller 2012; Goodfellow and Lindemann 2013). For example, in some cases "hybridity" is associated with reducing violent conflict, whilst in others it is associated with state fragility.

This indicates that the interplay and dynamics between rebel groups and state actors concerning complementarity, active arrangements, and contradiction/competition, remain relatively unknown and require empirical research (Mehler 2004). It remains especially unclear when and in what way rebel groups replace and/or become a part of state institutions, and in what way this institutionalization of rebel governance and practices affect the provision of services by rebel groups (Weinstein 2007; Mampilly 2011). For example, can the semi-autonomous Wajir County in North Eastern Kenya be considered to be a "state-within-a-state," or simply the state itself? And how is local governance driven, shaped, and affected by the (inter)national legitimacy of the different governance actors concerned?

Projecting Legitimacy

Whilst the weakness of the state is clearly a contributing factor in the non-state group's involvement in governance, research increasingly shows that instances of non-state governance cannot merely be seen as a result of state weakness, but have an autonomous dynamic as well (Migdal 2001; Mampilly 2007; Kalyvas et al. 2009; Arjona 2010; Raeymaekers et al. 2008). Processes of state de-legitimization resulting from engagement between rebel actors and local populations may explain long-term governance relationships beyond anti-state or singularly economic perspectives, in the form of a "social contract." These processes may in turn influence the provision of services by the rebel group and its relationship with other actors.

A social contract broadly constitutes an implicit understanding between a population and dominant power, whereby, "the people grant the state the right to rule over them in return for the state providing security from civil disorder and war" (Milliken and Krause 2002: 758), as well as other services. Discussion of rebel governance generally links social contracts to economic interests, whereby the pragmatic benefits of taxation, opposed to banditry, leads to a reciprocal supply of public goods (Weinstein 2007; Beardsley and McQuinn 2009). Olson asserts this to be less of a social contract, but more "rational self-interest among those who can organize the greatest capacity for violence" (1993: 568).

Yet, economic arguments only partially explain the phenomenon of rebel governance, and traditional perceptions commonly fail to move beyond viewing this phenomenon as a by-product of revenue extraction Mampilly demonstrates that a rebel group's decision to engage in governance tasks is a combination of influences from the population, internal group dynamics, and pressure from separate domestic and international actors (Mampilly 2007: 29).

Populations actively seek to negotiate a relationship with relevant elites and dominant groups, thus increasing pressure upon a rebel group to provide public goods (particularly security), without which it would struggle to maintain a hegemonic position. In studying the provision of governance tasks, the behavior and reaction of citizens should therefore be taken into account as "civilians are never passive or invisible actors, and can manipulate the structure of a rebel civil administration" (Mampilly 2007: 21; see also Kalyvas 2003). Also, recent studies show that rebel groups need to be strategic in their interaction with civilians in order to transition into legitimate and viable alternatives to the state, particularly in post-conflict settlements (Podder 2014).

Hence, one reason rebel groups perform governance tasks may therefore be to legitimize their existence in the political space (Milliken and Krause 2002: 756). Dahl (1971) demonstrates that it is easier to rule through perceived legitimacy,[3] compared to pure coercion. Evidence demonstrates that many rebel groups either actively seek legitimacy, or acquire it through their actions (Toft 2010; Podder 2012, 2013; Reno 2009; Branch and Mampilly 2005; Arjona 2010). A social contract may be constructed through both elite will and the capacity to provide public services, through the performance of these tasks and the extent to which a group becomes embedded in a population (Organisation for Economic Co-operation and Development 2008; Arjona 2010).

In fact, it is now recognized that legitimation is better viewed as a process, highly subjective and context dependent (Beetham 1991; Barker 2001; Thornhill 2008; Stel 2014), than as a fixed attribute of a state or rebel group. In a context of high insecurity, with multiple contesting groups, and an absent or abusive state,

---

3 For more on the legitimacy threshold see for example Stel (2014).

the provision of even a basic level of public services in itself constitutes a process of legitimation. Subsequent actions would contribute to this process, whether as an intentional goal, or as a longer-term result of rebel/population interaction (Arjona 2010).

Thus, a group's legitimacy is based on the "tacit social contract" with society (Podder 2013: 19). Within (situations of) violent conflict, the process of rebellion often involves criticism of the status quo and the highlighting of popular grievances (Toft 2010). Highlighting grievances in a post-conflict setting remains a crucial tool in maintaining a group's status and authority. In Libya, for example, rebel groups continued to justify their own (post-conflict) existence through so-called "revolutionary legitimacy" by stressing how they risked their lives during the revolution and successfully toppled the regime of Gaddafi (Sharqieh 2012; Jeursen and van der Borgh 2014).

Groups will often attempt to build recognition and legitimacy from international sources as well (Mampilly 2007). For example, non-state violence in Liberia in the 1990s focused extensively on the capital, Monrovia, which was attributed to the perception that the group controlling the capital and key symbols of statehood (i.e. the Presidential Palace) would be recognized as the predominant power, including by international actors (Duyvesteyn 2005). In other cases, ethnic identity has proven to be a crucial tenet in claiming legitimacy with a population, as was the case in Burundi for example in the early 1990s (Daley 2006).

Moreover, this pursuit of authority through legitimation includes more intangible processes of identity building, through symbols such as flags, songs, references to tradition, ethnicity. This process of building legitimacy through symbolism often involves "mimicry" of the state and state institutions to portray authority and cement claims of legitimacy portrayed to international actors (Hoehne 2009). For example in Somaliland and Puntland in Somalia, the contestants to the (absent) Somali state have gone to considerable lengths to portray elements of modern statehood, in a process of nation and identity building (Hoehne 2009). Podder highlights the use of nationalist propaganda by the SPLM/A in Sudan through the printing of a national currency (2014: 222).

These sources of legitimation have parallels with references to traditional and historical norms, particularly in contexts where there is little history of modern statehood. Then, governance can be argued to be less of a tool within violent conflict, but an attempt to cater for a specific constituency. Podder shows that rebel groups may actively establish partnerships with traditional authorities. The SPLM/A, for example, was partly dependent on traditional leadership as gatekeepers for mobilizing communities and establishing social trust (Podder 2014: 227–8). Box 3.2 exemplifies how the NRA in Uganda engaged with civilians.

Box 3.2   Engaging with civilians: National Resistance Army, Uganda

Upon the takeover by the NRA, the Baganda of the Luwero Triangle had been governed by a highly centralized system of chieftainships which faced a crisis of legitimacy. The NRA then put the power in the hands of the civilian population by setting up a structure of local governance (Weinstein 2007: 175–6). The NRA successfully rooted its movement in the civilian population, by providing public goods in exchange for civilian contributions. For instance security was provided with the use of a system of local "resistance committees", a network of local militias, to warn villages of approaching UNLA (government's) soldiers. Weinstein (2007) states that, at the high point of security in the liberated zone in 1983, a senior army official estimated that the NRA governed through 2,000 to 3,000 "resistance committees", each representing 40 homes. In addition, the NRA also delivered a basic set of health care services—including training of medical aides—to its constituents in the Triangle, where a lack of security had made the resupply of health care posts impossible (Weinstein 2007: 180).

Potential Partners in Statebuilding

Rebel groups may carry varying levels of legitimacy. Some may be "spoilers," but others may also require further engagement as potential partners in state- and peacebuilding. For instance, the Department for International Development recognizes the role of gangs, drug lords, youth militias and rebel groups in simultaneously perpetuating violence and exploitation, whilst also providing services, some level of security and their own claims to legitimacy (2010: 39). The majority of African policing is conducted by non-state actors, and "people look to them rather than to state actors for protection from and investigation of crime" (Baker 2007: in Organisation for Economic Co-operation and Development 2008: 38; also see Baker and Scheye 2007). Research by Diphoorn has shown in the case of South-African policing that state and non-state policing have always been interrelated. In contemporary South-Africa a climate has emerged even in which an increased contribution from non-state actors is encouraged alongside state representatives (2013: 267). Branch and Mampilly (2005) argue that in the case of Sudan, non-state governance structures are as crucial for long-term stability as negotiations between warring parties. Furthermore, Autesserre (2009) demonstrates that narrow perspectives of rebel groups have directly hindered efforts of international agencies in the DRC, where the United Nations and aid agencies are prohibited from engaging rebel groups, lest they risk *legitimizing* their status. Box 3.3 shows a similar case with regard to the UIC in Somalia.

Box 3.3   Narrative over local realities: Union of Islamic Courts (UIC), Somalia

From the 1990s onwards, following the collapse of the state in Somalia, an ad hoc alliance of non-state actors created their own Courts in order to create more stability within their communities. Although in the beginning these courts were very decentralized, the UIC finally gained a "politico-military momentum" and pushed warlords out of Mogadishu in 2006 (Verhoeven 2009: 406, 411). While the UIC presented itself as a force to bring order, unity and justice, the international community suspected the Courts of hosting East African terrorists, perceiving it as Somalia's "neo-Taliban". In December 2006, the US-backed Ethiopia's military overwhelmed UIC forces and Mogadishu was handed over to the Transitional Federal Government, a secular but self-appointed, powerless executive with local authority only. Hence, the dominant state failure/collapse narrative within the international community prevented the necessary connection to local realities, as such hindering the re-emergence of legitimate authority in Somalia (Verhoeven 2009: 411–12).

Conclusion

Returning to the central argument in this chapter: should our perception of rebel groups, otherwise regarded as "spoilers" and detrimental to development and governance be fundamentally reconsidered? The literature and cases discussed throughout this chapter have indicated that we should. It goes beyond the scope of this chapter to discuss the full emergence of the rebel groups used here to exemplify instances of rebel governance. Nonetheless, the case study observations of the SPLM/A, the NRA and the UIC show how a rebel group can set up a relatively well-functioning civil administration.

A rebel group may provide a genuine political order in response, or parallel to, a corrupt or ineffective government. Under an authoritarian or tyrannical government regime, rebel groups may have acquired wide support among segments of the population. The perception of rebels *solely* as "spoilers", therefore limits the potential for cooperation and negotiation with influential groups with a degree of legitimacy among local populations. Also, relying on this perception may lead analysis to be misrepresenting realities on the ground and may hamper effective international engagements, as the UIC case shows. Due to the dominant counter-terrorism discourse, a potential role for the UIC as a partner with legitimacy and authority in the creation of stability and order was rejected.

If rebel groups offer alternatives to an absent or even abusive state, development, state- and peacebuilding discourses should not automatically see the state as the main actor to address. Further research is necessary in order to specifically distinguish different types of rebel groups, with differing motives, financing and popular support. In addition, the conditions under which rebel groups are potential partners in "bottom-up-statebuilding" and legitimate partners in (future) peace settlements need to be analyzed. When and in what way do rebel groups merit further engagement by the international community in contexts of state fragility? Further research on rebel governance should aim to identify opportunities for cooperation and negotiation with rebel groups.

References

Arjona, A.M. (2010). *Social Order in Civil War.* PhD dissertation. New Haven: Yale University.

Autesserre, S. (2006). Local Violence, International Indifference? Post-Conflict"Settlement" in the Eastern D.R. Congo (2003–2005). PhD dissertation, New York University.

Autesserre, S. (2009). Hobbes and the Congo: Frames, Local Violence, and International Intervention. *International Organization,* 63(2): 249–80.

Baker, B. and Scheye E. (2007). Multi-layered Justice and Security Delivery in Post-Conflict and Fragile States, *Conflict, Security & Development,* 7(4): 503–28.

Barker, R. (2001). *Legitimating Identities: The Self-Presentations of Rulers and Subjects.* Cambridge: Cambridge University Press.

Beardsley, K. and McQuinn, B. (2009). Rebel Groups as Predatory Organizations: The Political Effects of the 2004 Tsunami in Indonesia and Sri Lanka. *The Journal of Conflict Resolution,* 53(4): 623–45.

Beetham, D. (1991). *The Legitimation of Power.* Basingstoke: Macmillan.

Boege, V., Brown, M., and Clements, K. (2009a). Hybrid Political Orders, Not Fragile States. *Peace Review: A Journal of Social Justice,* 21(1): 13–21.

Boege, V., Brown, M.A., Clements, K.P., and Nolan, A. (2009b). On Hybrid Political Orders and Emerging States: What is Failing—States in The Global South or Research and Politics in The West? *Berghof Handbook for Conflict Transformation Dialogue Series,* (8): 15–35.

Branch, A. and Mampilly, Z.C. (2005). Winning the War, but Losing the Peace? The Dilemma of SPLM/A Civil Administration and the Tasks Ahead. *Journal of Modern African Studies,* 43(1): 1–20.

Chandler, D. (2006). *From Kosovo to Kabul and Beyond: Human Rights and International Intervention.* London: Pluto Press.

Clements, K.P., Boege, V., Brown, A., Foley, W., and Nolan, A. (2007). State Building Reconsidered: The Role of Hybridity in the Formation of Political Order. *Political Science,* 59(1): 45–56.

Dahl, R. (1971). *Polyarchy: Participation and Opposition.* London: Yale University Press.

Daley, P. (2006). Ethnicity and Political Violence in Africa: The Challenge to the Burundi State. *Political Geography,* 25(6): 657–79.

Department for International Development (2010). *The Politics of Poverty: Elites, Citizens and States: Findings from ten years of DFID-funded research on Governance and Fragile States 2001–2010.* London: Department for International Development.

Diphoorn, T.G. (2013). Twilight Policing; Private Security in Durban, South Africa. PhD Thesis, Utrecht: Utrecht University.

Duffield, M. (1998). Post-modern Conflict: Warlords, Post-Adjustment States and Private Protection. *Civil Wars,* 1(1): 65–102.

Duffield, M. (2002). Social Reconstruction and the Radicalization of Development: Aid as a Relation of Global Liberal Governance. *Development and Change,* 33, 1049–71.

Duyvesteyn, I. (2005). *Clausewitz and African War: Politics and Strategy in Liberia and Somalia.* London: Frank Cass.

Gates, S. (2002). Recruitment and Allegiance: The Microfoundations of Rebellion. *Journal of Conflict Resolution,* 46(1): 111–30.

Goodfellow, T. and Lindemann, S. (2013). The Clash of Institutions: Traditional Authority, Conflict and the Failure of "Hybridity" in Buganda. *Commonwealth & Comparative Politics,* 51(1): 3–26.

Hagmann, T. and Péclard, D. (2010). Negotiating Statehood: Dynamics of Power and Domination in Africa. *Development and Change,* 41(4): 539–62.

Harvey, P., Holmes, R., Slater, R., and Martin, E. (2007). *Social Protection in Fragile States.* London: Overseas Development Institute (ODI).

Hibou, B. (2012). Economic Crime and Neoliberal Modes of Government: The Example of the Mediterranean. *Journal of Social History,* 45(3): 643–60.

Hoehne, M. (2009). Mimesis and Mimicry in Dynamics of State and Identity Formation in Northern Somalia. *Africa,* 79(2): 252–81.

Jackson, R. (1990). *Quasi-States: Sovereignty, International Relations and the Third World.* Cambridge: Cambridge University Press.

Jeursen, T. and van der Borgh, C. (2014). Security Provision after Regime Change: Local Militias and Political Entities in Post-Qaddafi Tripoli. *Journal of Intervention and Statebuilding*, 8(2–3): 173–91.

Johnson, D. (1998). The Sudan People's Liberation Army and the Problem of Factionalism. In C. Clapham (ed.), *African Guerrillas*. Oxford: James Currey Ltd, 53–72.

Kalyvas, S. (2003). The Ontology of "Political Violence": Action and Identity in Civil Wars. *Perspectives on Politics*, 1(3): 475–94.

Kalyvas, S., Shapiro, I., and Masoud, T. (eds) (2009). *Order, Conflict and Violence.* Cambridge: Cambridge University Press.

Krasner, S. (2004). Sharing Sovereignty: New Institutions for Collapsed and Failing States. *International Security*, 29(2): 85–120.

Krasner, S. (2005). The Case for Shared Sovereignty. *Journal of Democracy*, 16(1): 69–83.

Lund, C. (2006). Twilight Institutions: Public Authority and Local Politics in Africa. *Development and Change*, 37(4): 685–705.

Mampilly, Z. (2007). Stationary Bandits: Understanding Rebel Governance. PhD Thesis, Los Angeles: University of California.

Mampilly, Z. (2011). *Rebel Rulers. Insurgent Governance and Civilian Life During War.* Ithaca and London: Cornell University Press.

McIouglin, C. (2010). *Topic Guide on Fragile States*. Birmingham: Governance and Social Development Research Centre.

Mehler, A. (2004). *Oligopolies of Violence in Africa South of the Sahara.* GIGA Working Papers. Available at: http://giga-hamburg.de.

Menkhaus, K. (2007). Governance without Government in Somalia; Spoilers, State Building and the Politics of Coping. *International Security*, 31(3): 74–106.

Migdal, J.S. (2001). *State in Society; Studying how States and Societies Transform and Constitute One Another*. Cambridge: Cambridge University Press.

Milliken, J. and Krause, K. (2002). State Failure, State Collapse, and State Reconstruction: Concepts, Lessons and Strategies. *Development and Change*, 33(5): 753–74.

Müller, T.R. (2012). From Rebel Governance to State Consolidation—Dynamics of Loyalty and the Securitization of the State in Eritrea. *Geoforum*, 43(4): 793–803.

Naudé, W., Santos-Paulino, A.U., and McGillivray, M. (eds) (2011). *Fragile States; Causes, Costs, and Responses*. Oxford: Oxford University Press.

Olson, M. (1993). Dictatorship, Democracy, and Development. *The American Political Science Review*, 87(3): 567–76.

Organisation for Economic Co-Operation and Development (2008). *Concepts and Dilemmas of State Building in Fragile Situations: From Fragility to Resilience.* Paris: Organisation For Economic Co-Operation and Development.

Podder, S. (2012). From Spoilers to Statebuilders: Constructive Approaches to Engagement with Non-State Armed Groups in Fragile States. *OECD Development Cooperation Working Papers No. 5.*

Podder, S. (2013). Non-state Armed Groups and Stability: Reconsidering Legitimacy and Inclusion. *Contemporary Security Policy*, 34(1): 16–39.

Podder, S. (2014). Mainstreaming the Non-State in Bottom-up State-Building: Linkages between Rebel Governance and Post-Conflict Legitimacy. *Conflict, Security & Development*, 14(2): 213–43.

Rabasa, A., Boraz, S., Chalk, P., Cragin, K. Karasik, T., Moroney, J., O'Brien, K., and Peters, J. (2008). *Ungoverned Territories*. Pittsburgh, Arlington, Santa Monica: Rand Corporation.

Raeymaekers, T., Menkhaus, K., and Vlassenroot, K. (2008). State and Non-State Regulation in African Protracted Crises: Governance without Government? *Afrika Focus*, 21(2): 7–21.

Reno, W. (2009). Illicit Markets, Violence, Warlord, and Governance: West African Cases. *Crime, Law, and Social Change*, 52(3): 313–22.

Rice, S.E. and Patrick, S. (2008). *Index of State Weakness in the Developing World.* Brookings Foreign Policy Report.

Sharqieh, I. (2012). Imperatives for Post-conflict Reconstruction in Libya. http://www.brookings.edu/research/articles/2011/12/31-libya-sharqieh.

Siniawer, E.M. (2012). Befitting Bedfellows: Yakuza and the State in Modern Japan. *Journal of Social History*, 45(3): 623–41.

Stel, N. (2014). The Eye of the Beholder. Exploring the Relations between Service Delivery and State Legitimacy in Burundi. *Africa Focus, 49(3): 3–28.*

Stel, N. (2015). Lebanese-Palestinian Governance Interaction in the Palestinian Camp of Shabriha, South Lebanon—A Tentative Extension of the "Mediated State" from Africa to the Mediterranean. *Mediterranean Politics*. Forthcoming.

Stoker, G. (1998). Governance as Theory: Five Propositions. *International Social Science Journal*, 50(155): 17–28.

Thornhill, C. (2008). Towards a Historical Sociology of Constitutional Legitimacy. *Theory and Society*, 37(2): 161–97.

Toft, M. (2010). Ending Civil Wars: A Case for Rebel Victory? *International Security*, 4(34): 7–36.

Tull, D.M. (2003). A Reconfiguration of Political Order? The State of the State in North Kivu (Congo). *African Affairs*, 102(408): 429–46.

United Nations Development Programme (2012). *Governance for Peace: Securing the Social Contract*. New York: United Nations Development Programme.

Verhoeven, H. (2009). The Self-Fulfilling Prophecy of Failed States: Somalia, State Collapse and the Global War on Terror. *Journal of Eastern African Studies*, 3(3): 405–25.

Weinstein, J.M. (2007). *Inside Rebellion*. Cambridge: Cambridge University Press.

Chapter 4
Embracing Neo-Liberalism in Uganda and Rwanda

Noel Twagiramungu[1]

Abstract

In the 1980s and 1990s, a group of Marxist leaning rebels waged armed struggle and captured power in Uganda, Rwanda, Ethiopia and Eritrea, and went on to win warm accolades in the West as prominent darlings of the capitalist donor community. Over the last two decades, scholars and policy-makers have been divided over the performance of this new generation of African leaders—generally praised for bringing about stability and economic growth, yet blamed for their political repression, predatory behavior and involvement in proxy wars of plunder. This Chapter focuses on Museveni's Uganda and Kagame's Rwanda to empirically document and critically explain the real politics behind these paradoxical qualities. Findings underscore this new brand of leaders' remarkable ability to conduct militaro-political business as in a market. On their roads to power, they used the basic market laws of supply and demand to build complex networks of support within the Marxist–Capitalist ideological spectrum. Once in power, they hijacked the donor-driven enterprise of "democratic peace" to boost their hold on power. The result is a growing gap between the promises of democratic change and economic prosperity and the reality of state capture and mercantile militarism.

Introduction

In the late 1980s and early 1990s, the fall of authoritarian regimes, notably in Eastern Europe and Latin America, was deemed evidence of the era of democratic openings worldwide (Fukuyama 1989; 1992). In Africa, such prospects augured a sort of blueprint of the long-awaited African Renaissance,[2] a concept that received new meaning during US President Bill Clinton's state-visits to Africa in March 1998. Referring to former self-proclaimed Marxist revolutionaries, turned Heads of State including Yoweri Museveni of Uganda, Paul Kagame of Rwanda, Meles Zenawi of Ethiopia, and Isaias Afwerki of Eritrea, Clinton said he placed hope in "a new generation of African leaders devoted to democracy and economic reforms" (as quoted in Oloka-Onyango 2004: 29).

However, a combination of setbacks including worsening human rights records, authoritarian practices, predatory economic policies and proxy wars in which the so-called "new generation of African leaders" warred against each other (for, e.g., Museveni vs. Kagame in the DRC, Zenawi vs. Afwerki during the Ethiopian-Eritrean war) led some critics to dismiss the notion of "new generation" as nothing more than "irrational exuberance" (Rosenblum 2002: 195–202).

The first two leaders, Museveni and Kagame, along with their respective guerrilla movements and now ruling parties, the National Resistance Movement (NRM) in Uganda and the Rwandan Patriotic Front (RPF) in Rwanda, are the focus of this Chapter. The analysis is devoted to empirically documenting and critically explaining the real politics behind the rise of these revolutionaries from a Marxist leaning background to the center stage of power and international legitimacy as prominent darlings of the capitalist donor community.

---

1   Funding from World Peace Foundation at the Fletcher School of Law and Diplomacy, Tufts University, supported the research for this chapter.
2   The concept of African Renaissance was coined and popularized by Senegalese scholar Cheick Anta Diop in a series of essays written between 1946 and 1996 (see Diop 1990, 1996). For the development of this concept, see for example Okumu (2002).

Empirical findings suggest that the performance of the regimes incarnated by the two strongmen is less both a product of the Marxist background and a consequence of the efforts to embrace neo-liberalism as it is a distinctive feature of a new form of governance. To name this form of governance that needs to be understood on its own terms, I borrow Alex de Waal's concept of "political marketplace." The latter is understood as "a contemporary system of governance, characterized by pervasive rent-seeking and monetized patronage, which takes the form of exchange of political services or loyalty for payment" (de Waal 2014a). To this end, I hypothesize the governments led by NRM in Uganda and RPF in Rwanda as paradigmatic instances of "overt governance systems in which political business is actually conducted as in a market, with the price of the commodities of cooperation and allegiance determined by supply and demand, and regulated by violence and threat" (de Waal 2014b: 1–2). To make this case, a historical background is in order.

Historical Background

Both landlocked in the Great Lakes region of Africa, Uganda and Rwanda share much of the problems of post-independence African states, notably, ethnopolitics, military rule and refugee crisis. In Uganda for instance, the governing coalition that had led the country to independence in 1962 fell apart in 1966 when Milton Obote, then Prime Minister ousted King Edward Mutesa II, and went on to concentrate all the powers in his hands until 1971 when the army seized power in a coup d'état (Karugire 1980; 1996; Kasozi 1994). The new military leader, Idi Amin Dada, established a reign of terror that lasted for eight years and left more than 300,000 people massacred and another half-million forced into exile (Avirgan and Honey 1982; Bwengye 1985; Kyemba 1997). The exiled included a young man called Yoweri Museveni who founded a rebellion group, the Front for National Salvation (FRONASA) and sent his guerrillas to train in Mozambique. When Idi Amin arrogantly invaded Tanzania and occupied territory, Museveni's guerrillas joined Tanzanian forces which counter-attacked Amin's army and seized Kampala. After serving in the short-lived post-Amin government, Museveni contested and lost the 1980 presidential elections. Alleging massive fraud, he took up arms in February 1981 against the newly elect-president, Milton Obote, and went on to seize power by force in January 1986.

In Rwanda, the seed of trouble dates back to the colonial era when the colonial administration concentrated all the privileges associated with power and knowledge in the hands of the then ruling aristocracy, known as Tutsi, at the expense of the commoners, the Hutu. In 1959 however, a combination of factors including the sudden death of a progressive King, Charles Mutara Rudahigwa, and growing tensions between the aristocracy and colonial forces, notably the Catholic Church, paved the way for a Hutu uprising, generally referred to as the Hutu Revolution (Mamdani 2002; Newbury 1988; Prunier 1995; Lemarchand 1970). The ensuing bloodbath forced into exile the new King, Kigeri Ndahindurwa, along with thousands of sympathizers and followers.

Among these exiled, was a child named Paul Kagame. Born in 1957 and forced into exile in 1961, Paul Kagame grew up in a refugee camp in Uganda at a time when the Tutsi who remained in Rwanda were considered second-class citizens in a Hutu republic. After helping Museveni to seize power in Kampala in 1986, Kagame along with some four thousand of his comrades formed an armed rebellion of their own, the RPF which would eventually invade Rwanda on October 1, 1990 (Mamdani 2002; Prunier 1995; Twagiramungu 2014a). Following a peace agreement signed in August 1993 in Arusha, Tanzania, between the RPF and the then government of Rwanda, the RPF resumed war in April 1994 in the wake of the assassination of President Juvenal Habyariamana and the ensuing genocide, and seized power in July 1994.[3] Two years later, The RPF in tandem with the NRM went on to form a regional military coalition that invaded Zaire in 1996 and ousted the dictator Mobutu in 1997 before embarking on a controversial process of controlling, first in total and then in part, the eastern part of Zaire—now the Democratic Republic of Congo.

In retrospect, the roads that took Museveni and Kagame to power were unprecedented in many ways and, in many respects, were poised to signal a significant break from past patterns of governance. The remainder

---

3   The most comprehensive compendium to date of the evolution and effects of Kagame's political actions is Reyntjens (2013). For sympathetic accounts, see Clark and Kaufman (2009) and Crisafulli and Raymond (2014).

of this chapter accounts for what makes these roads to power, along with the resulting governance systems, pragmatic examples of the political marketplace model.

A Case for the Political Market Place

Empirical findings suggest two dynamics that made possible the political marketplace systems found today in Uganda and Rwanda. First, on their roads to power, the NRM and RPF used the basic market laws of supply and demand to master and defy dominant ideologies including the Marxist–Capitalist ideological spectrum. Second, once in power, the NRM and RPF hijacked the donor-driven enterprise of political and economic reforms to boost their hold on power.

Mastering and Defying the World's Ideologies

The NRM, and to some extent its offspring, the RPF, emerged from a Marxist ideological background, inextricably linked to the 1967 journey, that took the 23-year-old Yoweri Museveni from his native Uganda to the University of Dar es Salaam in Tanzania. Attracted at first sight by "Dar es Salaam's atmosphere of freedom fighters, socialists, nationalizations, [and] anti-imperialism," Museveni was disappointed to find "the students lacking in militancy" (Museveni 2010: 13). To fill this gap, Museveni founded and became the first chair of a radical student association, the University African Students' Front (UASF), whose overall goal was to advocate for Marxist ideologies and advance the struggle for Africa's liberation (Museveni 2010: 13–14). He went on to distinguish himself as a radical Marxist in his views and ideas some of which were published in a leftist magazine called Cheche (Hirji 2010: 35). After visiting the military camps of the Mozambique Liberation Front (*Frente de Libertação de Moçambique*—FRELIMO) in 1968, he started campaigning openly for the use of violence as the principal vehicle for the pursuit of political ideas. He passionately spelt out this theme in his graduation paper evocatively titled "Fanon's Theory on Violence: Its Verification in Liberated Mozambique" (Museveni 1971).

Ten years later, when Museveni launched in February 1981 the armed struggle that brought him to power in January 1986, his Marxist background won him massive support from top leftist regimes such as the USSR, China, Cuba and Libya (Amaza 1998: 167; Museveni 1997: 203). Upon his coming into power, his Marxist background did not prevent him from "see[ing] aid flowing in the country from conservative and radical governments at the same time" (Museveni 1997: 203–4). At the heart of Museveni's success in defying the world's ideological barriers was an interest-driven approach that he laid down in his very first speech to the UN General Assembly in October 1986. He stated inter alia that the "NRM is neither pro-west [n]or pro-east: it is pro-Uganda ... [We] have got our legitimate interests and we judge friend and foe according to how they relate to our interests." (Museveni 1997: 203–4). It thus comes as no surprise that

> [w]ithout severing his relations with Gaddafi, Museveni went on to establish cordial relations with Ronald Reagan and later George Bush, both of whom continued to regard the Libyan leader as a terrorist. He likewise established trade relations with Cuba based on contra-trade arrangements, and invited the Cubans to establish the Mbarara University of Science and Technology in western Uganda. He was at home with PLO leader Yasser Arafat and Egypt's Hosni Mubarak, at [the] time the two were hardly on talking terms. (Amaza 1998: 167)

This interest-driven approach became particularly evident in the wake of the collapse of the Soviet bloc when Museveni made history by establishing himself as the first African leader to have "traversed the whole ideological spectrum from a profound distrust of capitalism to a restored faith in market forces" (Mazrui 2006: 3).

The same approach is true for the RPF's military leader, Paul Kagame, who has distinguished himself as "the world's only head of state to have received military training in both Cuba ... and the United States" (Kinzer 2008: 12). When Kagame entered the Army Commander and General Staff College at Fort Leavenworth in Kansas in 1990, Herbert Walker Bush was busy pursuing Reagan's conservative policies. By the time Kagame's RPF captured power in Rwanda in 1994, the USA had just rejected the Reagan-era conservative policies to embrace the liberal agenda championed by his successor, Bill Clinton. This shift didn't prevent Kagame from winning special affection from Clinton and generous military, financial and diplomatic support from the US government from then onwards. At the same time, his close ties with Clinton's liberal administration did not prevent Kagame from winning the admiration and support from British Conservative government officials, notably Lady Linda Chalker, the then all-powerful Minister of Overseas Development and Africa. Nor did the fall of the Conservative government in 1997 prevent Kagame (and Museveni for that matter) from winning the hearts of the most combative socialists such as Clare Short in Tony Blair's Labour Party government.[4]

At first glance, the horrors of the 1994 genocide can be invoked to justify much of the donor communities' massive aid to Kagame's Rwanda—what some observers have described as a way to pay off western guilt over their failure to intervene during the bloodshed (Hintjens 2008: 5–41; Pottier 2002: 54–5; Reyntjens 2011: 27). The compassion argument sounds particularly compelling in explaining why Kagame's network of supporters includes religious figures like American evangelical superstar Rick Warren (McFadden and Gerstein 2008) or philanthropists like billionaire Bill Gates who spent USD$900,000 to build a training medical center specializing in treating infectious diseases in Rwanda (Kinzer 2008: 3). However, what this argument fails to explain is the naked truth that, alongside philanthropists and other moral authorities, Kagame's network of admirers and associates include not only the world's top corporations like Starbucks, but also multinational mining firms like Banro Gold, Casa Mining, Randgold, Loncor, and Moku Gold, all of whom have been repeatedly accused by the UN for being involved in criminal economic enterprises and activities aimed at financial extortion, money-laundering, racketeering, theft and plunder in the Democratic Republic of Congo (United Nations 2002; United Nations 2013).

Such paradoxical ties that Kagame has successfully built with both compassionate philanthropists and greedy corporations are consistent with the interest-driven marketplace approach. It is an approach to world affairs aptly articulated by Museveni when he asserts, "[We] have got our legitimate interests and we judge friend and foe according to how they relate to our interests" (Museveni 1997: 203–4).

As experience has shown, the business of judging friends and foes by the fluid changes in the interests of actors—states and non-states alike—is at odds with the neo-liberal expectations of democratic peace and principled free market economics. The following lines draw a bigger picture of the major contradictions resulting from such a strategic, but unhappy marriage.

Museveni's Uganda

In his inaugural speech of January 29, 1986, Museveni vowed to eradicate dictatorial practices and to build a strong economy free from all forms of corruption. Nearly three decades later, the true meaning of his political rhetoric of fundamental change in the politics of his country has become the reality of state capture. Ironically, the neo-liberal enterprise shares much of the blame in this endeavor. In fact, upon its coming to power, "the NRM government kept its distance from the IMF-World Bank conglomerate" whose emphasis was on "trade liberalization along with fiscal and monetary conditionalities" (Amaza 1998: 162). However, as one insider admitted, "the leadership of the NRM had, sooner or later, to reconcile themselves with the reality that the IMF is a reflection of the global distribution of power in a contemporary economic system in which Uganda happens to be pretty much on the margin" (Mugyenyi as quoted in Amaza 1998: 162). Citing another close aide to Museveni, Amaza (1998: 163) noted that "the dilly-dally could therefore only last for so long and no more, and when the orders of the IMF barons finally came they were the standard ones."

The process of heeding to the official demands of the IMF started on May 15, 1987, when President Museveni laid down an economic policy package for reconstruction and development, which was centered on the removal of price and wage controls, abolition of subsidies and devaluation of the Uganda shilling. The result was a political economy described by one Ugandan scholar as the one "of extensive and elusive corruption, in which prevail 'neo-patronage, power, and narrow interests'" (Asiimwe 2013: 129). Specifically,

---

4 The author thanks Professor David Newbury for his caution regarding the liberal nature of Bill Clinton's policies—and to some extent Tony Blair's—notably on welfare, on trade issues, and on the revision of banking laws which were clearly a turn to the right. So "liberal" here is relative to Reagan's or Thatcher's conservative stances.

Asiimwe presents a compelling case of how the donor-funded institutions failed "to effectively engage the inner-circle ruling elite due to a skewed power structure that serves narrow political interests" (Asiimwe 2013: 129). As a result, while the *zero tolerance* rhetoric won Museveni the donor community's approval for a while, corruption ended up becoming the law of the land. In Asiimwe's (2013: 129) view, "through its interplay of inclusion and exclusion political corruption has generated contestations which undermine it and challenge the National Resistance Movement (NRM) regime." To underscore this point, the US Ambassador to Uganda, Scott DeLisi, was recently quoted describing corruption as a pandemic threatening Uganda's future:

> Twenty years ago, the government of Uganda saw [the] "slim" disease, which we now know as HIV/Aids, as an existential threat to Uganda's future. Corruption is now the new slim. […]. We need to treat corruption as the pervasive and destructive evil and abuse of power and trust that it is, rather than allowing it to hide behind far less damning terms like "rent seeking." (Ninsiima 2014)

In this context, it comes as no surprise that what was believed to be a laboratory of rebel-led democratization has resulted in nothing more than the changing face of authoritarianism. As Tripp (2004: 3) aptly argues,

> [a]uthoritarianism has softened under Yoweri Museveni when compared with the earlier regimes of Idi Amin and Milton Obote. However, […] rulers have only gone as far with political reforms as they have felt they have needed to in order to satisfy domestic and donor pressures. Enormous constraints on civil and political liberties persist. (Tripp 2004: 3)

This process of softening authoritarianism evolved very slowly while patronage and military corruption regulated Ugandan politics (Mwenda and Tangri 2003: 539–52). In its first move, the NRM government, through its Ministry of Constitutional Affairs, engineered a no-party democracy system—or what it referred to as "the movement system," which was adopted in a popular referendum in 1995. The rationale for this system was that "before deeply torn African societies are subjugated to the divisive assault of multiparty competition, their community spirit must first be restored and nurtured back to health" (Assefa 1993: 25). Museveni sums up the point, claiming: "In spite of the interference of the international community, and pressure from international and local-enclave media, we, in the National Resistance Movement, were absolutely sure that our people did not want parties at this moment in our history." (Museveni 1997: 202). Thus, despite international pressures notably from the United States of America, Museveni "ruled out a swift return to multi-party system politics in Uganda, saying it was not up to the United States to decide on the best system for the country" (*New Vision* May 19, 1995 as quoted in Amaza 1998: 202).

As expected, Museveni and several NRM cadres won the so-called "no-party" democratic elections, first in 1996 and then in 2001 (Carbone 2008). When Museveni and his party finally resolved to embrace a multi-party system in 2005, the hope of change became the reality of "stayism," a phenomenon defined by Ugandan scholar Oloka-Onyango (2006: 1) as "the syndrome of seeking to remain in office and to entrench Presidents."

Under Museveni, the syndrome of "stayism" came in the form of constitutional amendments that culminated in the lifting of a sacrosanct principle of the 1995 Constitution, which had provided for a two-term limit on the tenure of the president, as a means of preventing the curse of centralization of power around a long-serving leader. Commenting on this move, former US Ambassador to Uganda Johnnie Carson lamented: "we may be looking at another Mugabe and Zimbabwe in the making" (Carson in *The Boston Globe*, May 1, 2005). The American public television broadcaster PBS underscored this concern in its documentary programme *Frontline* (screened September 7, 2004) stating: "Today, after arbitrary arrests, beatings, and harassment of the political opposition in the last presidential election in 2001, a new view is emerging of Museveni as a leader on the verge of becoming yet another African dictator" (Jones 2004: 1).Seen from a broader African perspective, such a view is of great relevance, especially in reference to Nzongala-Ntalaja's assessment of the general trends in postcolonial leadership struggles in Africa:

> For the neo-colonial state, a stable political order is one that is best captured by the slogan "one country, one leader." Relative stability requires that intra-elite conflicts be reduced to factional politics under the control and manipulation of the top leader. (Nzongala-Ntalaja 1993: 28)

To make sense of the real politics behind Museveni's grip on power, one has to take seriously a metaphor he used in a 2008 public speech: "I hunted my animal; and now I am being told to go; go where?" (Museveni as quoted in Kagoro 2013: 31). The endgame of this commitment to stayism is well captured in the title of a paper by a Ugandan scholar: "From Fundamental Change to No Change: The NRM and democratization in Uganda" (Muhumuza: 2013). In this context, while several donor countries including the United Kingdom, the USA, Sweden, and the Netherlands have, from time to time, withheld economic support to his government due to concerns about the country's democratic development and human rights, Museveni has thus far proved a master of the business of amassing and securing political power and the associated gains it has brought with it.

Kagame's Rwanda

Since the 1994 genocide that left nearly 20 percent of Rwanda's six million people dead and up to 50 percent forced into exile (Des Forges 1999; Guichaoua 2010; Twagiramungu 2014b), debates about the nature of the post-genocide regime led by General Paul Kagame have been both polarized and polarizing (Straus and Waldorf 2011: 8). Sympathetic accounts have praised Kagame for having pulled Rwanda from the abyss of violence to build an island of stability and economic growth in a volatile region (Blair and Buffet 2013; Clark 2010; Gourevitch 2009; Kinzer 2008). Critics have however tended to portray Kagame as the man whose fingerprints are to be found all over the sufferings of the people in Rwanda (see Ansoms 2011; Kayumba et al. 2010; Straus and Waldorf 2011; Reyntjens 2004) and the whole Great Lakes Region (see Pottier 2002; Stearns and Borello 2011; United Nations 2010; United Nations Security Council 2013).

Specifically, the pro-Kagame side in the theoretical-divide have argued that Rwanda "has become one of the most promising countries in the developing world, ... [a land where] killers and survivors have embarked on a breathtaking path toward reconciliation" (Kinzer 2008; see also Clark 2010; Gourevitch 2009). Beneath this rosy picture however, other sources reveal a move from genocide to dictatorship (Reyntjens 2004: 1) characterized by a climate of fear, abuse of power and exclusion (Human Rights Watch 2010; 2014; Kayumba et al. 2010; Kimenyi 1999; Reyntjens 2011; 2013).

While each side puts forth tangible facts to back its position, they both suffer from a static point of view as if Kagame's regime developed overnight as an outcome of unilateral stratagems cleverly devised and methodically implemented by RPF political engineers. Quite the contrary, as I have argued elsewhere (Twagiramungu 2010), the evolution of Kagame's regime can be best understood through the lens of the *Anatomy of Revolution* (Brinton 1965) according to which revolutionary regimes tend to begin in hope and moderation, then turn into radical dictatorships, that pave their own way for crisis in a reign of terror.

To begin with, when Kagame and his troops captured Kigali in July 1994, not only was the country in ruins, but also (and more importantly) they knew little about the country, the vast majority of them having been born and/or raised in exile, notably in Uganda, Burundi, Congo, Tanzania and Kenya (Mamdani 2002; Mushameza 2007; Reyntjens 2013; Rudasingwa 2013). Thus, once in power, Kagame contented himself with the post of Vice-President and Minister of Defense in a plural government where key positions including the presidency, the prime-minister, and ministries of foreign affairs, interior and justice were held by Hutu figures.[5] By the same token, a pluralistic parliament was put in place in November 1994 followed by the establishment of the Supreme Court in late 1995. This initial openness contributed to fostering the climate of hope and moderation for a while—at least in the south-western regions which were less affected by war-related violence and RPF reprisals—a fact that explains why not only the Tutsi survivors, but also the Hutu populations (who had resisted pressures to go into exile), along with the donor community, gave the RPF-led regime the benefit of the doubt, if not their full support. Alas, this honeymoon period was doomed to be short-lived.

5　Worth noting however that most of these Hutu figures ended up paying a high price for breaking up with Kagame: President Pasteur Bizimungu arrested in 2002 and sentenced to 15-year imprisonment; several officials including Prime Minister Faustin Twagiramungu forced into exile in 1995; others such as Seth Sendashonga would be assassinated. For a comprehensive account, see *Frontline* (2005: 8); Pottier (1996: 424–5); and Reyntjens (2011: 8–9, 28–9).

As early as November 1994, a group of Hutu figures led by the then Premier, Faustin Twagiramungu, publicly denounced the increasing abuses of power including summary executions, disappearances, massive arrests and other forms of harassment targeting prominent leaders and civil servants who defied military rule (Pottier 1996: 254). The result was a dual power regime comprising a powerless official government shadowed by a parallel government led by Kagame. As posited in Brinton's theory, when the radicals and the moderates clash, the former are likely to triumph because they are "better organized, better staffed, better obeyed" (Brinton 1965: 134). The so-called government of unity and reconciliation collapsed in August 1995, when 'the Hutu gang' resigned from the government only to be replaced by co-opted elements better known locally as *Hutu de service* (the Hired Hutu) (Smith 1996).

This period witnessed the rise of one-man rule through a gradual rough-and-ready centralization process. In fact, after ruling the country behind the scenes through his Hired Hutu, at a time when he was busy invading the DRC and fighting Hutu insurgency at home, Kagame went on to take control of the RPF as chairman in 1998, a position that allowed him to reshuffle, on his own terms, such top staffers in the three main state institutions—the parliament, the judiciary and the army—and to appoint his protégés in strategic political positions. The next move was to hijack the presidency in 2000 after forcing the then President, Pasteur Bizimungu, a Hutu, to resign, thus clearing the way for his candidacy for the 2003 elections. From then on,

> the rebel general-turned-civilian politician [has excelled in] cultivate[ing] a cult-image as the sole hero of the country's achievements [through] a hard-line, one-party, secretive police state with a façade of democracy [and in which] the government ensures its monopoly of power by means of draconian restrictions on the exercise of the fundamental human rights of citizens (Nyamwasa et al. 2010: 2; see also *Frontline* 2004; Human Rights Watch 2010; 2014; Reyntjens 2011).

Kagame himself has never shied away from advocating his iron-fisted leadership:

> nothing will change our way forward. […] I want to be clear on this now, and I have told [you] since long ago. […]. I am telling you that this process will continue and it will continue. I do not know why people do not believe in the truth that I always tell them. […]. To those who would pride themselves on having harvested abundant sorghum or maize, we will tell them that we have enough machines to crush the grains. (Kagame quoted in Rwanda Rugali 2006: 1)

Such is the context within which we need to understand how and why the western donor-funded game of democratic transition in Rwanda (Kimonyo et al. 2004) resulted in the move "from genocide to dictatorship" (Reyntjens 2004). One keen observer noted that "ironically, it is the genocide that has provided the government with a cover for repression. Under the guise of preventing another genocide, the government displays a marked intolerance of the most basic forms of dissent" (Roth 2009: 2).

The rise of this dictatorship has grown in tandem with politically motivated repression and discrimination on the basis of ethnicity. In that, "not only are the structures of power in Rwanda being Tutsified," as Mahmoud Mamdani (2002: 186) has noted, "civil organization—from the media to nongovernmental organizations—are being cleansed of any but a nominal Hutu presence" (Mamdani 2002: 186). Of greater concern is particularly what Mamdani found out to be the founding ideology behind the brand of the RPF's ethnocracy, namely the belief in "Tutsi power [as] the precondition for Tutsi survival" (Mamdani 2002:186). This concern is further aggravated by the government's failure to move beyond the victor's mentality of winners-take-all in its justice system revolving around two pillars: the imposition of collective guilt on Hutu (Waldorf 2011: 44–64) and the lack of official accountability for RPF war crimes (Gahima 2013; Twagiramungu 2014b).

Ironically, at a time when Kagame's rough-and-ready authoritarianism seemed to have reached its peak, strong evidence suggests that his political machine has now entered a new phase where, as Brinton would say, "the revolution, like Saturn, devours its children" (Brinton 1965: 121). To grasp the nature and extent of this power-surge and the subsequent consequences in the inner circle of the RPF machine, one is reminded how the military establishment had remained united around Kagame throughout his path to absolute power. However, his increasing authoritarianism, especially after the 2003 elections, has provoked sharp dissent within his inner circle of power. As an example of the RPF's "Saturnian curse"—devouring its own members

—former spy chief, Patrick Karegeya, was assassinated in South Africa on New Year's Eve 2014 (Gatehouse 2014; Findlay 2014; *The Independent* 2014); and a number of Kagame's closest comrades-in-arms have been forced into exile, including the once all-powerful general of staff of the army, Kayumba Nyamwasa, (who has also survived three assassination attempts in South Africa); Kagame's former cabinet director, Theogene Rudasingwa, and former deputy Chief Justice, Gerald Gahima, who now live in exile in the US.

Of great concern in post-genocide Rwanda is also the unhappy marriage between economic growth and political repression. "For the international investment community, the assumption is that the side effect of growth is nearly always better human rights in the long term" (Richardson 2012). Investors like Charles Robertson may genuinely believe that "the Rwandan government is producing growth and that's very positive for the Rwandan people and eventually for Rwandan human rights and Rwandan democracy" (Robertson quoted in Richardson 2012). However, Kagame's regime has an increasing record of cracking down on civil liberties and trampling on human rights, and this suggests otherwise. In fact, a combination of recent developments concur with the fear that "Rwanda is increasingly seen not as a nation emerging steadily out of the division of the past but as a country at risk of another cycle of violence" (Sebarenzi 2011: 351; see also Nyamwasa et al. 2010; Rudasingwa 2013; Conroy 2014). These developments include the donor community's disenchantment with the regime (Hudson 2014: 1; *The Economist* 2013); stormy relationships with neighboring countries including Tanzania, Burundi and DRC; worsening human rights records; and, more recently, increasing military build-up as evidenced by intensive recruitment and the purchase of TL-50 or Sky Dragon 50 air defense missiles from China (*Want China Times* 2014). All in all, the mixed success stories of governance in post-genocide Rwanda suggests inter alia, "that elections can reinforce authoritarian tendencies; … [and] that statebuilding can lead to a repressive peace" (Samset 2011: 265). So far, the RPF's 21-year long reign along with the on-going process of amending the constitution to allow President Kagame to stay in power beyond his current legal term suggests that "the repressive peace can be durable, at least in the short to medium term" (Samset 2011: 265). But for how long?

Conclusion

There is no question that the coming into power of NRM in Uganda and RPF in Rwanda was a watershed in the history of the two countries in many ways. Nor is it surprising that the horrors of the past—like Idi Amin's brutal dictatorship in Uganda, and the 1994 genocide in Rwanda—also played a role in winning Museveni, and to a greater extent Kagame, sympathy and the benefit of the doubt. What has received scant attention in the literature, however, which this chapter sought to address, is the extraordinary ability and propensity of these "liberators" to defy the world's ideological barriers and to hijack, to the dismay of the donor community, the neo-liberal enterprise of democratization and economic reforms.

To be sure, there is no question that the current ruling parties, NRM and RPF, inherited countries in such chaotic a situation that few if any conventional norms were appropriate to meet the enormity of post-war challenges. Nor was it without good reason that the hope for radical change incarnated by Museveni and Kagame won both leaders the sympathy, admiration, support and the benefit of the doubt from a great many local and international actors, including the donor community at various stages in time. At each stage, the core reason for hope was that, once basic conditions of order and security would be met and state institutions equipped with adequate human, logistical and financial resources, return to normalcy would gradually prevail and the leadership would regain enough confidence to conform to universally recognized standards of social, economic and political life. As of today however, the hope of democratic and economic reforms incarnated by this new generation of African leaders has become the reality of a "changing face of authoritarianism" (Tripp 2004: 3) embedded in the logic of personal rule, that is in Jackson and Rothberg's words,

> a dynamic world of political will and activity that is shaped less by institutions or impersonal social forces than by personal authorities and power; it is a world, therefore, of uncertainty, suspicion, rumour, agitation, intrigue, and sometimes fear, as well as of stratagem, diplomacy, conspiracy, dependency, reward, and threat. (Jackson and Rothberg 1984: 421; see also Jackson and Rothberg 1982)

In terms of economic reforms, strong evidence shows that twenty years since Museveni launched his much-vaunted anti-corruption zero tolerance policies, corruption is shockingly deemed "an existential threat to Uganda's future" (Ninsiima 2014). By the same token, while Kagame has won accolades over the world as a reformer who has turned Rwanda into a business friendly country and one of the fastest growing economies in Africa, reliable sources suggest that beneath the ambitious high modernism (Newbury 2011: 203) driving post-genocide Rwanda's economic reconstruction enterprise, lies a huge "mismatch between elite ambitions and rural realities" (Ansoms 2011: 240).

To make sense of such paradoxical outcomes, a close look at the real politics at work in contemporary Rwanda and Uganda through a business lens offers us three major empirical findings with overreaching theoretical insights and policy implications.

First, unlike what the much-vaunted from-Marxism-to-Neo-liberalism metamorphosis may suggest, NRM and RPF have excelled, on their roads to and exercise of power, in the art of mastering, embracing, and generally paying lip service to any ideology in tune with their ad-hoc needs, interests and positions. Their respective skills and abilities to work hand in hand with Chinese Communists, Russian Marxists and anti-Western leaders like Muammar Qaddafi and Fidel Castro, and then manage to win the hearts and generous funds of both Western conservative regimes, like Thatcher's government in Britain and Reagan's government in the US; and their counterparts, the Liberal governments, like Blair's and Clinton's, underscore this point. This observed reality is consistent with a key feature of the "political marketplace" model whose real politics "is integrated into the global order in a subordinate position, so that outside interests can intervene in its internal affairs" (de Waal 2014: 5–6).

Second, while the polarized debates about the nature of the governance systems led by NRM and RPF are far from over, much of these debates add little to our understanding of the real politics underlying these systems. For, by sifting the liberation politics through the sieve of democratic transition, with sympathizers highlighting selective success stories and apologetic excuses whereas critics are emphasizing failures and setbacks, dominant accounts fail to capture the essence of performance as defined, pursued and evaluated by the ruling elites themselves on their own terms. The growing disenchantment of the donor community towards both Uganda and Rwanda as evidenced by recent waves of aid cuts (*The Economist* 2013; Ninsiima 2014) speaks volumes about the gaps between donors' democratic values-based expectations and the recipient countries ruling elites' self-interests.

Third, the politics of "embracing neo-liberalism" as we know it today in Kigali and Kampala did not develop overnight. Rather, it emerged in specific contexts and developed gradually in a non-linear, yet self-reinforcing way in response to local, regional and international shifting patterns of constraints and opportunities involving various forms of transactional costs.

Put together, these findings draw our attention to the entrepreneurial performance that has allowed the self-proclaimed liberators to use a combination of guile and force to amass power and material gains in a way that confounds exuberant supporters and fierce critics alike. In this regard, a number of facts otherwise seen as contradictory, are best considered two faces of the same coin. One telling case was the ability of the Ugandan diplomatic machine, that led the UN General Assembly on June 14, 2014, to elect Sam Kutesa, the Minister for Foreign Affairs of Uganda (and Museveni's brother-in-law), as President of its 69th session, at a time when the Government of Uganda was under international fire for its new anti-Lesbian, Gay, Trans-gender and Bisexual (LGTB) legislation (Merrill 2015). Thus, Kutesa saw no contradiction in telling the General Assembly, "I'm motivated by putting people at the centre of everything we do," while justifying his country's sexual discriminatory policies. The same patterns of contradiction can be invoked with regard to President Paul Kagame—praised by some as the man whose "courage and triumph … show the beauty of reconciliation and of transcendent leadership" (Isaacson quoted in Kinzer 1998), yet seen by others as "[t]he Darling Dictator of the Day [whose country] … has the third-highest level of political exclusion in the world (behind Sudan and Syria)" (Sommers 2012).

All controversies aside, Museveni's NRM and Kagame's RPF stand out as two instances of a fascinating brand of political entrepreneurship. Judging from the odysseys that took them from guerrilla warfare to state governance and, in tandem, world affairs, via complex ideological barriers and donor-driven games of political and economic reforms, it is my contention that Yoweri Museveni and Paul Kagame fit well with Amit et al.'s (2002) concept of "new winners in the new business environment." In that, the most striking features of business life at the turn of the millennium are volatility, turbulence, and unpredictability. New winners emerge quickly and unexpectedly; established leaders decline or disappear. (Amit et al. 2002: 1)

While Marx's dialectic logic along with the growing disenchantment with the two former warlords begs caution, it is beyond the power of any scientific predictability to foretell what the future holds for the NRM and RPF. One thing is clear though: even as we wait and see, the business of controlling power and material gains by all means, ranging from cooperation and compromise to corruption and coercion, continues its course. To grasp what is going on, more efforts are needed to "develop alternative language, framework and metrics that are honest to the real politics of countries deceptively assumed to slowly transit toward liberal democracy" (de Waal 2014b: 15).

References

Amaza, O. (1998). *Museveni's Long March from Guerilla to Statesman*. Kampala: Fountain Publishers.

Amit, R., Hitt, M., Lucier, C., and Nixon, R. (2002). *Creating Value. Winners in the New Business Environment*. Oxford and Malden, USA: Blackwell Publishing.

Ansoms, A. (2011). Rwanda's Post-Genocide Economic Reconstruction. The Mismatch between Elite Ambitions and Rural Realities. In S. Straus and L. Waldorf (eds), *Remaking Rwanda. State Building and Human Rights after Mass Violence*. Madison: The University of Wisconsin Press, 240–51.

Asiimwe, G. (2013). Of Extensive and Elusive Corruption in Uganda: Neo-Patronage, Power, and Narrow Interests. *African Studies Review*, 56(2): 129–44.

Assefa, H. (1993). *Peace and Reconciliation as a Paradigm: A Philosophy of Peace and its Implications on Conflict, Governance, and Economic Growth in Africa*. Nairobi: Nairobi Peace Initiative.

Avirgan, T. and Honey, M., (1982). *War in Uganda: The Legacy of Idi Amin*. London: Zed Press.

Blair, T. and Buffet, H. (2013). Stand with Rwandans. Now is no time to cut aid to Kigali. *Foreign Policy*, February 21. http://foreignpolicy.com/2013/02/21/stand-with-rwanda/.

Brinton, C. (1965). *The Anatomy of Revolution*. New York: Vintage Books.

Bwengye, F. (1985). *The Agony of Uganda: From Idi Amin to Obote*. London: Regency Press.

Carbone, G. (2008). *No-party Democracy?: Ugandan Politics in Comparative Perspective*. Boulder, CO: Lynne Rienner Publishers.

Carson, J. (2005). A Threat to Africa's Success Story. *The Boston Globe*, May 1, http://www.boston.com/news/globe/editorial_opinion/oped/articles/2005/05/01/a_threat_to_africas_success_story/.

Clark, P. (2010). *The Gacaca Courts, Post-Genocide Justice and Reconciliation in Rwanda. Justice without Lawyers*. London: Cambridge University Press.

Conroy, J. (2014) *Rwanda: The Untold Story*. Documentary. London: BBC World Service. http://www.bbc.co.uk/programmes/b04kk03t.

De Waal, A. (2014b). The Concept of the "Political Marketplace." *Discussion Paper*, June 15, Somerville: World Peace Foundation.

De Waal, A. (2014a). *The Political Marketplace: Analyzing Political Entrepreneurs and Political Bargaining with a Business Lens*. http://sites.tufts.edu/reinventingpeace/2014/10/17/the-political-marketplace-analyzing-political-entrepreneurs-and-political-bargaining-with-a-business-lens/.

Des Forges, A. (1999). *Leave None to tell the story. Genocide in Rwanda*. New York: Human Rights Watch.

Diop, C.A. (1990). *Alerte Sous Les Tropiques*. Paris: The Estate of Cheikh Anta Diop and Présence Africaine.

Diop, C.A. (1996). *Towards the African Renaissance: Essays in Culture and Development, 1946–1960*. London: The Estate of Cheikh Anta Diop and Karnak House.

Economist, The. (2013). Aid to Rwanda. The pain of suspension. Will Rwanda's widely praised development plans now be stymied? January 12, http://www.economist.com/news/middle-east-and-africa/21569438-will-rwandas-widely-praised-development-plans-now-be-stymied-pain.

Findlay, S. (2014) Rwanda's president accused in death of ex-spy chief Patrick Karegeya. *Los Angeles Times.* January 3. http://www.latimes.com/world/worldnow/la-fg-wn-rwanda-former-spy-chief-patrick-karegeya-dead-20140103-story.html.

Frontline. (2005). *Front Line Rwanda. Disappearances, Arrests, Threats, Intimidation and Co-option of Human Rights Defenders 2001—2004.* Dublin, Ireland: Frontline.

Fukuyama, F. (1989). The End of History? In *The National Interest,* Summer, https://ps321.community.uaf.edu/files/2012/10/Fukuyama-End-of-history-article.pdf.

Fukuyama, F. (1992). *The End of History and the Last Man.* New York: The Free Press.

Gahima, G. (2013). *Transitional Justice in Rwanda. Accountability for Atrocity.* New York: Routledge.

Gatehouse, G. (2014) Patrick Karegeya: Mysterious death of a Rwandan exile. BBC News Africa, March 26, http://www.bbc.com/news/world-africa-26752838.

Gourevitch, P. (2009). The Life After. Fifteen years after the genocide in Rwanda, the reconciliation defies expectations. *The New Yorker,* May 4: 35–50.

Guichaoua, A. (2010). *Rwanda de la Guerre au Génocide. Les politiques criminelles au Rwanda (1990–1994).* Paris: La Découverte.

Hintjens, H. (2008). Post-genocide Identity Politics in Rwanda. *Ethnicities,* 8(1): 5–41.

Hirji, K. (2010). *Cheche. Reminiscences of a Radical Magazine.* Dar es Salaam: Mkuki na Nyota.

Hudson, J. (2014). Exclusive: Top Lawmaker Proposes Cuts to Rwanda Aid. *Foreign Policy,* April 2, http://foreignpolicy.com/2014/04/02/exclusive-top-lawmaker-proposes-cuts-to-rwanda-aid/.

Human Rights Watch (2010). *Rwanda: Silencing dissidents ahead of elections.* New York: Human Rights Watch, http://www.hrw.org/news/2010/08/02/rwanda-attacks-freedom-expressionfreedomassociation-and-freedom-assembly-run-presi.

Independent, The. (2014). Former Rwandan spy chief Patrick Karegeya murdered in Johannesburg. January 2, http://www.independent.co.uk/news/world/africa/former-rwandan-spy-chief-patrick-karegeya-murdered-in-johannesburg-9035481.html.

Jackson, R. and Rosberg, C. (1982). *Personal Rule in Black Africa: Prince, Autocrat, Prophet, Tyrant.* Berkeley: University of California Press.

Jackson, R. and Rosberg, C. (1984). Personal Rule: Theory and Practice in Africa. *Comparative Politics,* 16(4): 421–42.

Jones, J. (2004). Uganda: President for Life? PBS, Frontline/World, September 7, http://www.pbs.org/frontlineworld/elections/uganda/.

Kagoro, J. (2013). The Military Ethos in the Politics of Post-1986 Uganda. *Social Sciences Directory,* 2(2): 31–46.

Karugire, S.R. (1980). *A Political History of Uganda.* London and Nairobi: Heinemann.

Karugire, S.R. (1996). *The Roots of Instability in Uganda.* Kampala: Fountain Publishers.

Kimenyi, A. (1999). *Alexandre Kimenye Biography.* http://kimenyi.com/bio.php.

Kimonyo, J.P., Noel T., and Kayumba, C. (2004). *Supporting the Post-genocide Transition in Rwanda. The Role of the International Community.* The Hague: Clingendael-CRU, http://www.clingendael.nl/publications 2004/20041200_cru_working_paper_32.pdf.

Kinzer, S. (2008). *A Thousand Hills. Rwanda's Rebirth and the Man Who Dreamt about It.* Hoboken, NJ: John Wiley & Sons, Inc.

Kyemba, H. (1997). *A State of Blood: The Inside Story of Idi Amin.* Kampala: Fountain Publishers.

Lemarchand, R. (1970). *Rwanda and Burundi.* New York/Washington/London: Praeger Publishers.

Mamdani, M.(2002). *When Victims Become Killers: Colonialism, Nativism, and the Genocide in Rwanda.* Princeton, NJ: Princeton University Press.

Mazrui, A. (2006). The Role of the Academy in Politics and Economic Revival: Uganda in Comparative Perspective. Paper presented at Makerere University, August 15. http://www.binghamton.edu/igcs/docs/The%20Role%20of%20Academy%20in%20Politics%20and%20Economic%20Revival-Uganda%20in%20Comparative%20Perspective.pdf.

McFadden, C. and Gerstein, T. (2008). Rick Warren's "Long-Term Relationship" with Rwanda. ABC News, July 31, http://abcnews.go.com/Nightline/story?id=5479972.

Merrill, J. (2015). Gay rights activists defy Ugandan laws by publishing new LGBTI magazine. *The Independent*, January 4, http://www.independent.co.uk/news/media/press/gay-rights-activists-defy-ugandan-laws-by-publishing-new-lgbti-magazine-9955950.html.

Muhumuza, W.(2013). From Fundamental Change to No Change: The NRM and democratization in Uganda. *IFRA—Les Cahiers d'Afrique de l'Est*, 41, pp. 21–42. http://ifra-nairobi.net/wp-content/uploads/2013/12/2Muhumuza.pdf.

Museveni, Y. (1971). Fanon's Theory on Violence: Its Verification in Liberated Mozambique. In Nathan Shamuyarira (ed.) *Essays on the Liberation of Southern Africa*. Dar es Salaam: Tanzania Publishing House, 1–24.

Museveni, Y. (1997). *Sowing the Mustard Seed. The Struggle for Freedom and Démocratie in Uganda*. Oxford: Macmillan Publishers.

Museveni, Y. (2010). Activism at the Hill. In Karim Hirji (ed.), *Cheche. Reminiscences of a Radical Magazine*. Dar es Salaam: Mkuki na Nyota, 11–16.

Mushameza, E. (2007). *The Politics of Empowerment of Banyarwanda Refugees in Uganda 1959–2001*. Kampala: Fountain Publishers.

Mwenda, A. and Tangri, R. (2003). Military Corruption & Ugandan Politics since the Late 1990s. *Review of African Political Economy*, 30(98): 539–52.

Newbury, C. (1988). *The Cohesion of Oppression Clientship and Ethnicity in Rwanda 1860–1960*. New York: Columbia University Press.

Newbury, C. (2011). High Modernism at the Ground Level. The Imidugudu Policy in Rwanda. In S. Straus and L. Waldorf (eds), *Remaking Rwanda. State Building and Human Rights after Mass Violence*. Madison: The University of Wisconsin Press, 223–39.

Ninsiima, R. (2014). Corruption is now Uganda's Aids, says US envoy. *The Observer*, September 30, http://www.observer.ug/news-headlines/34145--corruption-is-now-ugandas-aids-says-us-envoy-?tmpl=component&print=1&layout=default&page=.

Nyamwasa, K., Karegeya, P., Rudasingwa, T., and Gahima, G. (2010). *Rwanda Briefing*. http://musabyimana.be/uploads/media/Rwanda_Briefing_August2010.pdf.

Okumu, W. (2002). *The African Renaissance*. Trenton, N.J. and Asmara, Eritrea: Africa World Press.

Oloka-Onyango, J. (2004). "New-Breed" Leadership, Conflict, and Reconstruction in the Great Lakes Region of Africa: A Sociopolitical Biography of Uganda's Yoweri Kaguta Museveni. *Africa Today*, 50(3): 29–52.

Oloka-Onyango, J. (2006). Dictatorship and Presidential Power in Post Kyankwanzi Uganda: Out of the Pot and into the Fire. *Rights and Democratic Governance Working Paper Series, No. 3*. Kampala: Makerere University.

Pottier, J. (1996). Relief and Repatriation: Views by Rwandan Refugees; Lessons for Humanitarian Aid Workers. *African Affairs*, 95(380): 403–29.

Pottier, J. (2002). *Re-imaging Rwanda. Conflict, Survival and Disinformation in the Late Twentieth Century*. Cambridge: Cambridge University Press.

Prunier, G. (1995). *The Rwanda Crisis. History of Genocide*. New York: Columbia University Press.

Reyntjens, F. (2004). Rwanda, Ten Years On: From Genocide to Dictatorship. *African Affairs*, 103: 177–210.

Reyntjens, F. (2011). Constructing the Truth, Dealing With Dissent, Domesticating the World: Governance in Postgenocide Rwanda. *African Affairs*, 110(438): 1–34.

Reyntjens, F. (2013). *Political Governance in Post-Genocide Rwanda*. New York: Cambridge University Press.

Richardson, P. (2012). Rwanda Gets Business Reformer Tag as Kagame Opponents Jailed. *Bloomberg News*, March 16. http://www.bloomberg.com/news/articles/2012–03–14/kagame-s-rwanda-earns-business-reformer-tag-as-opponents-jailed.

Rosenblum, P. (2002). Irrational Exuberance: The Clinton Administration in Africa. *Current History*, 101(655): 195–202. https://secure25.securewebsession.com/currenthistory.com/pdf_user_files/101_655_195.pdf.

Roth, K. (2009). The Power of Horror in Rwanda, *Los Angeles Times*, April 11, http://www.latimes.com/opinion/la-oe-roth11-2009apr11-story.html.

Rudasingwa, T. (2013). *Healing a Nation: A Testimony*. North Charleston: CreateSpace.

Rwanda Rugali (2006). Wounding speech. Speech by President Paul Kagame. International Water Day. Rebero, Bwisige District, Byumba Province, March 31, 2003. http://rwandarugali.tripod.com/rwanda/id383.html.

Samset, I. (2011). Building a Repressive Peace: The Case of Post-Genocide Rwanda. *Journal of Intervention and Statebuilding*, 5(3): 265–83.

Sebarenzi, Joseph. (2011). Justice and Human Rights for All Rwandans. In S. Straus and S. Waldorf (eds), *Remaking Rwanda. State Building and Human Rights after Mass Violence*. Madison: The University of Wisconsin Press, 343–53.

Smith, S. (1996). Au Rwanda, la disgrâce du—Hutu de service—du FPR. En exil, Seth Sendashonga a échappé à un attentat. *Liberation Monde*, March 21. http://www.liberation.fr/monde/1996/03/21/au-rwanda-la-disgrace-du-hutu-de-service-du-fpr-en-exil-seth-sendashonga-a-echappe-a-un-attentat_165332.

Sommers, M. (2012). The Darling Dictator of the Day. *New York Times*, May 27, http://www.nytimes.com/2012/05/28/opinion/Paul-Kagame-The-Darling-Dictator-of-the-day.html?_r=0.

Sterns, J. and Borello, F. (2011). Bad Karma: Accountability for Rwandan Crimes in the Congo. In S. Straus and L. Waldorf (eds), *Remaking Rwanda. State Building and Human Rights after Mass Violence*. Madison: The University of Wisconsin Press, 152–72.

Straus, S. and Waldorf, L. (eds) (2011). *Remaking Rwanda. State Building and Human Rights after Mass Violence*. Madison: The University of Wisconsin Press.

Tripp, A.M. (2004). The Changing Face of Authoritarianism in Africa: The Case of Uganda. *Africa Today*, 50(3): 3–26.

Twagiramungu, N. (2010). *The Anatomy of Leadership: A View-from-within of Post-genocide Rwanda*. Paper presented at the Annual Meeting of the African Studies Association, San Francisco, CA.

Twagiramungu, N. (2014a). Two Roads to Power: Explaining Variation in the Transition from Genocidal Violence to Rebel Governance in Contemporary Rwanda and Burundi. PhD dissertation. Medford: Tufts University.

Twagiramungu, N. (2014b). Can Be There Justice after Genocide? Lessons from Rwanda. *Al Jazeera Magazine*, May 1.

United Nations Human Rights (2010). *The Democratic Republic of the Congo, 1993–2003*. http://www.ohchr.org/Documents/Countries/CD/DRC_MAPPING_REPORT_FINAL_EN.pdf.

United Nations Security Council (2013). Letter dated June 20, 2013 from the Group of Experts on the Democratic Republic of the Congo addressed to the Chair of the Security Council Committee established pursuant to resolution 1533 (2004) concerning the Democratic Republic of the Congo. S/2013/433, http://www.securitycouncilreport.org/atf/cf./%7B65BFCF9B-6D27-4E9C-8CD3-CF6E4FF96FF9%7D/s_2013_433.pdf.

Want China Times (2014). Rwanda bought TL-50 air defense missiles from China: Kanwa, November 9, http://www.wantchinatimes.com/news-subclass-cnt.aspx?id=20141109000060&cid=1101.

Chapter 5

The International Responsibility to Protect and the Conflict in Darfur

John Idriss Lahai

Abstract

The political and legal dynamics surrounding the conflict in Darfur, Sudan threaten the entire structure of the international Responsibility to Protect (RtoP). General concern in the west and Africa has been expressed in different clusters of principles and policy directives. Collectively, they maintain that the primary responsibility of a state is to protect its citizens. Such protection should include prevention, reaction and rebuilding. In this chapter, I examine the origin and characteristics of the conflict and the nature of alternative dispute resolution and peacekeeping in Darfur. I argue that, political considerations in this conflict, as well as the competing interests of those interested in the conflict—i.e. the United Nations (UN), the African Union (AU), the International Criminal Court (ICC), and the United States (US) government—have led to (political and legal) tensions, especially with regards to the questions of genocide, Sudan's sovereignty and peacekeeping in the troubled region of Darfur.

Introduction

The conflict in Darfur has led to contentious arguments between two schools of thoughts: those that oppose the use of force and those that support an armed intervention in the country under the element of an international responsibility to react. Those opposed to the use of force have argued that reactionary peacekeeping forces have only succeeded in situations where the conflict is between two factions with well discipline armies with an identifiable command and control structure in place. Furthermore, in the case of Darfur, de Waal contends that:

> The knock-down argument against humanitarian invasion is that it won't work. The idea of foreign troops fighting their way into Darfur and disarming the *Janjaweed* militia by force is sheer fantasy. Practicality dictates that peacekeeping force in Darfur cannot enforce its will on any resisting armed groups without entering into a protracted and unwinnable counter-insurgency in which casualties are inevitable. The only way peacekeeping works is with consent: the agreement of the Sudan government and the support of the majority of the Darfurian populace […]. Without this, UN troops will not only fail but will make the plight of the Darfurians even worse. (de Waal 2014: 1)

For him, even if an international intervention force is able to engage in significant combat, it can only succeed in containing the national army of Sudan, and not the Darfurian insurgent groups, because most of these insurgent groups are peopled by men in the displaced camps. By day they are vulnerable civilians in need of protection, and by night they are insurgents. As such, finding a solution hinges on a sober assessment of what is practical and not on what would use the conflict to put to test the duty of care embedded in the international responsibility to protect, prevent and rebuild.

For those who believe that the inaction of the international community in Darfur is a missed opportunity have contended that the sobriety of any assessment of the conflict should be based on the realities on the ground and not on imaginative fears that the use of force in Darfur might lead to the destabilization of the country (Burr and Collins 2006).

In this chapter, I examine the question of genocide and the nature of peacekeeping in Darfur. The relevance of the discussions is not aimed at making a case for the use of force in Darfur (and by qualified extension, against the GoS). Rather to explain how international political considerations in the conflict have brought to the fore the challenges of legally legitimating and implementing the international responsibility to protect in Africa. The intention here is to also show how, by making the conflict a priority in its foreign policy, the United States have opened a window of opportunity for the African Union to criticize its stance on international law; including the emergence of an anti-colonial metanarrative against how the US and the UN have discursively interpreted Africa's place within the international system, and with it, the appearance of an African politico-legal objection to the activities of the International Criminal Court (ICC) in the continent.

The political and legal dynamics surrounding the conflict in Darfur, Sudan threaten the entire structure of the RtoP. General concern in the west and Africa has been expressed in different clusters of principles and policy directives. Collectively, they maintain that the primary responsibility of a state is to protect its citizens. Such protection should include prevention, reaction and rebuilding. In this chapter, I examine the origin and characteristics of the conflict and the nature of alternative dispute resolution and peacekeeping in Darfur. I argue that, political considerations in this conflict, as well as the competing interests of those interested in the conflict—i.e. the UN, the AU, the ICC, and the US government, have led to political and legal tensions, especially with regards to the questions of genocide, Sudan's sovereignty and peacekeeping in the troubled region of Darfur.

This chapter first presents the origins and the characteristics of the conflict, also taking into consideration how they impact the overall international effort to understand the trends of violence in the region. Secondly, the analysis shifts to the examination of the political and legal tensions surrounding the genocide question. Thirdly, the alternative dispute resolution mechanisms that have been used to resolve the crisis is discussed, as it gives us an understanding of the challenges of peacekeeping in Darfur. Finally, I discuss the politics surrounding attempts to deploy a robust reactionary peacekeeping force, to enforce the peace and protect civilians.

The Sources of the Conflict

The Darfur region is home to the Nilo-Saharan (Black African) Sudanese ethnic groups, the Fur, Zaghawa, Masaalit, Tungur, Bara and Tama, among others. However, to their fellow Arab Sudanese compatriots, they are derogatorily known as "Misseriya Zurug" (a derogatory Arabic word for *nigga*) (Bassil 2010: 89). Despite the dialectical differences, they all share the same Nilo-Saharan language, belief systems and cultural practices. Before the amalgamation of Darfur into Sudan by the British imperial government in 1917, Darfur was a strong and unified Sultanate (Bassil 2006). However, after 1917, the center of economic and political power shifted to the Khartoum government, which remains under the direct control of the northern Arab Sudanese ethnic groups.

Due to political neglect (Petterson 2003), coupled with structural inequality (Cock and Mironko 2006: 130) and the unresolved colonial constructions on the discourse of race, (Bassil 2010), amid the merciless desertification crisis—of drought and water scarcity that has resulted in frustrations, aggression, and increased levels of hatred between the nomadic Darfurians and their pastoralist Sudanese Arab neighbors (Mazo 2010: 85–6)—Darfur imploded into an internecine civil war in February 2003, when the group, the Sudan Liberation Front (SLF), led by Abd Al-Wahid Muhammed Ahmed Al-Nurr (hereafter, Al-Nurr), attacked and seized control of the townships of Aradyeb Al-Asharah and Gulu, the capital of Jabal Marra Province, Western Darfur (Flint and de Waal 2005). Equipped with mostly small arms, these rebels started attacking and destroying government military installations to steal weapons, which contributed to the long and deadly armed conflict.

Rather than seeking outright political independence, the aim of some of the Darfurian warring factions has been to fight for some autonomy within a Sudanese confederacy, which according to experts, offers the best possible outcomes of creating a political system whereby the people will get a fair share of the country's wealth, protect their scarce water resources, as well as preserve their cultural and ethnic identities (Bassil 2003).

However, inasmuch as the Darfurian warring factions share a common position against the Khartoum government and its protégé, the Janjaweed militia, they are also divided over the questions of political governance and military strategies. Through the complex interplay of the politics of deviance, ideologies and insurgent activism, these factions have broken-up and other splinter factions have emerged, with other minor factions merging to form a united front against the common enemy, the Government of Sudan (GoS) and its Janjaweed militia. For example, a few months after its formation, the Justice and Equality Movement (JEM) broke into two factions—The JEM-Khalil Ibrahim and JEM-Bahar Idriss Abu Garda (both supported by their Zaghawa-kodi kin). Whilst Khalil Ibrahim wanted outright independence, Abu Garda wanted a political outcome that would lead to the creation of a confederate Darfurian region under the political and military protection of a democratic national government in Khartoum (de Waal 2007: 1040). Interestingly also, before the split, both JEM factions were part of the Sheikh Hassan Al-Turabi-led National Islamic Front (NIF), which was advocating for the creation of a unified, but semi-autonomous Darfurian Islamic Sultanate. The key factions at the start of the conflict included the Sudan Liberation Front of Al Nurr (which is dominated by the Fur ethnic group), the Sudan Liberation Front, which is a breakaway group from the Sudan Liberation Army (SLA) created by Minni Mannawi (and dominated by the Zaghawa ethnic group), the Sudan Liberation Army formed by Abdul Wahid, SLA-Unity formed by Abdullah Yehya, the SLA-Ahmed Abdesh Shafi and the Free Will Movement of Abdel Rahman Musa.

Having said that, the level of intensity and severity of the conflict in Darfur cannot be understood by the mere quantification of battle-related deaths, but through an anthropocentric understanding of the character of the conflict itself, and how its characterization has impacted the politics of humanitarian intervention in Africa. Within such a volatile situation, it is expected that the mediators and peacekeepers should always emphasize their neutrality in the peace process, but neutrality should not prevent the need for military action to protect civilians and civilian installations in the region. Notwithstanding that, the main problem for the peacekeeping forces in Darfur is threefold.

First, how and where do they create a buffer between the belligerents, who are sparsely located and can hardly be contained under a central military command and control structure? Second, how do they create a balance between the military imperative for self-defense and the peremptory protection of civilians, on one hand, and the need for peacebuilding activities as stated in the hybrid African Union and United Nations (AU/UN) Status of Forces Agreements (SoFA)? Third, as in all ethnic conflicts—from Rwanda to Darfur—how do they reconstruct identities and create the platform for people to memorialize their shattered wartime identities in ways that do not lead to the emergence of new forms of identity induced grievances?

Characteristics of the Conflict and Patterns of Wartime Violence

The key characteristic features of this conflict revolve around the following: first, the identity question (Bassil 2006). The nuanced nature of that identity-of-same is determined by a hagiographical interpretation of one's origin, which leads to the nostalgic reflection on questions of *Who am I?*, and *Where do I come from?* In this sense, the individual does not exist without his/her roots (Horowitz 1985). In such a situation, whatever happens to the individual happens to the whole group; and the individual internalizes whatever happened to the group. It is this feeling of connectedness that leads people to become attached to those with whom they share the same physical and cultural beliefs. But when the idea of being connected emerges as an instrument in controlling a distinct ethnic group's collective agency, it becomes a tool for the political and military actions of the group. As such, belligerent ethnic groups are characterized by a politicized, albeit patriarchal, kinship political structures, which is needed, preferred and emphasized over matrilateral lineages in the creation of the foundations of a socio-political system of ethnic inequality, and the command structure in the conflict (or ethnic purging of the ethnic-other) that emerges mostly following a political interpretation of an incident.

Second, the nature of socio-affinal bonding of people towards their ethnic groups of-same, and the corresponding implications on the levels of hatred (and hate speech) between the competing racial groups in the region. Identity politics, social bonding and people metanarratives have a direct relationship to the trends in the patterns of recruitment into the warring factions. They have contributed to the emergence of a crowd psychology around the hagiographical interpretation of people's receptiveness to questions of "self" and "belongingness," which, in turn, create an agentive possibility for people to commit harm that they would not dare to commit when they are not under the influence of the psychological pull of the collective (Fearon et al. 2007).

Third, the dynamics of population density, and the corresponding migratory trajectories of the competing ethnic groups, for irrigable land and drinkable water: the more a particular group of people are concentrated in one area the higher the possibility that there will be higher levels of primordial bonding and the mobilization of people for militarized political adventurism (Green 2009: 10; see also Hameso 1997). However, mobilization rhetoric, as Horowitz (1985) argued, can only produce its intended impact if there is in existence deeply-rooted historical grievances of one group against the other. In the Darfur region, cultural, economic and political grievances have led to a situation whereby people's social and political energies are activated whenever one group feels a sense of being deprived by the dominant other (who may not necessarily be dominant in terms of numbers, but dominant in terms of its share of the national economy and control over national politics) or are contending against the attempt by the *other* to end that dominance. Population dynamics also has its own gendered implications—especially in feeding into the patterns of sexual and gender based violence. According to its 2004 report, the US State Department reported that about 60 percent of Darfurian children in the Chadian refugee camps reported seeing the gang raping of a female family member by the Janjaweed militia, and experiencing abduction themselves (United States Department 2004). Although the Khartoum government has long dismissed rape as an ignorable violation of military ethics by individual soldiers and rebels, Article 7(2)(f) of the ICC Statute notes that the rape of women, with the intent and motive of impregnation, constitutes a war crime of enforced population transfer (ICC 1998). Though this cannot be applied in all cases, in the case of Darfur this argument holds because within Sudan, questions of ancestral kinship and parentage are conditioned and paternalistically regulated through systems of patriarchy. Thus, when women are raped in this context, the children are automatically identified with their fathers' ethnicity. Women do not have rights to determine their reproductive rights. In fact they are culturally considered as property to be bought and owned by men, and where necessary, through the custom of *quwama*, the man has the unquestioned right to deprive their women of their basic human rights, including the right to life and religious beliefs all with the aim of sustaining the patriarchal status quo (Willemse 2007: 437).

Fourth, conflict escalation in the region is triggered when the political elites of the competing groups change their political, economic and cultural demands. Ethnic identity and its affinities to identity politics are socio-politically constructed by people with competing political interests that are not necessarily representative of those of the vulnerable civilians in the internal displaced camps. Through the use of identity-induced rhetoric and nationalistic mobilization strategies after 1917, when the independent sultanate of Darfur was amalgamated into Sudan, the identity-of-same bonding (against the other) have hardened to the point where cross-ethnic political appeals are unlikely to be made or even less likely to be tolerated by either the Arab Sudanese or the Darfurian people. In this situation, while the perceived or actual sense of annihilation has not always been an outcome of mutually exclusive socio-affinal differences, they have fed into the war narratives of the political elites.

Suffice to say, the ferocity with which the Khartoum government responded to this armed insurrection have been condemned outright by the international community. In a move to bring down the insurrection, the GoS had armed the pastoralist Arab groups in the Darfur region, transformed them into a Janjaweed (or "devils on horseback") militia, and unleased them on the Nilo-Saharan Darfurian population (Burr and Collins 2006). By arming one ethnic group that already had a deep-rooted hatred for, and grievance against the other, and by engaging in aerial bombardments of civilian targets, western countries, including the international legal community, believes the violations constitute grave breaches to international humanitarian law—to which the United States had called for armed humanitarian intervention under the threshold of an international responsibility to react.

Moreover, beyond arming the Janjaweed, another issue has to do with attempts at Arabizing the region. According to Burr and Collins, the Arabization policies of the GoS did not start with the eruption of war in 2003. Rather it started as far back as in 1980 when it sponsored the formation of the radical group, The Arab Gathering. This group it is believed was formed with the sole purpose of mobilizing the Arabs into a united front against the non-Arab ethnic groups in Darfur. In fact, the term *Misseriya Zurug* first appeared on the leaflets issued by the Arab Gathering in 1989 calling on all Arab Sudanese to declare a jihadist intifada (which was to be backed by a fatwa, i.e. a pledge of obedience) to exterminate the Darfurian people of Sirba, Silea and Abu Suroj townships (which were also attacked repeatedly, later on February 8, 2008). It should be noted that, while the use of derogatory anti-Darfurian narratives such as Zurug, for instance, do not amount to genocide, it has a huge psychological impact on the people. It has contributed to the emergence of constructs and stereotypes in the mobilization rhetoric of the ethnic others against the Darfurian people in the country—and many years later, it continues to act as a catalyst for Janjaweed recruitment.

Another characteristic that has been identified is the act of attacking food convoys with the calculated aim of preventing their arrival in the displaced camps of Darfur. While all factions are guilty of these kinds of violations, the UN Humanitarian Relief Coordinator, Ian Egalan (cited in Bellamy 2009: 158) has argued that the deliberate act of blocking humanitarian aid from reaching the displaced people, and the pillaging of the limited food aid in the displaced camps, as well as the burning down of villages and poisoning of the remaining draught affected water wells, is not only a violation of international law, it also transforms the conflict into one of the worst humanitarian disasters in Africa. It should, however, be noted that Egalan was more concerned with the inability of the UN to put in place a robust military presence in Darfur. In June 2005 he argued, during his briefing to the UN Security Council, that:

> We must provide better physical security. Humanitarian presence is not enough. The creation of a secure environment for displaced populations should be a primary objective of peacekeeping operations. We need strategic deployment around camps to provide area security for the displaced, we need it in areas of unrest to prevent new displacement, and in areas of origin to facilitate voluntary and safe return. (cited in Bellamy 2009: 158)

The Question of Genocide

The issue of whether there has been genocide in Darfur remains a legally contentious issue. Documentary evidence has shown that the Sudan government has used disproportionate force against the Darfurian population and their insurgent groups. But not everyone agrees that this should either warrant the use of military force, or for the conflict to be portrayed as genocide. However, if it cannot be defined as genocide, the issue then shifts from being a legal question to a political one—or a tension between the two.

To avoid the situation where a militarized attempt to save lives would inadvertently violate international humanitarian law, those who drafted the RtoP doctrine emphasized the need for cautious and affirmative action to prevent war crimes, crimes against humanity and genocide. They also called for the verification of reports of atrocities by highly credible, competent and impartial bodies (with an international legal personality) to prevent a situation whereby an isolated incident of, say, the accidental massacre of people, would result in full scale armed conflict (Thakur 2011). This, however, does not mean that the circumstantial lack of verified evidence would be a source for inaction to prevent or contain politically-motivated humanitarian catastrophes (Peters 2009: 514). As such, without precluding the relevance of grassroots perceptions in the conflict, the AU, the UN, the East African Intergovernmental Authority on Development (IGAD) and the Arab League (AL), among others have argued that all factions in the conflict have committed war crimes and crimes against humanity. It is estimated that between the years 2003–2008 hundreds of thousands of people had been killed, as well as the systemic massacre of livestock (UN News Centre 2008). For its part, the United States has argued that the severity and systematic nature of wartime violence should be a key determinant of the genocidal nature of the conflict, and the culpability of the GoS and its protégé, the Janjaweed militia (Junk 2014).

Conventional legal wisdom contends that for a conflict to be classified as genocide, the nature of violence should satisfy several thresholds—especially those outlined in the 1948 Genocide Convention. These thresholds emphasize that there should be—a) systematic use of mass imprisonment and the deprivation of the liberties of the people to suppress dissention; b) clear evidence that torture is being used; c) the elevation of sexualized forms of violence, such as rape, sexual slavery, enforced prostitution, forced pregnancy and enforced sterilization, with the intent and motive of destroying communities; d) targeted violence against a particular race of people; e) evidence of the enforced disappearance of persons-of-same; and f) evidence that other forms of inhumane acts, similar in character to those that have the potential of causing great suffering or serious injury to body or to mental or physical wellbeing, have been perpetrated (Quigley 2006; Thakur and Weiss 2009).

However, the mere allegation that there has been a severe breach of international law is not enough for the invocation of an international responsibility to react. The severity of the crimes should be judged against the question of whether the violence is high enough to be classified as a complex political emergency or a humanitarian catastrophe. Without engaging in legal argument per se, the focus here is to identify the tensions between those who believe there has been a genocide in Darfur and those who think otherwise. Despite its unwillingness to engage the US military in the conflicts, the administration of President George W. Bush, in 2004 had urged the United Nations Security Council to accept that the conflict in Darfur was a genocide because the severity of the conflict satisfied the 1948 Genocide Convention's definition of genocide (Junk 2014).

For them, despite the documented evidence at its disposal, the UN was, nonetheless, reluctant to accept the genocide argument of the US government. Instead, it relied on the January 2005 findings of the UN's International Commission of Inquiry on Darfur (ICID) to affirm that inasmuch as the Khartoum government of President Al Bashir, and the Janjaweed militia were in breach of international humanitarian law, the severity of its crimes, including rape, systematic killings, pillage and forced displacement, did not amount to genocidal crimes (United Nations Security Council 2005). Even though the ICID provided ample evidence of state culpability on the part of the GoS for refusing to regulate the military's conduct of its armed forces, coupled with the admissions from the field investigators that the Khartoum government had refused to grant them access to vital information on its military activities (and into some parts of Darfur), it nonetheless relied on anecdotal examples to conclude that there was no genocidal motive on the part of the Sudanese government.

As it would later emerge from the assessments of numerous international human rights reports and the analyses of scholars (such as Badescu 2009), the investigators did not take into consideration the level of devastation and the mass killings in some key townships such as Yassin, El-Geneina and Nyala, weeks before they submitted their report to the then UN Secretary General, Koffi Annan. They however conceded in their report that some of the key information they had requested that would have established whether genocide had taken place in Darfur was withheld by the GoS (United Nations Security Council 2005). With these revelations, coupled with the politics of deviance being played out by President Bashir and the African Union towards the international efforts to end the conflict, the commission can be criticized for not doing much in this regard.

Another shortcoming that can be identified in the UN report is the inability of the investigators to create a deconstructed, albeit a substantive (and a non-procedural), interpretation of the motive (i.e. the reasons behind the counterinsurgency in Darfur) and intent (.i.e. the very act of destroying, in whole or in part, the Darfurian people and their livelihoods) of the GoS and the Janjaweed militia in the conflict. The decision to emphasize that the offenses committed by the government can only be established using the inseparable principle of *mens rea* (the criminal intent—the state of mind indicating culpability which is required by law as an element of a crime) and *actus reus* (the act, or its omission thereof, that constitute the physical element of a crime required by law to establish culpability) was, unfortunately, a dangerous one, especially so when it comes from an international organization that had shown a legal commitment to regulate the actions of states and non-state actors to maintain regional peace and security. The danger is that it might be used by rogue states as a new precedence in international humanitarian law whenever they are implicated for war crimes and crimes against humanity.

The commission's attempt to distinguish between intent and motive without taking into consideration the roles that hate crimes and malice have played in the conflict makes their conclusions problematic. To some commentators, the counterinsurgency activities of the Khartoum government and the Janjaweed militia were nothing short of the intensification of its hatred for the people of Darfur. A case in point is the incident that occurred on August 6, 2003, prior to the attack on the town of Mukjar. On this date, Ahmed Mohammed Harun, the Humanitarian Minister in the government of President Umar Al-Bashir gave a speech in which he stated that "since the children of Fur had become rebels, all Fur and what they had, had become booty for the *Mujahidin*" (Totten 2011). This, according to Totten, meant that the conflict only offered an opportunity to the government to annihilate the Darfurian people.

That notwithstanding, the ICC seems to have disagreed with the incongruous interpretation of the UN investigators. The indictment that was issued in March 2009 against President Bashir clearly stated that the prosecutor believes there has been genocide in Darfur and, in explicit terms rejects procedural interpretation of *Actus Reus Non Facit Reum Nisi Mens Sit Rea* argument (that the conviction of a crime requires proof of a criminal act and intent). As such, the intent and motive behind the GoS' counterinsurgency in Darfur amounts to genocide as codified in Article 30 of the Rome Statute. The indictment states:

> Considering that there are also reasonable grounds to believe that, as part of the GoS's unlawful attack on the … civilian population of Darfur and with knowledge of such attack, Gos forces subjected, throughout the Darfur region, (i) hundreds of thousands of civilians, belonging primarily to the Fur, Masalit and Zaghawa groups, to acts of forcible transfer; (ii) thousands of civilian women, belonging primarily to these groups, to acts of rape; and (iii) civilians, belonging to the same groups, to acts of torture. (ICC 2009a)

Rejecting the Commission of Inquiry's political considerations of the genocide claims, the ICC prosecutor claimed in the indictment that, President Bashir is responsible for genocidal crimes that includes: genocide by killing (article 6[a]), genocide by causing serious bodily or mental harm (article 6[b]) and genocide by deliberately inflicting on each group conditions of life calculated to bring the group's physical destruction (article 6[c]) (ICC 2009a).

Alternative Dispute Resolution Mechanisms: Processes and Challenges

The 2001 report of the International Commission on Intervention and State Sovereignty, the 2005 *World Summit Outcome Document*, and the subsequent 2009 UN General Assembly's reports on the responsibility to protect, set a number of procedural and substantive criteria to be met before military intervention is evoked. One of these is the exhaustion of all (specified and non-specified) Alternative Dispute Resolution (ADR) strategies at the disposal of the international community, especially those listed in Chapter VI of the UN Charter and Article IV of the Constitutive Act of the African Union (AU), as well as those recommended in the outcome document of the 2005 Common African position on state responsibility, the *Ezulwini Consensus* (an outcomes document agreed by African heads of state and governments at the Swaziland city of Ezulwini. It included a set of recommendations to the UN that should act as the blueprint for the development of a comprehensive framework that would translate policy to action, and as well as safeguarding the authority of the UN and the AU in Africa). It has been established that,

> there is no better or more appropriate body than the United Nations Security Council to authorize military intervention for humanitarian purposes. The task, therefore, is not to find alternatives to the Security Council, as a source of authority, but alternatives that will make it work better than it has. (ICISS 2001: 12)

As such, the willingness of the UN to encourage alternatives to armed intervention is a demonstration that all strategies carry equal weight in the processes aimed at creating a universal acceptance of alternative dispute resolution mechanisms in international law and politics.

One of these ADR approaches being used is the ICC. With the understanding that there was not going to be a direct armed involvement involving AFRICOM, the US government's Africa Command, they requested that the matter be sent to the ICC (Junk 2014: 3). The acceptance of the *insurgency levels* by the US Congress was not good enough. On September 9, 2004, with the support of expert witnesses from the International Atrocity Documentation Team, the International Coalition for Justice, Amnesty International, Human Rights Watch, the International Crisis Group and the American Bar Association, the then US Secretary of State, Collin Powell (2004), during his testimony to the joint US Senate/congressional committee on Foreign Affairs (and few days later before the UN Security Council's Select Committee meeting on the crisis in Darfur), made a case for the matter to be reviewed because the political recognition of an ongoing conflict is not the same as acceptance of genocidal crimes against the Darfurian populations.

Through the US representative in the UN, Ambassador John Danforth, Powell was able to get the UN Security Council to pass Resolution 1593 in March 31, 2005 that referred the Darfur crisis to the ICC, in accordance with Article 13(b) of the Rome Statute of the international criminal court (Mendes 2014; Helmke 2010: 121). This referral was an interesting development because it exposes the double standards of both the governments of the USA and Sudan. For its part, the USA has always been very resilient in the defense of its national sovereignty against international encroachments. According to Thakur (2006: 252), the sovereigntists in the US have launched three lines of arguments. First, the emerging ICC legal order is vague and illegitimately intrusive on domestic affairs; Second, its internal law-making processes are unaccountable and the resulting laws are unenforceable; and, third, Washington DC can "opt out of international regimes as a matter of legal right to self-defence, constitutional duty to its people, and global power" (Thakur 2006: 252). What this means is that, while it has refused to accept the superiority of international criminal law over its national laws, it nonetheless accepts that the ICC has jurisdiction in Sudan. For its part, the GoS has refused to accept the legitimacy of the Rome Statute, and in 2008 it also withdrew its peremptory acceptance of the universal legitimacy of the International Court of Justice (ICJ). However, it has, on principle with some reservations, recognized the complementarity functions of the ICC. Despite its withdrawal, the US government objected that being a *de jure* member-state of the UN General Assembly implies that Sudan is still a party to a number of other non-peremptorily and binding international law instruments, including the UN Charter and the 1948 Genocide Convention (Arieff et al. 2010: 12).

Thus, after a thorough fact-finding investigation, the ICC invoked its complementarity clause and indicted some key figures in the Bashir government on the grounds that the GoS is unwilling to prosecute them for war crimes, crimes against humanity and genocide in Darfur. The Rome Statute states that by invoking its complementary prosecution powers (as stated in Article 58 of the Statute) the ICC is in effect performing its duty of care under international criminal law. However, this cardinal rule of a *duty of care* is subjected to the *principle of complementarity* (as stated in para. 10 of Article 58) which in substantive and procedural terms, states that the role of the ICC is to complement the national criminal justice systems of states. What this means it that, the ICC can only act after it has been proven beyond reasonable doubt that a government is unable and/or unwilling to prosecute suspected criminals. These indictments, as expected, created a political impasse with both the ICC Prosecutor and the Sudan government accusing each other of undermining the peace process. In reaction, the Sudan government issued a warrant of arrest on April 16, 2007, for ICC Prosecutor, Mr Luis Moreno Ocampo, whom they accused of subverting the peace process.

Furthermore, and in retrospect, to make mockery of its acceptance of the complementarity functions of the ICC, the GoS arrested the Minister for Humanitarian Affairs, Ahmed Mohammed Harun (who was accused by the ICC of being, at the time of his indictment, responsible for the attacks on the villages of Kodoom, Bindisi, Mukjar and Arawala in West Darfur between August 2003 and March 2004) and the leader of the notorious Janjaweed militia, Ali Kushayb. After a brief travesty of a trial, they were acquitted and discharged. However, despite this pretense that it has adhered to its state responsibility, Prosecutor Ocampo rejected the outcomes of the trials, and issued another indictment on March 4, 2009, this time for the President of Sudan, Omar Al Bashir (ICC 2009b). In the indictment, he was accused of war crimes (within the meaning of article 8[2][e][i] and 8[2][e][v]) and crimes against humanity.

It was expected that these indictments would have achieved the intended effect and put to an end the conflict. However, emboldened by its pan-Africanist, albeit anti-colonial stance on July 3, 2009 the AU during its 13th African Union Summit of Heads of States in Sirte, Libya, passed a hardline resolution that also criticizes the UN for disregarding its authority in Africa. To this, it decided that

> in view of the fact that the request by the African Union has never been acted upon [when it requested that the UN Security Council should ask the ICC to defer its investigation of the situation in The Sudan], the AU Member States shall not cooperate pursuant to the provisions of Article 98 of the Rome Statute of the ICC relating to immunities, for the arrest and surrender of President Omar El Bashir of The Sudan. (Meernik 2013: 323)

The imposition of sanctions and travel bans are other forms of ADR that have been employed to resolve the conflict. Under the constant jolting from Ambassador John Danforth, the UN Security Council adopted UNSC Resolutions 1556 (in July 2004) and 1564 (in September 2004) which imposed tough sanctions on key officials in the Al-Bashir government. Although both resolutions, like many others, did not authorize the deployment of a Chapter VII mandated peacekeeping force or made it mandatory for the peacekeepers in Darfur to monitor compliance, Resolution 1556, however, followed up on the recommendations made in the Ndjamena Humanitarian Ceasefire Agreement (signed on April 8, 2004) and called for the immediate cessation of hostilities and the disarmament of the Janjaweed militia.

Another form of ADR approach that has been attempted was getting the factions to agree to cease all forms of hostilities. Amid the mistrust that existed between the factions, the only way to create the enabling environment for the precarious peace processes to hold is to encourage them to agree to temporarily stop the fighting (de Waal 2014). In line with the recommendations of the UNSC resolution 1564, the UN Peacekeeping Department, in partnership with the AU and other multilateral agencies and governments, sponsored the Abuja negotiations in 2006. During the deliberations, it was agreed that a Ceasefire Commission should be created to monitor the activities of all warring factions. Despite its efforts, this commission was doomed to fail from its inception because both the UN and GoS could not agree on who should be included in it. According to deWaal (2007: 147), the mistake committed against the advice of the Security Commission of the African Union was to expel, on the insistence of GoS, the Darfur rebel factions that were not represented at the Abuja negotiations from the Commission. Soon after its formation, emboldened by the belief that they could use their marginality as an agency, these marginalized factions created an alliance, disregarded the ceasefire and kept on fighting. In February 2010, this alliance, which had grown to a ten-faction group, renamed itself the Liberation and Justice Movement and appointed Dr El Tijani El Sese, who also doubled as the Chairman of Dar Regional Authority, as their political and military leader.

The Moral Impossibilities of Reaching Lastness: The Politics of Armed Intervention and Peacekeeping

As a result of the lack of progress at the initial stages of the war, and amid the lack of clear cut answers to the genocide question, the African Union suggested a peacekeeping approach that would respect the sovereign authority of the Khartoum government and at the same time keep the peace in the country. This sovereignty question is a major political issue in this conflict because it represents the first test of the International community's commitment to the transformation of the meaning of state sovereignty and the prospect for the universalization of responsibility to protect doctrine. As Luise Arbour rightly pointed out, RtoP goes beyond the wishful humanitarian thinking of the past. It implies a much broader commitment than the impulsive right to intervene (politically and militarily) in the internal affairs of countries. Rather, "it is anchored in existing law, in institutions and in lessons learnt from practice. It virtually flows from its inherent soundness and justice, as well as from the concept's comparative advantage over formulations of humanitarian intervention" (Arbour 2008: 446–7). What this means, in practice is that, as a norm it calls for the respect for the national and constitutional sovereignty of states (Thakur 2006: 252) and at the same time, it rejects the argument that state sovereignty is an entitlement—although the selective application of this respect, when compared to the way how the United Nations relates to the core states of the West and the peripheral countries in Africa, raises the questions whether the Security Council is a respecter of its *erga omnes* obligations.

That notwithstanding, the RtoP is a norm that seeks to legitimate the argument that the authority and powers of states are not absolute but conditioned upon performance indicators of peace, human security and development (Shinoda 2008). However, these indicators according to Acharya (2013), once identified, do not remain uncontested and static. With the feedback to the UN and its specialized agencies, from individual states and non-state actors, all possible errors should be resolved as they emerge. Through this feedback, the interaction between policy and practice should further enable the international community to build the legitimating structures of *responsible sovereignty*. However, in an attempt to make sense of the dynamics involved in norm creation and consolidation, Amitav Acharya also reiterated that although the credit for the emergence of RtoP has generally been given to the International Commission on Intervention and State Sovereignty (ICISS), it has multiple prior sources and contexts-specific practical applications.

One of these sources is the persistency of complex political emergencies in Africa: a continent where there has been a relatively unsuccessful attempt to put to test the norm's criteria of last resort and proportionality, against the regime of the late Colonel Gaddafi in Libya (Acharya 2013: 466–7); and, as an addendum, greater operational accountability in humanitarian intervention to defend the norm has taken a dangerous turn, following the African Union's refusal to accept the international community's legal argument on the state responsibility of the GoS for genocidal crimes in Darfur.

To Thakur and Weiss (2009: 27) this shift in the legal legitimacy of states does not constitute a radical departure from established *jus cogens* principles of law and practice. That is, since the creation of the state system after Westphalia in 1648, the sovereign authority of the state is nowhere regarded as absolute. Against this backdrop, the argument in favor of a shift of sovereignty entitlement from being a must to a commitment by states to walk within the global framework of a liberal peace (the tenets on which the preamble of the UN Charter rests); and where a state is unable or is unwilling to keep up to that responsibility (to prevent conflicts, mitigate the incidences of systemic violations of human rights, and promote peacebuilding) it forfeits its sovereign entitlement to the international community, and has a strong theoretical support in the academic field (Jacobsen and Thakur: 2008; Peters 2009; Thakur 2011a; 2011b).

The International Commission on Intervention and State Sovereignty created in 2001 by the United Nations to draw up an international humanitarian protection framework, whose report was later adopted in 2009 in the UN General Assembly Resolution 63/308 (see UN Secretary-General 2009), had recommended that states should prioritize, first, the protection of their people by preventing situations that has the potential of resulting to grave breaches to the legal norms created for and regulated by the international humanitarian and human rights architecture. Second, where governments are unable to protect their people, the international community has a responsibility to complementarily assist by fulfilling that responsibility vacuum. Third, where it is evident that governments are unwilling to protect and prevent such violations, the international community has a peremptory obligation towards the people (Thakur 2006). It can intervene through conflict mediation, the imposition of economic sanctions, referrals to the ICC, and if all of these non-military actions are unsuccessful, it should intervene militarily. The UN Charter has provided the basis for and against military intervention for humanitarian purposes. Those against intervention are the crucial non-interventionist Articles 2(4) and 2(7). Those in favor of intervention are the Charter's preamble, its protection mandates such as Articles 1(2), 1(3) and 55, including the discretionary powers of the use of force it vests in the Security Council (Articles 39, 42 and 51); and the non-Charter conventions, for example the 1948 genocide convention.

However, this sovereignty changes do not only target the internal behaviors of states. According to Cohen, the newness of sovereign equality "based on shared political norms, involving mutual recognition, balance, and institutionalized cooperation" (Cohen 2004: 20), self-determination and non-intervention are about the transformative understanding that sovereign states should give up their sovereign right to go to war—where aggressive wars are considered illegal; where imperial (re)colonialization tendencies are deemed a violation of the principle of self-determination; and where sovereign states should begin to actively pursue cooperation in multiplicity of international institutions and accept, without reservation, that they are limited by human rights principles that frown against attempts to believe state/non-state actors are impermeable to international law.

The 2009 UN General Assembly Resolution 63/308 proposes three rudimentary thresholds: the responsibility to prevent, react and rebuild. The threshold of prevention calls on states and the international community to address the root causes of conflicts. The responsibility to react is somewhat more complex. It emphasizes the responsibility of states to respond to situations of compelling humanitarian and political emergences with appropriate measures—measures that may include non-militarized approaches to conflict resolutions like sanctions and the prosecution (at national and international or hybrid tribunals) of those with individual or collective criminal responsibilities for the violation of international law to, in extreme cases, direct military intervention, preferably under the direct command and control of the UN (Thakur 2006; Thakur 2013b; Sarkin 2009).

The threshold of reaction has some key sub-elements that should be met before an international armed intervention is justified. First, among these is the question of *Just Cause* to warrant the use of military force. For an armed action to be justified, serious and irreparable harm, such as instances of politically-motivated massacres of people, must have occurred or is most likely to occur, within a country either through the direct or indirect actions of the government and non-state actors (with or without legal personalities) (Arbour 2008). As a precautionary measure, the legality of intervention should be measured against the question of "right intention". Whether the troop contributing countries have their own political interests, they should clearly state and act towards the alleviation of the sufferings of the people (Peters 2009: 514). To prevent a situation whereby states would want to exploit this right intention argument and invade other countries, the RtoP doctrine recommends the use of a coalition of states with acceptable human rights records (ICISS 2011); or where the UN Security Council did not authorize an intervention, it should at least not be in opposition to the decision of any coalition of willing states to intervene. However, all intervention measures (non-militarized or otherwise) should be proportional in scale, intensity and duration, to the problem; and the intervening forces should make sure that their actions do not feed into the war and produce consequences that will worsen the situation (Arbour 2011a).

That said, the insistence of the African Union on a peacekeeping approach that would respect Sudan's sovereignty and at the same time keep the peace, however, raises the issue of whether the AU is willing to translate good intentions into action. Like the UN Security Council's interpretation of a Just Cause clause, Article 4(h) of the Constitutive Act of the AU affirms the right of the AU to intervene in the territories of member states to prevent or react to the crimes mentioned in Article 4(h) (war crimes, crimes against humanity and genocide) of the Constitutive Act. Of interest is its pronouncement in Article 4(j) that the AU does not need a UN Security Council authorization before it intervenes. Two reasons have been advanced to explain this radical constitutional framework, which would signal the first attempt by a regional organization to challenge the regulatory functions of the UN Security Council. First, according to Udombana (2005), this came about as a result of the political reawakening in the continent. African leaders have come to realize that the best way out of political servitude and negritude is to reject the conventional thinking that global peace and security should be decided by the five permanent members of the Security Council. Second, the legal counsel of the African Union, Ben Kioko posits that, the AU's decision "reflects a sense of frustration with the slow pace of reform of the continental order, and with instances in which the international community tended to focus attention on other parts of the world at the expense of more pressing problems in Africa" (2003: 807).

However, perchance, after a thoughtful evaluation of the legal consequences, amid the understanding that this bold step could lead to its isolation, the AU released a report on the RtoP in 2009, which was a follow-up resolution to the 2005 *Ezulwini Consensus*, in which it reaffirmed its recognition of the global reach of the role of the Security Council. During the deliberations at Ezulwini, Swaziland, if African leaders had accepted, without reservation, the recommendations of the 2004 UN High Level Panel Report on Threats, Challenges and Change, and had issued a communique agreeing that (1) the UN should continue its global leadership role in the development of a comprehensive framework that would translate inaction to action; (2) all AU member states have individual responsibility towards the safeguarding of the authority of the UN in Africa; (3) the UN should assess the military actions of the AU to make sure that it has not violated international law when and where it goes into action without prior UN Security Council approval; and (4) the UN's reform of the Security Council should also include, among others, allocation of a permanent membership seat with a veto powers status to an African country and should also support the peace and security priorities of the African Union (Sarkin 2009). The latter recommendation is in line with the International Commission on Intervention and State Sovereignty's reasoning that, "countries within the region are more sensitive to the issues and context behind the conflict headlines; more familiar with the actors and personalities involved in the conflict, and have a greater stake in overseeing a return to peace and prosperity" (ICISS 2001: 53–4).

With the sense of a duty of care, the AU deployed the African Union Mission in Sudan (AMIS), Darfur in 2004. However, this mission was doomed to fail from its very inception because its capacity did not match the scale, duration and intensity of the conflict. The Status of Forces Agreement (SoFA) of the peacekeepers exposed the ineffectiveness of the AU to combat genocide, war crimes and crimes against humanity as codified in Article 4(h) of its Constitutive Act. Despite it reaffirmation of this commitment, in Article 3(f) of SoFA (on the mode of military operation in Darfur) of the said agreement between the AU Secretary General and the GoS, that AMIS will only protect civilians who happen to be within the vicinity of the peacekeepers, and where AMIS have the capability and capacity to protect them (Udombana 2005: 1190). The inability to translate policy into action meant that the legal imperative of humanitarian intervention was subverted by behind-the-scenes negotiations between the AU and the GoS.

Frustrated by the inability of the AU to put words into action, the neo-hawks in the United States Congress and cabinet of then President George W. Bush began to lobby for a more radical approach that would have circumvented the last resort threshold of the responsibility to protect to put an end to the conflict. In November

2006, the United States Presidential Special Envoy to Sudan Andrew Natsios issued an ultimatum to Khartoum with a January 1, 2007, deadline. He demanded that the Sudan government must cease its attacks on Darfurian populations; and should allow the deployment of a robust international force into the region, or face harsh consequences, which would not only be limited to the possibility of the use of force by the North Atlantic Treaty Organization's (NATO) Rapid Response Force (Rice 2007: 3).

The talk of harsh consequences by the US government, was exactly the kind of political thinking that the RtoP doctrine was designed to manage when it argued that military action should only be considered after the exhaustion of all ADR mechanisms. However, it is morally impossible to exhaust all ADR approaches within a limited time frame. Though resistant to the just war principle of "lastness"—in the sense of when to intervene as a last resort, and in favor of the need for further research into the issue of the "reasonableness" standards, suggested by international relations theorist James Childress (1982), Walzer (2004: 88) contends that:

> Taken literally ... "last resort" would make war morally impossible. For we can never reach lastness, or we can never know that we have reached it. There is always something else to do: another diplomatic note, another United Nations resolution, another meeting.

Fast forward the discussion to 2006, the inability of AMIS to effectively maintain a buffer between the factions, led the AU representative, Ambassador Salim Ahmed Salim, to reach an agreement with the UN (in the presence of the Deputy US Secretary of State, Robert B. Zoelick), during the 2006 Abuja peace talks between the GoS and the Darfurian warring factions, to deploy a more robust joint peacekeeping force, The African Union–United Nations Hybrid Operation in Darfur (UNAMID).

Despite its ongoing successes, this hybrid mission, with a UN Chapter VI mandate, signaled the start of a series of operational related challenges for the peacekeepers. Apart from the problem of how to frame an exit strategy that would sustain peace after they would have left, de Waal tells us that, during the negotiations there was tension between the AU and the US over the question of mandate (de Waal 2007: 1048–9). While Zoelick and the leaders of the Darfur rebel groups were hoping for the presence of a strong peacekeeping force with a mandate to use all necessary means to end the conflict, the AU and GoS successfully made a case for the adoption of a peacekeeping strategy that prioritized mediation with the right of the UNAMID forces to defend themselves when attacked. The latter, though it has been ineffective, remains the preferred mode of intervention in Darfur because it has been endorsed in the 2011 Doha peace processes between the GoS and Dr. Tijani El Sese's Liberation and Justice Movement (Ahmed and Sorbo 2013: 245).

Conclusion

In this chapter I have discussed the conflict in Darfur with reference to the emergent doctrine of the international responsibility to protect. The nature and character of the war was presented as a template on which the genocide question was anchored. Here, by looking at the intersecting roles that law and politics play in establishing whether there has been a genocide in the region, I drew attention to the often neglected issue in this conflict, the politics of otherness and of self-serving national interests. Alternative dispute resolutions and approaches that have been used to end the conflict were discussed; however, unfortunately, the desired outcomes have not been achieved. It is this mixed result that has led to tensions and contradictions in the proposed means of keeping the peace. Postcolonial narratives of otherness on the part of the Sudanese government and the AU against the neo-liberal desires of the United States government also played a major role in the framing of an ineffective peacekeeping agenda for the region.

That notwithstanding, the UNSC and the AU remain seized of their responsibility to peace and security in Africa, their preferred mode of intervention in the conflict in Sudan, is far from being a consolidated, comprehensive and systematic approach. What is needed, therefore, is a paradigm shift from the political culture of "wait-and-see." Millions have lost their lives in Cambodia, Rwanda, Srebrenica, and Darfur. After each of these conflicts, the international community would renew its pledge of "Never Again," only to look back each next time, with varying degrees of incredulity and horror, and propose new norms on intervention, state sovereignty and humanitarian law in the face of the politicized processes of alternative dispute resolution.

References

Acharya, A. (2013). The R2P and Norm Diffusion: Towards A Framework of Norm Circulation, *Global Responsibility to Protect*, 5(4): 466–79.

Ahmed, A.G.M. and Sorbo, G.M. (2013). *Sudan Divided: Continuing Conflict in a Contested State*, New York: Palgrave Macmillan.

Arbour, L. (2008). The Responsibility to Protect as a Duty of Care in International Law and Practice, *Review of International Studies*, 34(3): 445–58.

Arieff, A., et al. (2010). *International Criminal Court Cases in Africa: Status and Policy Issues*, Washington DC: Congressional Research Service.

Badescu, C.G. (2009). The Responsibility to Protect and the Conflict in Darfur: The Big Let-Down, *Security Dialogue*, 40: 287–309.

Bassil, N.R. (2003). *The Crisis of the Post-Colonial Sudanese State: Origins of the Conflict in Darfur*, London: I.B. Tauris and Co.

Bassil, N.R. (2006). A Brief History of the Keira Sultanate of Dar Fur, Western Sudan, *Journal of North African Studies*, 11(4): 347–64.

Bassil, N.R. (2010). Colonial Constructions of Race in Sudan. In Joseph Pugliese (ed.), *Relational Dis/locations: Mediterranean Cultures in Translocal and Transnational Contexts*. Brussels: Peter Lang Publishers, 85–104.

Bellamy, A. (2009). *Responsibility to Protect*. Cambridge: Polity Press.

Burr, J.M. and Collins, R.O. (2006). *Darfur: The Long Road to Disaster*. Princeton, NJ: Markus Wiener.

Cohen, J.L. (2004). Whose Sovereignty? Empire Versus International Law, *Ethics and International Affairs*, 18(3): 1–24.

de Waal, A. (2004). *The Book was Closed too soon on Peace in Darfur: Restoring stability is a long-term task of nine parts politics and one part force. We need fair representation and time* (September), http://www.theguardian.com/commentisfree/2006/sep/29/comment.sudan.

de Waal, A. (2007). Darfur and the Failure of the Responsibility to Protect, *International Affairs*, 83(6): 1039–54.

de Waal, A. (2006). *The Future of the Movements' Combatants*. London: All Africa Global Media, http://allafrica.com/stories/200607140761.html.

Fearon, J., Kasara, K., and Laitin, D. (2007). Ethnic Minority Rule and Civil War Onset. *American Political Science Review*, 101(1): 187–93.

Flint, J. and de Waal, A. (2005). *Darfur: A New History of a Long War*. London: Zed Books.

Green, E.D. (2009). *The Political Demography of Conflict in Modern Africa*. London: London School of Economics, Development Studies Institute.

Hameso, S. (1997). *Ethnicity and Nationalism in Africa*. New York: Nova Science Publishers.

Helmke, B. (2010). *Under Attack: Challenges to the Rules Governing the International Use of Force*, Farnham: Ashgate.

Horowitz, D.L. (1985). *Ethnic Groups in Conflict*. Berkeley: University of California Press.

International Commission on Intervention and State Sovereignty (ICISS) (2001). *The Responsibility to Protect*, Ottawa: IDRC.

International Criminal Court (1998) Rome Statute of the International Criminal Court: A/CONF.183/9 of July 17, 1998 which entered into force on July 1, 2002.

International Criminal Court (2009a) Trial Chamber I, Situation in Darfur, Sudan: Warrant of arrest. In the Case of The Prosecutor v Omar Hassan Al Bashir. [No.: ICC-02/05-01/09] (March 4).

International Criminal Court (2009b) Situation in Darfur, Sudan, in the case of The Prosecutor v. Omar Hassan Ahmed Al Bashir ("Omar Al Bashir"), No.: ICC-02/05-01/09, March 4, http://www.icc-cpi.int/iccdocs/doc/doc639078.pdf.

Jacobsen, T., Sampford, C., and Thakur, R. (eds) (2008). *Re-envisioning Sovereignty: The End of Westphalia?* Aldershot: Ashgate.

Junk, J. (2014). The two-level politics of support—US Foreign Policy and the Responsibility to Protect. *Conflict, Security and Development*, 14(4): 535–64.

Kioko, B. (2003). *The right of intervention under the African Union's Constitutive Act: From non-interference to non-intervention.* www.icrc.org/Wed/eng/siteeng0.nsf/htmlall/5WNJDL/$File/IRRC_852_kioko.pdf.

Mazo, J. (2010). *Climate Conflict: How Global Warming Threatens Security and What to do About it.* Oxford: Routledge.

Meernik, J.D. (2013). Public Support for the International Criminal Court. In D.L. Rothe, J. Meernik, and T. Ingadóttir (eds), *The Realities of International Criminal Justice.* Leiden, The Netherlands: Martinus Nijhof Press, 319–37.

Mendes, E.P. (2014). *Global Governance, Human Rights and International Law: Combating the Tragic Flaw,* Abingdon: Routledge.

Peters, A. (2009). Humanity as the A and Ω of Sovereignty, *European Journal of International Law,* 20(3): 513–44.

Petterson, D. (2003). *Inside Sudan.* Boulder, CO: Westview Press.

Powell, C. (2004). *Crisis in Darfur.* Testimony before the Senate Foreign Relations Committee, September 9, http://www.state.gov/secretary/former/powell/remarks/36042/htm.

Quigley, J. (2006). *The Genocide Convention: An International Law Analysis.* Aldershot: Ashgate.

Rice, S.E. (2007). *The Genocide in Darfur: America must do more to fulfill the Responsibility to Protect.* Washington, DC: Brookings Institution.

Sarkin, J. (2009). The Role of the United Nations, the African Union and Africa's Sub-Regional Organisations in Dealing with Africa's Human Rights Problems: Connecting Humanitarian Intervention and the Responsibility to Protect, *Journal of African Law,* 53(1): 1–33.

Shinoda, H. (2008). *Re-examining Sovereignty: From Classical Theory to the Global Age,* New York: St Martin's Press.

Thakur, R. (2006). *The United Nations, Peace and Security: From Collective Security to the Responsibility to Protect,* Cambridge: Cambridge University Press.

Thakur, R. (2011a). The Responsibility to Protect and the North-South Divide. In S.R. Silverburg (ed.), *International Law: Contemporary Issues and Future Developments.* Boulder, CO: Westview, 32–47.

Thakur, R. (2011b). *The People vs. the State: Reflections on UN Authority, US Power and the Responsibility to Protect,* Tokyo: United Nations University Press.

Thakur, R. (2013b). The Use of International Force to Prevent or Halt Atrocities: From Humanitarian Intervention to the Responsibility to Protect. In Dinah Shelton (ed.), *The Oxford Handbook of International Human Rights Law.* Oxford: Oxford University Press, 815–40.

Thakur, R. and T.G. Weiss (2009). R2P: From Idea to Norm—and Action? *Global Responsibility to Protect,* 1(1): 22–53.

Totten, S. (2011). *An Oral and Documentary History of The Darfur Genocide.* Santa Barbara: Praeger.

Udombana, N. (2005). When Neutrality Is a Sin: The Darfur Crisis and the Crisis of Humanitarian Intervention in Sudan. *Human Rights Quarterly,* 27(4): 1149–99.

UN News Centre. (2008). At five-year mark, Darfur crisis is only worsening—UN aid chief, April 28, http://www.un.org/apps/news/story.asp?NewsID=26422&Cr=darfur&Cr1#.VRYGCR1TOAg.

United Nations Security Council (2005) *Report of the International Commission of Inquiry on Darfur to the United Nations Secretary General,* http://www.un.org/news/dh/sudan/com_inq_darfur.pdf.

United States Department of State. (2004). *Documenting Atrocities in Darfur.* Washington, DC: The Bureau of Democracy, Human Rights, and Labor and the Bureau of Intelligence and Research.

Walzer, M. (2004). *Arguing about War.* New Haven, CT: Yale University Press.

Willemse, K. (2007). *One Foot in Heaven: Narratives on Gender and Islam in Darfur, West-Sudan.* Leiden, NL: Martinus Nijhoff Publishers.

Chapter 6
State Collapse, Counter-Insurgency and Security Governance in Somalia

Oscar Gakuo Mwangi

Abstract

Somalia is a collapsed state where both insurgent activism and counter-insurgency operations are complex. This chapter examines the relationship between state collapse, counter-insurgency and security governance in Somalia. It pays attention to the insurgent movement in Somalia, al-Shabaab and the Kenya Defence Forces' peacekeeping component of the African Union Mission in Somalia, which has positioned itself as a counter-insurgency against armed insurgency in the country. In this chapter I adopt the political process approach as a framework of analysis raising arguments that under conditions of state collapse, the African Union Mission in Somalia counter-insurgency operations have adversely affected both internal security in Somalia and regional security. The counter-insurgency operations have provided al-Shabaab with political opportunities to sustain their insurgent activities at the same time compromising their capacity to offer local-level security governance alternatives in the areas under their control. The operations have not gained the support of the Somali populace nor have they enhanced the capacity of the state to provide citizens with minimum levels of security. Counter-insurgency operations have, therefore, hindered peacebuilding and governance efforts in the country. The chapter concludes by offering recommendations on how to deal with insurgent activism in Somalia and simultaneously promote peacebuilding and good governance.

Introduction

This chapter examines the relationship between state collapse, counter-insurgency and security governance in Somalia. It focuses on the insurgent movement in Somalia, Harakat Al-Shabaab Al Mujaheddin (commonly known as al-Shabaab) and the Kenya Defence Forces (KDF) peacekeeping component of the African Union Mission in Somalia (AMISOM), which has positioned itself as a counter-insurgency force against armed insurgency in the country. Using the political process approach the arguments raised are that under conditions of state collapse, AMISOM's counter-insurgency operations, conducted by these external actors have adversely affected internal security in Somalia and regional security within the Intergovernmental Authority on Development (IGAD) region. The counter-insurgency operations have provided al-Shabaab with political opportunities to sustain their insurgent activities at the same time compromising their capacity to offer local-level security governance alternatives in the areas under their control. Hence counter-insurgency operations have impacted negatively upon peacebuilding and governance efforts in the country. The chapter concludes by offering recommendations on how to deal with insurgent activism in Somalia and, in tandem, promote peacebuilding and good governance.

Social Movements and the Political Process Approach

In recent years, social movement research, which is mostly concerned with non-violent social movements, has turned a spotlight on violent movements. This is due, in part, to the impact of globalization on the domestic politics and international relations of states. The focus on violent movements links social movement theory, mainly, to the field of terrorism studies. Terrorism studies and social movement studies, however, continue to be distinct areas (Porta 2009: 5–8). This chapter examines violent movements through the political process approach embedded in social movement theory.

The political process approach pays attention to the political, organizational and structural aspects of social movements. It emphasizes that the emergence and operations of social movements are analyzed and understood in the context of the external political environment in which they operate (Eisinger 1973: 11–28; Tarrow 1998; McAdam 1999). The approach points to the existence of a political opportunity structure that determines the emergence of, strategies for, and success of social movements, activities and collective actions (McAdam 1999). It postulates that social movements emerge when change in political opportunities increase the possibilities for such movements to mobilize by opening up new and existing channels of aspiration. Movements arise because, by and large, political social conditions are favorable for successful and sustained contention (Beck 2008: 1569; Weissman 2008: 9–10). In other words, political opportunities combine with the organizational capacity for mobilization to allow the emergence of social movements. The key point of the political process approach is that movements do not choose goals, strategies, and tactics in a vacuum (Meyer 2004: 126–8). The insight, ingenuity, and outcomes of movement choices—their agency—is best understood and assessed by examining the political environment and the rules of the games in which those choices are made—that is, structure (Meyer 2004: 128).

As a framework of analysis, Porta (1996) contends that, the political process approach distinguishes between three sets of variables, namely structures, power configurations, and contexts of interaction. The first set refers to the political opportunity structure as already explained, is the fundamental component of the approach. The second set refers to the configuration of actors comprising three major components: the protagonists, antagonists, and bystanders. The power configuration of these actors explains not only the level of potential conflict but also an analysis of the situation. The third level of analysis, the interaction context, refers to the level of socio-political and economic processes that link structures and configurations to agency and action. It is at this level that the strategies of social movements and their opponents manifest themselves. Despite its popularity as a framework, the political process approach has, however, been criticized for its conceptual complexity (Kriesi 2004: 69–77).

It is the context of the foregoing framework that this chapter examines the relationship between state collapse, counter-insurgency and security governance in Somalia. The chapter focuses on the largest insurgent movement in Somalia, al-Shabaab and the military component of the AMISOM as a counter-insurgency operation largely meant to suppress the insurgent activities of militants. In this chapter al-Shabaab, is analyzed interchangeably, as a terrorist network and as an insurgent group. The arguments raised are that under conditions of state collapse, AMISOM's counter-insurgency operations, conducted by the KDF, have adversely affected both human and physical security in Somalia as well as regional security. The counter-insurgency operations have provided al-Shabaab with new political opportunities to sustain violent action while at the same time compromising its capacity to offer local-level security governance as part of its service delivery in areas under its control. Hence counter-insurgency operations have impacted negatively upon peacebuilding and governance efforts in Somalia. The chapter concludes by offering recommendations on how to deal with insurgent activism in Somalia and, in tandem, promote peacebuilding and good governance.

State Collapse and Counter-Insurgency in Somalia

The nature of counter-insurgency in Somalia is complex. Counter-insurgency operations are determined by the prevailing situation in the country. They increase when conflict escalates and decrease when there is a lull in the fighting between the competing armed groups, and between them and the peacekeeping forces. Therefore, counter-insurgency has no constant set of operational techniques. Its primary aim is to suppress an insurgency by any means possible. Classical counter-insurgency theory points out that an insurgent primarily challenges a functioning, though more often a fragile state. The insurgent challenges the status quo, while the counter-insurgent seeks to strengthen the state thereby suppressing the insurgency. Modern counter-insurgency, in the context of failed or collapsed states, indicates that "insurgency today follows state failure, and is not directed at taking over a functioning body politic, but at dismembering or scavenging its carcass, or contesting an 'ungoverned space'" (Kilcullen 2006–7: 112). In contemporary African politics, the counter-insurgent embodies revolutionary change, while the insurgent fights to preserve the status quo of ungoverned spaces, or to repel an occupier (Byman 2005: 5–6). Insurgents normally use three related methods to achieve their objectives: guerrilla war, political mobilization, and terrorism. Thus, according to Williams,

> "Counterinsurgency," then, refers to both a type of war and a style of warfare. The term describes a kind of military operation outside of conventional army-vs.-army war-fighting, and is sometimes called "low-intensity" or "asymmetrical" combat. (Williams 2011: 83)

Somalia's on-going conflict is thus complex as it involves insurgents comprising clan militias, nationalist, and terrorist groups (ICG 2008: 11). Furthermore, Somalia is a failed state. It has had no effective and functional centralized government since President Siad Barre's rule came to an end in 1991 (Mwangi 2010: 88). The Transitional Federal Government (TFG) established in 2004 and whose interim mandate came to an end in 2012, was replaced by the Federal Government of Somalia (FGS) in the same year. These governments have largely failed to provide basic political and economic goods to the citizens. Islamists militants are competing with the dysfunctional government in providing basic services to the largely displaced population. Since 1991, a variety of Islamist movements have emerged in the country. These include among others, Ahlu Sunna Wal Jama'a (ASWJ), Union of Islamic Courts (UIC), and Hizb al Islam (ICG 2010: 9–14). Some have even been inspired or sponsored by foreign interests (ICG 2005: i). The rise of militant Islamism in Somalia has been accentuated by state collapse, civil war, and counter-insurgency (Hoehne 2009: 25–7; Mwangi 2012: 517–20).

Several counter-insurgency operations, in the form of regional and international peacekeeping missions, have, therefore, been effected in Somalia since 1991. Many of these have been driven by concerns regarding the impact of war in Somalia on international security. The most notable military interventions are the United Nations Operation in Somalia I (UNOSOM), April—December 1992, the United States-led Unified Task Force (UNITAF), December 1992—May 1993, UNOSOM II, March 1993—March 1995, Ethiopia's military interventions of 2006 and 2011, Kenya's Operation Linda Nchi (Protect the Country) (October 2011–June 2012) and AMISOM, January 2007—to date). UNISOM I, UNITAF, and UNISOM II (see Bradbury and Healy 2010; Hamilton 2013), while not the focus of this chapter, were considered failures as they did not abate, but rather escalated the conflict in Somalia. The Ethiopian, Kenyan, and AMISOM military interventions are therefore more appropriate for analysis in this chapter.

Ethiopia's military interventions in Somalia can also be described as counter-insurgency operations. Ethiopia has vast security interests in Somalia, some of which have led it into direct confrontation with Somalia. The Somali crisis has had a negative impact on Ethiopia's internal security (Mesfin 2013: 103). Ethiopia's motivations have been driven by its strategic interests to contain the conflict and the radicalization processes that follow it. These counter-insurgency operations have, however, contributed to the radicalization of a small group of dedicated jihadists, providing the basis for the emergence of extremist violence in Somalia (Hoehne 2009: 8–9). The Ethiopian military intervention of 2006 primarily aimed at suppressing the UIC that rose to political prominence in June 2006. The UIC leadership fled Somalia but al-Shabaab and others launched an insurgency against the TFG and Ethiopian troops, assuming the role of liberating Somalia from what it called "occupying forces." Though Ethiopian troops officially departed Somalia in January 2009 (Dersso 2010: 6–7), their strategic interest in Somalia remains. In that, they fear that the continuation of conflict in Somalia will lead to a permanent state of war in the Somali inhabited region of Ogaden in Ethiopia where the Ogaden National Liberation Front (ONLF) is fighting a war with the sole aim of forcing the Ethiopian government to relinquish its hold of the region to Somalia. Consequently, the Ethiopian government has launched a series of counter-insurgency operations placing the Ogaden issue as part of its reasons for war against Somalia (Eriksson 2013: 37; Mesfin 2013: 103). Ethiopia also launched a military incursion into Somalia in late 2011 with the aim of assisting the FGS recapture some al-Shabaab-occupied territories (BBC News 2011).

Kenya officially launched Operation Linda Nchi (Protect the Country) on October 16, 2011. The government cited Article 51 of the UN Charter (Mkawale 2011), which allows a country to defend itself from external aggression, as well as to prevent attacks, to emphasize that Kenya was exercising its right given the threats posed by al-Shabaab on the country's economy and security. The government had accused al-Shabaab of kidnappings of foreign tourists and humanitarian aid workers in Kenya to which al-Shabaab immediately denied involvement, warning of retaliatory attacks. Kenya's strategic interests in Somalia have since moved beyond direct physical threats posed by the movement. They now include economic and socio-political interests (ICG 2012: 10–11; HIPS 2013: 2; UNSC 2013b). At the request of the AU, the Kenya government agreed to place the KDF under the command of AMISOM one month after the launch of Operation Linda Nchi. The KDF were formally integrated into AMISOM on February 22, 2012 after the UN Security Council passed Resolution 2036 (2012). On June 2, 2012, the Government of Kenya signed a memorandum of understanding with the AU that would formally integrate KDF into the command and control structures of AMISOM (UNSC 2013a: 27).

Power Configurations and Counter-Insurgency in Somalia

The configuration of actors as instruments of power in Somalia has divided the parties in the conflict into three major groups: the protagonists, antagonists, and bystanders—though through their actions, it is difficult to ascertain their differences. The power configuration of these actors explains not only the level of potential conflict, but it also provides us with a template to analyze the conflict. The protagonists discussed in this chapter are the members of the coalition consisting of the KDF component of AMISOM and its state and non-state allies, the Somali National Army (SNA) of the FGS, and the Ras Kamboni Brigade, a local militia respectively. The antagonist examined is al-Shabaab, while the bystanders are largely the ordinary citizens of Somalia and the neighboring states that have adopted a non-interventionist foreign policy towards Somalia.

A description of AMISOM and its composition is given in order to provide background information on its role in the coalition and its counter-insurgency strategies. The different manifestations of al-Shabaab are also examined in order to understand its organizational and structural capacity as an antagonist. By doing so it becomes easier to understand the power configurations among these components. The AMISOM is a regional peacekeeping mission operated by the AU with the approval of the UN. It is also backed by the FGS. The AMISOM has been mandated to take all necessary measures, in full compliance with its obligations under international humanitarian law and human rights law, while fully respecting the sovereignty, territorial integrity, political independence and unity of Somalia, to assist in the creational and establishment of a functional government in the country. AMISOM's detailed mandate is outlined in UN Security Council Resolution 2093 (2013) (UNSC 2013a: 3–4). The AMISOM comprises three components: military, police, and civilian. The military component is the biggest of the three components. Currently the military component comprises of troops who are deployed in six sectors covering south and central Somalia. Ugandan troops are deployed in Sector 1 comprising Banadir and Lower Shaballe regions. Kenyan forces are responsible for Sector 2 comprising Lower and Middle Juba. Sector 3 covering Bay, Bakool and Gedo comes under Ethiopian command. Djiboutian forces are in charge of Sector 4 comprising Hiiraan and Galgadoud, while Burundian forces are in charge of Sector 5 covering Middle Shabelle region. Sierra Leone forces are in charge of Sector Kismayo covering the port city and its environs (AMISOM 2014a).

Al-Shabaab expresses itself in several different forms as a result of the international response against it. According to Menkhaus (2014: 6–7), there are four significant manifestations that define the organizational and structural capacity of the movement, which also explains the threat levels in the country. These include al-Shabaab as: a network, that is, Amniyat; as an armed force; as an administration; and as an extortionist movement. The covert Amniyat network is the most intact and feared part of the movement, serving both as an effective intelligence network and an operational arm of al-Shabaab, with specialized tactical units. The military component of al-Shabaab, known as Jaysh al-Usra (the Army of Hardship), is mainly composed of young inexperienced recruits in comparison with the superior and experienced AMISOM forces. This military group includes paid fighters and martyrs—the latter of whom are both suicide bombers and suicide infantry. As an administration, Menkhaus tells us that, al-Shabaab continues to provide basic administration, including various social services and security governance in areas it controls. Communities under its control enjoy higher levels of security governance than when liberated by AMISOM and left in the hands of the predatory and poorly controlled SNA. Al-Shabaab's ability to provide local-level security governance makes it acquire some legitimacy in the rural areas. Its service delivery has been weakened with the movement's loss of territory due to counter-insurgency. As an extortion racket, al-Shabaab's systematic collection of taxes from

Somali businesses is little more than extortion. It is acting increasingly like the Mafia in much of Somalia, although it has not yet degenerated into a criminal racket the way many protracted insurgencies do. The bystanders to this configuration of actors are the people and states who are the most affected by the unintended consequences or outcomes of counter-insurgency.

The power configuration of these actors gives us an illustration of the situation in Somalia. While the protagonists seem to have an upper hand against the antagonist, the latter has nonetheless, been able to use guerrilla warfare and suicide bombings to create a balance in the conflict. The AMISOM's operations in Somalia, including those conducted by the KDF have presented great challenges for al-Shabaab. The battle for Kismayo in south-central Somalia, for instance, was conducted by the coalition comprising SNA, KDF battalion within AMISOM peacekeeping forces, and the Ras Kamboni Brigade against al-Shabaab. The offensive began on September 28, 2012, when these forces coordinated an assault against Kismayo, and after several days of fighting they captured it from al-Shabaab militants. The loss of this port city was a major blow for al-Shabaab, because it was the economic hub for the militant group, which had established a government in the region (AMISOM 2014b: 3; Homeland Security Policy Institute 2013: 9–10). However, though they lost this city, al-Shabaab continues to use guerrilla warfare tactics against the peacekeeping forces. They have also used the subtle means of Amniyat to get recruits to fill their ranks. Given that its infantry forces, Jaysh al-Usra, operates mainly in rural areas and generally avoids major engagements with the coalition forces, al-Shabaab relies heavily on anti-Western rhetoric—which has been translated into violent martyrdom warfare—to demonstrate to ordinary Somalis the reasons why war against the peacekeepers is an obligation for them. However, al-Shabaab's increasing levels of violence in areas it controls is beginning to cause strained relationships between it and the local-level populations. Arrests, detentions and executions of civilians for alleged spying within al-Shabaab strongholds have increased, as has guerrilla-style tactics on both military and civilian targets in areas it has lost to the coalition forces (see Dowd 2013: 2–3).

The devastating July 2010 Kampala bombing that killed over 70 people and the September 2013 Nairobi Westgate Mall attack that killed at least 67 and wounded over 175, are demonstrations of how, in desperation to balance the odds against them, al-Shabaab militants have adopted martyrdom operations as part of their war tactics. These attacks offer important insights into the evolution of al-Shabaab's Martyrdom Brigade and development of its tactics, techniques and procedures. The Westgate attack is an indicator of the coalition's relative successes in regaining control of much of south-central Somalia. Al-Shabaab claimed responsibility for both the Kampala and Westgate attacks citing Uganda's and Kenya's participation in AMISOM's operations as justifications for their violent attacks on civilians.

The Uganda People's Defence Force (UPDF) and the KDF are deployed in Sectors 1 and 2 respectively. The capital and strategic port city Mogadishu falls under Sector 1 while the strategic post city of Kismayo falls under Sector 2. Al-Shabaab has blamed Kenya and Uganda for the loss of these cities and their strategic resources. It also blames the RAS Kamboni Brigade, which fights alongside the KDF in Kismayo (Dowd 2013: 1–3; OFS 2013: 19; Bryden 2014: 7–8; Menkhaus 2014: 5). It is in this context that al-Shabaab has enhanced asymmetrical warfare against the protagonists, that is, the coalition forces' counter-insurgency operations. This shift in tactics indicates a change in al-Shabaab's wider strategy of ensuring that the coalition forces are unable to promote peacebuilding and good governance in the country (Bryden 2014: 7–8; Menkhaus 2014: 5; US Department of State 2014: 25–6).

Contexts of Interaction and Security Governance in Somalia

Given the current political situation in the country, it is important to discuss the nature of interaction between actors and its implications on governance in Somalia. It should be noted here that, the successes or failures of insurgent and counter-insurgent activities in Somalia depends on the support it receives from the people, and the role of the state. In Somalia, the three rudimentary ways in which insurgent activities of the insurgent groups have prolonged the conflict has a direct relationship to the outcomes that the peacekeeping operation is having on people's livelihoods and state building (Gregg 2009: 18). That said, in this sub-section a discussion of these interrelationships are discussed.

Population Engagement

In conventional wars, one military aims to weaken another on the battlefield. In civil wars, however, the focus is on the people—not excluding the need to protect or kill them (or both). The state and insurgents fight for the loyalty and support of the population. Insurgents cannot survive without the support of the population, but neither can the state, if both are to maintain legitimacy. The success of the counter-insurgency strategy of the state (and peacekeeping forces, in the case of Somalia) is to win the population away from insurgents (Gregg 2009: 19). So far, the counter-insurgency strategies in Somalia conducted by the coalition forces have been unable to achieve their intended outcomes because they have so far been unable to gain the support of the people. The Somali populace perceives these counter-insurgency efforts as externally driven and extremely hesitant to engage, positively, with the fundamental Somali sociopolitical structures such as the clan structure and Islam. These socio-political structures play a significant role in local-level peacebuilding and governance processes (Sandstrom 2013: 49–50). In Somalia, al-Shabaab, as the insurgent group has an upper hand in gaining the support of Somalis particularly through the use of (Islamic) religious and political narratives, which describe the former transitional government and current federal government as being imposed on them by the international community of liberal states. Moreover, the al-Shabaab led insurgency has gained popular support among the local-level communities, largely due to the social services and more importantly the local-level security governance it provides, in the absence of a functional state (Mwangi 2012: 527). The movement was very effective in the provision of alternative governance structures at the local-level prior to the pre-2010 military intervention of AMISOM (see Mwangi 2012: 524–7). This, however, changed following the intervention.

While the counter-insurgency operations of the peacekeeping forces provided al-Shabaab with new opportunities, they have at the same time compromised their capacity to continue with governance in the areas under their control. Al-Shabaab often points out its relative success in providing meaningful security governance prior to the intervention (Turbiville et al. 2014: 98). Having being driven out and strategically withdrawing from areas many believed would remain under their control, the movement embarked on a propaganda campaign aimed at discrediting AMISOM and its local allies as spoilers of the peace that it had established in its stronghold (Cilliers et al. 2010: 14–17; Turbiville et al. 2014: 76). The security vacuum created by al-Shabaab's departure in these areas has led to an increase in the levels of insecurity, prompting affected Somalis and some non-governmental organizations to point out that life was more secure, and better, under al-Shabaab (Dagne 2011: i; Bruton and Williams 2014: 87–9). AMISOM also acknowledged that there was a "security vacuum" created by its advancing forces, and insisted that the vacuum would be filled by the SNA and other Somali security forces (Turbiville et al. 2014: 76–7). Therefore, there is a need to emphasize the importance of delivering security to the population during counter-insurgency campaigns if counter-insurgency operations are to achieve their intended outcomes (Bruton and Williams 2014: 98–100; Turbiville et al. 2014: 98–100).

Al-Shabaab continues to use religion in order to gain popular support for armed insurgent activism. It has portrayed the coalition's counter-insurgency operations as an infidel invasion that compels Muslims to support its insurgency (Menkhaus et al. 2010: 321–50; Turbiville et al. 2014: 59). The aim is to portray, a common narrative among insurgent groups in the country, that conflict in Somalia, especially where external forces are involved, is a direct attack on Islam (see Chopra et al. 1995; Clarke and Herbst 1996: 70–85; Dersso 2009: 6–8; Lewis 2002; Menkhaus 2008: 220–40; Mwangi 2012: 520–21). As the International Crisis Group has pointed out,

> AMISOM (especially [troops from] Ethiopia and Kenya) are [depicted as] "African crusaders" spreading Christianity and falsehood. The SNA are [portrayed as] *murtadiin* (apostates). A common line is that the *murtadiin* value the lives only of foreigners, not fellow Somalis. SNA soldiers and SFG officials are ridiculed and portrayed as "weak" in their faith, their lives disgraced and facing the prospect of hell-fire in the hereafter (akhera). Mujahidin who fight with Al-Shabaab are glorified. The efficacy of a message fusing patriotism with the duties of Islam should not be underestimated. (ICG 2014:18)

Stability Operations

Population engagement is thus part of the broader stability operations that all factions and stakeholders of the conflict require. For example, the actions undertaken to build credibility and trust in the early stages of AMISOM's counter-insurgency, determine the levels of stability needed for the FGS to govern the country. Population engagement and stability operations are preconditions for the success of the armed sections of the peacekeeping forces. Stability operations are however the most difficult phase of peace building because it is at this stage that the military operations component and its corresponding non-military capacity-building responsibilities are handed over to the civilian populations (Gregg 2009: 19–20).

The actions taken by coalition forces to build credibility and trust requires meticulous planning before any military incursion begins. There are a number of indicators that suggest in the early stages, AMISOM neither planned nor implemented an effective counter-insurgency strategy. Kenya's initial objective was not peace enforcement in Somalia, but to counter the direct physical threats posed by al-Shabaab on its territory. Kenya's incorporation into AMISOM was also driven by socio-political and economic interests rather than peacebuilding in Somalia (ICG 2012: 10–11). AMISOM was, arguably, initially a peacekeeping mission which later became a peace enforcement mission when its operational scope was widened by UN Resolution 2036 (2012) in February 2012 (UN 2012). Hence, initially, its use of force to enhance peace was limited. Furthermore, a good counter-insurgency strategy takes into account an exit strategy, and both KDF's and AMISOM's entry strategies into Somalia initially did not take into account exit strategies. This is evident by the conflicting accounts of an exit strategy given by both the KDF and AMISOM. It is in the context of these shortcomings that AMISOM did not initially have an effective counterinsurgency strategy (Turbiville et al. 2014: 70).

The lack of or an effective implementation strategy by AMISOM was further compounded by the need to govern the new areas captured from the insurgents. In Kismayo, for instance, the KDF had to keep the peace by providing street patrols. Yet winning the hearts and minds of the hardline Islamist population was too difficult, because of the peacekeepers' inability to convince the local population that they were not an occupying force, and had a temporal mandate (Turbiville and Forest 2013: 66–9). Thus, while al-Shabaab was able to consistently attack (see Raleigh and Dowd 2013: 6), some progress was made, and the FGS was gradually attempting to build its capacity ultimately to enhance security, peace and good governance (Dowd 2013: 3).

Functioning State

The long-term goal of a counter-insurgency campaign requires the creation of a functioning state that supports a government that can govern with minimal external technical support; a government that is able to provide for its citizens; and complement the regional and international efforts to promote peace and stability in the region (Gregg 2009: 30). However, the goal of creating a functional state in Somalia has been compromised by the manner in which the above mentioned regional and international peacekeeping efforts, were conducted in the country. For example, the UN Monitoring Group on Somalia accused the KDF of violating AMISOM's mandate. AMISOM was not taking the appropriate measures aimed at supporting the creation of a functionally effective state due to the strategic interests of its member states. This compromised peacebuilding and security governance in the country (Dowd 2013: 3). Kenya was thus accused of pursuing its own national interests at the expense of the sanctioned IGAD AMISOM plan which led to "strains in the alliance" (Turbiville and Forest 2013: 75).

The KDF's participation in AMISOM was also criticized for further weakening the FGS's efforts at building its own capacity to be an effective central authority. Therefore, further opportunities for al-Shabaab and other violent and non-state actors to conduct their violent attacks in the region were developed. The UN Monitoring Group on Somalia pointed out that the KDF component of AMISOM significantly affected the resources required to support the FGS enhance its capacity to perform its basic functions. The Monitoring Group also accused the KDF of pursuing Kenya's strategic interests at the expense of implementing the AMISOM mandate and most of their assigned tasks (UNSC 2013b). The KDF to some degree, was unwilling, to clarify its operational status and allegiance within AMISOM—for example, that its operational presence was more theoretical than practical. The Group pointed out that KDF took a partisan approach especially in its association with the Ras Kamboni Brigade, hence it was not collaborating with the FGS to reduce the threat posed by al-Shabaab. The KDF was also accused of not supporting dialogue and reconciliation in Somalia, and not assisting with the implementation of the Somali national security plan, among others. The FGS has also occasionally accused the KDF of not operationally confining itself to AMISOM's mandate as well as undermining its authority. To this extent, Kenya's strategic interests in Somalia were perceived as hindering the FGS's capacity to manage the conflict and provide security thereby providing more opportunities for more non-state transnational security threats to emerge (UNSC 2013b).

The KDF's counter-insurgency operations thus created a local-level governance vacuum, and al-Shabaab took advantage of this vacuum to provide the required local-level governance in Somalia. The objective was to legitimize its military action so as to contest the ungoverned spaces created by conditions of state collapse. Al-Shabaab's task was simplified because of the lack of consensus within the FGS over post-liberation governance arrangements. A good example is the consultative and participatory National Stabilisation Strategy (NSS) for south-central Somalia, coordinated by the Prime Minister's office. The hostility that exists between the FGS and local/sub-regional authorities, raises doubt over who is responsible for implementing the NSS. The top-down (re-)appointments of governors based on the recommendations of the NSS, in newly liberated areas, has raised old and political new criticisms among the local communities. Kenya, though operating under AMISOM, has promoted its long-standing ally, Ras Kamboni, in areas it has liberated such as Kismayo. These appointments, endorsed by AMISOM rather than Somalis, are detrimental to the governance processes, as they do not adhere to the procedures and with the affirmed intent of bottom-up processes of establishing local governance as per the NSS. Al-Shabaab has taken advantage of these and other unsettled local political conflicts to co-opt some of the local Somali actors it its own governance processes (ICG 2014: 3–4). It is in the context of the foregoing analysis that the governance processes are adversely affected, given that AMISOM was partisan in its approach.

Conclusion

Counter-insurgency operations have impacted negatively upon peacebuilding and governance efforts in the Somalia as they have exacerbated rather than mitigated insurgent activism in the country. Counter-insurgency operations in Somalia can be enhanced so as to effectively deal with insurgent activism and promote peacebuilding and good governance in the country by adopting both goal-oriented and process-oriented methods. Both goal-oriented and process-oriented methods can be adopted to ensure that counter-insurgency efforts enhance state-capacity building and attract population support.

Goal-oriented methods are formal and tend to focus on strengthening the capacity of formal institutions to achieve their objectives. Such methods tend to be based on power relationships. Goal-oriented methods can be used to enhance the functional capacity of the FGS to deal with insurgent activism while at the same time promote peacebuilding and good governance in Somalia. While the establishment of a functioning state is a long-term goal, the capacity of the FGS can be enhanced in the short and medium-term by strengthening AMISOM's operational capacity to strictly and effectively adhere to its peace enforcement mandate. This can be achieved by increasing the quantity and quality of its financial, human and military resources so that it has the relative autonomy required for it to formulate and implement, independently, effective repressive counter-insurgency measures. The aim is to further weaken the military capabilities of insurgent groups particularly al-Shabaab so as to enhance the physical security of the Somali populace. External support to improve the quantity and quality of AMISOM's resources can be sourced from various donor countries, international and regional organizations. Strengthening the repressive operations of the coalition forces in Somalia, as spelt out in their mandates, will begin creating the enabling security environment for the FGS to become functionally effective in promoting peacebuilding and good governance.

Process-oriented counter-insurgency methods can also be used to promote peacebuilding and good governance in Somalia. Process-oriented methods, unlike goal-oriented ones that are based on power and fear, are more informal, humane, and based on mutual trust and respect. The coalition forces should adopt process-oriented counter-insurgency measures that target population support. These are measures that take into account the fundamental Somali socio-political structures such as the role of clans, and the role of Islam. The aim of incorporating such structures is to win population support and encourage community participation in effective counter-insurgency efforts. Such efforts will achieve their intended outcomes of dealing with insurgent activism and peacebuilding and good governance in the country.

References

Africa Union Mission in Somalia (AMISOM). (2014a). *About AMISOM*. http://amisom-au.org.

Africa Union Mission in Somalia (AMISOM). (2014b). *Sector II Profile: Kismayo*. http://amisom-au.org.

Beck, C. (2008). The Contribution of Social Movement Theory to Understanding Terrorism. *Sociology Compass*, 2(5): 1565–81.

Bradbury, M., and Healy, S. (2010). A Brief History of the Somali Conflict. *Accord: An International Review of Peace Initiatives*, 21: 10–14.

BBC News (2011). Ethiopian troops capture Beledwenye from Somalia militants, December 31, http://www.bbc.com/news/world-africa-16372453.

Bruton, B. and Williams, P. (2014). *Counter-insurgency in Somalia: Lessons Learned from the African Union Mission in Somalia, 2007–2013*. Joint Special Operations University Report 14–5, September 2014. Tampa Point Boulevard: Joint Special Operations University.

Bryden, M. (2014). *The Reinvention of Al-Shabaab: A Strategy of Choice or Necessity? A Report of the CSIS Africa Program*, February. Washington: Center for Strategic & International Studies.

Byman, D. (2005). *Going to War with Allies You Have: Allies, Counter-insurgency and the War on Terrorism*. Carlisle: Strategic Research Institute.

Chopra, J., Eknes, A., and Nordbo, T. (1995). Fighting for Hope in Somalia. *Norwegian Institute of International Affairs. Peacekeeping and Multinational Operations*, No. 6. http://sites.tufts.edu/jha/archives/102.

Cilliers, J., Boshoff, H., Aboagye, F. (2010). Somalia: The Intervention Dilemma, *ISS Policy Brief*. No. 20. Pretoria: Institute for Security Studies.

Clarke, W. and Herbst, J. (1996). Somalia and the Future of Humanitarian Intervention: Learning the Right Lessons. *Foreign Affairs*, 75(2): 70–85.

Dagne, T. (2011). *Somalia: Current Conditions and Prospects for a Lasting Peace*. CRS Report, RL33911, August 2011.

Della Porta, D. (1996). Social Movements and the State: Thoughts on the Policing of Protest. In D. McAdam, J. McCarthy, and M. Zald (eds), *Comparative Perspectives on Social Movements: Political Opportunities, Mobilizing Structures, and Cultural Framings*. Cambridge: Cambridge University Press, 62–92.

Della Porta, D. (2009). *Social Movement Studies and Political Violence*. Centre for Studies in Islamism and Radicalisation (CIR) Series. Arhus: CIR.

Dersso, S. (2009). The Somali Conflict: Implications for Peacemaking and Peacekeeping Efforts. *ISS Paper 198*. Pretoria: Institute for Security Studies.

Dersso, S. (2010). Somalia Dilemma: Changing Security Dynamics but Limited Policy Choices. *ISS Paper 218*. Pretoria: Institute for Security Studies.

Dowd, C. (2013). *Country Report: Somalia, Armed Conflict Location & Event Database* (ACLED), April 2013.

Eisinger, P. (1973). The Conditions of Protest Behaviour in American Cities. *American Political Science Review*, 67(1): 11–28.

Eriksson, M. (2013). Conclusion. In M. Eriksson (ed.), *External Intervention in Somalia's Civil War: Security Promotion and National Interests?* Report No. FOI-R-3718-SE (pp. 34–40). Stockholm: FOI, Swedish Defence Research Agency.

Gregg, H. (2009). Beyond Population Engagement: Understanding Counterinsurgency. *Parameters*, Autumn 2009: 19–31.

Hamilton, L. (2013) Feature Analysis: Somalia's Post Civil War Renewal. *Africa Conflict Monitor*, May edition: 8–11.

Heritage Institute for Policy Studies (HIPS). (2013). The Kismaayo Crisis: Options for Compromise. *HIPS Policy Briefing Issue 4*, June 2013. http://www.heritageinstitute.org/wp-content/uploads/2013/06/HIPS_ Policy_Brief_004-2013_ENGLISH.pdf.

Hoehne, M. (2009). *Counter-terrorism in Somalia: How External Influence Helped To Produce Militant Islamism*. Max Plank Institute for Social Anthropology. Halle/Saale, Germany, 2009.

Homeland Security Policy Institute (HSPI). (2013). Somalia's Al-shabaab: Down but Not Out, *HSPI Issue Brief 22*, August 27. Washington: HSPI.

International Crisis Group (ICG). (2005). Somalia's Divided Islamists. *Africa Report No. 100*, Nairobi/ Brussels, December 12, 2005.

International Crisis Group (ICG). (2008). Somalia: To Move Beyond the Failed State. *Africa Report No. 147*, Nairobi/Brussels, December 23, 2008.

International Crisis Group (ICG). (2012). The Kenyan Military Intervention in Somalia, *Africa Report No. 184*, Nairobi/Brussels, February 15, 2012.

International Crisis Group (ICG) (2014). Somalia: Al-shabaab—It Will Be a Long War, Policy Briefing, *Africa Briefing No. 99*, Nairobi/Brussels, June 26, 2014.

Kilcullen, D. (2006–7). Counter-insurgency *Redux, Survival*, 48(4): 111–30, doi: 10.1080/00396330601062790.

Kriesi, H. (2004). Political Context and Opportunity. In D. Snow, S. Soule, and H. Kriesi (eds), *The Blackwell Companion to Social Movements*. Oxford: Blackwell, 67–90.

Lewis, I. (2002). *A Modern History of the Somali*. Oxford: James Currey.

McAdam, D. (1999). *Political Process and the Development of Black Insurgency, 1930–1970*, 2nd edition. Chicago: Chicago University Press.

Menkhaus, K. (2007). The Crisis in Somalia: Tragedy in Five Acts. *African Affairs*, 106(204): 357–90.

Menkhaus, K. (2014). Al-Shabab's Capabilities Post-Westgate. *CTC Sentinel*. Special Issue, February, 7(2): 4–9.

Menkhaus, K., Sheikh, H., Quinn, S., and Farah, I. (2010). Somalia: Civil Society in a Collapsed State. In T. Paffenholz (ed.), *Civil Society and Peacebuilding: A Critical Assessment*. London: Lynne Rienner Publishers, 321–50.

Mesfin, B. (2013). Ethiopia—Somalia Relations after 2012. In M. Eriksson (ed.). *External Intervention in Somalia's Civil War: Security Promotion and National Interests?* Report No. FOI-R-3718-SE (pp. 95–115). Stockholm: FOI, Swedish Defence Research Agency.

Meyer, D. (2004). Protest and Political Opportunities. *Annual Review of Sociology*, 30: 125–6.

Mkawale, S. (2011). Kenya to fight Al-shabaab. *The Standard*, October 16. http://www.statndardmedia.co.ke/ print.php?id=2000044910&cid=4.

Mwangi, O.G. (2010). The Union of Islamic Courts and Security Governance in Somalia. *African Security Review*, 19(1): 88–94, doi: 10.1080/10246021001736674.

Mwangi, O.G. (2012). State Collapse, Al-shabaab, Islamism, and Legitimacy in Somalia. *Politics, Religion & Ideology*, 13(4): 513–27, doi: 10.1080/21567689.2012.725659.

Raleigh, C., and Dowd, C. (2014). Real-Time Analysis of African Political Violence. *Conflict Trends (No. 25)*, Armed Conflict Location & Event Database (ACLED), April.

Sandstrom, K. (2013). Contextual Disconnect: The Failure of the "International Community" in Somalia. In E. Leonard and G. Ramsey (eds), *Globalizing Somalia: Multilateral, International and Transnational Repercussions of Conflict*. New York: Bloomsbury, 49–69.

Tarrow, S. (1998). *Power in Movement: Social Movements and Contentious Politics*, 2nd edition. Cambridge: Cambridge University Press.

Turbiville, G., and Forest, J. (2013). Al-shabaab. *JSOU Report 14–1*, December. Tampa Point Blvd: Joint Special Operations University.

Turbiville, G., Meservey, J., and Forrest, J. (2014). Countering the al-shabaab Insurgency in Somalia: Lessons for U.S. Special Operations Forces. *JSOU Report* 14–1, February 2014. Tampa Point Blvd: Joint Special Operations University.

United Nations Security Council (UNSC). (2012). *Resolution 2036 (2012)*. Adopted by the Security Council at its 6718th meeting, on February 22, 2012, S/RES/2036 (2012).

United Nations Security Council (UNSC). (2013a). *Resolution 2093 (2013).* Adopted by the Security Council at its 6969th meeting, on March 6, 2013, S/RES/2093 (2013).

United Nations Security Council (UNSC). (2013b). *Report of the Monitoring Group on Somalia and Eritrea pursuant to Security Council Resolution 2060 (2012)*, S/2013/413, July, 12, 2013.

United States Department of State. (2014). *Country Reports on Terrorism 2013*, US Bureau of Counterterrorism.

Weissman, M. (2008). The Missing Link: Bridging Between Social Movement Theory and Conflict Resolution. GARNET Working Paper No. 60/80.

Williams, K. (2011). The Other Side of the COIN Counter-Insurgency and Community Policing. *Interface: A Journal for and about Social Movements*, 3(1): 81–117.

Chapter 7
Nigerian State Responses to Insurgency[1]

Daniel E. Agbiboa

Abstract

Boko Haram remains arguably the biggest problem confronting Nigeria today, with consequences going beyond security into the political and socio-economic aspects of governance. This Islamist group from north-eastern Nigeria has killed at least 13,000 people since 2009 when it first launched its Islamic insurgency to wrest power from the Nigerian government and create an Islamic state under the supreme law of sharia. The group's active gnawing at the religious, ethnic, and regional fault-lines of Nigeria not only threatens the country's peace and unity, but holds serious transnational implications. The objective of this chapter is to answer three fundamental questions about the extremist group: Who is Boko Haram? Why does the group rebel? How has the Nigerian State responded? The chapter also touches on Boko Haram's growing connection to transnational terrorist groups like the transcontinental al-Qaeda movement and the al-Shabaab group of Somalia as a form of survival strategy.

> Religion is not the cause of religious conflict; rather for many … it frequently supplies the fault line along which intergroup identity and resource competition occurs. (Seul 1999: 58)

Introduction

There is an ongoing campaign of terror in Nigeria. Since July 2009 Boko Haram, an extremist Islamist group from the north-eastern part of Nigeria began a violent campaign that has resulted in the deaths of over 13,000 people, with the death toll rising on an almost daily basis (*Africa Check* 2014; See Table 7.1 at the end of this chapter for a comprehensive timeline of Boko Haram attacks and related violence 2002–2015). The group has carried out frequent attacks and bombings, in some cases using suicide bombers. In a January 2015 bomb attack, which killed at least 19 at a crowded market in Maiduguri, Boko Haram is reported to have used a young girl of about 10 for the suicide mission explosion (*The Guardian* 2015). Targeted locations have included police stations, military facilities, churches, schools, beer halls, newspaper offices, and the United Nations building in Abuja. In addition, the group has assassinated Muslim clerics and traditional leaders in the north for allegedly leaking information about their activities to state authorities (Agbiboa 2013a; 2013b). Boko Haram's increasingly sophisticated and coordinated attacks have targeted Nigeria's ethno-religious fault lines and security agents in an attempt to wrest power from the Nigerian government and create an Islamic state governed by strict sharia law (Forest 2012; Mustapha 2012). Since January 2013, Boko Haram has taken (and lost) control of various local government areas in Borno. including "Gwoza, Marte, Mobbar, Gubio, Guzamala, Abadam, Kukawa, Kala Balge, and Gamboru Ngala" (*Premium Times* 2013; Allison and Ogunlesi 2014). So critical is the threat posed by Boko Haram that in January 2012 Nigerian President Goodluck Jonathan lamented, "[t]he situation we have in our hands is even worse than the civil war [1967–1970] that we fought" (cited in Agbiboa 2013c: 65). On February 7, 2015, Nigeria, through the Nigerian Independent Electoral Commission (INEC), was forced to postpone its general elections for six weeks to allow its armed forces to control parts of the country currently controlled by Boko Haram (see Table 7.1). Unfortunately, numerous attempts at negotiating with Boko Haram, including the April 2013 presidential amnesty offer

---

1   This chapter is an updated version of Agbiboa (2013e). The paper is revised here with copyright permission.

extended to its members (BBC News Africa 2013a), have stalled due to distrust on both sides, and the factionalized leadership of the group.

The central goal of this chapter is to understand who Boko Haram is, why the group rebels, and how the Nigerian state has responded. The chapter also seeks to briefly explore Boko Haram's growing connection to transnational terrorist groups like al-Qaeda and al-Shabaab as a form of survival strategy. The chapter is divided into four main sections. The first provides an historical background to religious militancy in northern Nigeria. The second section seeks to answer the question: Who is Boko Haram? This involves exploring Boko Haram's origins, ideology, demands, *modus operandi*, and sources of funding. The third section looks closely at why Boko Haram rebels. The fourth section explores how the Nigerian state has responded to the threat of Boko Haram; this section involves a critical examination of the soft-handed and heavy-handed approaches of the Nigerian state.

Militant Religiosity in Northern Nigeria

Northern Nigeria, a region with a predominantly Muslim population, has a well-documented history of militant religiosity dating back to the highly successful holy war (jihad) fought by Sheik Usman dan Fodio (1754–1817) in the early nineteenth century (Hickey 1984: 251). Usman dan Fodio launched a jihad against what he saw as the hopelessly corrupt and apostate Hausa ruling elite of the time and established the sharia-governed Sokoto Caliphate—one of the largest and most powerful empires in sub-Saharan Africa—across much of northern Nigeria, although it is important to note that much of the area now known as the middle belt or North Central State resisted the jihadists (Marchal 2012: 2; Agbiboa 2013c). What began as a search for religious purification soon became a search for a political kingdom (Crowder 1978; International Crisis Group 2010), with the outcome being that "Islam has remained the focal veneer for the legitimacy of the northern ruling class," and consequently, "its politicians have always prided themselves as soldiers for the defense of the faith" (Udoidem 1997: 156).

Some authors have argued that the British conquest of the Sokoto Caliphate in 1903, and its subsequent dealings with colonial and postcolonial states, opened it up to the corrupting influence of secular political power (Agbiboa 2013b; Falola 1998; Ekot 2009; Adesoji 2010). Ever since, "there has been resistance among the area's Muslims to Western education" (Marchal 2012: 2). For example, in the first two decades following Nigeria's independence in October 1960, northern Nigeria experienced a violent confrontation between a radical Islamist sect known as *Maitatsine* (in Hausa "he who curses") and the Nigerian Police Force in Kano (December 1980) and Maiduguri (October 1982). Hickey argues that the Maitatsine uprisings had their roots in the "deeply conservative practice of Islam" (1984: 251) which has been dominant in the region since Usman Dan Fodio's holy war. Muhammed Marwa, was an Islamic scholar who migrated from the town of Marwa in northern Cameroon to the city of Kano in 1945. In Kano, Marwa became an Islamic zealot preoccupied with the purification of Islam. He believed that Islam had come under the corrupting influence of modernization (and Westernization) and the formation of the modern state (Agbiboa 2013d). The Nigerian historian Toyin Falola (1998: 146) describes Marwa thus:

> He was a Qur'anic teacher and preacher. Forceful, persuasive, and charismatic, he rebelled against many popular opinions among Kano Islamic circles, denouncing certain parts of the Holy Qur'an and even criticizing Prophet Mohammed ... He was opposed to most aspects of modernization and to all Western influence. He decried such technological commonplace as radios, wrist watches, automobiles, motorcycles, and even bicycles. Those who use these things or who read books other than the Qur'an were viewed as hell-bound "pagans."

Marwa attracted the urban poor in the northern city of Kano with his message that "denounced the affluent elites as infidels, opposed Western Influence, and refused to recognize secular authorities" (Human Rights Watch [HRW] 2012: 22; Lubeck 1985). The urban Muslim poor were attracted to Marwa because "he condemned the hypocrisy and ostentation of the *nouveau riche* and promised redemption and salvation to God's righteous people" (Hickey 1984: 253). Among the groups attracted by Marwa were the Almajiris—that is, a group of young itinerant students of the Qur'an who had a very simple lifestyle made a living by begging on the city streets. Maitatsine extremists lived in secluded areas to avoid contact with Muslims who, in their eyes, had gone astray. They also rejected material wealth on the grounds that it was associated with Western values.

The Maitatsine uprisings led to eleven days of violent confrontations with state security forces in Kano in December 1980. A tribunal inquiry set up by the federal government in 1981 found that 4,177 people were killed in the violence, excluding members of the police force who also lost their lives (Agbiboa 2013c). Although the Nigerian government used its military might to crush the Maitatsine uprisings and kill its leader, hundreds more people lost their lives in reprisal attacks over the next five years (HRW 2012).

Sheik Abubaka Mahmoud Gumi (1922–1992) was another noteworthy Muslim that promoted militant Islam during the 1980s. He was renowned as the most distinguished Islamic scholar in Nigeria of the 1980s (Agbiboa 2013c; Falola 1998). Sheik campaigned against sorcery and witchcraft and promoted Islamic education for women (Marchal 2012: 3). He further promoted the implementation of Sharia courts in Nigeria's Christian south, arguing that Nigeria should be brought under sharia law (Agbiboa 2013a). He once openly declared that "once you are a Muslim, you cannot accept to choose a non-Muslim as a leader" (cited in Aguwa 1997: 338). Sheik Abubaka's speeches and ideas radicalized many Muslims in Nigeria and led to increased tensions between Muslims and Christians, especially in northern Nigeria. The burning of eight prominent churches in Kano by Muslims in October 1982 signaled the beginning of a religious war. According to a government tribunal, the violent act was caused by two factors. First, Kano was predominantly an Islamic city where the growing influence of Christianity was a constant source of worry for Muslims. Second, the tribunal argued that the radical Islamic literature imported from Iran motivated Muslims to begin fighting (Falola 1998: 169).

Notably, since the early days of Nigeria's political sovereignty in 1960 power has shifted from the Muslim north to the Christian south. The Iranian revolution of 1979 resulted in growing demand for sharia law to be adopted across Nigeria. In addition, Saudi-sponsored missionaries from Saudi Arabia, Sudan, Syria, Libya, Pakistan, and other countries were sent to Nigeria to promote Wahhabi doctrine and orthodoxy beginning in the 1990s (Umar 2011). This led to the adoption of sharia law in twelve northern states between 1999 and 2001, beginning with Zamfara State. The then-Zamfara governor, Ahmed Sani, once said, "Whoever administers or governs any society not based on Sharia is an unbeliever" (Agbiboa 2013a). Following his example, many northern governors also introduced Sharia, reinforcing the 'Movement of Restoration'—an attempt by conservative Muslims in northern Nigeria to restore Sharia to its status as the supreme law of the land, as it was pioneered by Usman dan Fodio's Sokoto Caliphate two centuries earlier. However, there was a strong resistance in Kaduna State, where half of the population is Christian. In February 2000, protests by Christians against Sharia in the ancient city of Kaduna resulted in clashes that resulted in over 2,000 deaths (Ekot 2009).

In light of the above facts, this chapter argues that extremist Islamic movements in northern Nigeria (such as Maitatsine and Boko Haram) should be seen as part of the Movement of Restoration, since their overriding goal continues to be the enforcement of Sharia in the spirit of earlier times as inspired by Usman dan Fodio and the sharia-governed Sokoto Caliphate. Boko Haram, which this chapter considers next, is the latest and most violent manifestation of this Movement of Restoration.

Who is Boko Haram?

Mohammed Yusuf, born on January 29, 1970 in the village of Girgir in Yobe State, founded Boko Haram in 2002 in the city of Maiduguri with the goal of establishing sharia government in Borno State under then-Senator Ali Modu Sheriff (Adesoji 2010). As a student of Sheik Gumi, Yusuf received instruction in Salafi radicalism and was greatly influenced by Ibn Taymiyyah, an Islamic scholar (Alim) born 1263CE in the town of Harran in Upper Mesopotamia, into an Arabophone family. Boko Haram was led by Yusuf until he was killed by Nigerian security forces following sectarian violence that broke out in July 2009 and during which over 700 people were killed. At the time of his death, Yusuf was the commander-in-chief (Amir ul-Aam) of Boko Haram. He had two deputies (Na'ib Amir ul-Aam I and II) and each state and local government where Boko Haram existed had its own commander (Amir). Yusuf established a religious complex in his hometown that included a mosque and a school where many poor families from across Nigeria and from neighboring countries enrolled their children. However, the center had ulterior political goals and soon it was also working as a recruiting ground for future jihadists (Agbiboa 2013c; Adesoji 2010; Isa 2010). Boko Haram thus includes members who came from neighboring Chad and Niger and speak only Arabic. The sect was able to attract more than 280,000 members across northern Nigeria and these two countries (Umar 2011; Agbiboa 2013c; Forest 2012).

Boko Haram's membership comprises university lecturers, bankers, political elites, drug addicts, unemployed graduates, *almajiris*, and migrants from neighboring countries. Members are drawn primarily from the Kanuri tribe, which makes up roughly 4 percent of the Nigerian population, and is concentrated in the northeastern states of Nigeria, including Bauchi and Borno, as well as from the Hausa-Fulani 29 percent of the population, who are spread throughout most of the northern states (Agbiboa 2013c).

Recent reports have also revealed that some members in the Nigerian security sector have strong links to Boko Haram (*Punch* 2012; *Vanguard* 2012). In January 2012, The Nigerian President Goodluck Jonathan claimed, "Some [members of Boko Haram] are also in the armed forces, the police and other security agencies" (*Punch* 2012). In February 2012, the commissioner of police in charge of criminal investigations in Abuja, Zakari Biu, was dismissed from the Nigerian police force for allegedly facilitating the escape of Boko Haram suspect Kabiru Sokoto (*Vanguard* 2012). Sokoto is believed to be the mastermind of the bombing of St Theresa's Catholic Church in Madalla, Niger State, in which over 40 people died. Sokoto's escape also led to the sacking of the former Inspector General of Police, Hafiz Ringim (*Elombah* 2012). Like the Maitatsine movement, many of the members attracted by Boko Haram are motivated by deep-seated socio-economic and political grievances such as corruption and poor governance (Kukah 2012). Already, Campbell noted, "Boko Haram, once an obscure, radical Islamic cult in the North, is evolving into an insurrection with support among the impoverished and alienated Northern population" (Campbell and Harwood 2011). Abdul Raufu Mustapha (2012) argues that Boko Haram makes education and informal jobs available to its marginalized members. Governor of the northeastern state of Borno, Kashim Shettima, explains the appeal of Boko Haram. Despite its misguided ideology, Shettima argues that Boko Haram's slain leader Mohammed Yusuf

> retained the loyalty of his supporters by providing one meal a day to each of his disciples. He also had a youth empowerment scheme, under which he helped his disciples to go into petty trading and wheelbarrow pushing. He also arranged cheap marriages between sect members, which enabled many of them to marry, which gave them personal dignity and self-worth. (Shettima cited in Mustapha 2012)

Boko Haram's main affiliation is the Jama't Izalat al Bida'aWaIqamat as Sunna (Society of Removal of Innovation and Reestablishment of the Sunna). This movement is a Wahhabi, anti-Sufi movement established in 1978 in the city of Jos, by Sheikh Ismaila Idris (1937–2000). It was one of the fast-growing Islamic reform movements in Nigeria, shaped by the teachings of Sheikh Abubakar Gumi (Marchal 2012: 3). Boko Haram's ideology is embedded in deeply traditional Islamism and is but one of several variants of radical Islamism to have emerged in northern Nigeria. Its adherents are reportedly influenced by the Qur'anic phrase: "Anyone who is not governed by what Allah has revealed is among the transgressors" (Thurston 2011). Boko Haram is strongly opposed to what it sees as a Western-based incursion that threatens traditional values, beliefs, and customs among Muslim communities in northern Nigeria (Isa 2010). Mohammed Yusuf told the BBC in 2009, "Western-style education is mixed with issues that run contrary to our beliefs in Islam" (Boyle 2009). Elsewhere, the "charismatic" leader argued, "Our land was an Islamic state before the colonial masters turned it to a *kafir* (infidel) land. The current system is contrary to true Islamic beliefs" (Boyle 2009). In January 2012, a spokesman for the group, Abubakar Shekau, accused the US of waging war on Islam (Agbiboa 2013b: 19).

The Boko Haram Revolt

Boko Haram became a full-fledged insurgency following confrontations between the group and Bauchi State's security agency, charged with enforcing a newly introduced law that required motorcyclists in the entire country to wear crash-helmets (Uzodike and Maiangwa 2012). Members of Boko Haram refused to obey this law. This led to a violent clash between the state's enforcement agency and the group which left 17 Boko

Haram members dead. The group's hideout in Bauchi State was also ransacked and materials for making explosives were confiscated. Following this crackdown, the group mobilized its members for reprisal attacks which led to the deaths of several policemen and civilians (Agbiboa 2013c). The riot was temporarily quelled after Nigerian forces captured and killed the Boko Haram leader, Yusuf. Following the death of Yusuf, and the arrest of several of Boko Haram members, the group retreated for a while, but only to recuperate. According to Marchal (2012: 3), "this major blow [the killing of their founder] pushed the movement to transform itself into a network of underground cells with a hidden leadership—a situation that today makes any military solution illusory." Boko Haram soon announced its re-emergence with more advanced tactics and devastating attacks, e.g. the bombing of police headquarters in Abuja in June 2011 and the United Nations (UN) Headquarters in August 2011. In the first ten months of 2012 alone more than 900 people died in attacks perpetrated by the group—more than in 2010 and 2011 combined (Mshellizza 2011).

Boko Haram's modus operandi has involved the use of gunmen on motorbikes, assassinating policemen, politicians, or anyone critical of the group, including Muslim clerics who disclose information regarding their whereabouts to state security services (HRW 2012). Increasingly, suicide bombing has become a major strategy for Boko Haram. For many members, the extrajudicial killing of their founder served to foment pre-existing animosities toward the Nigerian government and its security forces. In the group's bid to avenge the death of its founder, almost every individual and group outside Boko Haram's network was impacted, particularly the Nigerian police and army. Boko Haram's most frequent targets have been police stations, patrols, and individual policemen at home or in public including those who were off-duty or retired (Agbiboa 2013d). They have used petrol bombs, improvised explosive devices, and armed assaults in these violent attacks (Forest 2012). From early 2012, Boko Haram began targeting telecommunication infrastructure, especially around Mubi, Gongola State. The group believes that GSM (Global System for Mobile Communications) companies are aiding security agencies by providing them with call information (HRW 2012). In 2012, Boko Haram launched several attacks against police officers, Christians, and perceived moderate or liberal Muslims who allegedly cooperated with the government or opposed the group (Forest 2012). Among the demands of Boko Haram are the release of its imprisoned members and the prosecution of those responsible for the killing of their founder. However, Boko Haram's number one aim is the overthrow of the Nigerian government and the creation of an Islamic state (Uzodike and Maiangwa 2012).

It is important to note that Boko Haram is not a monolithic entity with a unified purpose. There are separate factions within the movement who disagree about tactics and strategic directions, competing at times for attention and followers (Forest 2012). According to a recent United States House of Representatives report on Boko Haram, one faction of the group might be focused on domestic issues while another on violent international extremism (Agbiboa 2013c; United States House of Representatives 2011). The report further indicated that the group may have even split into three factions: one that remains moderate and welcomes an end to the violence, another that wants a peace agreement, and a third that refuses to negotiate, wanting instead to implement strict sharia law across Nigeria by force (Forest 2012; United States House of Representatives 2011). In July 2011, a group calling itself the Yusufiyya Islamic Movement distributed leaflets throughout Maiduguri denouncing other Boko Haram factions as "evil." Invoking the legacy of founder Mohammed Yusuf, the authors of the leaflets distanced themselves from violent attacks on civilians and on churches (Agbiboa 2013d: 151). Against this backdrop, a jihadist splinter group, commonly known as Ansaru, emerged in northern Nigeria, led by a man that uses the pseudonym Abu Usamatul Ansar. The group has pledged to defend the interests of Muslims in Africa, claiming a different understanding of Jihad. Ansaru, which officially calls itself Jama'atu Ansarul Musilimina fi Biladin Sudan (or Supporters of Islam in the Land of Sudan), has said in a video recently posted on the internet that they will not target non-Muslims except "in self-defense or if they attack Muslims" (*Al Arabiya* 2013). Ansar noted that the "rampant massacre of Muslims in Nigeria will no longer be tolerated" (*Al Arabiya* 2013). The leader also stated that one of the group's main goals is "restoring the dignity of the Muslims as it was in the time of the Caliphate … [and] the method of achieving these aims and goals is 'jihad'" (*Al Arabiya* 2013).

On February 17, 2012, Ansaru kidnapped, and later killed, seven foreigners from Britain, Italy, Greece, Lebanon, and the Philippines. According to a statement released by the group, the kidnappings were in response to "alleged transgressions perpetrated against Islam by European countries in many places such as Afghanistan and Mali" (Roggio 2013). On November 26, 2012, 40 Ansaru fighters stormed the Special Anti-

Robbery Squad prison in Abuja and freed senior Boko Haram commanders, an action praised by Shekau, Boko Haram's current supreme leader. According to Jacob Zenn (2013: 3–4), "Ansaru's freeing of Boko Haram prisoners suggested that despite the circumstances surrounding Ansaru's formation, the two groups were capable of supporting each other's mutual objectives." But these mutual objectives go beyond Nigeria to include global jihadist organizations like the transcontinental al-Qaeda movement and the al-Shabaab group of Somalia, East Africa.

Indeed, one of Boko Haram's main ambitions is to become a key player in the global jihad. In one of its early statements, the group declared that "Boko Haram is just a version of al-Qaeda which we align with and respect. We support Osama bin Laden, we shall carry out his command in Nigeria until the country is totally Islamized which is according to the wish of Allah" (*Vanguard* 2009). Members of Boko Haram are known to have fought in Mali alongside groups affiliated to al-Qaeda. Its members have also received training with Somali-based al-Shabaab. Boko Haram members were reportedly significantly involved in the April 2012 invasion of the Algerian embassy in the Malian city of Gao, which resulted in the hostage-taking of seven Algerian diplomats. A local official in Mali confirmed that "there are a good 100 Boko Haram fighters in Gao. They are Nigerians and from Nigeria ... they're not hiding. Some are even able to speak in the local tongue, explaining that they are Boko Haram" (*Punch* 2012).

In the past, Nigerian officials have been criticized for being unable to trace much of the funding that Boko Haram has received. However, in February 2012, recently arrested Boko Haram officials revealed that while the organization initially relied on donations from members, its links with al-Qaeda in the Islamic Maghreb (AQIM) opened it up to more funding from groups in Saudi Arabia and the UK (Agbiboa 2013b). Furthermore, the arrested officials divulged that other sources of funding included the Al Muntada Trust Fund and the Islamic World Society. Additionally, a spokesman of Boko Haram claimed that Kano State Governor Ibrahim Shekarau and Bauchi State Governor Isa Yuguda had placed them (as members of the Boko Haram group) on a monthly salary (Aziken et al. 2012). Boko Haram also self-finances by robbing local banks. For example on January 12, 2010, four Boko Haram members attempted to rob a bank in Bakori, Katsina State according to local Police Commissioner Umaru Abubakar (Leigh 2011). On December 4, 2011 Bauchi Police Commissioner Ikechukwu Aduba claimed that members of Boko Haram had robbed local branches of Guaranty Trust Bank PLC and Intercontinental Bank PLC (Ibrahim 2011). And on December 10, 2011, Mohammed Abdullahi of the Central Bank of Nigeria claimed that "At least 30 bank attacks attributed to Boko Haram have been reported this year" (Mbachu, Onu and Muhammad 2011). Beyond bank robberies and individual financiers, some sources have linked Boko Haram to illicit weapon trafficking (Agbiboa 2013c; Forest 2012; *ThisDayLive* 2013; Study of Terrorism and Responses to Terrorism [START] 2014: 3). In August 2011, General Carter Ham, Commander of the US Africa Command (AFRICOM), claimed that al-Qaeda and al-Shabaab were financing Boko Haram and also said that both global Jihadist terrorist groups shared training facilities and fighters with Boko Haram. He described it as "the most dangerous thing to happen not only to the Africans, but to us as well" (International Institute for Strategic Studies 2011: 3). This is all the more likely as Boko Haram has expanded its propaganda efforts to show solidarity with al-Qaeda and its affiliates.

In July 2010 Shekau reportedly released an online statement praising al-Qaeda and offering condolences to al-Qaeda of Iraq for its loss of Abu Ayyub al Masri and Abu Omar al Baghdadi, two top al-Qaeda operatives in Iraq (Radin 2012). In another video released in November 2012, Shekau said that he and his fighters supported the ongoing jihads in Afghanistan, Pakistan, in the Indian/Pakistani region of Kashmir, in the Russian territory of Chechnya, Iraq, Saudi Arabia, Yemen, Somalia, Algeria, Libya, and Mali. Shekau's speech, which was received and translated by the SITE Intelligence Group, was issued in Arabic, which suggests that the Boko Haram leader is seeking to appeal to both the wider jihadist community and al-Qaeda's leaders. The 39 minute-long videotape includes various clips of Boko Haram men in training, as well as videos of weapons seized by the group during raids (Roggio 2013). Shekau also repeatedly refers to the fighters in the jihadist theatres as his "brothers." He directly addresses

> the soldiers of the Islamic State in Mali ... our brothers and sheikhs in beloved Somalia ... our brothers and sheikhs in Libya ... our brothers and sheikhs in oppressed Afghanistan ... our brothers and sheikhs in wounded Iraq ... our brothers and sheikhs in Pakistan ... our brothers and sheikhs in blessed Yemen ... our brothers and sheikhs in usurped Palestine, and other places where our brothers are doing jihad in the Cause of Allah. (Roggio 2013: 4)

Shekau warned the US that jihad is far from over and is quoted as saying: "O America, die with your fury" (Roggio 2013: 4). Early in its violent campaign, Boko Haram spokesperson Musa Tanko had warned that: "[The] United States is the number one target for its oppression and aggression against Muslim nations particularly in Iraq and Afghanistan and its blind support to Israel in its killings of our Palestine brethren" (quoted in *Dawn News* 2010).

Given the increased frequency of bomb attacks and shootings carried out by Boko Haram, the prospect for human security remains grim in Nigeria, with potentially serious ramifications for the international community. For one thing, Boko Haram provides al-Qaeda with an avenue to expand its operations in Africa, should the two groups become affiliated. Leaders of both organizations have publicly pledged mutual support (Uzodike and Maiangwa 2012). Shekau, the current head of Boko Haram, has linked the jihad being fought by Boko Haram with the global jihad. He has threatened attacks not only in Nigeria but also against "outposts of Western culture" (Radin 2012). In association with al-Qaeda, Boko Haram could pose a major threat not only to Nigeria, but also transnationally, since Nigeria is Africa's largest oil producer. The increasing sophistication of Boko Haram's attacks and its adoption of suicide bombings may be a sign that the group is indeed receiving tactical and operational assistance from a foreign militant group. Since AQIM has attacked UN targets in Algeria, and al-Shabaab has attacked United Nations' (UN) targets in Somalia, Boko Haram's decision to attack the UN building in Abuja is unlikely to be a coincidence. According to Forest (2012: 81), "this attack on a distinctly non-Nigerian target was a first for Boko Haram, and may indicate a major shift in its ideology and strategic goals."

Awakened to the threat posed by Boko Haram to the international community, the United States State Department in 2012 added Shekau, Boko Haram's most visible leader, to its list of specially designated global terrorists. Khalid al-Barnawi and Abubakar Adam Kambar were also included in the list, because of their ties to Boko Haram and close links with AQIM (United States State Department 2012). The United States also recently announced a USD$7 million bounty for the capture of Shekau, putting him in the top echelon of wanted jihadist leaders (Patel 2013). Four al-Qaeda leaders in Africa where also included in the "Rewards for Justice" list. The State Department noted that that Boko Haram and al-Qaeda's affiliate in Yemen and Saudi Arabia are cooperating to "strengthen Boko Haram's capacity to conduct terrorist attacks" (Roggio 2013).

Why does Boko Haram Rebel?

The extent of relative poverty and inequality in the north has led several analysts and organizations to argue that socio-economic deprivation is the main factor behind Boko Haram's campaign of violence in northern Nigeria (Agbiboa 2013d; International Crisis Group 2010). Isa, for example, argues that Boko Haram communities are wrecked by "poverty, deteriorating social services and infrastructure, educational backwardness, rising numbers of unemployed graduates, massive numbers of unemployed youths, dwindling fortunes in agriculture ... and the weak and dwindling productive base of the northern economy" (2010: 329). Kwaja toes a similar line in arguing that "religious dimensions of the conflict have been misconstrued as the primary driver of violence when, in fact, disenfranchisement and inequality are the root causes" (2011: 1). Sope Elegbe, research director at the Nigerian Economic Summit Group (NESG) argues, "[t]he increasing poverty in Nigeria is accompanied by increasing unemployment. Unemployment is higher in the north than in the south. Mix this situation with radical Islam, which promises a better life for martyrs, and you can understand the growing violence in the north" (cited in Oxford Research Group 2011: 4). In his personal account of the Nigerian Civil War (1967–1970), the late Nigerian writer Chinua Achebe described Boko Haram as a product of economic deprivation and corruption in northern Nigeria. In his words, "economic deprivation and corruption produce and exacerbate financial and social inequities in a population, which in turn fuel political instability" (Achebe 2012). In the final analysis, says Mustapha (2012), "Boko Haram is the symptom of the failure of nation-building and democratic politics in Nigeria. It is the misguided cry of a disgruntled youth crushed by the socio-economic system on the one hand and then repressed by the state on the other." Marchal (2012: 2) highlights the issue of the divergent (and largely unequal) economic and social dynamics of northern versus southern states in Nigeria as a main factor in the Boko Haram rebellion: "Boko Haram is an ultra-violent social movement that has deep roots in the social and economic marginalization of a large section of Nigeria's northern population." (Marchal 2012: 2). With Rev. Fr. Kukah (2012: 3) a scholarly northern clergyman, we observe a somewhat nuanced analysis from the poverty-conflict nexus to the bad governance-conflict nexus. Kukah argues that religion is used to mobilize against modernity, which is seen as the root cause of social anomalies:

> The evil effects of bad governance, corruption, total lack of security and welfare have all become part of our daily lives. Clearly, in the eyes of the sect members, the persistence of corruption, collapse of public morality, injustice and so on could only be attributed to those who govern. In their reasoning, those who govern us do so because they have acquired their tools by gaining Western education. (Kukah 2012: 3)

Kukah finds an ally in scholars like Clapham, who argues more broadly that "the breakdown of law and order in African states was basically the result of the legacy of bad governance" (Clapham 2004: 200). Other scholars like Evans argue that

> a downward spiral of economic decline, often exacerbated by official corruption and mismanagement, has created governments that are at or near the point of collapse and that are being challenged, often violently, by their own citizens. Economic decline has hastened the process of national disintegration and vice versa. (Evans 1994: 3)

Furthermore, Evans argues that "it is no accident that those countries whose economies are declining ... should also be the ones experiencing the greatest amounts of violence and turmoil" (1994: 3). Similarly, in their book entitled *Breaking the Conflict Trap*, Collier et al. adopt an economic approach to the causes of intrastate conflict. They argue that

> [c]ountries with low, stagnant, and unequally distributed *per capita* incomes that have remained dependent on primary commodities for exports face dangerously high risks of prolonged conflict. In the absence of economic development, neither good political institutions, nor ethnic and religious homogeneity or high military spending, provide significant defenses against large scale violence. (Collier et al. 2003: 53)

Explanations such as these often draw on the human needs theory of social conflicts which holds that all human beings have basic needs which they seek to fulfil; and failure to meet these needs could lead to the outbreak of violent conflict (Rosati, Carroll and Roger 1990). The human needs theory resonates with the frustration-aggression theory of violence which argues that the occurrence of aggressive behavior presupposes the existence of frustration (Pear 1950; McNeil 1959). The frustration-aggression theory, in turn, provides the psychological dynamic for the relative deprivation theory—the proposed nexus between the intensity of deprivation and the potential for collective violence (Gurr 1970; Birrel 1972). Drawing on his studies of relative deprivation and conflict in Northern Ireland, Birrel argues that group tensions develop from a discrepancy between the *ought* and the *is* of collective value satisfaction. According to Davies, "this discrepancy is a frustrating experience that is sufficiently intense and focused to result in either rebellion or revolution" (Davies 1962: 5).

Despite the above socio-economic explanations, it is important to emphasize that the link between terrorism and poverty remains unclear and the debate unsettled. In fact, in recent years the poverty-conflict thesis has been criticized as overly simplistic. This is largely because it fails to explain why some poor people or places do not participate in violence, and because it offers very little in the way of clear recommendations for policy-makers (Agbiboa 2013a).

Krieger and Meierrieks (2011) examine a host of possible influences on terrorism including global order, contagion, modernization, institutional order, and identity conflict among other factors. They concluded that "there is only limited evidence to support the hypothesis that economic deprivation causes terrorism ... poor economic conditions matter less to terrorism once it is controlled for institutional and political factors." Instead, they argue that "terrorism is closely linked to political instability, sharp divides within the populace, country size, and further demographic, institutional, and international factors" (Krieger and Meierrieks 2011: 3).

In addition to the history of militant Islam and relative deprivation in northern Nigeria, this chapter has argued that the ultra-violent turn of Boko Haram can be traced back to the extrajudicial killing of its leader, and the bloodletting of its members. Until 2009 Boko Haram was seen as radical, but not ultra-violent (Onuoha 2012). The killing of the group's leader "provoked a staunch reaction from Boko Haram members who primarily want to settle their scores with the police and army" (Marchal 2012: 2).

State Responses and Nigerian Reactions

The Nigerian state has responded to the Boko Haram crisis with both a soft-hand and a heavy-hand, two approaches best understood as running concurrently rather than sequentially. The soft-handed approach has involved an attempt to engage Boko Haram members in political negotiations and/or dialogue. At the state level, this approach has involved overtures and rapprochements to Boko Haram insurgents. For example, the former governor of Borno State, Ali Modu Sheriff, allegedly paid the sum of N100 million (USD $620,000), to mollify the anger of the group when their leader was killed in 2009. Current Governor Kashim Shettima called on Boko Haram to come forward for dialogue on July 16, 2011 (Aghedo and Osumah 2012: 866). In 2012, Datti Ahmad, president of the National Supreme Council on Sharia, who is believed to have had the respect of Yusuf, attempted to reach out to the group. However, contact was broken off by leaders of Boko Haram who accused the Nigerian state of bad faith after the media got wind of, and published, the talks (Anyadike 2012).

In April 2013, Nigerian President Goodluck Jonathan established a 26 member amnesty Committee on Dialogue and Peaceful Resolution of Security Challenges in the North, headed by Nigerian Special Duties Minister Kabiru Tanimu comprising former and current government officials, religious authorities, and human rights activists (Agbiboa 2013d). This committee had a three-month mandate to try to convince Boko Haram to surrender its arms in exchange for a state pardon and social integration (*IRIN* 2013; Thurston 2013).

However, Boko Haram leader Shekau responded to the amnesty entreaties by saying that his group had done no wrong and that an amnesty would not be applicable to them, arguing that it was the Nigerian government committing the atrocities (Chiles 2013; Agbiboa 2013c). In a video released on May 13, 2013, Shekau vowed not to cease his group's violent campaigns to establish an Islamic state in Nigeria (*IRIN* 2013). Barely a week after Boko Haram refused Nigeria's amnesty offer, the group launched two devastating attacks in the north of the country. In the first attack, members of Boko Haram, disguised in military uniforms, driving buses and machine gun-mounted trucks, laid siege to the town of Bama, Borno State, killing 55 people, mostly police and security forces, and freeing over 100 prison inmates (Fox News 2013). In the second attack only a few days later, Boko Haram members killed 53 people and burnt down 13 villages in central Nigeria's Benue State where violent confrontations between pastoralists and nomads had been commonplace (Ross 2013).

In a pre-recorded address broadcast to the Nigerian public on May 14, 2013, President Jonathan said, "What we are facing is not just militancy or criminality, but a rebellion and insurgency by terrorist groups which pose a very serious threat to national unity and territorial integrity" (Ross 2013). Jonathan further stated that "it would appear that there is a systematic effort by insurgents and terrorists to destabilize the Nigerian state and test our collective resolve." Jonathan's speech threw the ongoing Islamic insurgency into stark relief, at one point describing how Islamist fighters had laid waste to state buildings and "had taken women and children hostage." According to Jonathan, "These actions amount to a declaration of war and a deliberate attempt to undermine the authority of the Nigerian state and threaten [its] territorial integrity. As a responsible government, we will not tolerate this" (Jonathan cited in Agbiboa 2013c: 65). These two violent attacks thus led the Nigerian president to declare a state of emergency on May 15, 2013 in Borno, Adamawa and Yobe—all three northern states where Boko Haram has been most active—in an attempt to restore order and reclaim control of the territories (Agbiboa 2013a; see also Table 7.1).

Against this backdrop, the Nigerian president vowed to "'take all necessary action ... to put an end to the impunity of insurgents and terrorists,' including the arrest and detention of suspects, assaults on Boko Haram hideouts, the lockdown of suspected Boko Haram enclaves, raids, and the arrests of anyone possessing illegal weapons" (*IRIN* 2013).

This brings us to the Nigerian state's heavy-handed response—the preferred option, involving the use of the state's security forces—to "mount [an] aggressive pursuit and crackdown of [Boko Haram] members" (Onuoha 2012: 5). To this end, the Nigerian government established a special Joint Task Force (JTF), known as Joint Task Operation Restore Order (JTORO). President Jonathan ordered some 8,000 soldiers to the region in a direct military offensive against Boko Haram members (Omonobi 2013), the largest military deployment since Nigeria's Civil War.

However, far too often, members of the JTF have been accused of killing innocent people in the name of counter-terrorism. In Borno State, for example, the JTF resorted to extra-legal killings, dragnet arrests, and intimidation of the hapless Borno residents (HRW 2012). As noted by Solomon (2012: 9) "[f]ar from conducting intelligence-driven operations, the JTF simply cordoned off areas and carried out house-to-house searches, at times shooting young men in these homes." In a series of interviews with residents in the city of Maiduguri, Human Rights Watch reported that

> During raids in communities, often in the aftermath of Boko Haram attacks, members of the security forces have executed men in front of their families; arbitrarily arrested or beaten members of the community; burned houses, shops, and cars; stolen money while searching homes; and, in at least one case, raped a woman. [In addition] Government security agencies routinely hold suspects incommunicado without charge or trial in secret detention facilities and have subjected detainees to torture or other physical abuse. (HRW 2012: 58)

In a firefight between the JTF and Boko Haram in Baga, a village on Lake Chad near Nigeria's border with Cameroon, up to 187 people were allegedly killed, and 77 others were injured (*Premium Times* 2013). At least 2,000 houses, 64 motorcycles, and 40 cars were burnt in the wake of the attack (ibid.). Baga residents have accused the JTF, not Boko Haram, of firing indiscriminately at civilians and setting fire to much of the fishing town (Chiles 2013). According to Marchal the Nigerian state apparatus allegedly "kills even more civilians than Boko Haram does" (Marchal 2012: 1).

It is important to note that both the soft and heavy-handed approaches of the Nigerian government have divided Nigerians: those who support the use of coercion, and those who support conciliation. Advocates of the coercive approach argue that force rather than dialogue is more effective in dealing with terrorist organizations. As argued by a prominent Nigerian constitutional lawyer, Yahaya Mahmud, the Nigerian government had no choice but to take military actions against Boko Haram:

> No government anywhere will allow a group to usurp part of its territorial sovereignty. The declaration of a state of emergency was necessitated by the constitutional obligation to restore a portion of Nigeria's territory taken over by [Boko Haram] which involves the suspension of constitutional provisions relating to civic rights. (Mahmud cited in Anyadike 2012)

However, there is a legitimate concern that coercive responses will force Boko Haram to simply shift their bases and arena of violence, with grave consequences for Nigeria's neighbors. As Nigerian political scientist Kyari Tijani has pointed out, "Boko Haram cannot face Nigerian troops in conventional war; the troop deployment to northern Borno means they will move out to other towns and cities with less military presence and launch guerrilla warfare" (Tijani cited in Anyadike 2012).

Conclusion

This chapter has addressed three fundamental questions regarding Boko Haram's ongoing campaign of terror in Nigeria: Who are Boko Haram? Why do they rebel? And how has the Nigerian state responded? The chapter has also touched on Boko Haram's growing connections with the transnational terrorist groups like al-Qaeda and al-Shabaab and the subsequent transnational ramifications. The emergence of Boko Haram is not *sui generis* but rather may be understood in the context of a long history of militant Islam in northern Nigeria, along with the movement towards the full restoration of Sharia as pioneered by Usman dan Fodio's Sokoto Caliphate.

Boko Haram remains a major security problem confronting the Nigerian state today, stretching its security apparatuses to their limits. The frustration of the Nigerian government with the worsening security situation in northern Nigeria is evidenced in its declaration of a state of emergency and its changing approach from a soft hand (amnesty talks) to a heavy hand (deployment of troops and the declaration of outright war against Boko Haram) in less than two weeks. These factors have coalesced to further complicate the task of the Amnesty Committee—that is, winning the trust of Boko Haram, crucial in bringing them to the negotiating table.

According to Thurston, the questions facing the Amnesty Committee are serious: "How will the new Committee on Dialogue identify credible interlocutors? Can anyone speak for Boko Haram particularly if the group is proving increasingly fragmented and prone to splinter groups? If Boko Haram has already rejected the Amnesty offer, what conditions would induce a change of mind? Will the state of emergency and efforts towards amnesty prove mutually reinforcing, constituting a soft-hand and heavy-hand approach to Boko Haram, or does the state of emergency signal that Nigeria lacks a clear response strategy?" (Thurston 2013).

While military crackdowns on Boko Haram have the potential to significantly degrade the group's operational capability to mount devastating attacks on a large-scale, it must be considered that such an approach may increasingly force ultra-radical elements within Boko Haram to establish terrorist networks with AQIM and al-Shabaab as a form of survival strategy, with serious ramifications for the international community.

Table 7.1   Timeline of Boko Haram attacks and related violence

Timeline	Incidents
2002	Mohammed Yusuf founded Boko Haram in 2002, establishing a mosque called *Markaz* as the headquarters of his movement, following his expulsion from two mosques in Maiduguri by Muslim clerics for propagating his radical views. November 20–23: Miss World riots, around 250 are killed during riots by Muslims across northern Nigeria as a response to an article deemed blasphemous
2003	
December 23–31	A group of about 200 members of a Boko Haram splinter group launched attacks on police stations in the towns of Kanamma and Geidam in Yob state from their enclave outside Kanamma on the Nigerian border with Niger. The militant killed several police men and requisitioned police weapons and vehicles. Following the deployment of military troops to contain the insurrection, 18 militants were killed and a number arrested.
2004	
June	Four members of Boko Haram were killed by prison guards in a foiled jail break in Yobe state capital Damaturu.
January 7	Seven members of Boko Haram killed and three others arrested by a team of local vigilantes outside the town of Damboa, Borno state, near border with Chad. Bags containing AK-47 rifles were recovered from sect members.
September 23	A Boko Haram group launches a militia attack on police stations in the towns of Gwoza and Bama in Borno state, killing four policemen and two civilians. They took to the Mandra mountains along the Nigeria-Cameroon border. Soldiers and two gunships were deployed in the mountains and after two days of battle 27 sect members were killed while the rest slipped away. Five Boko Haram members who crossed into Cameroon were arrested by Cameroonian gendarmes who had been alerted by Nigerian authorities. The five were deported and handed over to Nigerian authorities.
October 10	Gunmen from a Boko Haram splinter group attack a convoy of 60 policemen in an ambush near the town of Kala-Balge on the border with Chad. The militants took 12 policemen hostage and police authorities presumed they were killed by the gunmen because all attempts to trace them failed.

continued ...

Timeline	Incidents
2005–2008	Boko Haram concentrated on recruiting new members and shoring up its resources. As evidence of their growing popularity, Borno state governor Ali Modu Sheriff appoints an influential Boko Haram member, Buju Foi, as his commissioner of religious affairs in 2007. November 28–29: Jos riots, 381 people are killed in sectarian rioting between Christians and Muslims in Jos.
2009	
June 11–12	Boko Haram leader Mohammed Yusuf threatens reprisals in a video recording to the president following the killing of 17 Boko Haram members in a joint military and police operation in Borno state. This was after a disagreement over Boko Haram members' alleged refusal to use crash helmets while in a funeral procession to bury members who had died in a car accident
July 26	Boko Haram launches a short-lived uprising in parts of the north, which is quelled by a military crackdown that leaves more than 800 dead—mostly sect members, including Boko Haram leader Mohammed Yusuf. A mosque in the capital of Borno state (Maiduguri) that served as a sect headquarter is burnt down
2010	
December 7	A group of Boko Haram gunmen free over 700 inmates including over 100 sect members from a prison in Bauchi. Four people including a soldier, one policemen and two residents were killed in the raid
December 24 & 27	A series of attacks claimed by Boko Haram in the central city of Jos and Maiduguri kill at least 86 people
December 29	Suspected Boko Haram gunmen shoot dead eight people in Maiduguri, including the governorship candidate of the ruling All Nigeria Peoples Party (ANPP) in Borno state
2011	
April 22	Boko Haram frees 14 prisoners during a jailbreak in Yola, Adamawa state
May 27	A group of around 70 suspected Boko Haram gunmen kill eight people including four policemen in simultaneous gun and bomb attacks on a police station, a police barracks and a bank in Damboa, Borno state, near the border with Chad.
May 29	Three bombs rip through a beer garden in a military barracks in the northern city of Bauchi, killing 13 and wounding 33. Boko Haram claims responsibility
June 6	Muslim cleric Ibrahim Birkuti, critical of Boko Haram, short dead by two motorcycle-riding Boko Haram gunmen outside his house in Biu, 200km from Maidguri
June 7	Attacks on a church and two police posts in Maiduguri, blamed on the sect, leave at least 14 dead.
June 16	Boko Haram claims responsibility for the 2011 Abuja police headquarters bombings that killed two
June 26	Bombing attack on a beer garden in Maiduguri, leaving 25 dead and 12 injured
July 10	Bombing at the All Christian Fellowship Church in Suleja, Niger state
July 11	The University of Maiduguri temporarily closes down its campus citing security concerns
July 27	Boko Haram's gun and bomb attack on a beer garden in Maiduguri leaves at least 25 dead and dozens injured
August 3	The government rejects negotiations with Boko Haram

Timeline	Incidents
August 12	Prominent Muslim Cleric Liman Bana is shot dead by Boko Haram
August 25	Gun and bomb attacks by Boko Haram on two police stations and two banks in Gombi, Adamawa State, kill at least 16 people, including seven policemen.
August 26	Boko Haram claims responsibility for a suicide bomb blast on the UN compound in Abuja, killing 23 people.
September 1	A shootout between Boko Haram gunmen and soldiers in Song, Adamawa state, kills one sect members while another is injured and captured
September 4	Muslim Cleric Malam Dala short dead by two Boko Haram members outside his home in the Zinnari area of Maiduguri
September 12	Seven men, including four policemen, are killed by Boko Haram gunmen in bomb and shooting attacks on a police station and a bank in Misau, Bauchi state. The attackers rob the bank.
September 13	Four soldiers shot and wounded in an ambush by Boko Haram members in Maiduguri shortly after the arrest of 15 sect members in military raids on Boko Haram hideouts in the city.
September 17	Babakura Fugu, brother-in-law to slain Boko Haram leader Mohammed Yusuf, is short dead outside his house in Maiduguri two days after attending a peace meeting with Nigeria's ex-president Olusegun Obasanjo in the city. Boko Haram denies any involvement in the incident
October 1	A butcher and his assistant are killed by Boko Haram gunmen at Baga market in Maiduguri in a targeted killing. In a separate incident, three people are killed in a shoot-out following Boko Haram bomb and shooting attacks on a military patrol vehicle delivering food to soldiers at a checkpoint in Maiduguri. All three victims are civilians.
October 3	Three killed in Boko Haram attacks on Baga market in Maiduguri, Borno state. The victims included a tea-seller, a drug store owner and a passer-by
October 23	Sect members open fire on a market in the town of Katari in Kaduna state, killing two. Boko Haram members kill a policeman and a bank security guard in bombing and shooting attacks on a police station and two banks in Saminaka, Kaduna state.
October 25	A policeman is shot dead in his house in a targeted attack by Boko Haram gunmen in Damaturu
October 29	Boko Haram gunmen shoot dead Muslim Cleric Sheikh Ali Jana'a outside his home in the Bulabulin Ngarnam neighborhood of Maiduguri. Jana'a is known to have provided information to security forces regarding the sect.
November 2	A soldier on duty is shot dead by sect members outside Maiduguri's main market. Boko Haram says it will not dialogue with the government until all of its members who have been arrested are released.
November 4	The motorcade of Borno state governor Kashim Shettima comes under Boko Haram bomb attack in Maiduguri on its way from the airport to the governor's residence as he returns from a trip to Abuja. Around 150 are killed in coordinated Boko Haram bombing and shooting attacks on police facilities in Damaturu and Potiskum in Yobe state. Two Boko Haram suicide-bombers blow themselves up outside the military Joint Task Force headquarters in Maiduguri in a botched suicide attack
November 9	Boko Haram members bomb a police station and the office of Nigeria's road safety agency in Maina village, Borno state. No one is hurt.

continued ...

Timeline	Incidents
November 26	Three policemen and a civilian are wounded in Boko Haram bomb and shooting attacks in Geidam, Yobe state. Six churches, a police station, a beer parlour, a shopping complex, a high court, a local council building and 11 cars are burnt in the attacks
November 27	A Borno state protocol officer in the officer of the governor is shot dead by motorcycle-riding sect members while driving home.
December 4	A soldier, a policeman and a civilian are killed in bomb and gun attacks on police buildings and two banks in Azare, Bauchi state. Boko Haram open fire at a wedding in Maiduguri, killing the groom and a guest.
December 7	An explosion linked to Boko Haram kills eight in the Oriyapata district of Kaduna city
December 13	A bomb attack on a military checkpoint by Boko haram and resulting shooting by soldiers in Maiduguri leaves 10 dead and 30 injured
December 17	A shootout between sect members and policemen following a raid on the hideout of a Boko Haram sect leader in the Darmanawa area of Kano state kills seven, including three police officers. Police arrest 14 Boko Haram suspects and seize large amounts of arms and bombs. Three Boko Haram members die in an accidental explosion while assembling home-made bombs in a hideout on the outskirts of Maiduguri
December 19	One suspected Boko Haram member dies and two others wounded in an accidental explosion while assembling a home-made bomb in a hideout in Damaturu
December 22	Boko Haram bombs in parts of Maiduguri kill 20. Four policemen and a civilian are killed in gun and bomb attacks on a police building in Potiskum, Yobe state. Around 100 are killed following multiple bomb and shooting attacks by Boko Haram gunmen and ensuing gun battles with troops in the Pompomari outskirts of Damaturu.
December 25	A Christmas Day Boko Haram bomb attack on Saint Theresa Catholic Church in Madalla town near Abuja kills 42 worshippers. Three secret police operatives and a Boko Haram bomber are killed in a suicide attack when the bomber rams his bomb-laden car into a military convoy at the gates of SSS headquarters in Damaturu. A policeman is killed in a botched Boko Haram bomb attack on a church in the Ray Field area of Jos, capital of Plateau state
December 28	A bombing and shooting attack by Boko Haram on a beer parlour in the town of Mubi, Adamawa state, wounds 15
December 30	Four Muslim worshippers are killed in a Boko Haram bomb and shooting attack targeting a military checkpoint in Maiduguri as worshippers leave a mosque after attending Friday prayers
2012	
January 1	President Goodluck Jonathan imposes a state of emergency on 15 local government areas hardest-hit by Boko Haram attacks, in Borno, Yobe, and Plateau states. He orders the closure of Nigerian borders in the north.
January 3	Boko Haram gunmen attack a police station in the town of Birniwa in Jigawa state killing a teenage girl and wounding a police officer.
January 5	Six worshippers are killed and 10 others wounded when Boko Haram gunmen attack a church in Gombe city
January 7	Eight worshippers are killed in a shooting attack on a church in Yola. Boko Haram gunmen shoot dead 17 Christian mourners in the town of Mubi in the northeastern state of Adamawa. The victims are friends and relations of one of five people killed in a Boko Haram attack on a hotel the previous day

Timeline	Incidents
January 9	Boko Haram gunmen shoot dead a secret police operative along with his civilian friend as they leave a mosque in Biu, Borno state, 200km south of the state capital Maiduguri. The president says Boko Haram has infiltrated the executive, parliamentary and judicial wings of government.
January 10	A Boko Haram attack on a beer garden kills eight, including five policemen and a teenage girl, in Damaturu, capital of Yobe State
January 11	Four Christians killed by Gunmen in Potiskum, Yobe state, when gunmen open fire on their car as they stop for fuel. The victims had been fleeing Maiduguri to their hometown in Eastern Nigeria
January 13	Boko Haram kills four and injures two others, including a policeman, in two separate attacks on pubs in Yola (Adamawa state) and Gombe city in neighboring Gombe state.
January 17	Two soldiers and four Boko Haram gunmen are killed in an attack on a military checkpoint in Maiduguri, Borno state. Soldiers arrest six high-profile Boko Haram members in a raid on a sect hideout in the city.
January 20	January 2012 Kano bombings
January 28	Nigerian army says it killed 11 Boko Haram insurgents
February 8	Boko Haram claims responsibility for a suicide bombing at the army headquarters in Kaduna
February 16	Another prison break staged in central Nigeria; 119 prisoners are released, one warden killed
March 8	During a British hostage rescue attempt to free Italian engineer Franco Lamolinara and Briton Christopher McManus, abducted in 2011 by Boko Haram, both hostages were killed
May 31	During a Joint Task Force raid on a Boko Haram hideout, it was reported that five sect members and a German hostage were killed
June 3	15 church-goers were killed and several injured in a church bombing in Bauchi state. Boko Haram claimed responsibility through Spokesperson Abu Qaqa
June 17	Suicide bombers strike three churches in Kaduna state. At least 50 people were killed
June 17	130 bodies were found in Plateau state. It is presumed they were killed by Boko Haram members
2013	
April 24	Jonathan sets up Boko Haram amnesty committee
May 7	At least 55 killed and 105 inmates freed in coordinated attacks on army barracks, a prison and police post in Bama town
May 14	Jonathan declares state of emergency in Borno, Yobe, Adamawa states over Boko Haram attacks
August	Abubakar Shekau said to have been shot and deposed by members
2014	
April 14	Boko Haram kidnaps Chibok schoolgirls at Government Secondary School, Chibok, Borno
April 14	Boko Haram suicide bombers attack Nyanya bus station in Abuja, 90 killed
May 1	Car bomb attack in Nyanya area of Abuja, 19 killed, scores injured

continued ...

Timeline	Incidents
May 18	Boko Haram suicide bomb attack in Kano, five killed
May 20	Twin bomb explosions in Jos, 118 killed
September 17	Nigeria military claims it killed Abubakar Shekau "again"
September	Australian Stephen Davis names some alleged "sponsors" of Boko Haram
September	Nigeria's military fought back Boko Haram's attack to retake Konduga, killing about 115 of the militants, several insurgents surrender their weapons
September	Boko Haram claimed it shot down a Nigerian military jet and captured one of the pilots alive. It released the video of how it beheaded one of the pilots.
September 19	Around 30 people are killed by Boko Haram militants at a busy market in Mainok, Borno State
October 17	VOA reports a meeting of a delegation of the Federal Government and Boko Haram members on Saudi Arabia
October 31	At least 4 people are killed, 32 injured and 13 vehicles destroyed by an explosion at a bus station in Gombe
November 2	Kogi prison break, 99 inmates in Kogi State are freed by suspected Boko Haram militants
November 3–10	Yobe State attacks, a double suicide bombing in Yobe State kills 15 Shiites on the 3rd and 46 students on the 10th
November 25	Over 45 people are killed by two suicide bombers in Maiduguri, Borno State
November 27	Around 50 people are killed in Damasak by Boko Haram militants
November 28	2014 Kano bombing, at least 120 Muslim followers of the Emir of Kano, Mohammed Sanusi II, are killed during a suicide bombing and gun attack by Boko Haram. The 4 gunmen are subsequently killed by an angry mob.
December 1–5	People are killed by two female suicide bombers who detonated explosions at a crowded market place in Maiduguri, Bornu State
December 6	Minna prison break, 270 prisoners are freed from a prison in Minna, Boko Haram is not suspected to be involved in the attack
December 13	Gumsuri kidnappings, between 32 and 55 are killed and between 172 and 185 are kidnapped by Boko Haram in Borno State
December 22	Gombe bus station bombing, at least 27 people are killed at a bus station by a bomb in Gombe State
December 28–29	Cameroon clashes, 85 civilians, 94 militants, and 2 Cameroonian soldiers are killed following a failed Boko Haram offensive into Cameroon's Far North Region.
2015	
January 2	Boko Haram militants attack a bus in Waza, Cameroon, killing eleven people and injuring six
January 3–7	Baga massacre, Boko Haram militants raze the entire town of Baga in north-east Nigeria. Bodies lay strewn on Baga's streets with as many as 2,000 people having been killed (actual figures are disputed). Boko Haram now controls 70% of Borno State, which is the worst affected by the insurgency.
January 3	Fleeing villagers from a remote part of the Borno State report that Boko Haram had three days prior kidnapped around 40 boys and young men

Timeline	Incidents
January 5	News emerges that two days prior hundreds of Boko Haram militants had overrun several towns in northeast Nigeria and captured the military base in Baga
January 9	Refugees flee Nigeria's Bornu State following the Boko Haram massacre in the town of Baga. 7,300 flee to neighboring Chad while over 1,000 are trapped on the island of Kangala in Lake Chad. Nigeria's army vows to recapture the town, while Niger and Chad withdraw their forces from a transnational force tasked with combating militants
January 10	A female suicide bomber, believed to be aged around 10-years-old, killed herself and 19 others, possibly against her will, at a market in the northwestern city of Maiduguri, Nigeria
January 11	More female suicide bombers, this time two, and again each believed to be around 10 years old, kill themselves and three others at a market in the northeastern city of Potiskum, Nigeria
January 12	Kolofata raid, Boko Haram militants launch a failed raid on Kolofata in Cameroon. The Cameroonian military claims the army lost only one officer while the Islamic group lost between 143–300 rebels
January 16	The Military of Chad enters Cameroon to assist in fighting against Boko Haram insurgents
January 17	Following the January 16 Chad authorities decision to send troops to Nigeria and Cameroon to fight Boko Haram militants, the Russian ambassador to the country pledges to supply Cameroon with more modern weapons to combat the Islamist insurgents
January 18	Boko Haram militants kidnap 80 people and kill three others from villages in north Cameroon
January 20	Boko Haram leader Abubakar Shekau claims responsibility for the attack on the town of Baga, Nigeria in which an unknown number of civilians were killed
January 25	Boko Haram rebels launch a large offensive against Nigerian forces in Maiduguri, the capital of Borno State, leading to the deaths of at least 8 civilians, up to 53 militants, and an unknown number of soldiers. Although the attack fails, the rebels manage to capture the nearby strategic town of Monguno. The status of the 1,400 soldiers stationed in Monguno is unknown. As a result of these attacks, Boko Haram now controls four out of five roads leading into the major city, prompting fears that it will be taken as well
January 28	Boko Haram fighters killed 40 people while on a rampage in Adamawa State
January 29	The Nigerian military, in collaboration with Chadian soldiers, captures the border town of Michika from Boko Haram rebels
January 31	The African Union pledges to send up to 7,500 international soldiers to aid Nigeria's fight against Boko Haram. Chadian forces claim to have killed 120 Boko Haram fighters while losing only 3 soldiers of their own during fighting in the north of Cameroon
February 1	Boko Haram again attacks the capital city of Borno State, Maiduguri. This time, the city is attacked from four out of the five sides. The attack is unsuccessful, but many civilians inside the city panic. Also, a suspected Boko Haram suicide bomber kills himself and eight others at the residence of a politician in Potiskum. Another suicide bomber kills five people outside a mosque in Gombe.
February 2	A female suicide bomber attacks minutes after the President of Nigeria leaves an election in the city of Gombe resulting in at least one death and 18 people injured

continued ...

Timeline	Incidents
February 4	Boko Haram militant reportedly raid the Cameroonian town of Fotokol in Cameroon's Far North Region with scores of people killed. Also on February 4th, the Chad Army claims to have killed 200 militants and lost nine soldiers while capturing the border town of Gamboru Ngala
February 6	Niger raid, Boko Haram forces launch riads on the towns of Bosso and Diffa, both in Niger, marking the first time that the group has attacked the country. The Chadian military assists the Nigerien Armed Forces in repelling the attack. 5 Nigeriens are killed while the government claims 109 Boko Haram militants are killed as well.
February 7	Nigeria postpones its general election for six weeks to allow its armed forces to control parts of the country currently controlled by Boko Haram
February 9	Boko Haram launch a raid on a prison in the town of Diffa in Niger. Authorities repel the attack
February 12	The West African Allied Forces, led by Nigeria and supported by Cameroon, Chad and Niger, invade the Sambisa Forest in Borno State, a stronghold of Boko Haram, killing scores of the insurgents. Elsewhere, the town of Mbuta, 15 miles northeast of Maiduguri is raided by Boko Haram, resulting in the deaths of 8 residents. A dozen people are also killed in a suicide blast at Biu, 100 miles southwest of Maiduguri.
February 13	Boko Haram militants attack Chad for the first time after 30 fighters crossed Lake Chad in four motorboats and attacked the village of Ngouboua. Chad recently joined Nigeria, Niger, and Cameroon in a military coalition against Boko Haram
February 14	Boko Haram forces assault Gombe, the capital city of Gombe State, for the first time. The Nigerian military repels the attack, although the militants managed to overrun a checkpoint on the edge of the city before retreating. The attack coincides with the beginning of a Nigerian offensive to rollback Boko Haram forces around the northeast
February 15	A suicide bomber kills 16 and wounds 30 in the Nigerian city of Damaturu
February 16	Nigeria regains the key town of Monguno from Boko Haram. The town had previously fallen to the militants on January 25th.
February 18	The Nigerian Army claims to have killed 300 militants in northeastern Nigeria. A warplane bombs a funeral ceremony in Niger killing 37 civilians. The warplane remains unidentified, with the Nigerian government denying responsibility.
February 20	Boko Haram militants kill 34 people in attacks across Borno State, 21 from the town of Chibok
February 21	Nigerian army retakes Baga, which had fallen to Boko Haram on January 3rd
February 22	A suicide bomber kills five and wounds dozens outside a market in Potiskum
February 24	Two suicide bombers kill at least 27 people at bus stations in Potiskum and Kano
February 24	Chadian soldiers kill over 200 Boko Haram fighters in a clash near the town of Garambu, close to Nigeria's border with Cameroon. One Chad Army solider is killed and nine are wounded
February 26	At least 35 people are killed in two attacks targeting the cities of Biu and Jos
February 28	Two female suicide bombers kill up to four civilians near Damaturu
March 2	A senior military officer claims that 73 Boko Haram militants disguised as herders were killed near Kondunga town in Bornu State. In addition, the Chadian military recaptures the town of Dikwa, also in Borno State
March 7	Five suicide bomb blasts leave 54 dead and 143 wounded in Maiduguri. After the explosions, Boko Haram formally declares allegiance to the Islamic State.

Sources: compiled with data retrieved from *IRIN* (2012); and *Punch* (2014)

References

Achebe, C. (2012). *There Was a Country: A Personal History of Biafra*. London: Allen Lane.

Adesoji, A. (2010). The Boko Haram Uprising and Islamic Revivalism in Nigeria. *Africa Spectrum*, 45(2): 95–108.

Agbiboa, D.E. (2013a). Boko Haram, the Nigerian State, and Spiraling Violence in Nigeria. *The African Executive*, June 2–12, www.africanexecutive.com/modules/magazine/articles.php?article=7259.

Agbiboa, D.E. (2013b). The Nigerian Burden: Religious Identity, Conflict and the Current Terrorism of Boko Haram. *Conflict, Security and Development*, 13(1): 1–29, DOI: http://dx.doi.org/10.1080/14678802.2013.770257.

Agbiboa, D.E. (2013c). No Retreat, No Surrender: Understanding the Religious Terrorism of Boko Haram in Nigeria. *African Study Monographs*, 34(2): 65–84.

Agbiboa, D.E. (2013d). Why Boko Haram Exists: The Relative Deprivation Perspective. *African Conflict and Peacebuilding Review*, 3(1): 146–59.

Agbiboa, D.E. (2013e). The Ongoing Campaign of Terror in Nigeria: Boko Haram versus the State. *Stability: International Journal of Security and Development*, 2(3): 1–18.

Aghedo, I. and Osumah, O. (2012). The Boko Haram Uprising: How Should Nigeria Respond? *Third World Quarterly*, 33(5): 853–69, DOI: http://dx.doi.org/10.1080/01436597.2012.674701.

Aguwa, J.C. (1997). Religious Conflict in Nigeria: Impact on Nation Building. *Dialectical Anthropology*, 22(3–4): 335–51, DOI: http://dx.doi.org/10.1023/A:1006866525049.

Al Arabiya (2013). New Islamic Group Emerges in Nigeria: Claims Different "Understanding" of Jihad, May 27, http://english.alarabiya.net/articles/2012/06/03/218371.html.

Allison S. and Ogunlesi, T. (2014). Analysis: In Nigeria, Boko Haram follows in the footsteps of Iraq's Islamic State. *Daily Maverick*, August 14, http://www.dailymaverick.co.za/article/2014-08-14-analysis-in-nigeria-boko-haram-follows-in-the-footsteps-of-iraqs-islamic-state/#.VQEY9h1TOAg.

Anyadike, O. (2012). Analysis: Carrot or Stick? Nigerians Divided over Boko Haram. *IRIN Humanitarian News and Analysis*, July 16, www.irinnews.org/report/95874/analysis-carrot-or-stick-nigerians-divided-over-boko-haram.

Aziken, E., Muhammad, A., Ojeme, V., and Marama, N. (2012). We're On Northern Govs' Payroll—Boko Haram. *Vanguard*, January 24, www.vanguardngr.com/2012/01/we-re-on-northern-govspayroll-boko-haram.

BBC News Africa (2013a). Nigeria's Boko Haram rejects Jonathan's amnesty Idea, April 11, http://www.bbc.com/news/world-africa-22105476.

Birrel, D. (1972). Relative Deprivation as a Factor in Conflict in Northern Ireland. *Sociological Review*, 20(3): 317–43, DOI: http://dx.doi.org/10.1111/j.1467-954X.1972.tb00213.x.

Boyle, J. (2009). Nigeria's Taliban Enigma. BBC News, July 31, http://news.bbc.co.uk/2/hi/8172270.stm.

Campbell, J., and Harwood, A. (2011). Nigeria's Challenge. *The Atlantic*, June 24, www.theatlantic.com/international/archive/2011/06/nigerias-challenge/240961/.

Chiles, N. (2013). After Rejecting Nigeria's Amnesty Offer: Boko Haram Continues to Kill. *Atlanta Blackstar*, April 23, http://atlantablackstar.com/2013/04/23/after-rejecting-nigerias-amnesty-offer-boko-haram-continues-to-kill.

Clapham, C. (2004). Problems of Peace Enforcement: Lessons to be Drawn from Multinational Peacekeeping Operations in Ongoing Conflicts in Africa. In Z. Williams (ed.), *Africa in Crisis*. London: Pluto Press, 196–215.

Collier, P., Elliott, V.L., Hegre, H., Hoeffler, A., Reynal-Querol, M., and Sambanis, N. (2003). *Breaking the Conflict Trap: Civil War and Development Policy*. Washington, DC: World Bank.

Crowder, M. (1978). *The Story of Nigeria*. London: Faber and Faber.

Davies, J.C. (1962). Towards a Theory of Revolution. *American Sociological Review*, 27(1): 5–19.

Dawn News (2010). Nigeria Islamist Sect Threatens to Widen Attacks. March 29, http://www.dawn.com/news/910613/nigerian-islamist-sect-threaten-to-widen-attacks.

Ekot, B. (2009). Conflict, Religion and Ethnicity in the Postcolonial Nigerian State. *The Australasian Review of African Studies*, 30(2): 47–67.

Elombah (2012). Boko Haram Escape: Zackary Biu Fired from the Nigerian Police, February 22, http://www. elombah.com/index.php/reports/9994-Boko-Haram-Escape-Zackary-Biu-Fired-from-the-Nigerian-Police.

Elombah (2013). Boko Haram Leader, Shekau say will burn Schools, Kill Teachers, but not Children, July 13, www.elombah.com/index.php/reports/16640-boko-haram-leader-shekau-say-will-burn-schools-kill-teachers-but-not-children.

Evans, G. (1994). Cooperative Security and Intrastate Conflict. *Foreign Policy*, 96 (Autumn): 3–20.

Falola, T. (1998). *Violence in Nigeria: The Crisis of Religious Politics and Secular Ideologies*. New York: University of Rochester Press.

Forest, J.J.F. (2012). *Confronting the Terrorism of Boko Haram in Nigeria*. Florida: The JSOU Press.

Fox News (2013). Nigerian President Declares State of Emergency, May 14, www.foxnews.com/world/2013/05/14/state-emergency-declared-in-nigeria.

Guardian, The (2015). Nigeria: Bomb Blast Kills at Least 19 at Crowded Market in Maiduguri, January 10, http://www.theguardian.com/world/2015/jan/10/nigeria-bomb-blast-maiduguri-young-girl-borno-state.

Gurr, T.R. (1970). *Why Men Rebel*. Princeton, NJ: Princeton University Press.

Hickey, R. (1984). The 1982 Maitatsine Uprisings in Nigeria: A Note. *African Affairs*, 83(331): 251–6.

Human Rights Watch (2012). *Spiraling Violence: Boko Haram Attacks and Security Forces Abuses in Nigeria*, www.hrw.org/sites/default/files/reports/nigeria1012webwcover.pdf.

Ibrahim, L. (2011). Nigeria: Bank Robbery Suspects Boko Haram Members. *Daily Trust*, February 4.

International Crisis Group (2010). Northern Nigeria: Background to Conflict. *Africa Report*. 168: December 20, http://www.crisisgroup.org/en/regions/africa/west-africa/nigeria/168-northern-nigeria-background-to-conflict.aspx.

International Institute for Strategic Studies (2011). Boko Haram: Nigeria's Growing New Headache. *Strategic Comments*, 17(9): 1–3, DOI: http://dx.doi.org/10.1080/13567888.2011.646168.

IRIN (2012). Nigeria: Timeline of Boko Haram Attacks and Related Violence. *IRIN Humanitarian News and Analysis*, January 20, http://www.irinnews.org/Report/94691/NIGERIA-Timeline-of-Boko-Haram-attacks-and-related-violence.

IRIN (2013). Nigerians on the Run as Military Combat Boko Haram. *IRIN Humanitarian News and Analysis*, May 22, http://www.irinnews.org/report/98076/analysis-nigerians-on-the-run-as-military-combat-boko-haram.

Isa, M.K. (2010). Militant Islamist Groups in Northern Nigeria. In W. Okumu and A. Ikelegbe (eds), *Militias, Rebels and Islamists Militants: Human Security and State Crises in Africa*. Pretoria: Institute for Security Studies, 313–40.

Krieger, T. and Meierrieks, D. (2011). What Causes Terrorism? *Public Choice*, 147(1): 3–27.

Kukah, M.H. (2012). Nigeria: Country as an Emerging Democracy: The Dilemma and the Promise. *Daily Trust (Abuja)*, September 9.

Kwaja, C. (2011). Nigeria's Pernicious Drivers of Ethno-Religious Conflicts. *Africa Security Brief*, July 14: 1–8, http://africacenter.org/wp-content/uploads/2011/06/AfricaBriefFinal_14.pdf.

Leigh, K. (2011). Nigeria's Boko Haram: Al Qaeda's New Friend in Africa? *Time*, August 31, http://content.time.com/time/world/article/0,8599,2091137,00.html.

Lubeck, P.M. (1985). Islamic Protest under Semi-Industrial Capitalism: Yan Tatsine Explained. *Africa: Journal of the International African Institute*, 55(4): 370–86.

Marchal, R. (2012). Boko Haram and the Resilience of Militant Islam in Northern Nigeria. *NOREF Report*, June, Norwegian Peacebuilding Resource Centre,http://www.peacebuilding.no/var/ezflow_site/storage/original/application/dc58a110fb362470133354efb8fee228.pdf.

Mbachu, D., Onu, E., and Muhammad, M. (2011). Nigeria Bank Raids Reach 100 this Year on Boko Haram Attacks. *Bloomberg Business*, December 10, http://www.bloomberg.com/news/articles/2011-12-09/nigeria-bank-raids-reach-100-this-year-on-boko-haram-attacks.

McNeil, E.D. (1959). Psychology and Aggression. *Journal of Conflict Resolution*, 3(3): 195–294, DOI: http://dx.doi.org/10.1177/002200275900300301.

Mshellizza, I. (2011). Islamist Sect Boko Haram Claims U.N. Bombing, August 29, www.reuters.com/article/2011/08/29/us-nigeria-bombing-claim-idUSTRE77S3ZO20110829.

Mustapha, A.R. (2012). Boko Haram: Killing in God's Name. *Mail and Guardian*, April 5, http://mg.co.za/article/2012-04-05-boko-haram-killing-in-gods-name.

Omonobi, K. (2013). Jonathan creates new army division, sends 8,000 troops after Boko Haram. *Vanguard*, August 18, http://www.vanguardngr.com/2013/08/jonathan-creates-new-army-division-sends-8000-troops-after-boko-haram/.

Onuoha, F.C. (2012). *Boko Haram: Nigeria's Extremist Islamic Sect. Al Jazeera Centre for Studies*, February 29: 1–6. http://studies.aljazeera.net/ResourceGallery/media/Documents/2012/2/29/20122291133417937 34BOKO%20HARAM%20NIGERIAS%20EXTREMIST%20ISLAMIC%20SECT.pdf.

Patel, A. (2013). Boko Haram Banned in Nigeria after US Bounty Announced. BBC News Africa, June 5, www.bbc.co.uk/news/world-africa-22777817.

Pear, T.H. (1950). *Psychological Factors of Peace and War*. London: Hutchinson.

Premium Times (2013). 185 Killed in Borno Town, Baga, as Soldiers, Boko Haram Fight, April 22, http://premiumtimesng.com/news/130680-185-killed-in-borno-town-baga-as-soldiers-boko-haram-fight.html.

Punch (2014). Timeline on Boko Haram Activities, October 17, http://www.punchng.com/news/timeline-on-boko-haram-activities/.

Punch. (2012). Boko Haram Spreads Terror Campaign To Mali. April 10 www.punchng.com/news/boko-haram-spreads-terror-campaign-to-mali.

Radin, C.J. (2012). The Threat of Boko Haram for Nigeria, Africa, and Beyond. *The Long War Journal*, April 23, http://www.longwarjournal.org/archives/2012/04/the_threat_of_boko_haram_for_n.php.

Roggio, B. (2013). Nigerian Jihadist Group Executes Seven Foreigners. *The Long War Journal*, March 9, http://www.longwarjournal.org/archives/2013/03/nigerian_jihadist_gr.php.

Rosati, J.A., Carroll, D.J., and Roger, A.C. (1990). A Critical Assessment of the Power of Human Needs in World Society. In J. Burton and F. Dukes (eds), *Conflict: Readings in Management and Resolution*. Basingstoke: B Press, 156–9.

Ross, W. (2013). Nigeria: Goodluck Jonathan Declares Emergency in States. BBC News Africa, May 15, www.bbc.co.uk/news/world-africa-22533974.

Seul, J.R. (1999). Ours is the Way of God: Religion, Identity and Intergroup Conflict. *Journal of Peace Research*, 36(5): 553–69.

Solomon, H. (2012). Counter-terrorism in Nigeria: Responding to Boko Haram. *The RUSI Journal*, 157(4): 6–11, DOI: http://dx.doi.org/10.1080/03071847.2012.714183.

Study of Terrorism and Responses to Terrorism (START) (2014). *Background Report: Boko Haram Recent Attacks*, http://www.start.umd.edu/news/background-report-boko-haram-recent-attacks.

ThisDayLive (2013). Seven Boko Haram Members Arraigned for Bank Robbery, February 21, http://www.thisdaylive.com/articles/seven-boko-haram-members-arraigned-for-bank-robbery/140114.

Thurston, A. (2011). Threat of Militancy in Nigeria. Commentary for Carnegie Endowment for International Peace, September 1, http://carnegieendowment.org/2011/09/01/threat-of-militancy-in-Nigeria/4yk8.

Thurston, A. (2013). Amnesty for Boko Haram: Lessons from the Past. *Africa Futures*, May 20, http://forums.ssrc.org/african-futures/2013/05/20/amnesty-for-boko-haram-lessons-from-the-past/.

Udoidem, S. (1997). Religion in the Political Life of Nigeria: A Survey of Religious-Related Crises in Nigeria since Independence. In F.U. Okafo (ed.), *New Strategies for Curbing Ethnic and Religious Conflicts in Nigeria*. Enugu: Fourth Dimension, 154–60.

Umar, S. (2011). *The Discourses of Salafi Radicalism and Salafi Counter-Radicalism in Nigeria, 2008–2009*. Abuja: United Nations Development Programme.

United States House of Representatives (2011). *Boko Haram—Emerging Threat to the U.S. Homeland*. 112th Congress, 1st Session. Report by United States House of Representatives Committee on Homeland Security. Subcommittee on Counterterrorism and Intelligence. http://homeland.house.gov/sites/homeland.house.gov/files/Boko%20Haram-%20Emerging%20Threat%20to%20the%20US%20Homeland.pdf.

Uzodike, O.U. and Maiangwa, B. (2012). Boko Haram Terrorism in Nigeria: Causal Factors and Central Problematic. *African Renaissance: Terrorism in Africa*, 9(1): 91–118.

Vanguard (2009). *Boko Haram Resurrects, Declares Total Jihad*, August 14, http://allafrica.com/stories/200908140646.html.

Vanguard (2012). Nigeria: Kabiru's Sokoto Escape, February 22, http://allafrica.com/stories/201202230251.html.

Zenn, J. (2013). Cooperation or Competition: Boko Haram and Ansaru after Mali Intervention. *CTC Sentinel*, March 27, 1–4, https://www.ctc.usma.edu/posts/cooperation-or-competition-boko-haram-and-ansaru-after-the-mali-intervention.

PART II
Peacebuilding

Chapter 8

Coping with Vulnerability: Civil War Avoidance in Guinea 1984–2010

Mamadou Diouma Bah

Abstract

Guinea exhibits many of the major risk factors commonly associated with the onset of civil war and/or armed conflicts, including deep ethnic divisions; a politicized military; an abundance of natural resources alongside extreme poverty; and being located in a conflict ridden neighborhood. Yet, the constant presence of these violent risk variables has failed to ignite a broader conflict or to destabilize the central power structure of the state, therefore sparing the nation from the types of armed conflicts often associated with similar contexts in many West African nations. This chapter identifies mitigating factors against the onset of large-scale violence in such contexts and explains why Guinea has been spared from civil war despite these unfavorable conditions for peace. The chapter reveals that the presence of such violent conflict risk variables in Guinea failed to be associated with the onset of large-scale violence in the country largely due to measures taken by the Guinean state and its international partners. This outcome contrasts with much literature on the incidence of armed conflicts in such contexts.

> Guinea almost slid into the kind of civil war that plagued almost all of its neighbours ... yet managed several times to pull back from the brink. (Macgovern 2012: 235)

Introduction

In this chapter I discuss why the existence of significant opportunities for large-scale violence did not turn into civil war in Guinea. In recent years, a number of countries in the region of West Africa have succumbed to civil wars. The causes of these wars have been attributed to deep ethnic divisions, a politicized military, an abundance of natural resources alongside extreme poverty, and also simply being located in a conflict ridden neighborhood (Collier and Hoeffler 1998; Collier and Hoeffler 2004; Collier 2000; Fearon and Laitin 2003; Sambanis 2004a; Ross 2003; Zartman 1995; Ellis 1999; Utas 2003; Abdullah 1998; Keen 2005; McGovern 2011). The Republic of Guinea has exhibited many of these causes and factors, but the country has avoided falling into a civil war. In many respects, Guinea resembles its West African neighbors that have had civil wars. The country is endowed with large amounts of mineral resources, alongside the abject poverty of its population, which is deeply divided along clear ethno-regional affiliations. Guinea has also been under military dictatorship for nearly three decades. Similarly, during the 1990s, the outbreak of civil wars in its neighboring countries was added to Guinea's recurrent and violent domestic unrest—such as communal clashes and state repression—involving the armed forces. Each of these conditions should have encouraged rebellion and civil war, yet the situation in Guinea did not translate into civil war. More importantly, the frequent unrest in the country has not involved rebel groups fighting for secession or to dislodge the government, and therefore did not result in significant casualties on the government side. By all measures then, Guinea has not had a civil war since independence. So, we need to ask why Guinea has been spared from civil war.

A Definition of Civil War

Here I adopt the definition of civil war as those armed conflicts which are "fought by well-organized groups with political agendas, challenging the sovereign authority, and [where] violence was reciprocal" (Sambanis 2004b: 820). This means that in order for an armed conflict to be considered a civil war, the conflict must be: (1) an organized armed conflict; (2) that has challenged the sovereignty of an internationally recognized state; (3) which occurred within the recognized boundaries of that state; (4) that involved rebel elements consisting wholly or mainly of nationals of the state; (5) with a clearly articulated political agenda; and, (6) over 1000 people (civilians and combatants) have lost their lives (Souaré 2006: 28; Elbadawi and Sambanis 2000: 247–8). As such, in this chapter the terms armed conflict and civil war apply to a situation where armed forces are used between two parties, of which at least one is the government of a state that involves organized armed groups that are able to mount sustained resistance against the state with local recruitment, and a clearly articulated political agenda. These characteristics exclude other forms of violence, such as coups, communal violence, political repression, massacre, crime and cross-border attacks (Blattman and Miguel 2010: 6). This definition is particularly important for this study, since in a number of incidences, as discussed later, Guinea has had its fair share of violent conflicts, such as attempted coup d'état, communal violence, political repression, and cross-border attacks, with varied numbers of fatalities, nevertheless, none of them can be classified as civil war. This differentiation is particularly relevant to this study's assertion that Guinea is the exception to the rest of its West African neighbors in escaping civil war. The following section discusses some of the relevant literature on the causes of armed conflicts in West Africa and places Guinea's exception in this regional context.

Ethnic Rivalry

A significant body of literature maintains that civil wars are often the feature of countries with deep ethnic divisions (Montalvo and Reynal-Querol 2005: 796; Guelke 2012: 33). A society is described as deeply ethnically divided if it is "both ethnically diverse and where ethnicity is a politically salient cleavage around which interests are organized for political purpose" (Reilly 2001: 4); and if "ethnic divisions [are] severe enough to threaten the very existence or nature of the state" (O'Flynn 2010: 281). Ellingsen (2000) found that countries with fewer "groups (3–4) have higher risk of civil conflict than countries with many groups (5 or more)" (p. 241). In particular, where two groups are comparable in size, Horowitz (1985) found that the frequency of ethnic conflict was greater. This view is echoed by others whose findings demonstrate that deep ethnic divisions put a nation at "a higher risk of suffering a civil war" (Reynal-Querol 2002: 30). In fact, there is a general agreement that countries with fewer ethnic groups are more prone to armed conflicts than highly diverse societies (Elbadawi and Sambanis 2000: 10; Nordlinger 1972: 6–7; Lustick 1979: 325; Peleg 2004: 7–9; Guelke 2012: 20).

The situation in Guinea fits well into the above description of ethno-regional affiliations. The country is divided into four major geographical regions whereby each region is dominated by a major ethno-linguistic grouping (see Counsel 2009; O'Toole 1978: xvii; Person 1971: 272; Rivière 1977: 27). Lower Guinea is inhabited mainly by the Soussou ethnic group who represent around 15 percent of the population. In Middle Guinea, the Fulani people are the dominant ethnic group and represent around 40 percent of Guinea's population. Upper Guinea is predominantly inhabited by the ethnic Manlinké who constitute around 30 percent of Guineans. In the Forest Region, the Guerzé, Toma and Kissi constitute three very different linguistic groups but are bound together by their regional affiliations and represent around 10 percent of the population. In addition to these major ethno-linguistic groups, a number of other minor ethnic groups exist in Guinea but without distinctive geographical domination (see O'Toole 1978: xix). This type of ethnic composition whereby ethnic groups are few in number but large in size, has put Guinea among those nations categorized as having deep ethnic divisions and is thereby vulnerable to large-scale violence. This vulnerability to armed conflict was exacerbated by the introduction of multiparty politics in the early 1990s that produced a system whereby political parties were mainly based on ethnic and/or regional affiliations (Groelsema 1998a; 1998b; International Crisis Group 2011; Philipps 2013; Smith 2013; Arieff and McGovern 2013). According to Horowitz such situations are strongly linked with the onset of ethnically motivated armed conflicts (1985: 291–332).

Politicized Military

Similar to ethnic divisions, recent literature has identified a strong relationship between military intervention in politics and armed conflicts in West Africa (McGowan 2006; Collier 2007; 2009). Evidence shows that coups—whether successful or otherwise—often trigger counter-coups, military factionalism, ethnic polarization, chaotic politics, and communal violence in West African nations (Collier and Hoeffler 2005: 3). In fact, there is a cyclical relation between coups and armed conflicts in West Africa. Just as coups have been principal triggers of a number of West African civil wars in recent decades, in several other instances coups have been triggered by armed conflicts in the region (McGowan 2006: 247; Baégas and Marshal-Fratani 2007: 81–111). In Guinea, the military has been an important political actor in the country's history, being at the heart of Guinean politics for more than a quarter of a century. It helped usher Lansana Conté to the presidency after the sudden death of President Ahmad Sékou Touré in 1984. In the following decades, the military establishment gradually entrenched itself in the political, economic, and legal systems of the country (Bah 2015: 75–85). It formally ceded power in 2010 after enormous domestic and international pressure following a violent suppression of a pro-democratic rally in September 2009 that claimed many civilian lives (Counsel 2010). As discussed above, such entrenchment of the military in politics has often been associated with the outbreak of large scale violence in a number of West African nations. Yet, despite the protracted military involvement in Guinean politics, the country did not experience large-scale armed conflicts.

Duality of Poverty and Wealth

Beside ethnic rivalry and militarized politics, a body of research links recent civil wars in West Africa with the availability of abundant natural resources, combined with extreme poverty (Zartman 1995; Sambanis 2004; Reno 1995; Abdullah 1998: 206; Boås 2001: 721). A number of scholars suggest that the availability of these resources tends to weaken the state because it relies on revenue derived from primary commodity exports of these resources, and neglects investment in other sectors of the economy (Fearon and Laitin 2003; Humphreys 2005; Ross 1999, 2003). In addition, some research concludes that an abundance of natural resources provides both motivation and opportunity for armed rebellion (Collier and Hoeffler 1998, 2004; Collier 2000). Guinea possesses mineral deposits of bauxite, gold, diamond and iron ore that puts it among the resource-rich countries in Africa (World Bank 1990a; Campbell and Clapp 1995; Keefe 2013). Ironically, many reports of Guinea's economic potential are often contrasted with the poverty and misery of most Guineans (United Nations Development Programme [UNDP] 1992; 1993; 1994; 1996; 2009; 2013; Tinti 2013). According to the International Crisis Group (2007), "the depth of poverty [and] the dilapidation of the infrastructure … makes the country look like it has just emerged from a civil war'" (p. 5). Thus, in the last few decades "Guinea has remained at the bottom twenty of the least developed countries in the World" (Soumah 2007: 183). As discussed above, the presence of abundant natural resources alongside extreme poverty makes for a dangerous combination that often leads to large-scale violent civil conflicts. Yet, despite this seemingly toxic combination in Guinea, the state has managed to avoid large-scale civil violence.

The Spill-Over Effect

Akin to the point made above, what is now known as "bad neighborhood effects" has been linked with armed conflicts in West Africa (Bøås 2001; International Crisis Group 2002). In the early 1980s, within the Cold War context, Most and Star (1980: 932) highlighted the theoretical importance of the diffusion approach, that is, war contagion across borders as a new phenomenon in international relations. By the early 1990s the debate had narrowed on the term "bad neighborhood effect" and became associated with the idea that geographic proximity to armed conflicts increases vulnerability to an outbreak of civil wars through spillover effects (Fearon and Laitin 2003; Iqbal and Starr 2008: 318). As such, the outbreak of civil wars in Guinea's neighboring countries during the last two decades of President Conté's rule (1989–2008), led observers to suggest that all the pieces were in place for an onset of a large-scale-war in the country (Gberie 2001;

Kaplan 1994; Sawyer 2004; Silberfein and Conteh 2006). During this period each of Guinea's immediate six neighbors (Mali, Senegal, Liberia, Sierra Leone, Guinea Bissau and Ivory Coast) have all experienced civil wars. This begs the question of why Guinea did not descend into civil war? The remainder of the discussion addresses this question through the demonstration of how a model based on the analysis of: an ethic minority president; a selective redistribution mechanism and; an external conflict and internal cohesion, provides the explanation of why Guinea has been spared from civil war.

Political Stability of an Ethnic Minority President

The link between politics and ethnicity in Guinea since 1984 evinces a mixture of primordial and instrumental features of ethnic identity. Scholars that focus on the primordial features emphasize the immutable cultural character of ethnic identity (Isaacs 1975: 28, 30, 33; Hameso 1997: 33; Smith 1983; Keyes 1981: 5–6: Zirker, Danopoulos and Simpson 2008: 333; Barth 1969) and its destructive tendency when confronted with civil sentiments (Zirker et al. 2008: 334; Young 1993: 22). In contrast, those that focus on instrumental features emphasize the material interpretation of ethnic identity (Barrington 2006: 14; Rothschild 1981: 2; Olzak and Nagel 1986: 1–14) and its potential for constructive competition among groups within the state. The following discussion examines the political circumstances under which both tendencies have flourished in Guinea since 1984 and its resultant relative stability.

Although noted scholars have argued that the rule of a demographic minority in deeply divided societies tends to lead to large-scale violence (Gellner 1983: 1; Cederman and Girardin 2007: 176; Fearon, Kasara and Laitin 2007: 187), in Guinea this outcome was avoided during President Conté's rule (1984–2008). In fact, the ethnic minority factor of President Conté can be said to have dissuaded opposition groups from initiating a violent overthrow of his regime. This situation can be attributed to: (1) the strong primordial attachment of Guinea's two largest ethnic groups, the Fulanis and the Malinkés, to their ethnicity which prevented them from political compromises among themselves and; (2) President Conté's inability to rely on his own minority, ethnic Sossou, to dominate the main opposition groups, thereby leading him to a more *inclusive* approach to ethnicity and politics.

Colonel Lansana Conté came to power on April 3, 1984 in a bloodless military take-over after the sudden death of President Sékou Touré a few weeks earlier. One of the significant results of the 1984 military coup—in terms of ethnic relations in Guinea—was the change of the president's ethnicity from Malinké to Soussou. Unlike his predecessor, who was from the Malinké ethnic group, which constituted Guinea's second largest ethnic group, President Conté was a Soussou, whose ethnic group represented a small minority of the population. Considering this situation, President Conté had to maintain a delicate ethnic balance. The first major challenge to President Conté's rule, which could have degenerated into a major ethnic conflict, came in July 1985. Colonel Diarra Traoré, the Prime Minister after the 1984 military coup, was demoted to minister of education in December of the same year. In July of the following year, Traoré staged a failed military coup. Both Traoré and former President Touré were of Malinké origin, therefore the coup was seen by some Guineans as an attempt on the part of the Malinkés "to re-establish their dominance lost with the passing of Sékou Touré" (Schissel 1986: 22). The coup therefore "unleashed a susu [Soussou] looting spree of Malinké shops, and harassment of Malinkés living in Conakry" (Groelsema 1998a: 11) and other towns. Initially, President Conté "welcomed the ethnically targeted attacks" on Malinké owned shops and businesses in a speech delivered in his native Soussou language "in an expression that became famous in Guinea, 'Wofatara,' which means 'well done'" in Soussou (International Crisis Group 2007: 3). Nevertheless, the government tried to downplay the ethnic nexus behind the coup by placing the blame on "Traoré's ruthless quest for power" (Schissel 1986: 22), therefore suggesting a leadership struggle between Conté and Traoré rather than "a clash between Soussou and Malinké ethnic groups" (Masayuki 2009: 10).

Similarly, the introduction of multiparty politics in the early 1990s significantly increased Guinea's vulnerability to civil war. In 1990, Guinea introduced the first example of political pluralism since independence by holding a national referendum to adopt a new constitution. As a result, a multi-party electoral system was established, resulting in the 1993 presidential election and the subsequent local, municipal and legislative elections. However, with the introduction of political pluralism, ethnic politics became a focal point in Guinea. This new process of multiparty politics moved the country "toward a politics of identity" which was led by "parties imagined by many of their supporters as representing the ethnic group" they belonged to (International Crisis Group 2007: 1). Consequently, as the democratic process goes on, "ethnic identity became a principal source of conflict" turning elections into ethnic contests (Groelsema 1998a: 14–15).

During the electoral campaign, the Malinkés "reflected their perception of Malinké claims [of] their right to political domination on the basis of historical events and processes" (Groelsema 1998b: 418). As a result, the Malinké based political party, Rassemblement du Peuple de Guinee (RPG), led by Alpha Condé dominated the Upper Guinea region. The Fulanis made a similar cultural and historical claim of their right for political domination in the country. Thus, the Fulani based political parties, the Union pour la Nouvelle République (UNR) led by Mamadou Ba and the Party du Renouveau et Progrès (PRP) led by Siradiou Diallo, largely dominated Middle Guinea. Because of this primordial attachment, "opposition parties failed to form a lasting alliance" (Groelsema 1998a: 17) thereby allowing the ruling Parti de l'Unité et du Progrès (PUP) led by President Conté, to strengthen its hold on power. One analyst states that the behavior of the opposition in Guinea

> had less to do with personal rivalry than ethnic difference. Leaders and parties became captives of their ethnic constituencies. The intellectual and cultural underpinnings of Peulh [Fulani] and Malinké worldviews precluded compromise with each other. Acting upon history and traditions, their cultural leaders and ethnic politicians orchestrated the marriage between culture and politics, excluding outsider identification with party and group goals (Groelsema 1998a: 18).

This culturally based impediment of electoral alliances which could have been advantageous to the opposition can be explained by the primordial attachment of the Malinké and the Fulani to their ethnic groups. The political behavior of the Fulanis and Malinkés drew "from a deep cultural reservoir of symbols and myths anchored in history" (Groelsema 1998a: 40) which left the two groups "unable to resolve [their] immutable and irreconcilable differences" (Groelsema 1998a: 33). According to a recent study, "political coalitions on issues that cut across the main societal divide" (Guelke 2012: 29) are a rare commodity in deeply divided societies. Thus, from the primordialist standpoint, such a situation often leads to "destructive competition among ethnic groups" (Nnoli 1995: 3) giving rise to violent political struggle.

In contrast, President Conté's instrumental approach to ethnicity mitigated this danger by drawing support from both the Malinké and the Fulani, and from the "less cohesive Foresters [who] lacked the raw materials for political mobilization" based on cultural affiliation (Groelsema 1998a: 41). In an apparent attempt to win Foresters' support in the 1993 elections, President Conté deliberately evoked their identity against the Malinké community in N'zérékoré (Bah 2014b: 58), therefore reinforcing his instrumental approach to ethnicity. A long and violent history of ethnic tension exists between the two groups which originated at the end of the nineteenth century (Bybee 2013). Back then, the French colonial authorities used the Malinké ethnic group as "allies in their colonial project and granted them access to strategic posts in the area, drawing a fierce reaction from other communities in the region" (*IRIN* 2005: 18). This historical animosity between the Malinkés and Foresters was often utilized by President Conté's regime in order to consolidate power in a context where primordial attachments among the larger ethnic groups—the Fulani and the Malinké—dominated.

As mentioned above, President Conté was from the minority Soussou ethnic group which represents only 15 percent of the population and therefore he seemed unlikely to be able to rely on his own ethnic Soussou to dominate the main opposition groups, the Fulanis 40 percent and the Malinkés 35 percent. This situation led President Conté to a degree of political inclusiveness, therefore reinforcing Conté's appeal as a unifying figure (Bah 2014b: 59). Equally important was the fact that the Fulanis and the Malinkés were locked in a primordial competition for power since independence which prevented them from political compromises among themselves. At the same time, the two groups were nearly matched in number and probably resources so that the outcome of any attempt for the violent removal of President Conté was uncertain. As such, both groups seemed to have settled with the demographically minority president whose ethnic group was less likely to be able to perpetually dominate the state and threaten any of the two groups' long term vital interests.

A Political Stability of Selective Redistribution

The dichotomy of wealth and poverty, existing alongside a relative peace and political stability in Guinea, owes much to the existence of a centralized rent-seeking and selective redistribution system. Under this system, resource revenues have often been distributed among a relatively small group of elites as a strategy for maintaining stability by accommodating potential political rivals. Studies show that the system of selective redistribution often enables governments in natural resource rich countries to spend revenue from abundant natural resources to buy off opposition in order to dissuade armed rebellion (Basedau and Lay 2009: 762; Le Billon 2003: 416; Fjelde 2009; Johnston 1986). Accordingly, successive Guinean regimes have been able to use selective redistribution as a mechanism for maintaining political stability by channeling resources from revenues of bauxite, diamonds and other minerals to a small circle of elites (Bah 2014a).

During President Conté's rule, Guinea's selective redistribution system consisted mainly of a primary and a secondary group. The primary group was composed of a small host of individuals close to the presidency, also known as the presidential entourage. Membership of this group was comprised of powerful ministers, higher echelons of the military hierarchy, the presidential guards and those business people close to the Presidency. A study put the total number of this group at no more than 120 people in any given time (Picarda and Moudoud 2010: 59). In contrast, the secondary group is the patronage network that, according to Picarda and Moudoud, "may incorporate as many as 3500 middle-level administrators, military officers and private-sector businessmen" (2010: 59), and according to Bah "other privileged sections of the population, including religious leaders and tribal dynastic families" (2014b: 163). The two groups monopolized much of the import and export businesses, non-competitive state contracts, tax exemptions and other favors, thereby giving them "a stranglehold on the economy" (International Crisis Group 2005: 13).

Despite the fact that these two groups constituted a small portion of the population, individuals in both groups had their own networks through which the resources that were channeled to them from above could trickle down in order to ensure loyalty from below and maintain the system's cohesion (Bah 2014b: 163). For instance, a degree of loyalty was often maintained in the military by rewarding high-ranking officers with business opportunities and/or lucrative contracts which "through the military clientele system these benefits trickle[d] down to both [lower-ranking] officers and ordinary soldiers in a way that ensures their loyalty to their superiors and to the political elites" (Bah 2015: 80). Available sources indicate that President Conté often settled "problems or tensions within the armed forces [by immediate] promotions of all serving personnel" (International Crisis Group 2010: 8). This unregulated promotion resulted in disproportionate number of officers compared with the numbers of common soldiers yet, its accompanying benefits ensured the officers' loyalty to the regime (Bah 2014b: 89).

A recent study describes the privileges and favors guaranteed to this group as "monumental" in their scale (International Crisis Group 2005: 12), including, for instance, "a plush villa and a share in rackets worth up to $50,000 a month" for the lucky holder of a post in Guinea's presidential guard (Samb 2011), and access to "non-competitive state contracts and tax exemptions" for business people closely associated with the presidency (Bah 2014b: 121). The mining sector was particularly singled out as an area where lack of transparency appears to have contributed immensely to a large-scale corruption. Contracts between the government and investors in this sector were often secret. Therefore, it was difficult to know the details of contracts and to hold officials accountable (Bah 2014b: 122). In an interview in 2006, President Conté admitted that the mining sector was the most corrupt area of the Guinean economy, where the politico-military-business elites enrich themselves at the expense of the larger population (Michel 2006). This was a staggering admission from the chief executive of the country, yet, the system of selective redistribution of mineral and state rents remained intact and served to strengthen the relationship between Conté's semi-military regime and the politico-business elites vis-à-vis domestic and external destabilizing forces. Thus, through the passage of time, the maintenance of this relationship became of mutual concern to both entities. As such, when Guinea became a victim of a series of coordinated armed attacks from rebels backed by Liberia and Sierra Leone between 2000 and 2001, "the Guinean business class created a war fund" to support the government (Gbaydee Doe 2003: 154). This was in sharp contrast with what happened in Liberia and Sierra Leone, where business people and politicians saw "their respective wars" as opportunities to negotiate "profitable deals with rebels" thereby exacerbating the conflicts (Gbaydee Doe 2003: 154). On the contrary, the business class in Guinea has consistently been "reluctant to push conflict to the brink, recognizing they have the most to lose" (Smith 2013: 3). In short, a selective redistribution mechanism of mineral and other state revenues have spared the Guinean economy from total collapse, allowed for a degree of public services to be maintained, enabled President Conté's regime to keep most Guineans in extreme poverty, yet to avoid large-scale violent resistance.

External Conflict—Internal Cohesion

During the 1990s and 2000s, Guinea's surrounding regional instability provided opportunities for the consolidation of domestic peace. The aforementioned widespread incidences of wars in West Africa and the influx of refugees fleeing these conflicts provided the Guinean government the framework through which to emphasize the value of the country's stability against external and internal threats in a region marked by violent conflicts. This framing of external threats for domestic stability was aimed at both international and domestic audiences.

For the international community, Guinean officials presented the country as an "island of stability" (Kanafani 2006) in a region marked by instability, rogue regimes, transnational networks of domestic opponents, regional warlords, and foreign refugees (Jourde 2007:493). The state-owned radio was used to explain to its international audience that Guinea "more than any other regional country, has been harboring the greatest number of [refugees] and it is doing so with remarkable hospitality" (Radio diffusion nationale de Guinee, March 15, 1993 cited in Jourde 2007: 493). In a similar fashion in 2001, President Conté reassured visiting French and British officials of Guinea's determination to assist the refugees and encouraged them to support "Guinea's efforts to restore and consolidate peace and security in the sub-region" (Radio diffusion nationale de Guinee, April 19, 2001, cited in Jourde 2005: 493). This promotion of Guinea's stability as a necessary factor for resolving the sub-region's conflicts was meant to mobilize Western support for Guinea's stability, capitalizing on their concerns over the region's instability.

Apparently, the Guinean government's narrative found a positive response among western policy makers. A spokesperson from the US State Department stated that, "Guinea is one of Africa's most hospitable nations because it has hosted more than 500,000 refugees over the past decade" (Jourde 2005: 498). This view was echoed by the American ambassador to Guinea, Barrie Walkley, who reminded the Senate Foreign Relations Committee that "despite its security concerns, Guinea has been the primary haven for up to 700,000 refugees fleeing West Africa's brutal wars" (Jourde 2005: 498). Similarly, General Wilford, the head of an American delegation of military officers to Guinea in 2001, praised Guinea for its role "in strengthening peace and stability in the sub-region [and reaffirmed his] firm willingness to support Guinea's efforts in favor of security in West Africa" (Radio diffusion nationale de Guinee, August 29, 2001 cited in Jourde 2005: 498). The British Minister of Foreign Affairs, Clare Short, commended "General Lansana Conté and his government's actions towards the restoration and preservation of peace in the sub-region" (Radio diffusion nationale de Guinee, April 19, 2001, cited in Jourde 2005: 498).

For the domestic audience, the state controlled mass media continued broadcasting images of devastation and horror stories of civil wars in neighboring countries narrated by refugees. It also frequently depicted domestic political opponents as extremists aiming to destabilize the country in collaboration with regional rebel networks (Bah 2012). In the 2003 election campaign, which was boycotted by the opposition, the President explained to the people that the opposition refused to participate in the electoral process because "they want to take over [power] by other means [and that their aim is] to see disorder in Guinea just like in the neighboring countries" (Jourde 2005: 495). Similarly, the Guinean government often utilized domestic unrest, to mobilize support for internal stability by directly accusing the opposition of trying to import instability with the help of regional rebels and rogue regimes. On January 19, 2005, several armed men shot at President Conté's motorcade in Conakry, wounding a bodyguard. The attackers escaped and were never identified and their motives never revealed, yet the official statement referred to them as "those who receive orders from abroad" (International Crisis Group 2005: 22–3).

This framing of stability provided an opportunity for the government to attract foreign military assistance and justify increased spending on training, equipment and, armed forces' budgets. The fear that regional conflict might spread to Guinea, therefore creating another humanitarian crisis in the region, invoked the interest of major powers in the political stability of Guinea. This presented the Guinean government with opportunities to attract military aid from donor countries in order to prevent it collapsing from rebellions. The military aid sought by the Guinean government varied from training and equipment to cash to cover salary increases often demanded by the security forces (Bah 2012). In 1998, the US State Department and its Embassy in Guinea requested the US Special Operations Command to send "a Joint Combined Exchange Training Program (JCET) team to work with Guinean forces on military activities designed to protect the Guinean border" (Smith 2006: 434). As a result, a resident military attaché was assigned to the US Embassy in Conakry for the first time and the JCET was initiated. The US military sent a second training team in 2000, which provided basic training to Guinean forces in border security, small weapons, and martial arts. The total military training aid increased from USD$100,000 in 1998 to USD$300,000 in 2001. The US also increased its military support to Guinea in the aftermath of the September 2000 attacks on Guinean frontier villages, launching a program in 2001 to "train an 800-man ranger battalion over a 6-month period as a rapid reaction force" (Smith 2006: 434). As a result of this program, the Guinean army received vehicles, communications equipment and uniforms. According to Smith, the composition of the battalion was carefully chosen to include representatives from Guinea's different ethnic groups, and the Guinean government committed itself to maintain the battalion as an integrated unit (Smith 2006: 434). During the same time period, the Chinese government trained several hundred Guinean army commandos (Arieff 2009). Thus, due to the widespread of civil wars in Guinea's neighbors, the international community invested a lot of diplomatic time and economic aid in an effort to maintain stability in the country. More importantly, the Guinean government and its international partners paid particular attention to the strengthening of the Guinean armed forces through military aid and training in border control.

On the domestic front, the external threats provided the Guinean government with the basis for justifying the increased expenditure on the military, an excuse for the army's impunity and, the introduction of extra security measures. During the 1990s, the Guinean Army was estimated at around 9,700 soldiers (O'Toole 2005: 9–10). However, in the decade since 2001 the army saw a dramatic increase in its numbers, recently estimated as comprising around 45,000 soldiers (Human Rights Watch 2011: 50; International Crisis Group 2010: 15, 97) This rapid growth of the army was explained by the government in terms of the security threats posed by Guinea's neighboring civil wars in the 1990s and 2000s (Bah 2014a). There was a series of cross-border attacks on Guinea by Sierra Leonean rebels and Liberian government forces between 2000 and 2001 (Bah 2012). While the security threats of neighboring civil wars cannot be discounted, analysts argue that Guinea did not need a military of this size (Bah 2015). Yet, the threats of these wars were used to justify the increases of military expenditure, and therefore, the military was sized to support the large-scale military patronage of the regime (International Crisis Group 2010: 15; Arieff 2009: 340–42). In return, there was a non-written agreement between the ruling elites and the military establishment to preserve the system for the mutual benefits it provided the two entities, which led to a degree of stability despite the vulnerability of the system to armed conflict (Bah 2014b).

Similarly, the external threat provided an excuse for the army's bad behavior domestically. Recent studies of the Guinean armed forces conclude that brutality and impunity run deep in the armed forces' culture (Bah 2015: 82; International Crisis Group 2010: 16; Counsel 2010). According to International Crisis Group, the armed forces of Guinea "have a well-deserved reputation for human rights abuses, including suppressing opposition, torture and extra-judicial killings" (2010: 17). According to Human Rights Watch during Conté's era the army was "well protected: and not worried about any possibility of accountability measures" for their abuses (2011:14). The brutality of the armed forces against the civilian population was exacerbated by the military's formal return to power in the 2008 coup, when a political rally was violently repressed on September 28, 2009 by military forces resulting in 157 deaths of unarmed civilians and with over 1,700 injured (International Crisis Group 2009: 2; Counsel 2010: 109; Koko 2010: 103–4). Despite national and international pressure, successive Guinean governments have "failed to bring to justice even one member of the security forces credibly implicated in killings and other serious abuses" (Human Rights Watch 2009:14).

Following the election of Alpha Condé to the presidency in November 2010, Guinea embarked on a Security Sector Reform (SSR) program led by the Economic Community of West African States (ECOWAS) and supported by the UN, France and the European Union (EU). Since the programs started in 2011, some important measures have been taken, including the retirement of 3,928 troops (Gil 2013: 7). Optimists argue that the 2010 landmark democratic elections and the introduction of the SSR programs are clear indications that Guinea has turned toward democracy, with a subordinated military (Gil 2013: 7). There is no denial that the SSR programs are a major step in the right direction towards military subordination to civilian rule in Guinea. Yet, despite this strong international support, reinforcing the army's capabilities whilst bringing it under civilian control have proven to be arduous tasks for the new democratic government. The attack on President Condé's residence in July 2011 (see Foucher 2011), and the fact that military officers are still holding key government offices, including ministerial posts, are stark reminders that the army still retains a great degree of economic power and political influence.

Likewise, the external threats enabled the Guinean government to justify extreme security measures. One of these measures is the introduction of roadblocks across the country. These roadblocks served both economic and security purposes. Economically, the extortion from roadblocks enriches the rank and file of security forces, informally supplementing their salaries (see McGovern 2011: 186). Roadblocks also served as a security guarantor for various regimes against potential rebellion from inside the country (International Crisis Group 2005: 15–16). Studies show that roadblocks in West Africa are often linked "to the proliferation of repressive state structures for putting down social movements, or undertaking shakedowns by police, gendarmes, militias and presidential guards" (Mbember 1990, quoted in McGovern 2011: 185).

Conclusion

The central objective of this chapter has been to investigate why Guinea has been spared from civil war despite the availability of significant opportunities for large scale violence to occur. The chapter discussed ethnic rivalry; protracted military involvement in political affairs; natural resource abundance alongside extreme poverty; and the contagion of proximate conflicts as significant causes of recent West African civil wars. The chapter reveals that a model based on the analysis of: an ethically minority president; a selective redistribution mechanism and; an external conflict and internal cohesion, can best explain why Guinea has been spared from civil war.

It was revealed that in the period between 1984 and 2008 Guinea witnessed a change of presidents, and thereby a change in their respective ethnicities, presenting an additional risk of ethnically based armed conflicts. Nevertheless, this risk was largely mitigated. First, hailing from a small minority, incoming President Conté could not afford to alienate the larger ethnic groups and therefore adopted a rather more inclusive rule during his time in office. This degree of inclusiveness reduced the chances of ethnically based grievances against the regime from escalating to large-scale violence. Secondly, none of the larger ethnic groups, who constituted the main opposition group, perceived a serious threat to its interests from a president who hailed from a minority group. Therefore, due to their primordial rivalry and the uncertain outcome of an armed rebellion in deep ethnically divided societies, the opposition groups were unable and/or unwilling to mount an armed rebellion for the removal of President Conté. Yet, since 2008, political pluralism has been reintroduced in Guinea and primordial attachments to ethnic politics have dramatically increased, resulting in significant election related violence. Thus, the question of whether deep ethnic divisions will lead Guinea to the kind of armed conflicts that ravaged most of Guinea's neighbors in recent decades or towards sustained stability remains open-ended, but the answer is likely to depend on how ethnicity is used and/or misused by the political elites.

The adoption of a selective redistribution mechanism of revenues from Guinea's vast natural resources contributed towards a degree of political stability, thereby mitigating against the onset of armed conflicts in the country. Nevertheless, it also perpetuated a politico-economic system where enormous inequality prevailed, keeping most Guineans under abject poverty. Thus, with the reintroduction of political pluralism in the early 2010s, it is less likely that political stability can be sustained unless Guineans receive a greater share of the country's natural resources than they used to from previous regimes.

Likewise, it was found that the Guinean government was able to use the outbreak of civil wars in neighboring countries and the subsequent influx of refugees fleeing from these wars, to frame stability as a narrative of what constituted a threat to regional security and the importance of Guinea's stability in mitigating such threats. This Guinean narrative of peace and conflict in the West African region was successfully *sold* to the domestic audience and to Guinea's international partners, resulting in the strengthening of the national armed forces' capacity. As such, the Guinean armed forces were well trained, equipped and compensated. They were able to deter internal rebellion and to secure the country's border against the spread of neighboring wars. These findings lead to the conclusion that the combined efforts of the Guinean state and its international partners worked against the onset of civil war in the country despite the unfavorable conditions for such outcome.

References

Abdullah, I. (1998). Bush Path to Destruction: The Origin and Character of the Revolutionary United Front/ Sierra Leone. *The Journal of Modern African Studies*, 36(2): 203–35.

Arieff, A. and McGovern, M. (2013). History is Stubborn: Talk about Truth, Justice, and National Reconciliation in the Republic of Guinea. *Comparative Studies in Society and History*, 55(1): 198–225.

Arieff, A. (2009). Still Standing: Neighbourhood Wars and Political Stability in Guinea. *Journal of Modern African Studies*, 47(3): 331–48.

Basedau, M. and Lay, J. (2009). Resource Curse or Rentier Peace? The Ambiguous Effects of Oil Wealth and Oil Dependence on Violent Conflict. *Journal of Peace Research*, 46(6): 757–76.

Bah, M.D. (2015). The Military and Politics in Guinea: An Instrumental Explanation of Political Stability. *Armed Forces & Society*, 41(1): 69–95.

Bah, M.D. (2014a). Mining for Peace: Diamonds, Bauxite, Iron-ore and Political Stability in Guinea. *Review of African Political Economy*, 41(142): 500–515.

Bah, M.D. (2014b). Coping with Vulnerability: State Resilience to Armed Conflict in Guinea. PhD dissertation, The University of Waikato.

Bah, M.D. (2012). State Resilience in Guinea: Mitigating the "Bad Neighbourhood Effect" of Civil War Next Door. *The Australasian Review of African Studies*, 33(1): 13–33.

Baégas, R. and Marshal-Fratani, R. (2007). Côte d'Ivoire: Negotiating Identity and Citizenship. In M. Boas and K.C. Dunn (eds), *African Guerrillas, Raging against the* Machine. London: Lynne Rienner, 81–111.

Blattman, C. and Miguel, E. (2010). Civil War. *Journal of Economic Literature*, 48(1): 3–57.

Barrington, L. (2006). *After Independence*. Ann Arbor: University of Michigan Press.

Barth, F. (1969). Ethnic groups and boundaries. In F. Barth (ed.), *Ethnic Groups and Boundaries*. Boston: Little, Brown and Company, 9–38.

BBC (2009). Guinea calls for unity government, September 30, http://news.bbc.co.uk/2/hi/africa/8284128.stm.

Bermúdez-Lugo, O. (2004). The Mineral Industry of Guinea. *Minerals Yearbook 2004*. United States Geological Survey.

Bøås, M. (2001). Liberia and Sierra Leone: Dead Ringers? The Logic of Neo-patrimonial Rule. *Third World Quarterly*, 22(5): 697–723.

Bybee, A. (2013). Encouraging Developments to Ease Guinea's Political Paralysis? *Africa Watch*, 1 (August 1), https://www.ida.org/upload/africawatch/africawatch-aug-1-2013-vol1.pdf.

Campbell, B. and Clapp J. (1995). Guinea's Economic Performance under Structural Adjustment: Importance of Mining and Agriculture. *The Journal of Modern African Studies*, 33(3): 425–49.

Cederman, Land Girardin L. (2007). Beyond Fractionalization: Mapping Ethnicity onto Nationalist Insurgencies. *The American Political Science Review*, 101(1): 173–85.

Collier, P. (2000). Rebellion as a Quasi-criminal Activity. *Journal of Conflict Resolution*, 44(6): 839–53.

Collier, P. and Hoeffler, A. (1998). On Economic Causes of Civil War. *Oxford Economic Papers*, 50(14): 563–73.

Collier, P. and Hoeffler, A. (2004). Greed and Grievance in Civil War. *Oxford Economic Papers*, 56(4): 563–96.

Collier, P. (2007). *The Bottom Billion, Why the Poorest Countries are Failing and What Can Be Done About It*. Oxford: Oxford University Press.

Collier, P. (2009). *Wars, Guns and Votes: Democracy in Dangerous Places*. London: Vintage.

Collier, P and Hoeffler, A. (2005) *Coup Traps: Why Does Africa Have So Many Coups D'etat?* Centre for the Study of African Economies, Department of Economics, University of Oxford.

Counsel, G. (2010). Music for a Coup "Armee Guineenne": An Overview of Guinea's Recent Political Turmoil. *The Australasian Review of African Studies*, 31(2): 94–112.

Elbadawi, I. and Sambanis, N. (2000). Why Are There So Many Civil Wars in Africa? Understanding and Preventing Violent Conflict. *Journal of African Economies*, 9(3): 244–69.

Ellingsen, T. (2000). Colorful Community or Ethnic Witches' Brew? Multiethnicity and Domestic Conflict during and after the Cold War. *Journal of Conflict Resolution*, 44(2): 228–49.

Ellis, S. (1999). *The Mask of Anarchy: The Destruction of Liberia and the Religious Dimension of an African Civil War*. London: C. Hurst & Co. Ltd.

Fjelde, H. (2009). Buying Peace? Oil Wealth, Corruption and Civil War, 1985–99. *Journal of Peace Research*, 46(2): 199–218.

Fearon, J. and Laitin, D. (2003). Ethnicity, Insurgency, and Civil War. *American Political Science Review*, 97(1): 75–90.

Fearon, J., Kasara, K., and Laitin, D. (2007). Ethnic Minority Rule and Civil War Onset. *American Political Science Review*, 101(1): 187–93.

Gbaydee Doe, S. (2003). Preventive Peacebuilding in the Republic of Guinea: Building Peace by Cultivating the Positives. In Cynthia Sampson, M. Abu-Nimer, C. Liebler, and D. Whitney (eds), *Positive Approaches to Peacebuilding: A Resource for Innovators*. Washington DC: Pact Publications, 147–67.

Gberie, L. (2001). *Destabilizing Guinea: Diamonds, Charles Taylor and the Potential for a Wider Human Catastrophe*. Partnership Africa-Canada. The Diamond and Human Security Project, Occasional Paper No. 1.

Gellner, E. (1983). *Nations and Nationalism*. Ithaca, NY: Cornell University Press.

Gil, M.M. (2013). The Democratic Transition in Guinea reaches a Critical Point. *European Parliament Policy briefing*. DG EXPO/B/PolDep/Note/2013_160, June, http://www.europarl.europa.eu/RegData/etudes/briefing_note/join/2013/491507/EXPO-DEVE_SP%282013%29491507_EN.pdf.

Guelke, A. (2012). *Politics in Deeply Divided Societies*. Cambridge: Polity Press.

Groelsema, R.J. (1998b). The Dialectics of Citizenship and Ethnicity in Guinea. *Africa Today*, 45(3/4): 411–22.

Groelsema, R.J. (1998a). The Politics of Ethnicity: The Cultural Basis of Political Parties in Guinea. PhD dissertation, Indiana University.

Hameso, S. (1997). *Ethnicity and Nationalism in Africa*. New York: Nova Science Publishers.

Horowitz, D.L. (1985). *Ethnic Groups in Conflict*. Berkeley: University of California Press.

Human Rights Watch (2011). "We Have Lived in Darkness": A Human Rights Agenda for Guinea's New Government. Human Rights Watch, May 2011, http://www.hrw.org/sites/default/files/reports/guinea0511webwcover_1.pdf.

Human Rights Watch (2009). Guinea: Stadium Massacre, Rape Likely Crimes against Humanity. Human Rights Watch, December 17, http://www.hrw.org/news/2009/12/17/guinea-stadium-massacre-rape-likely-crimes-against-humanity.

Humphreys, M. (2005). Natural Resources, Conflict, and Conflict Resolution: Uncovering the Mechanisms. *Journal of Conflict Resolution*, 49(4): 508–37.

International Crisis Group (2010). Guinea: reforming the army. *Africa Report*, September 23, 164: http://www.crisisgroup.org/en/regions/africa/west-africa/guinea/164-guinea-reforming-the-army.aspx.

International Crisis Group (2011). Guinea: Putting the transition back on track. *Africa Report*, September 23, 178: http://www.crisisgroup.org/en/regions/africa/west-africa/guinea/178-guinea-putting-the-transition-back-on-track.aspx.

International Crisis Group (2003). Tackling Liberia: The Eye of the Regional Storm. *Africa Report*, April 30, 62: http://www.crisisgroup.org/en/regions/africa/west-africa/liberia/062-tackling-liberia-the-eye-of-the-regional-storm.aspx.

International Crisis Group. (2009). Guinea: Military Rule Must End. *International Crisis Group Policy Briefing: Africa Briefing*. Dakar/Brussels, October 16, 66: http://www.crisisgroup.org/~/media/Files/africa/west-africa/guinea/B066%20Guinea%20Military%20Rule%20Must%20End.pdf.

International Crisis Group. (2005). Stopping Guinea's Slide. *Africa Report*, June 14, 94: http://www.crisisgroup.org/~/media/Files/africa/west-africa/guinea/Stopping%20Guineas%20Slide.pdf.

International Crisis Group. (2007). Guinea: Change or Chaos. *Africa Report*, February 14, 121: http://www.crisisgroup.org/en/regions/africa/west-africa/guinea/121-guinea-change-or-chaos.aspx.

Isaacs, H.R. (1975). *Idols of Tribes: Group Identity and Political Change*. New York: Harper & Row.

Iqbal, Z. and Starr, H. (2008). Bad Neighbours: Failed States and Their Consequences. *Conflict Management and Peace Science*, 25(4): 315–31.

IRIN (2005). Guinea: Living on the edge. *IRIN Web special*, January, http://www.irinnews.org/pdf/in-depth/guinea-living-on-the-edge-irin-in-depth.pdf.

Johnston, M. (1986). The Political Consequences of Corruption. A Reassessment. *Comparative Politics*, 18(4): 459–77.

Jourde, C. (2007). The International Relations of Small Neo-authoritarian States: Islamism, Warlordism, and the Framing of Stability. *International Studies Quarterly*, 51(2): 481–503.

Kanafani, Sarah Birgitta. (2006). Guinea: An Island of Stability? *Georgetown Journal of International Affairs*, 7(1): 153–9.

Kaplan, R.D. (1994). The Coming Anarchy: How Scarcity, Crime, Overpopulation and Diseases are Rapidly Destroying the Social Fabric of Our Planet. *The Atlantic Monthly*. 273(2): 44–76.

Keefe, P.R. (2013). Buried Secrets. *The New Yorker*. July 8, http://www.newyorker.com/magazine/2013/07/08/buried-secrets?currentPage=all&goback=.gde_1520727_member_256292429.

Keen, D. (2005). *Conflict and Collusion in Sierra Leone*. Oxford: James Currey/Palgrave Macmillan.

Keyes, C.F. (1981). Ethnic Change. In C.F. Keyes (ed.), *Ethnic Change*. Seattle: University of Washington Press, 3–30.

Koko, Sadiki. 2010). Challenges for a Return to Civilian Rule in Guinea. *African Security Review*, 19(1): 101–7.

Le Billon, P. (2003). Buying Peace or Fuelling War: The Role of Corruption in Armed Conflicts. *Journal of International Development*, 15(4): 413–26.

Lustick, I. (1997). Stability in Deeply Divided Societies: Consociationalism versus Control. *World Politics*, 31(3): 325–44.

Mbember, A. (1990). Pouvoir, violence et accumulation. *Politique Africaine*, 39: 7–24 (L'Afrique Autrement, 1990).

Masayuki, K. (2009). *Ethnic Favoritism: Micro Evidence from Guinea* (July 28). http://ssrn.com/abstract=1440303 or http://dx.doi.org/10.2139/ssrn.1440303.

McGovern, M. (2012). *Unmasking the State: Making Guinea Modern*. Chicago and London: The University of Chicago Press.

McGovern, M. (2011). *Making War in Côte d'Ivoire*. London: Hurst & Co. Ltd.

McGowan, P.J. (2006). Coups and Conflict in West Africa, 1955–2004: Part II, Empirical Findings. *Armed Forces & Society*, 32(2): 234–53.

Michel, S. (2006). Le vieux président et les voleurs. *Le Monde* (November 30). http://www.lemonde.fr/a-la-une/article/2006/11/30/guinee-le-vieux-president-et-les-voleurs_840337_3208.html.

Montalvo, J.G and Reynal-Querol, M. (2005). Ethnic Polarization, Potential Conflict, and Civil Wars. *The American Economic Review*. 95(3): 796–816.

Nnoli, O. (1995). *Ethnicity and Development in Nigeria*. Aldershot: Avebury.

Nordlinger, E. (1972). *Conflict Regulation in Divided Societies*. Cambridge, MA: Center for International Affairs, Harvard University.

Olzak, S., and Nagel, J. (1986). Introduction, Competitive Ethnic Relations: An Overview. In S. Olzak and J. Nagel (eds), *Competitive Ethnic Relations*. New York: Academic Press, 1–14.

O'Flynn, I. (2010). Democratic Theory and Practice in Deeply Divided Societies. *Representation*, 46(3): 281–93.

O'Toole, T.E. (2005). *Historical Dictionary of Guinea*. Metuchen, NJ: Scarecrow Press.

Peleg, I. (2004). Transforming Ethnic Orders into Pluralist Regimes: Theoretical, Comparative and Historical Analysis. In A. Guelke (ed.), *Democracy and Ethnic Conflict: Advancing Peace in Deeply Divided Societies*. New York: Palgrave Macmillan, 7–25.

Philipps, J. (2013). *Ambivalent Rage: Youth Gangs and Urban Protest in Conakry Guinea*. Paris: L'Harmattan.

Picarda, L.A. and Moudoud, E. (2010). The 2008 Guinea Conakry Coup: Neither Inevitable nor Inexorable. *Journal of Contemporary African Studies*, 28(1): 51–69.

Reilly, B. (2001). *Democracy in Divided Societies: Electoral Engineering for Conflict Management*. Cambridge: Cambridge University Press.

Reynal-Querol, M. (2002). Ethnicity, Political Systems, and Civil Wars. *The Journal of Conflict Resolution*, 46(1): 29–54.

Reno, William. (1995). Reinvention of an African Patrimonial State: Charles Taylor's Liberia. *Third World Quarterly*, 16(1): 109–20.

Ross, M.L. (1999). The Political Economy of the Resource Curse. *World Politics*, 51(2): 297–322.

Ross, M.L. (2003). *Natural Resources and Civil War: An Overview*. UCLA Department of Political Science.

Rothschild, J. (1981). *Ethnopolitics: A Conceptual Framework*. New York: Colombia University Press.

Samb, S. (2011). End of the Good Life Stirs Discontent in Guinea's Army. *Reuters*, July 22, http://www.trust.org/item/?map=analysis-end-of-the-good-life-stirs-discontent-in-guineas-army/.

Sambanis, N. (2004a). Using Case Studies to Expand Economic Models of Civil War. *Perspectives on Politics*, 2(2): 259–79.

Sambanis, N. (2004b). What Is Civil War?: Conceptual and Empirical Complexities of an Operational Definition. *Journal of Conflict Resolution*, 48(6): 814–58.

Schissel, H. (1986). Conté in control. *Africa Report*, 31 (November–December): 21–5.

Scott, J. (2005). Afterword to "Moral Economies, State Spaces, and Categorical Violence." *American Anthropologist*, 107(3): 395–402.

Silberfein, M. and Conteh, A. (2006). Boundaries and Conflict in the Mano River Region of West Africa. *Conflict Management and Peace Science*, 23(4): 343–61.

Smith, A. (1983). *State and National in the Third World*. New York: St Martin's Press.

Smith, D.F. Jr. (2006). US–Guinea Relations during the Rise and Fall of Charles Taylor. *Journal of Modern African Studies*, 44(3): 415–39.

Smith, D.F. Jr. (2013). Guinea Inches toward Stability. *World Politics Review*. Briefing, May 13: 1–3.

Souaré, I.K. (2006). *Civil Wars and Coups d'état in West Africa: An Attempt to Understand the Roots and Prescribe Possible Solutions*. Lanham, MD: University Press of America.

Soumah, I. (2007). *Avenir de l'industrie minièr en Guinée*. Paris: L'Harmattan.

Tinti, P. (2013). In Mineral-Rich Guinea, can Reform Leader Keep it Together? *The Christian Science Monitor*, July 3, http://www.csmonitor.com/World/Africa/2013/0703/In-mineral-rich-Guinea-can-reform-leader-keep-it-together.

United Nations Development Programme (1992). *Human Development Report 1992*. New York: Oxford University Press.

United Nations Development Programme (1993). *Human Development Report 1993*. New York: Oxford University Press.

United Nations Development Programme (1994). *Human Development Report 1994*. New York: Oxford University Press.

United Nations Development Programme (1996). *Human Development Report 1996*. New York: Oxford University Press.

United Nations Development Programme (2009). *Human Development Report 2009*. New York: Palgrave Macmillan.

United Nations Development Programme (2013). *Human Development Report 2013*. New York: UNDP.

Utas, M. (2003). *Sweet Battlefield: Youth and the Liberian Civil War*. Uppsala: Uppsala University.

World Bank (1990). *Guinea: Mining Sector Review*, Report No. 8692 (July 10). Washington, DC.

Young, C. (1993). The Dialectics of Cultural Pluralism: Concept and Reality. In C. Young (ed.), *The Rising Tide of Cultural Pluralism: The Nation-State at Bay?* Wisconsin: The University of Wisconsin Press, 3–35.

Zartman, W. (1995). Dynamics and Constraints in Negotiations in Internal Conflicts. In W. Zartman (ed.), *Elusive Peace: Negotiating an End to Civil Wars*. Washington, DC: Brookings Institute, 3–39.

Zirker, D., Danopoulos, C.P., and Simpson, A. (2008). The Military as a Distinct Ethnic or Quasi-Ethnic Identity in Developing Countries. *Armed Forces & Society*, 34(2): 314–37.

Chapter 9

Breaks with the Past: Conflict, Displacement, Resettlement and the Evolution of Forest Socio-Ecologies in Sierra Leone[1]

Paul Munro and Greg van der Horst

Abstract

In contrast to media fixation on the physical violence of recent West African conflicts, scholars have emphasized the lasting effects of massive population displacements. In Sierra Leone, for example, roughly 2 million of a total 3.8 million people had to migrate internally and several hundred thousand more fled to neighboring countries. As many have noted, both the experiences of those who were displaced and later returned home, as well as the dramatic shifts in population geography caused by those who did not, have had considerable impacts on important social issues including ethnic relations, identity formation, (macro)economic patterns and medical services provision. What remain less well understood, however, are the effects of these disruptions and reconfigurations on rural livelihoods and, by extension, on the (re) production of human-environmental relationships across broad swathes of landscape. These are of critical importance to processes of post-war stabilization and reconstruction, since most of Africa's mainly agrarian populations rely almost entirely on the productivity of their immediate landscapes for subsistence and small-scale commercial production. Focusing on Sierra Leone, in this chapter we draw on extensive field data to describe how rural residents' responses to both the vagaries of intense and chaotic conflict as well as the unstable conditions of peacebuilding have produced a considerable transformation of people-forest relationships across the country.

Introduction

In contrast to media fixation on the immediate brutalities of the Mano River War(s)[2] in Sierra Leone (1991–2001) and Liberia (1989–1996; 1999–2003), a key emphasis in scholarly work has been the equally important and in many ways more lasting disruptions produced by war-induced displacement of more than half of the two national populations (Chimni 2002; Crisp 2000). In Sierra Leone, for example, an estimated 2 million of its then 3.8 million people were forced to migrate internally and several hundred thousand more fled to neighboring Guinea and Liberia (Norwegian Refugee Council 2002). While many people endured such exile for several years, many more abandoned their old lives, resettling themselves in new parts of the country (Binns and Maconachie 2005; Maconachie, Binns, Tengbe and Johnson 2006). As a number of scholars have noted, both the experiences of those who were displaced and later returned, as well as the dramatic shifts in population geography caused by those who did not, have had considerable effects on a wide range of important issues. A range of studies have illuminated the effects of these dynamics on various aspects of

1   Funding for this research was provided by the European Union and the UN Food and Agricultural Organisation (FAO) through the Forest Law Enforcement, Governance and Trade (FLEGT) support program, as well as the Promoting Agriculture, Governance and the Environment (PAGE) program sponsored by USAID, and the Social Sciences and Humanities Research Council (SSHRC) of Canada.
2   This term is used by Danny Hoffman (2011) to illustrate the close connections between the broader political economies of the individual Liberian and Sierra Leone civil wars.

national life, such as social relations and identity formation, (macro)economic patterns and medical services provision among others (Binns and Maconachie 2005; Grant 2005; Maconachie et al. 2006; Medeiros 2007).

Much less well understood, however, are the effects these experiences and population flows have had on how rural people have gotten back to the business of making a living and, by extension, the socio-political and material characteristics of human-environmental relationships across the majority of Sierra Leone and Liberia's landscapes (Maconachie et al. 2006). In the post-war context such concerns have been largely obscured from view by more dramatic immediate concerns such as disease control, fiscal collapse and electoral violence. Nonetheless, they have been and remain critically important as the two countries move forward with their self-reconstruction since the majority agrarian populations rely almost entirely on immediate forest and savanna environs for subsistence and small-scale commercial livelihood production. During the conflicts and their aftermath, rural residents (displaced or otherwise) have had to formulate new livelihood strategies not only in new environments, but also in considerably changed social and economic contexts (Maconachie et al. 2006).

Focusing on the Sierra Leonean case, in this chapter we draw on extensive field data to describe how rural residents' responses to the vagaries of chaotic conflict and the unstable conditions of peacebuilding have produced a considerable transformation of people-forest relationships across the country. We argue that the civil war and its fallout, by producing a range of novel necessities, experiences and opportunities, created the political and economic space for new forest livelihood activities to be established and expanded. We contextualize this socio-ecological dynamic in the broader political economy of the colonial and postcolonial Sierra Leone nation state, illustrating how this transformation has challenged notions of the state's centralized hegemony in forest governance, that have been prevalent since the colonial era.

Following this introduction, the remainder of this chapter is divided into four sections. In the next section we provide a brief overview of Sierra Leone's political and economic history demonstrating how formal forestry governance in Sierra Leone was (and continues to be) couched in a colonialist mindset focused on "rationalized" large-scale timber exploitation. Building on this analysis, the third section moves on to describe the Sierra Leonean civil war (1991–2001) and its aftermath, explaining how it produced new socio-political spaces in which novel forms of human-forest relations could emerge. In the fourth section we analyze current dynamics in the evolution of Sierra Leone's new forest socio-ecologies at the grass-roots level and the tensions between these and the centralizing ambitions of the Forestry Division. Finally, in the fifth section we offer a summary and concluding thoughts.

Origins of the "Rationalizing" Urge: Colonialism and the Birth of Formal Forestry in Sierra Leone

The modern state of Sierra Leone owes its earliest existence to a late-eighteenth-century experimental attempt, partly initiated by the British Government, to provide a form of redress to former slaves from England, Eastern Canada and the Caribbean (Braidwood 1994) by "repatriating" them to a small Colony founded in the Freetown Peninsula. While for some time Imperial ambitions were limited to this small holding, during the 1890s "scramble for Africa" the British annexed a deep and broad swathe of adjoining territory, expanding colonial hegemony to include the "Protectorate"—a domain largely matching the current borders of the country. As the colonial adventure was intended to be profitable (or at least self-supporting) (Kaindaneh 1993; Meredith 1986), however, the motive for this act was less to acquire territory per se than to establish control over (and increase) the extraction of valuable commodities for the benefit of the imperial core (Munro and Hiemstra-van der Horst 2011). The formalization and institutionalization of natural resource exploitation for export was therefore a key focus of the Colonial Government during the early 1900s, pursued through the establishment of managing bureaucracies (Akiwumi 2006a, 2006b; Munro and Hiemstra-van der Horst 2011), such as the Sierra Leonean Forestry Department founded in 1911.

At root, the organization and operations of the Forestry Department were premised on two key systems of ideas. The first was an overtly racist and thorough-going distrust of native environmental competence, which itself was deeply linked to a systematic misreading of the Sierra Leonean landscape through the lenses of pseudo-scientific ecological notions such as "succession," "equilibrium" and (deforestation-induced) desiccation. In essence, the colonial perspective held that the agricultural practices of the indigenous population had destroyed (and continued to destroy) the tropical moist forests which, it was believed, had once covered the majority of the country (Fairhead and Leach 1998, 2000; Munro and van der Horst forthcoming). The second was a particular ideal of professionalized forest management based largely on a German cameralist model of forestry practice that had been developed during the 1800s. This approach was predicated on the simplification and rationalization of arboreal resources for easy and efficient economic exploitation by separating forests from people, altering their ecologies to enhance production of higher-priced species, and increasing harvesting rates with mechanized industrial equipment (Munro 2015). In simple terms, the objective was to manufacture forests that were easier to count, manipulate, measure, assess and hence to exploit for maximum yield and profits (Neumann 2005). Indeed, the very establishment of forestry departments in Sierra Leone and the rest of Africa at the start of the twentieth century was itself considerably a product of a broadly-based belief that the continent's forests were in immediate danger of destruction by the local population and required urgent intervention by rational, scientific—and of course European—professionals. The appropriation of control was thus justified within the moral-economic framework of colonization (Endfield and Nash 2002) and the sequestration of resource-rich areas was easily framed as a beneficent gesture protecting ignorant locals from themselves.

Despite its urgent initial pursuit and the "civilizing" rhetoric under which it paraded, however, the colonization process in Sierra Leone that began with the Scramble for Africa in the 1890s proved neither quick nor socio-politically motivated but rather a protracted attempt to subsume the territory, its resources and its peoples under the hegemony of imperial capitalism. As Hoogvelt and Tinker argue, colonial-era exploitation was expressly designed to feed capitalist development in the imperial homeland, not to develop capitalist economies in the colonial periphery, and was:

> [n]ot, therefore, just exploitative, but super exploitative. It was rapacious rather than reproductive, bent on quick returns rather than long-term exchange. It was destructive of the soil and resources, yet failing to provide alternative forms of livelihood. It was content to work in makeshift technological and capitalist enclaves, allowing itself to be supported by the surrounding social formation, rather than attempting to change or improve it. (Hoogvelt and Tinker 1978: 73)

On the whole, then, the colonial period was characterized by—or indeed predicated on—nearly wholesale exploitation of the colonial hinterland for maximum profitability at the least possible cost by a system in which Sierra Leoneans (like many other peoples) were effectively made to pay for their own colonization.

Despite the economic and strategic importance of the Sierra Leonean territory, however, the British authorities never achieved truly systematic control over the country, partly due to the relatively short period of formal colonization (1896 to 1961) and the distraction of the First World War which drew Imperial attention and investment largely elsewhere. In this context the colonial Forestry Department struggled, particularly since its potential profitability was a much longer-term and less lucrative prospect than the opportunities for filling imperial coffers offered by the agricultural and mining sectors.

Between 1921 and 1941, for example, investment in agriculture was increased by 400 percent while expenditure on forestry remained stagnant (Blood 1941) with the result that during this period Sierra Leone was heavily reliant on imported timber to meet domestic needs. Importantly, the Second World War offered a strategic opportunity for the Department which secured for itself four large-scale sawmills with the rationale of contributing supplies to meet the timber demand of the war effort (Cline-Cole 1993; Munro and Hiemstra-van der Horst 2011). When the conflict ended the Department retained the mills and attempted to transform itself from a peripheral bureaucracy draining the colonial treasury into the progenitor of an efficient industry producing enough timber for domestic needs. As one observer exclaimed at the time: "[s]awmilling, which was an outcome of wartime necessity ha[d] come to stay" (Pelly 1952: 10).

These notable developments notwithstanding, at independence in 1961 the institutionalization of formal industrial forestry was still very much an unfinished project. British investment had been haphazard and self-serving and offered little to the rural majority of Sierra Leoneans still dependent on direct access to land to meet the bulk of their daily needs. Still, the role of natural resources in the socio-economic development of the country had been profoundly altered (Colson 1971) and the lives of rural Sierra Leoneans had on the whole become more linked and vulnerable to the vagaries of volatile national and global markets. As a consequence, the independent government that took over Sierra Leone did not inherit a stable polity, but instead a fragmented one that was in many ways coming apart at the seams (Phillips 1989). Despite its efforts to the contrary, the British Administration in Freetown had always been reliant on financial support from the colonial office in London, and the governance structure inherited at liberation was financially unsustainable (Harris 2014). Nevertheless, in line with the modernization discourse of the time, industrialization remained a principal concern for the postcolonial Sierra Leonean Government, as was the pride associated with the idea of new nationhood, which mandated spending on prestige projects to impress visiting foreign officials and prospective investors (Siddle and Swindell 1990). As a result, promoting the development of a more formalized and technologically sophisticated forestry sector remained an important focus in the postcolonial era. This effort was led in both policy and practice by the state itself which directly conducted the majority of large-scale logging operations through the centrally-owned Forest Industries Corporation (FIC). By 1968 the FIC had become one of the most prominent industrial actors in the country (outside of the mining sector) employing around 1,000 people (*Sierra Leone Trade Journal* 1968).

Just as during the late colonial period, however, the promising initial successes of the nascent industrialized forestry sector in Sierra Leone were again relatively short lived, in this case due to broad-based political-economic decline. Already in the 1960s there were problems of political insecurity—notably marked by three *coups d'état*—as the country attempted to adjust to democratic governance. Although stability was increased in the 1970s, it came in the form of an authoritarian regime headed by Siaka Probyn Stevens whose pursuit of a "state hegemonic project" (Zack-Williams 1999: 125) gathered pace with the reconstitution of the country as a single party democracy in 1978 (Abraham 1993). Determined to consolidate and maintain his power, Stevens targeted any and all forms of opposition using a combination of cunning manipulation, intimidation and violence. At the same time, he constructed a "shadow state" (Reno 1995), building a neopatrimonial network of personalized support paid for with wealth looted from Sierra Leone's rich mineral extraction industry (Bøås 2001; Richards 1996).

The implications of these developments for the forestry sector were significant, changing the nature of both the formal timber production industry and the Department charged with its oversight in ways that remain salient in the present day. On one hand, the autonomy and capacity of the Department itself were reduced quite dramatically by the patterns of Stevens' rule and his increasing focus on mineral—and particularly diamond—wealth. In order to consolidate his grip on power, Stevens increasingly centralized the political and economic functions of the state in the capital city of Freetown, using the state and its resources to distribute patronage to his cronies while the rest of the country was neglected (Riddell 1985, 2005). Forestry was no exception, and the authority of the Department in this period became highly concentrated in the Chief Conservator of Forests, a figure tied by personalized neopatrimonial connections to the president, ensuring "that the Forestry [Department] literally spoke with a 'single voice' in policy formulation" (Grainger and Konteh 2007: 54). At the same time, however, the Department's relevance waned as mineral resources, especially, diamonds, proved to be much more congenial to realizing profits with little state investment (Forde 2011).

An intriguing aspect of the forestry sector's decline during this period is its paradoxical relationship with the central state which both promoted it and allowed it to sink into ruin. In a number of ways—and particularly earlier on—Stevens' government exhibited considerable enthusiasm for commercial forestry. In 1975, for example it succeeded in negotiating establishment of the Sierra Leone Timber Industries (SILETI), a timber company co-owned by the state and operated by an Italian enterprise, set up to exploit forests in the south-east of the country. The company was given a 25 year logging concession, however, only just eight years later the regime reversed its position and "things fell apart." The Government accused SILETI of engaging in "the unauthorised felling of trees by using forged stamps to mark trees, ... smuggl[ing] logs out of [the country] ... via neighbouring Liberia and paying no royalties to the government even on logs legally felled" (Tuboku-Metzger 1983: 241). SILETI's concession (due to expire in 2000) was cancelled in 1983 and the company was expelled from the country. Moreover, the government-owned FIC fared little better during the same period. Despite Stevens' early emphasis on increasing exports, by the late-1970s the Corporation was in dire financial straits. In order to revive it, in 1978, the government negotiated with the UK government for a Le 3 million loan (around US$2.8 million) to purchase logging trucks and a new sawmill production line. As well, that same year the West German government was prevailed upon to provide the FIC with 30 million DM (around US$14.2 million) for the construction of a new timber complex (Office of the President, 1980;

Tuboku-Metzger 1983). Despite these interventions, however, due to subsequent neglect the FIC fell quickly back into a state of decay and logging operations came to a halt in 1989 largely due to the inoperability of its sawmill which had fallen into disrepair. Overall, with the demise of SILETI and FIC, by the early 1990s only a few small-scale logging operations mainly run by wealthy Lebanese families were still operational in the country (Hartley 1992; Leach 1990, 1994).

Ruptures and Reconfigurations: Civil War, Displacement and Political-Ecological Shifts

The 1980s were ultimately the beginning of the end for the Siaka Stevens' patrimonial government, and marked the beginning of a slide into chaotic conflict that would prove transformative for the country. In 1985 Stevens, citing "fatigue," stepped down as president installing the erstwhile head of the army, Brigadier Joseph Saidu Momoh, as his successor (Alie 1990; Davies 2000; Zack-Williams 1999). Momoh however, inherited a situation of increasing economic and political disintegration (Kpundeh 1994; Luke and Riley 1989) which, lacking the charisma and political nous of his predecessor, he failed to contain and by the early 1990s the country was ripe for conflict (Zack-Williams 1999). The national debt rose at a pace still more dramatic than that of the previous decade while corruption became truly pervasive, spreading throughout the furthest reaches of the state apparatus (Keen 2005). In this context the political and economic disenfranchisement of the country's populace—especially rural youth—during the 1970s and 1980s had created widespread frustration and anger (Abdullah 1998; Kandeh 1999). In 1991 hostilities spilled across the eastern border from neighboring Liberia creating the necessary catalyst for conflict and alluvial diamond fields provided the necessary resources to finance its perpetuation.

The war itself (1991–2001) was a complex affair involving a variety of combatants including *sobels* (soldiers colluding with and/or sometimes posing as rebels in strategic areas), foreign mercenaries, village level militias, West African peacekeeping forces and—during its later stages—British troops (Abdullah 2004; Gberie 2005; Zack-Williams 1997). More importantly, however, it was also intensely disruptive and violent. Over the course of its 10 year duration more than 50,000 people were killed, many more were maimed, raped or otherwise violated and over half of the population was displaced in a torrent of violence that left no Sierra Leonean unaffected (Hoffman 2011; Keen 2005; Richards 1996). Importantly, the rebel/sobel onslaught also caused major destruction to the governance regime, shattering vestigial illusions of central state control over the country—not least the forests of the rural hinterland, many of which provided cover for rebel bases and movements (Richards 1996, 2005). The Forestry Department, already in decline for the previous two decades, saw its activities nearly completely halted: any notions of reviving the FIC were thoroughly quashed and during the latter part of the 1990s its staff could hardly even conduct field trips to areas outside of Freetown. Moreover, at times the capital itself was not safe from the ravages of the conflict and during its occupation by the rebels in 1999, Prince Palmer, then Head of the Forestry Department, was killed (Munro 2015). Largely abandoned by the state and left to fend for themselves, rural residents in many areas across the country took matters into their own hands, building networks of cooperation for provisioning and defense famously exemplified by the rise of the Kamajors and other ethnic militias that emerged to (quite successfully) challenge the Revolutionary United Front (Rebel) menace (Hoffman 2007, 2011; Zack-Williams 1997). Sierra Leone's forest was often allegorized as an actor within these conflicts. As Paul Richards notes, the rebels presented themselves as "bush revolutionaries" revolting against an urban (patrimonial) elite and many protagonists of the war viewed it as a crisis in which the "bush" came to "town" (phrased in Krio: *lepet dcn kam na tcn*—the leopard has entered the city) (Richards 1996). Equally, the civil militias such as the kamajors who were considered to have had power over bush paths, as well as the secrets and medicine (*hale*) of the forest in their societies. Through this unique access to the resources of the forests (physically and symbolically) the kamajors could mobilize power outside the usual channels to develop a village-level defense (Hoffman 2011). Historically, the kamajors protected their villages from the various animal, human, and extra-human forces of the forest (bush devils, wild animals) (Hoffman 2007); and, to an extent, protecting villages against bush revolutionaries was seen as an extension of this earlier role.

At the same time as the ever tenuous authority of the state was falling to pieces, the relationship between the Freetown urban core and the marginalized rural periphery was also being considerably disrupted. In this a key factor was the massive influx of rural residents that produced acute changes in Freetown's structure and population (Munro 2009). Until 1997, Freetown was relatively insulated from the excesses of the conflict and was generally seen as a haven of safety from rebel atrocities. As a result, large numbers of provincial people driven from their homes by the war relocated to the capital and its surroundings, increasing the number of its residents as much as threefold (Abdullah 2002; Boadi, Kuitunen, Raheem and Hanninen 2005). This major shift in population geography was to prove critically transformative for the forestry sector, creating foundations for new markets, commodity chain networks and livelihoods for the generally cash-poor rural majority. For one thing—and particularly in the later context of post-war recovery and reconstruction—the arrival of so many new migrants created a major upsurge in demand for materials to supply housing construction and household energy needs creating the basis for effectively new industries. As well, they also brought with them the social means by which to organize these novel economies: close ties to their villages of origin provided the basis for the establishment of strategic trade networks linking rural producers of lumber, firewood and charcoal to urban markets where demand was rising rapidly. The establishment of refugee and internally displaced peoples (IDP) camps augmented these patterns. Located both on the outskirts of Freetown and in the east of the country, the camps essentially became new towns and many functioned for over a decade while others evolved into permanent settlements. Growing rapidly, they became key sites of economic activity and trade in firewood became an important micro-industry (Leach 1992; Sargent 1993) while sales of building poles received a considerable boost from the demand for refugee shelters (Alieu 2001; Munro and van der Horst 2012a).

Beneath the more obvious patterns of state disintegration and the relatively simple dynamics of supply and demand, however, deeper processes were also at work that caused fundamental shifts in the relationship between rural Sierra Leoneans and the forest and savanna landscapes that most call home. In essence, through the processes of displacement and resettlement, the civil war and its aftermath exposed large numbers of rural people to new technologies and ways of thinking about forest-based products and livelihood strategies. Certainly the rapid post-war growth in urban material needs provided a vibrant market for rural goods encouraging a rapid increase in their production. Nonetheless, it was largely the conflict itself and the strategies of state and donor agencies for immediate post-war rehabilitation efforts which produced technological and ontological shifts transforming forests from *sources* of micro-scale subsistence into *resources* for commercially-oriented production. The now national-scale commercialization of firewood and building poles, for example, was actually largely a product of experiences in the IDP camps where many displaced rural residents began for the first time to think of these normally subsistence products as tradeable commodities (Munro and van der Horst 2012a, 2012b).

Still more illustrative, however, is the dramatic rise in charcoal production and trade which emerged during the conflict and has since grown rapidly into a notable industry. Until the mid-1990s, charcoal was a largely peripheral and uncommoditized product—consumed mainly by rural blacksmiths, and of marginal importance relative to firewood which was used as a household fuel—and a material which few Sierra Leoneans knew how to produce.[3] During the civil war, however, a variety of population movements resulted in technological transfers that gave birth to a new commercial subsector that ultimately revolutionized urban household energy markets across the country. In the context of relocation to IDP camps near Freetown, displacement over the borders to Liberia and Guinea and interaction with Liberian refugees (and in one case Liberian prisoners of war) based in different camps across Sierra Leone, a wide range of people learned both the techniques of charcoal making and its potential profitability from skilled artisanal producers in these areas. Following the end of the war, a great many brought this new knowledge back during resettlement to start production in their home villages. As well, since the war, Guinean traders and semi-nomadic charcoal making teams have stayed in or near many Sierra Leonean villages in the border regions, teaching the trade to a considerable number of people particularly in the north of the country. In the post-war context the results of this revolution have been nothing short of dramatic. Village-level production of charcoal for urban markets has become widespread across many areas of the country, particularly in areas within reach of major transportation arteries. Illustrating the trade's socio-economic importance, residents of charcoal producing

---

3   The charcoal used by blacksmiths differs from cooking charcoal. They are made through different processes, with the blacksmith charcoal producing smaller charcoal pieces that produce a more intense heat.

villages emphasized in interviews that through it, they had acquired economic freedom, earning enough to marry and set up their own households as well as to buy costly but important items such as motorcycles and other much-desired goods. Indeed, one charcoal trading village encountered during field research was made up entirely of ex-combatants who had established their own settlement after the disarmament program and turned to cooperative charcoal production as an exclusive source of income (Munro and van der Horst 2012a).

Another critical example of these trends is the massive expansion of rural lumber production. Prior to the 1990s, chainsaws were rare in Sierra Leone and used almost exclusively by large commercial timber operations such as FIC and SILETI, while village-level lumber production was modest in scale and based almost exclusively on labor-intensive pit-sawing. Following the end of the civil war, this situation began to change rapidly as a number of developments combined to stimulate the rapid proliferation of chainsaws in the country (Munro and van der Horst 2012a, 2012b). First, as part of the effort to resettle citizens displaced during the conflict, government agencies provided chainsaws to chiefdoms all over the country, training local residents (and notably a fair number of *re-integrated* ex-combatants) in their use, in order to facilitate land clearing and lumber production for the resettlement program. Second, in subsequent years, the government of neighboring Guinea increasingly cracked down on illegal timber exploitation activities, eventually placing a ban on timber exports. In response, a number of Guinean chainsaw operators migrated to Sierra Leone, taking up residence in Sierra Leone villages and passing on chainsaw milling skills to their host communities. Finally, outbreaks of illegal logging for export in Sierra Leone itself have also contributed significantly to both the proliferation of chainsaws in the country and the ways in which the board production industry has developed. In 2007, a number of Chinese timber merchants crossed the border from Guinea and started making arrangements with northern communities, often providing chainsaws as direct payment for timber (Hiemstra-van der Horst 2011; Hiemstra-van der Horst, Munro, and Batterbury 2011; Munro and van der Horst 2012a). This development not only furthered the dissemination of saws and training in their use for on-site Chain Saw Milling (CSM) of lumber materials, but also illustrated to many rural youths, entrepreneurs (and ex-combatants) the profitability of the practice, in turn stimulating the growth of this informal sub-sector and fostering a high demand for chainsaws in rural areas as well as the near disappearance of pit-sawing operations. Thus the decline in domestic large-scale timber production during the 1980s did not result in a return to high reliance on timber imports for Sierra Leone—instead the formal sector was supplanted by a plethora of small-scale producers operating in off-reserve rural areas across the country who, via complex and varied transportation and trade networks, have rendered the country self-sufficient in timber for the first time since the 1970s (Munro and van der Horst 2012a).

Markets for timber and other forest products have continued to expand in the post-war era, due to continued processes of urbanization and the rebuilding of infrastructure. This has allowed for the continual expansion of trade in firewood and poles and most villages within a few kilometers of a highway or an urban center are involved in the selling these commodities, acquiring an important supplement to agricultural income (Munro and van der Horst 2012a). Moreover, the increase in production capacities has combined with the rapid growth of many urban centers to perpetuate the growth of the charcoal and lumber trades over the past decade. Thus, a wide variety of the political, demographic technological and conceptual shifts produced by the war and its aftermath have now become entrenched in the political-economic structures and functioning of the country as a whole. Supply chains—while remaining flexible—have become institutionalized and expanded and a nascent process of capitalization has emerged.

Policy vs Praxis: Formality, Informality and Tensions in the New Sierra Leonean Forest Socio-Ecologies

As illustrated by the preceding analysis, the Sierra Leonean civil war and its aftermath have proved both brutally destructive and creatively productive, dismantling the status quo and generating a range of novel necessities, experiences and opportunities leading to important reconfigurations of thinking and practice with respect to forests and the forestry sector. In essence, the shifts and changes described above ultimately created a space of possibility in which the transformation of forest socio-ecologies across Sierra Leone could—and almost inevitably would—take place. The disintegration of formal governance in rural areas, the undermining of agrarian livelihood strategies, mass human displacement and the creation of both new and expanded economic markets all combined to produce a critical political-economic context in which novel rural-urban productive networks could emerge and the nature and role of forests in rural life could be re-imagined. Key to these processes, of course, were technological shifts facilitated by new social relations within novel human networks of knowledge exchange, collaboration and entrepreneurial mobilization.

The result of these disruptions and re-formations has been a national scale shift at the grass-roots level away from the previous externally imposed vision of a formally managed and centrally directed forestry sector to the development of vibrant and spontaneous informal practice that allows for the participation of a wide range of new actors. Rural residents' responses to the vagaries of chaotic conflict and the unstable conditions of peacebuilding have thus produced a considerable transformation of people-forest relationships across the country. These, in turn, are supported and reproduced by new rural-urban political and economic relationships via the emergence of capitalized and (more-or-less) systematized, but also informal, flexible and even (spatially) ephemeral forest product supply networks. This has been facilitated by the emergence of a new political and socio-ecological dispensation in which ongoing population movements and rising urbanization continue to drive the growth and evolution that has not only reshaped forest-society and urban-rural linkages but also spun them away from *de jure* centralized control. The small-scale domestic trading networks of forest products that emerged during the civil war have been increasingly extensified, institutionalized and capitalized in the post-war era even as state influence over forest management across the country crumbled into near non-existence. In its place a *de facto* process of democratization and localization of socio-ecological governance has begun to emerge despite an adversarial legislative environment that continues to emphasize the importance of reviving centralized bureaucratic control and large-scale industrial timber production.

Indeed, the nascent small-scale commercial forestry industry in Sierra Leone currently sits in significant tension with the orientation, rhetoric and goals of the Forestry Division (née Department)[4] which is trying to swim against the popular current to re-establish export-oriented forestry in the country and more direct control over the country's forest resources *in toto*. Not long ago, for example, it oversaw both the sale of the FIC's former rights and production infrastructure to a Nigerian company (Munro and van der Horst 2012b) as well as the announcement (though not effective implementation) of a national system of fees and regulations that effectively criminalized small-scale producers (Hiemstra-van der Horst 2011). This orientation, however, is merely an extension of the agency's historical struggle to mold a commercial forestry sector—both domestic and export-oriented—that conforms to its own image of "proper practice" rooted in colonial era perceptions and ideology. While a lively domestic commercial sector did emerge during the civil war it was not one aligned to the model of large-scale, spatially stable and centrally supervised heavy industry envisaged by Sierra Leone's professional foresters. Instead it is informal, mobile, dynamic and conducted by a mosaic of small-scale producers working in complex rural-urban networks effectively beyond the ability of the Division to contain. As a result, the Division has become not the progenitor and stern "parent" of a modern internationally oriented industry but rather little more than a spectator observing with apprehension the development and rapid growth of a spontaneous and vibrant grass-roots driven suite of forest-based production chains delivering much needed simple and low cost materials to domestic markets. In essence, the initiative has shifted considerably from the center to the periphery as forest-based lives and livelihoods have been reconceived and a new socio-ecological dispensation has emerged.

Conclusion: The Roads Ahead

Despite the relatively dramatic nature of these developments, it is difficult to speculate what the future holds for forestry and its subsectors in Sierra Leone. The transformations produced by the civil war and its aftermath have considerably changed the rules of the game with respect to forest industry and governance but in ways that have raised the concerns and ire of central regulators. Importantly, as the Forestry Division continues to work toward the re-centralization of control, it is increasingly supported both technically and financially by the international community via a range of initiatives tied to the broader Global Forest Governance (GFG) regime (Hiemstra-van der Horst et al. 2011). As progress is made toward implementation of national-level

---

4   The Forestry Department was renamed the Forestry Division during the 1990s.

programs under the United Nations' Reducing Emissions from Deforestation and Forest Degradation UN-REDD+, the European Unions' Forest Law Enforcement, Governance and Trade (EU-FLEGT) program, and the Extractive Industries Transparency Initiative (EITI) (although the last has not yet been extended to the forestry sector in Sierra Leone as it has elsewhere, such as in Liberia) it is almost certain that the monitoring and regulatory capacity of the Division will be considerably strengthened (indeed this is a key pre-requisite for participation in either of the first two initiatives which are already in development).

At the same time, however, the very nature of the new informal forestry practices and their flexible, ephemeral and diffuse networks makes them extremely unamenable to classic modernist command and control approaches to resource management. Moreover, in line with current discourses of pro-poor development and stakeholder participation these initiatives also come with their own prescriptions for negotiation and resolution of tensions and conflicts within the sector to ensure that lower income and less formally established actors are not unfairly treated or unreasonably disadvantaged. This is a critical consideration in the context of peacebuilding in Sierra Leone where widespread employment—especially for youth—is seen as a critical ingredient for maintaining stability (Peeters, Cunningham, Acharya and Van Adams 2009; Peters 2011). The change in the productivity regime of the forestry sector can therefore be contextualized within the broader shift in Sierra Leone from an externally conditioned formal economic sector (since devastated by the war) to a more spontaneous informal economic sector (Lahai 2012). As has been noted by Lahai (2012), such a post-war informal economy has been critical to Sierra Leoneans (particularly the youth) striving to carve out pioneering survival strategies. The small-scale productive forest sector has thus created a critical space—not only economically, but also in terms of identity- for communities to occupy in their path towards reconstruction. Therefore, any approach based on either rigid control or simple eradication of the existing charcoal, lumber and other commodity chains is not only impracticable from a capacity perspective, but a political non-starter given the income it provides to a sizeable section of the populace as well as the urgency of broad based social demands for their products. As a result, it seems evident that current pressures strongly favor the evolution of a compromise in which formal central policy and informal peripheral practice will both have to adapt and change meeting somewhere in the middle. How, when and to what extent this may occur, however, remains an open question.

References

Abdullah, I. (1998). Bush Path to Destruction: The Origin and Character of the Revolutionary United Front/ Sierra Leone. *The Journal of Modern African Studies*, 36(2): 203–35.

Abdullah, I. (2002). Space Culture and Agency in Contemporary Freetown: The Making and Remaking of a Postcolonial City. In O. Enwezor, C. Basualdo, U.M. Bauer, S. Ghez, S. Maharaj, M. Nash, and O. Zaya (eds), *Under Siege: Four African Cities, Freetown, Johannesburg, Kinshasa, Lagos*. Germany: Hatje Cantz Publishers, 201–12.

Abdullah, I. (2004). *Between Democracy and Terror: The Sierra Leone Civil War*. South Africa: Unisa Press.

Abraham, A. (1993). Local Government and the Provision of Social Services in Sierra Leone. In C.M. Fyle (ed.), *The State and the Provision of Social Services in Sierra Leone since Independence, 1961–1991*. Oxford: CODESRIA.

Akiwumi, F.A. (2006a). Conflict Timber, Conflict Diamonds: Parallels in the Political Ecology of 19th and 20th Century Resource Exploitation in Sierra Leone. In K. Konadu-Agyemang (ed.), *Africa's Development in the Twenty-first Century: Pertinent Socio-Economic and Development Issues*. Aldershot: Ashgate, 109–25.

Akiwumi, F.A. (2006b). Environmental and Social Change in Southwestern Sierra Leone: Timber Extraction (1832–1898) and Rutile Mining (1967–2005). PhD dissertation, Texas State University.

Alie, J. (1990). *A New History of Sierra Leone*. London: MacMillan.

Alieu, E.K. (2001). *FOSA Country Report: Sierra Leone*. Ministry of Natural Resources and Tourism, Sierra Leone, Sierra Leone.

Binns, T. and Maconachie, R. (2005). "Going Home" in Postconflict Sierra Leone: Diamonds, Agriculture and re-Building Rural Livelihoods in the Eastern Province. *Geography*, 90(1), 67–78, doi: 10.2307/40574030.

Blood, H.R. (1941). *Reorganisation and Expansion of the Forestry Department*. Freetown: Government Printer.

Boadi, K., Kuitunen, M., Raheem, K. and Hanninen, K. (2005). Urbanisation without Development: Environmental and Health Implications in African Cities. *Environment, Development and Sustainability*, 7(4): 465–500.

Bøås, M. (2001). Liberia and Sierra Leone—Dead Ringers? The Logic of Neopatrimonial Rule. *Third World Quarterly*, 22(5): 697–723.

Braidwood, S.J. (1994). *Black Poor and White Philanthropists: London's Blacks and the Foundation of the Sierra Leone Settlement 1786–1791*. Liverpool: Liverpool University Press.

Chimni, B.S. (2002). Refugees, Return and Reconstruction of "Post-Conflict" Societies: A Critical Perspective. *International Peacekeeping*, 9(2): 163–80, doi: 10.1080/714002734.

Cline-Cole, R.A. (1993). Wartime Forest Energy Policy and Practice in British West Africa: Social and Economic Impact on the Labouring Classes 1939–45. *Africa*, 63(1): 56–79.

Colson, E. (1971). The Impact of the Colonial Period on the Definition of Land Rights. In P. Duignam and L.H. Gann (eds), *Colonialism in Africa 1870–1960: Volume 3*. Cambridge: Cambridge University Press, 193–215.

Crisp, J. (2000). Africa's Refugees: Patterns, Problems and Policy Challenges. *Journal of Contemporary African Studies*, 18(2), 157–78. doi: 10.1080/02589000050080986.

Davies, V.A.B. (2000). Sierra Leone: Ironic Tragedy. *Journal of African Economies*, 9(3): 349–69.

Endfield, G.H. and Nash, D.J. (2002). Missionaries and Morals: Climatic Discourse in Nineteenth-Century Central Southern Africa. *Annals of the Association of American Geographers*, 92(4): 727–42.

Fairhead, J. and Leach, M. (1998). *Reframing Deforestation: Global Analyses and Local Realities With Studies in West Africa*. London: Routledge.

Fairhead, J. and Leach, M. (2000). Shaping Socio-Ecological and Historical Knowledge if Deforestation in Sierra Leone, Liberia and Togo. In R.A. Cline-Cole and C. Madge (eds), *Contesting Forestry in West Africa*. Ashgate: Aldershot, 64–95.

Forde, W. (2011). *The Story of Mining in Sierra Leone*. Xlibris Corporation.

Gberie, L. (2005). *A Dirty War in West Africa: the RUF and the Destruction of Sierra Leone*. Bloomington: Indiana University Press.

Grainger, A. and Konteh, W. (2007). Autonomy, Ambiguity and Symbolism in African Politics: The Development of Forest Policy in Sierra Leone. *Land Use Policy*, 24(1): 42–61.

Grant, J.A. (2005). Diamonds, Foreign Aid and the Uncertain Prospects for Post-Conflict Reconstruction in Sierra Leone. *The Round Table*, 94(381): 443–57, doi: 10.1080/00358530500243690.

Harris, D. (2014). *Sierra Leone: A Political History*. Oxford: Oxford University Press.

Hartley, D. (1992). Forest Resource Use and Subsistence in Sierra Leone. PhD dissertation, UCL.

Hiemstra-van der Horst, G.A. (2011). "We are Scared to Say No": Facing Foreign Timber Companies in Sierra Leone's Community Woodlands. *Journal of Development Studies*, 47(4), 574–94.

Hiemstra-van der Horst, G.A., Munro, P.G., and Batterbury, S.P.J. (2011). Les réseaux illégaux du pillage: La demande globale de bois et la (re)commercialisation des forêts d'Afrique de l'Ouest. *Écologie & Politique*, 42: 47–58.

Hoffman, D. (2007). The Meaning of a Militia: Understanding the Civil Defence Forces of Sierra Leone. *African Affairs*, 106(425): 639–62.

Hoffman, D. (2011). *The War Machines: Young men and violence in Sierra Leone and Liberia*. Durham, NC: Duke University Press.

Hoogvelt, A.M.M. and Tinker, A.M. (1978). The Role of Colonial and Post-Colonial States in Imperialism-a Case-Study of the Sierra Leone Development Company. *The Journal of Modern African Studies*, 16(1): 67–79.

Kaindaneh, P. (1993). State Provision of Transport and Communication Services in Sierra Leone. In C.M. Fyle (ed.), *The State and the Provision of Social Service in Sierra Leone Since Independence, 1961–91*. Oxford: CODESRIA Book Series, 20–43.

Kandeh, J.D. (1999). Ransoming the State: Elite Origins of Subaltern Terror in Sierra Leone. *Review of African Political Economy*, 26(81): 349–66.

Keen, D. (2005). *Conflict & Collusion in Sierra Leone*. London: James Currey Oxford.

Kpundeh, S.J. (1994). Limiting Administrative Corruption in Sierra Leone. *The Journal of Modern African Studies*, 32(1): 139–57.

Lahai, J.I. (2012). Youth Agency and Survival Strategies in Sierra Leone's Postwar Informal Economy. In M.O. Ensor (ed.), *African Childhoods: Education, Development, Peacebuilding, and the Youngest Continent*: Palgrave Macmillan, 47–60.

Leach, M. (1990). Images of Propriety: The Reciprocal Constitution of Gender and Resource use in the Life of a Sierra Leonean Forest Village. PhD thesis, University of London.

Leach, M. (1992). *Dealing with Displacement: Refugee-Host Relations, Food and Forest Resources in Sierra Leonean Mende Communities during the Liberian Influx, 1990–91*. Sussex: Institute of Development Studies.

Leach, M. (1994). *Rainforest Relations: Gender and Resource Use among the Mende of Gola, Sierra Leone*. Edinburgh: Edinburgh University Press.

Luke, D.F. and Riley, S.P. (1989). The Politics of Economic Decline in Sierra Leone. *Journal of Modern African Studies*, 27(1): 133–41.

Maconachie, R., Binns, T., Tengbe, P., and Johnson, R. (2006). Temporary Labour Migration and Sustainable Post-conflict Return in Sierra Leone. *GeoJournal*, 67(3): 223–40, doi: 10.1007/s10708-007-9056-1.

Medeiros, E. (2007). Integrating Mental Health into Post-conflict Rehabilitation The Case of Sierra Leonean and Liberian Child Soldiers. *Journal of Health Psychology*, 12(3): 498–504.

Meredith, D. (1986). State Controlled Marketing and Economic "Development": The Case of West African Produce during the Second World War. *The Economic History Review*, 39(1): 77–91.

Munro, P.G. (2009). Deforestation: Constructing Problems and Solutions on Sierra Leone's Freetown Peninsula. *The Journal of Political Ecology*, 16(1): 104–24.

Munro, P.G. (2015). A Critical History of Forest Conservation in Sierra Leone. PhD thesis, University of Melbourne, Melbourne.

Munro, P.G. and Hiemstra-van der Horst, G.A. (2011). Conserving Exploitation?: A Political Ecology of Forestry Policy in Sierra Leone. *The Australasian Review of African Studies*, 32(1): 59–72.

Munro, P.G. and van der Horst, G. (forthcoming). Contesting African Landscapes: a critical reappraisal of Sierra Leone's competing forest cover histories. *Environment and Planning D: Society and Space*, under submission.

Munro, P.G. and van der Horst, G.A. (2012a). The Domestic Trade in Timber and Fuelwood Products in Sierra Leone: Current Dynamics and Issues. Freetown: FAO/EU.

Munro, P.G. and van der Horst, G.A. (2012b). *The Governance and Trade of Wood-based Products in and around the Kambui Hills North Forest Reserve*. Freetown: USAID ACDI/VOCA.

Neumann, R.P. (2005). *Making Political Ecology*. London: Hodder Arnold.

Norwegian Refugee Council (2002). *Internally Displaced People: A Global Survey* (2nd edn). London: Earthscan.

Office of the President (1980). *Sierra Leone: 12 Years of Economic Achievement and Political Consolidation under the APC and Dr Siaka Stevens: 1968–1980*. Freetown: State House.

Peeters, P., Cunningham, W., Acharya, G., and Van Adams, A. (2009). *Youth Employment in Sierra Leone: Sustainable Livelihood Opportunities in a Post-conflict Setting*. Washington DC: World Bank Publication.

Pelly, R.S. (1952). Statement by the Forest Authority, Sierra Leone Prepared for the Sixth Commonwealth Forestry Conference, 1952. Freetown: Government Printer.

Peters, K. (2011). *War and the Crisis of Youth in Sierra Leone*. Cambridge: Cambridge University Press.

Phillips, A. (1989). *The Enigma of Colonialism: British Policy in West Africa*. London: Currey.

Reno, W. (1995). *Corruption and State Politics in Sierra Leone*. Cambridge: Cambridge University Press.

Richards, P. (1996). *Fighting for the Rain Forest: War Youth and Resources in Sierra Leone*. Oxford: James Currey.

Richards, P. (2005). The Mano River Conflicts as Forest Wars. *ETRFN News*, 43–4.

Riddell, J.B. (1985). Urban Bias in Underdevelopment: Appropriation from the Countryside in Post-Colonial Sierra Leone. *Tijdschrift voor economische en sociale geografie*, 76(5): 374–83.

Riddell, J.B. (2005). Sierra Leone: Urban-elite bias, atrocity & debt. *Review of African Political Economy*, 32(103): 115–33.

Sargent, J.S. (1993). A Fieldtrip Report: Displaced Sierra Leoneans and Liberian Refugees in Sierra Leone. Dartmouth College.

Siddle, D., and Swindell, K. (1990). *Rural Change in Tropical Africa: From Colonies to Nation States.* London: Blackwell.

Sierra Leone Trade Journal. (1968). Sierra Leone Forest Industries Corporation. 8(2): 38–41.

Tuboku-Metzger, D. (1983). Forest Exploitation in Sierra Leone: A Tale of Devastation. *The Ecologist,* 13(6): 239–41.

Zack-Williams, A.B. (1997). Kamajors, "Sober" & the Militariat: Civil Society & the Return of the Military in Sierra Leonean Politics. *Review of African Political Economy,* 24(73): 373–80, doi: 10.1080/03056249708704269.

Zack-Williams, A.B. (1999). Sierra Leone: The Political Economy of Civil War, 1991–98. *Third World Quarterly,* 20(1): 143–62.

Chapter 10

Arming Community Vigilantes in the Niger Delta: Implications for Peacebuilding

Kialee Nyiayaana

Abstract

This chapter explores the complexity and dimensions of arming vigilante groups in Nigeria's oil-rich Niger Delta, which has been confronted with conflicts and insurgencies since the 1990s. It argues that contrary to common assumptions that local communities arm vigilante groups primarily for protection purposes, state governments, local political elites and Multinational Oil Companies with different motives are also involved in arming vigilante groups in the region. Significantly, the arming of vigilante groups by these different actors contributes to the proliferation and availability of arms in local communities in the Niger Delta with implications for the militarization of the region. The key argument is that since arms availability in villages act as incentives for local hostilities in Nigeria, local communities in the Niger Delta face greater difficulties in sustaining post-conflict intercommunity reconciliation and peace. Accordingly, the continuing availability of weapons in villages in the region problematizes the distinction drawn between conflict zones and post-conflict settings.

Introduction

In most African States, citizens depend on a variety of private security organizations and vigilante groups to cope with the growing challenges of insecurity and crime in both urban and rural communities. This has called into question, the predominant assumptions about the social role of the State as security provider. Yet, issues of legitimacy, legality and effectiveness of vigilante groups in community protection are at the center of emerging debates amongst scholars. Some have argued that the practices of vigilante groups as local modes of collective security and justice promotion fall below acceptable community norms and cultural values for protecting and advancing human rights (Human Rights Watch 2002; Higazi 2008). Others conclude that vigilante policing activities tend to reproduce and reinforce the very structures and conditions of repression, domination and insecurity in the society (Anderson 2002; Ruteere and Pommerolle 2003). On the other hand, some contend that rather than supplement State policing, vigilante groups have emerged, in some contexts, as effective and viable alternatives to state security institutions in which the people turn to for crime prevention and crime fighting and ultimately physical safety (Abrahams 1987; Comaroff and Comaroff 2006; Adamu 2008).

Thus, the nature of the States in Africa has been identified as a crucial factor in the growth and reliance of vigilantism by the citizenry for protection. In fact, reflecting largely the deterministic Weberian notions of the state and neo-liberal conceptions of state building that also politicize it, the proliferation of armed vigilantes and more broadly militia groups, in much of Africa, has been attributed to state failure (Reno 2002; Raleigh 2014; Bates 2008; Young 2004). Again, while not completely rejecting the view that African States undoubtedly suffer from functional failure rather than structural collapse (Naanen and Nyiayaana 2013), others see the issue of state capacity differently. Abrahamsem and Williams (2007) argue that the increased visibility of vigilante policing in Africa is complex, relating not only to globalization, but also to the liberalization and privatization of the security space and changing dynamics of the provision and governance of political and social order, a process that has redefined the nature and role of the state globally.

The nature of this complexity is well articulated by Ian Loader who observes: "across the developed and the developing world there is a broad and diverse network of policing that not only works through government but, above, below and beyond government" (Loader 2000: 328). Accordingly, vigilantism may not necessarily arise as a response to the breakdown of state services as popularly conceived (see Johnston 1996). Rather, vigilant groups collaborate with the state to provide services to the people in complex ways that drawing a clear distinction between the state and vigilante groups as non-state bottom-up mechanisms for fighting crime and protecting local communities becomes increasingly difficult (Kirschner 2011).

Importantly, also, some have maintained that the phenomenon of vigilantism as citizen-led provision and governance of security is neither new in history across cultures (Killingray 1986; Abrahams 1987; Gore and Pratten 2003; Leach 2004; Fourchard 2008), nor are vigilante activities in modern times are uniquely peculiar to African social formations. In precolonial Africa, vigilantism finds expression in the activities of secret societies, warrior bands and night guards which perform diverse functions of law enforcement, extra-judicial practice of adjudication, external defense and peacemaking (Pratten 2008a, 2008b). Similarly in North America, vigilantism dates back to the eighteenth century (Brown 1975) and remains relevant to-date. Brian Newby's recent research suggests that the continuing use of a variety of vigilante groups in different contexts in the United States is part of the efforts to protect and create a perfect democracy (Newby 2012).

What can be gleaned from the above is that " ... vigilantism obeys not only the logics of neo-liberalism but its own local and national historical and cultural logics" (Pratten 2008a: 5). Broadly then, the resurgence of vigilantism in Africa is not necessarily a response to the politics of plunder and disorder (Gore and Pratten 2003; see also Membe 2001; Branch and Cheeseman 2008) or "retraditionalization" as Chabal and Daloz (1999: 45) would argue. After all, state-making especially, if the European experience is anything to go by, is historically and inherently conflictual, a process that is not necessarily unilineal and determinate (Tilly 1992). Given this therefore, it is argued here that the growing significance of vigilantism in Africa's security architecture reflects continuity and change in relation to state-building processes and peacebuilding conversations taking place in the continent.

In summary, extant scholarships have made important insights into the nature of these conversations, either by presenting vigilante groups as a threat to public order and social stability through their engagement in violent and criminal activities; or as a mechanism for advancing ethno-nationalist claims, cultural and political identity of a group (Last 2008; Nolte 2007); or as a means of promoting justice, security and social control in local communities in collaboration with the State in ways that are complex (Kirschner 2011). But in undertaking the foregoing activities especially physical protection, the use or misuse of weapons by vigilante groups has been a key determinant factor in the acceptance or rejection of vigilante policing by the society. As Laurent Fourchard has observed, "In each case, vigilante groups interrogate the relationships between the society and law enforcement agents, the issue being to know whether such groups are tolerated or even supported by the police or if they are forbidden because they are considered to be a threat to the state monopoly of legitimate violence" (Fourchard 2008: 16). Yet, the question of who arms vigilante groups, for what purpose, and the risks that arms proliferation associated with vigilantism pose for peacebuilding in local communities has only received partial scholarly attention.

This chapter contributes to the literature on vigilantism in Africa by exploring the complexity and dimensions of arming village vigilante groups in Nigeria's oil rich Niger Delta. It argues that contrary to common assumptions that local communities themselves arm vigilante groups primarily for community protection purposes, evidence from the Niger Delta, which has been confronted with violent communal conflicts, armed insurgencies and criminality especially since the post-Cold War suggests otherwise. This chapter identifies the government, Multinational Oil Companies (MNOCs) and local communities as key actors involved in arming youth-based vigilante groups in the Niger Delta for purposes that are sometimes contradictory. Community chiefs and local political elites, for instance, may arm vigilante groups not only to provide security for the local populations in the region, but also as a means of consolidating their local authority and power bases as well as demonstrating local power. In this regard, constitutive of broader aspects of community arming patterns, vigilante arming, contributes to the proliferation of Small Arms and Light Weapons (SALW) and militarization of local communities in the Niger Delta. For example, when youth/vigilante security structures collapse in the region, in some instances, notably the case of the vigilante group called the Bakassi Boys in 2002, the arms used by the group resurfaced in criminal activities and communal conflicts. This has had serious implications and complications for community security and sustainable peacebuilding in the Delta region.

In advancing the above argument, the chapter progresses with a conceptualization of the Niger Delta, while also examining the historical context of the ways and manners ethnic communities in the region have been involved the maintenance of peace, security and social order. This is then followed by an exploration of community vigilante arming patterns in the Niger Delta, describing the key actors involved and explaining their varying motivations. Finally, the analysis is centered on the peacebuilding implications of vigilante arming in the region.

Historical, Social and Political Contexts of Community Vigilante Arming in the Niger Delta

It is pertinent to define the area that constitutes the Niger Delta before exploring the historical, economic and social forces that have shaped vigilante activities in the region since the 1990s. By the Niger Delta Development Commission (NNDC) Act of 2000, the Niger Delta comprises nine of Nigeria's 36 states: Abia, Akwa Ibom, Bayelsa, Cross River, Delta, Edo, Imo, Ondo and Rivers states. All these states have been lumped together on the basis of oil possession and it is more or less a reflection of the larger politics of oil in Nigeria. Until the creation of the NDDC, for instance, the Niger Delta has been conceived as the territory recognized by the Willinks Commission Report of 1958, which contains oil and has a very difficult terrain. This territory includes Bayelsa, Delta and Rivers states, which not only has larger deposit of oil and gas but has also been the worst hit by oil-related violence (Okorobia and Olali 2013). These states are regarded by some scholars as core Niger Delta (Isumunah 2013).

By and large, and despite this recent political permutation, the Niger Delta consists primarily of ethnic minority groups such as the Andoni, Efik, Ibibio, Ijaw, Ikwerre, Itshekiri, Kalabari, Ogoni, and Urhobo. These minority groups have been excluded from the benefits of oil wealth generated from their land. Accordingly poverty is endemic in the region in the midst of plenty, and is complicated by environmental pollution and dearth of social infrastructure. These socio-economic and political conditions have underpinned the struggle for self-determination and armed insurgencies for the control of their resources by ethnic communities in the region since the 1990s. Indeed, the region has a history of local resistance and violent conflicts dating back to precolonial time in which the existence of strong and effective security institutions and vigilante structures were central to promoting internal social stability and external defense. Secret societies such as the Amanikpo, Ekpo and Egbesu are rooted in precolonial Niger Delta history and cosmology amongst the Ogoni, Ibibio and Ijaw ethnic groups. These societies responded effectively to issues of public accountability, security, peacemaking, social justice and crime fighting in the region in several ways.

The Amanikpo society, for instance, occupied an important place in local arbitration processes, the administration and dispensation of justice and social control in precolonial Ogoni. This is because the Amanikpo was both a secret society and an oath system. The Egbesu deity is well respected amongst the Ijaws for spiritual protection in warfare. In key respects, these societies may be may be regarded as precursor to contemporary armed vigilante groups not only in the provision of security-related services but also in behavior and practices (Leach 2004). The claims of invincibility of members of the Bakassi Boys as well as the ability of the group to detect criminals through the local medium of juju spirits and occult power has been well popularized in the *Isakaba* video film (McCall 2004). Isakaba is a popular Nigerian film that reflects the cultural underpinnings and complexities of the practice of vigilantism in Nigeria. In some sense, for instance, it demonstrates not only the continuing relevance of local cultural beliefs in the power of the juju spirits but also a dramatization of the superiority of charms as a means of protection. This is because the armed robbers themselves also wear charms for protection. David Pratten's ethnographic study of Annang vigilante groups in the Niger Delta shows that the swearing of oaths, an important means of promoting trust, cooperation and solidarity amongst group members is critical to the effectiveness of vigilante activities (Pratten 2008a; 2008b). It has also been argued that the Igbesu deity provided both spiritual and moral foundations for the Ijaw struggle for resource control in the Niger Delta in the 1990s.

It is also important to note that, in addition to the vigilante structure of secret societies and the night guards organized for the protection of person and property (Pratten 2008; 2008b), ethnic communities in the

Niger Delta as elsewhere in much of West Africa acquire weapons and had local armories prior to European contacts. Weapons systems like clubs, bows and arrows were commonly used for internal security and warfare in the region in pre-colonial times. However, the introduction of European fire arms—Portuguese hand guns in the fifteenth century, and the "Dane guns" in the seventeenth century—enabled access to better weaponry in West Africa (Smith 1989) including the Niger Delta (Isomunah 2013). In fact, Inikori (1977) has shown that by the second half of the eighteenth century, Bonny was the largest firearms importer in West Africa due mainly to but not entirely limited to slave trading.

Interestingly, neither British colonial rule nor the postcolonial administration in Nigeria completely destroyed the well-established community security structures in the Niger Delta especially vigilante structures and practices. Instead, vigilante groups became entrenched in the political, social and leadership structure of several communities in the region particularly after the Cold War. For example, faced with complex and violent insurgencies characterized by a variety of ethnic militia organizations such as the Niger Delta Vigilante Group (NDVG), Niger Delta People Volunteer Force (NDPVF) and the Movement for the Emancipation of the Niger Delta (MEND), demanding local political autonomy to control oil resources in the Niger Delta and embarking on "oil bunkering" (oil thefts) and kidnapping as strategies for funding rebellion, the region has become increasingly insecure since the 1990s. In fact, in 2007, "the State and the international community led by United States and Britain had reacted to the security challenges by designating the Niger Delta as a dangerous and insecure place inhabited by criminals, vandals, hostage takers, kidnappers, restive youths, oil thieves and terrorists" (Joab-Peterside 2007: 2).

Responding to the insurgency and armed insurrections in the Niger Delta, the Federal Government initiated the amnesty program for youths and militant groups in the region in 2009. Conceived and implemented in the context of a Disarmament, Demobilization and Reintegration (DDR) program, all Niger Delta militants were directed to disarm within 60 days, August 6 and October 4, 2009, and be free from criminal prosecution. Militants who accepted the State's offer of amnesty and handed in their weapons were not fewer than 26,358 (Kuku 2013). As part of the demobilization and reintegration processes, the ex-militants were trained in peaceful conflict resolution strategies and paid monthly stipends of N65,000.00. They were also trained both within and outside Nigeria in several trades including under-water welders, pilots, medical doctors, boat builders, seafarers, marine engineers, fashion designers, furniture makers, agriculturalists, information technologists amongst others, to enable them acquire skills and become self-reliant. Some enrolled for various academic programs in selected universities in Nigeria, South Africa, Europe and North America (Kuku 2013).

Importantly, since its implementation in 2009, the amnesty program has contributed to the reduction of militia violence and relative peace in the region, and oil exploration and production have fully resumed. However, focusing primarily on militants and failing to address the structural roots of militancy, which include but are not restricted to environmental insecurity and political and social exclusions of the Niger Delta people from their oil wealth, the amnesty program falls short of lasting solutions to resource conflict in the region. In fact, the amnesty program may best be described as a peacebuilding policy designed primarily to remove the militant youths from the scene in order to create stability and order necessary for oil production activities to resume in the region. As Sofiri Joab-Peterside has argued, security, peace and stability in Niger Delta have largely been conceived in the context of uninterrupted oil flow in the region rather than from a human security perspective (Joab-Peterside 2007).

Thus, in the post amnesty era, oil bunkering activities especially artisanal oil production by local youths, has been on the increase in the Niger Delta, not least because oil-producing communities have turned a blind eye to oil thefts as a result of deeply rooted grievances and perceptions of structural exclusion from the benefits of oil as well as the involvement and support provided by political and military elites (Naanen and Tolani 2014). Oil bunkering business, whether its local version of artisanal crude oil refining is an organized crime that is facilitated by the use of weapons by the youths involved. Yet, the sale of crude oil provides the youth the financial means to purchase better weaponry. Accordingly, oil bunkering and arms proliferation in the region are mutually reinforcing, what Badmus (2010: 323) has described as "gunning for oil and oiling the gun." However, beyond the rising incidence of oil thefts in the post-amnesty era, the Niger Delta has seen several rural communities engulfed in intercommunity conflicts and youth-based cult violence caused mainly by the armed Deebam and Deewell cult groups, while also contending with rape, kidnapping and armed robbery attacks perpetrated by their members (Nyiayaana 2011). In October 2012, four students of the University of

Port Harcourt suspected to be cult members were brutally murdered by the Aluu community vigilante group in Ikwerre on allegations of armed robbery (Iyang 2012). Until the 1990s, armed robbery was rare or non-existent in most rural communities in the Niger Delta. However, today, it has become commonplace.

Given the foregoing, there has been an increasing demand for, and reliance on vigilante groups as bottom-up mechanisms for confronting rising insecurities in almost all villages in the Niger Delta. Pratten (2008b) argues that the killing of a villager, by armed robbers in 1995 was the catalyst for the rise and arming of vigilante groups in various communities that make up Annang. A key observation, however, is that oil politics and the nature and character of elites' competition for power and wealth in the region has interfered with the activities of vigilante groups in such a way that the ultimate goal of promoting collective community security interests is sometimes compromised. The case of the creation of the Bakassi Boys, detailed below, is illustrative of the nature of this complexity. In other words, the complex interplay of the internal dynamics and imperatives of creating vigilante groups for protection and the varying motivations for funding them by actors with convergent and divergent interests has become a key problematic in promoting security and peace in the region. This complexity is illustrated in relation to local communities, state governments and multinational oil companies as key actors in community vigilante arming processes in the Niger Delta.

Vigilante Arming, Actors and Processes: Reflections on Local Communities

A core assumption in the literature on community policing is that local communities arm vigilante groups primarily for the promotion and protection of internal and external security interests of the local population (Johnston 1996). In the Niger Delta, this is true to some extent especially in the face of intercommunity conflicts in which arms have been procured by ethnic communities to prosecute in order to protect themselves (Bisina 2003). These forms of conflicts have come to define the region since the 1990s mainly due but not limited to the changing dynamics of oil politics. For example, why ethnic militia groups have engaged the state in contestations of the right to self-determination to control oil resources in the region, there have also been struggles between local communities themselves over who owns the lands on which oil is found or where oil facilities are situated. The protracted dispute between the Okrika and Eleme over the ownership of the land where the Port Harcourt Oil Refinery Company is located reflects this form of ethnic community contestations and tensions. In an effort to prosecute this communal conflict, the Chiefs and people of Okrika had to task each War-Canoe House to nominate two able men for defense of the community who were armed by the Houses. Importantly, as Sofiri Joab-Peterside (2007) points out, it was within the context of protecting the Okrika against the Eleme people that the vigilante group known as the "Bush Boys" emerged among former Okrika combatants who were treated as nationalists by the traditional political leadership" (Joab-Peterside 2007: 6). Indeed, "after the Okrika/Eleme dispute, the Okrika community maintained the group, which became known as Peace Makers because of the services they rendered" (Joab-Peterside 2007: 6) to their community.

Besides intercommunity clashes, there have been intra-community conflicts that also reflect the peculiar dynamics of the struggle for the control of oil governable space in the region. Of particular relevance here is the struggle to control the chieftaincy institutional space. Today, occupying chieftaincy positions in the Niger Delta confers on the Chief or King the right to access oil companies and government contracts, scholarships and employment opportunities including government and political party patronage. Accordingly, the politicization and privatization of the traditional leadership structures in the region has not only led to intense competitions among aspirants to the chieftaincy/kingship positions but also chieftaincy tussles. In most cases, chieftaincy tussles, as in Kula, Nembe, Rumuekpe and Zaakpon have led to protracted violent conflicts and factionalization of local communities along chieftaincy lines in which rival Chiefs/Kings have armed and used youth/vigilante groups to fight in an effort to claim their right to the throne. Similarly, some incumbent chiefs have recruited and armed youth/vigilante members who fight on their behalf as they struggle to retain their positions, what Koblentz (2013) aptly calls the struggle for regime security rather than the security of the people. In either or both ways, vigilante arming and chieftaincy conflicts have been mutually reinforcing and constitutive, thus counterproductive to the promotion and protection community security.

Related to the above point also is the arming and use of youth/vigilante groups by local politicians as structures for rigging elections and subverting of the democratic process to capture political power. In 1999, the Ateke Tom's led Niger Delta Vigilante Group was employed, sufficiently armed and funded by the People's Democratic Party led by Governor Peter Odili, to rig elections in Rivers State. Given the nature and extent of involvement of armed cult and vigilante groups in the rigging of the 1999, 2003, and to some extent the 2007 elections, Human Rights Watch (2007) described the elections as criminal politics. Since then, local political elites continue to arm and use village youth groups/vigilante members not only for their personal security but also as a demonstration of their power. This is because the higher the number of highly armed militant youths a local politician has, the more he/she is recognized as being able to deliver electoral victory for his/her party. Expanding their power base, therefore, means that they have to control youth and vigilante structures of power in local communities. All of these, however, are counterproductive to the collective security interests of the society.

Multinational Oil Companies and the Dynamics of Arming Youth and vigilante Organizations

Multinational Oil Companies (MNOCs) operating in the Niger Delta, especially Shell are structurally embedded in the conflict dynamics of the region in several ways that undermine sustainable peace and security. Shell has in active collusion with the Nigerian state, what Ken Saro-Wiwa (1995) calls "slik alliance" clamped down on local peaceful protests against its environmental degradation activities in the region. The Ogoni case amply illustrates this. It would be recalled that the Ogoni, led by Ken Saro-Wiwa, had under the aegis of the Movement for the Survival of the Ogoni People (MOSOP) in the 1990s embarked on campaigns, locally and internationally, against Shell's environmental damage and lack of corporate social responsibility in Ogoni. In fact, by 1993, MOSOP had declared Shell *persona non grata* in Ogoni and the company seized operating in the area with attendant loss of oil revenue, the soul of Nigeria's economy. Based on a particular conception of sovereignty and security, the Nigerian State in 1994 responded to the Ogoni agitation by establishing a special Rivers State Internal Security Task Force code-named Operation Restore Order and Stability. The Task Force was headed by Major Paul Okuntimo and stationed in Ogoni mainly to protect oil and Shell. It was well resourced: militarily by the Nigerian State and financially, by Shell Oil Company (Amusan 2014) with an implicit mandate to suppress the Ogoni struggle and broadly any form of local resistance that directly threatens oil production in the region (Obi 1999). Human rights abuses and atrocities committed by the Security Task Force in Ogoni have been well documented (see Odoemene 2012). Similarly in the context of corporate militarism, Shell has been involved in procuring weapons not only for its Shell police but also for the Nigerian security institutions, what Jedrzej George Frynas describes as security cooperation for the destruction of oil-producing communities in the Niger Delta (Frynas 1998).

Closely related to the above and particularly central to this chapter is that Shell has also adopted the British colonial divide and conquer tactics to create and reinforce alternate structures of power in local communities by funding and arming of different youth/vigilante groups. This strategic move is both to reduce the assertiveness of youths in fighting against the company's recklessness in environmental pollution, and to control governable oil space in the region. According to Ike Okonta, "oil companies in the region often offer 'protection work' to youths, arming them with arms in a tactical and cynical move to divide emergent and politically assertive youth organizations that were beginning to emerge" (Okonta 2006: 11). Recently, these behaviors and motivations were evident in Shell's activities in Rumuekpe, an oil-producing community in Ikwerre, Rivers State. Ben Amunwa has shown that field work testimonies and evidence of contracts awarded by Shell implicate the company in regularly assisting armed youth/vigilante groups with lucrative payments in Rumuekpe (Amunwa 2011). Amunwa further notes that in "one case in 2010, Shell was alleged to have transferred over $159,000 to a group credibly linked to militia violence" (Amunwa 2011: 1). Thus, while "the 2005–2008 Rumuekpe crisis was caused by a multi-layered struggle over land, power and access to oil contracts and payments ... it is possible to identify several ways in which Shell's routine practices increased the likelihood of conflict" (Amunwa 2011: 33). Shell distributed community development funds and contracts via Friday Edu, a youth leader and Shell Community Liaison Officer (Amunwa 2011: 35). Clearly the Rumuekpe community strikingly illustrates Shell's role in promoting and sustaining violence by awarding security contracts and making payments to armed youth/vigilante leaders and their members in the community. Michael Watts has also noted that Shell uses some of the funds allocated in its annual budget for the development of the company's host communities to promote community hostilities. In his words, "They represent in practice to a massive infusion of cash designed to purchase consent or compliance—but in practice they are central to the dynamics of rebellion and community violence" (Watts 2008: 27). Thus, contrary to conventional wisdom that conflicts and insecurity are a disincentive to business operations, Shell as a rational actor, has profited much more from conflicts and insecurity in the Niger Delta (Frynas 1998).

State Governments in Vigilante Arming

The transition from military dictatorships to civilian rule in Nigeria in 1999 saw a fundamental shift in the practice of vigilantism in some sense. State governments have been directly involved in the sponsorship, financing, arming as well as the creation of vigilante groups such as the Hisba and the Bakassi Boys. More recently, local vigilante groups popularly referred to as the Civilian Joint Security Task Force, which have been very useful in fighting the Boko Haram insurgency in the Northeast of Nigeria have received significant support from state governments in the region. A combination of factors and dynamics accounts for the growing involvement of state governments in vigilante activities since 2000. For example, while the motivation for supporting the Civilian Joint Security Task Force by the state governments in the Northeast has been primarily driven by the security challenges of the Boko Haram terrorist group, the creation of hisba vigilantes by 12 state governments in Northern Nigeria upon the return to multiparty democracy in 1999 to implement and monitor compliance with Sharia reflected the politics of ethnicity, identity, citizenship and religion in Nigeria. As Last (2008) has argued, the hisba enforcers of the Sharia code introduced in 12 states in the North in 2000 was much more concerned with issues of physical and spiritual insecurity of Muslims. Accordingly, the non-Muslim population in the North defined as the *other* became targets of the hisba vigilante attacks, which sometimes resulted in violence especially in Kano (Last 2008). The hisba, to some extent differ from the O'odua People's Congress (OPC) in Yoruba, western Nigeria. Though, it emerged in the mid-1990s, the OPC doubles as an ethnic militia fighting for Yoruba political autonomy within a decentralized federal structure in Nigeria and also as a vigilante group involved in fighting crime especially in Lagos. It was officially recognized by the Lagos State House of Assembly and therefore has the support and backing of the Lagos state government (Reno 2002).

The Bakassi Boys in Abia's Niger Delta on the other hand, were a case of cooption by the Abia government to help complement security services in the state. The social origins of the Bakassi Boys were primarily to confront rampant criminality, particularly armed robbery in the urban city of Aba amongst the Igbo traders. Although it has been largely criticized by some for its instant systems of judgment and barbaric killing of thieves based on automatic presumptions of guilt (Human Rights Watch 2002), the success and popularity of the Bakassi Boys in combating the menace of armed robbery in Aba led to its adoption in neighboring Anambra state. But as it turned out, the Bakassi Boys soon became a tool in the hands of both rival market trade unions and the governor of Abia state for scoring political points in terms of fighting perceived and real enemies (Harnischfeger 2008). The consequence of this political interference was that the Bakassi Boys lost their autonomy; and its leadership degenerated to the extent that the federal government had to ban the organization in 2002. But the key question remains: what happened to the weapons used by the Boys, which were given to them by state governments?

Peacebuilding and Security Implications of Vigilante Arming

Arguably, in the face of declining effectiveness of the state's capacity to control SALW acquisition and use in the Niger Delta, vigilante arming involving multiple actors such as local communities, political elites and MNOCs with diverse goals, motivations and agendas does constitute an enduring source of weapons diffusion and availability in the region. While it is widely acknowledged that the presence of arms does not directly cause conflict, it has also been shown that arms availability, and arms transfer to areas of conflict may lead to the escalation of violence (Bourne 2004). As it has been noted earlier, communal conflicts and arms proliferation in the region are not mutually exclusive. Yet, when conflicts end, arms remain in the local communities with implications for their recirculation and use in future conflicts. The ready availability of arms thus undermines intercommunity reconciliation and peace in the region. Accordingly, the continuing availability of arms in villages, in this case, community weapons problematize the distinction drawn between conflict zones and post-conflict settings (Rogers 2009: 5).

Furthermore, the renting of community vigilante arms by vigilante leaders to armed robbers and communities in conflicts in the Niger Delta has emerged as a key structural factor that feeds and escalates crime, insecurity and conflicts in local communities in the region. In 2008, a vigilante leader in charge of the Kono Boue community weaponry, was arrested by the Joint Military Task Force (JTF) for renting community weapons to armed robbers. This is another form of commodification of violence in the Niger Delta that is synonymous with the practice of renting arms by military personnel to insurgent groups in the region (Agwu 2011).

Yet, youths have also exploited the vigilante space and their access to, and control of community weapons to contest the authorities and powers of chiefs and elders of local communities in their struggle to have a share of the natural resource wealth of the region. In several communities, youth/vigilante groups have been transformed into parallel leadership structures to chieftaincy institutions with implications for armed conflicts. In its complexity, the Rumuekpe conflict of 2005–2008 in which no fewer than 100 people died, is a notable example (Akpobari and Obodoekwe 2009). Some scholars like Obi (2006) have described such violent youth agitation as intergenerational struggle for inclusion and participation in community leadership processes as well as a general dissatisfaction with hierarchies of power, paternalism and patrimonial domination, which they consider as a structural barrier to their own advancement.

From the above, it can be argued that the dynamics of, and risks associated with community vigilante arming in the Niger Delta pose a significant threat to sustainable peacebuilding and security in the region. Paradoxically, however, local communities and their vigilantes have been excluded from various government arms control and disarmament programming in the region (Davidheiser and Nyiayaana 2011). This policy gap therefore has implications for how we seek to transform social relations between vigilante groups and local communities in the context of enhancing the "guarding of the guardians" especially in the face of collapsing traditional means of arms control. It also has implications for how we approach arms proliferation dynamics and arms control in the Niger Delta in the context of the growing involvement of MNOCs and state actors.

Conclusion

Vigilante policing has occupied a central place in peace and security discourse in Africa. Questions of legitimacy, legality and effectiveness of vigilante groups in community protection have dominated debates amongst scholars. This chapter shifts attention from the legitimacy and effectiveness arguments and advances our understanding of post-Cold War vigilantism in Africa by examining the actors involved in the arming of vigilante groups, their motivations and implications for sustainable peacebuilding and security in Nigeria's Niger Delta. It argues that community policing has a long history in the protection of village-communities in the Niger Delta. However, the logic and contradiction of the diverse interests of local political elites, MNOCs and state governments, which are the key actors involved in the financing and arming of vigilante groups have fundamentally altered the nature, character and purpose of community policing.

For example, while chiefs and political elites arm vigilante groups to acquire political power or in pursuit of regime security, MNOCs particularly Shell, on the other hand, finance vigilante groups in local communities to protect and advance their business goals. Accordingly, community vigilantism in the Niger Delta has acquired a political character, in which there is a shift away from people's collective security to the security of local elites, chiefs and oil companies. Yet, all the various arms procurement patterns of the actors leave the local communities with highly sophisticated weaponry, thus contributing significantly to the proliferation of SALW in the Niger Delta in ways that fuel insecurity, crime and conflicts in the region. This chapter therefore draws attention to the need for arms control and a peace policy that addresses the risks associated with vigilante arming in the region. This is because disarmament and arms control policies initiated in the region have ignored local communities and vigilante arming processes (Davidheiser and Nyiayaana 2011).

References

Abrahams, R.G. (1987). Sungusungu: Village vigilante groups in Tanzania. *African Affairs*, 86(343): 179–96.

Abrahamsen, R. and Williams, M.C. (2007). Securing the City: Private Security Companies and Non-State Authority in Global Governance. *International Relations*, 21(2): 237–53, doi: 10.1177/0047117807077006.

Adamu, F.L. (2008). Gender, *Hisba* and the Enforcement of Morality in Northern Nigeria. *Africa*, 78(1): 136–52, doi: 10.3366/E0001972008000089.

Agwu, F.A. (2011). *From Rebellion, Insurgency to Belligerency: The Niger Delta Oil War in International Law*. Ibadan: Ibadan University Press.

Akpobari, C. and Obodoekwe, S. (2009). *Fueling Discord: Oil and Three Niger Delta Communities*. A Report of Social Integrated Development Centre (Social Action), Port Harcourt, Nigeria.

Amunwa, B. (2011). *Counting the Cost: Corporations and Human Rights Abuses in the Niger Delta*. Platform, London. http://platformlondon.org/nigeria/Counting_the_Cost.pdf.

Amusan, L. (2014). From Operation Law and Order to Operation Restore Hope: Human Security Crisis in the Niger Delta. In Christopher Lamonica and J. Shola Omotola (eds), *Horror in Paradise: Frameworks for Understanding the Crises of the Niger Delta region of Nigeria*. North Carolina: Carolina Academic Press, 144–69.

Anderson, D.M. (2002).Vigilantes, Violence and the Politics of Public Order in Kenya. *African Affairs*, 101(405): 531–55, doi: 10.1093/afraf/101.405.531.

Badmus, I.A. (2010). Oiling the Guns and Gunning for Oil: Oil Violence, Arms Proliferation and the Destruction of Nigeria's Niger-Delta. *Journal of Alternative Perspectives in the Social Sciences*, 2(1): 323–63, http://e-publications.une.edu.au/1959.11/6581.

Bates, R.H. (2008). *When Things Fell Apart: State Failure in Late-Century Africa*. New York: Cambridge University Press.

Bisina, J. (2003). *Reducing Small Arms, Increasing Safety and Security and Minimising Conflicts in the Niger Delta Region*. A paper presented at a Roundtable organized by African Strategic and Peace Research Group (AFSTRAG) at Motel Benin Plaza, Benin City, Nigeria. http://nidprodev.org/files/ND percent20small percent20arms percent20analysis.pdf.

Bourne, M. (2004). An Examination of Small Arms Proliferation and Areas of Conflict. Unpublished PhD Dissertation, University of Bradford, UK.

Branch, D. and Cheeseman, N. (2008). Democratisation, Sequencing, and State Failure in Africa: Lessons from Kenya. *African Affairs*, 108(430): 1–26, doi: 10.1093/afraf/adn065.

Brown, R.M. (1975). *Strain of Violence*. New York: Oxford University Press.

Chabal, P. and Daloz, J.P. (1999). *Africa Works: The Political Instrumentalisation of Disorder*. London: James Currey.

Comaroff, J. and Comaroff, J.L. (2006). Figuring Crime: Quantifacts and the Production of the Un/real. *Public Culture*, 18(1): 209–46, doi:10.1215/08992363-18-1-209.

Davidheiser, M. and Nyiayaana, K. (2011). Demobilization or Remobilization? The Amnesty Programme and the Search for Peace in the Niger Delta. *African Security*, 4(1): 44–64, doi: 10.1080/19392206.2011.551063.

Fourchard, L. (2008). A New Name for an Old Practice: Vigilantes in South-western Nigeria. *Africa*, 78(1): 535–58, doi: 10.3366/e000197200800003x.

Frynas, J.G. (1998). Political Instability and Business: Focus on Shell in Nigeria. *Third World Quarterly*, 19(3): 457–78.

Gore, C. and Pratten, D. (2003). The Politics of Plunder: The Rhetorics of Order and Disorder in Southern Nigeria. *African Affairs*, 102: 211–40, doi:10.1093/afraf/adg014.

Harnischfeger, J. (2008). Balance of Terror Rival Militias and Vigilantes in Nigeria. *Afrikanistik-Aegyptologie-Online*, http://www.afrikanistik-online.de/archiv/2008/1756.

Higazi, A. (2008). Social Mobilisation and Collective Violence: Vigilantes and Militias in the Lowlands of Plateau State, Central Nigeria. *Africa*, 78(1): 106–35, doi: 10.3366/E0001972008000077.

Human Rights Watch (2002). Nigeria: Bakassi Boys: The Legitimization of Murder and Torture. *Human Rights Watch Report*, May, 14 (5a) http://www.hrw.org/reports/2002/nigeria2/nigeria0502.pdf.

Human Rights Watch (2007). Criminal Politics, Violence, "Godfathers" and Corruption in Nigeria. *Human Rights Watch Report*, October, 19 (16a) http://www.hrw.org/reports/2007/nigeria1007/nigeria1007web.pdf.

Inikori, J.E. (1977). The Import of Firearms into West Africa 1750–1807: A Quantitative Analysis. *Journal of African History*, 18(3): 339–68, doi: http://dx.doi.org/10.1017/S0021853700027304.

Isumonah, V.A. (2013). Armed Society in the Niger Delta. *Armed Forces & Society*, 39(2): 331–58, doi: 10.1177/0095327X12446925.

Iyang, F. (2012). Murder of 4 UNIPORT Students: An Exclusive Story Behind their Death. *Daily Post*, October 8, http://dailypost.ng/2012/10/08/murder-4-uniport-students-an-exclusive-story-behind-death/.

Joab-Peterside, S. (2007). *On the Militarization of Nigeria's Niger Delta: The Genesis of Ethnic Militia in Rivers State, Nigeria Niger Delta*. Economies of Violence Working Paper, No. 21, Berkeley: Institute of International Studies, University of California.

Johnston, L. (1996). What is Vigilantism? *British Journal of Criminology*, 36(2): 220–36.

Killingray, D. (1986). The Maintenance of Law and Order in British Colonial Africa. *African Affairs*, 85(340): 411–37.

Kirschner, A. (2011). Putting out the Fire with Gasoline? Violence Control in Fragile States: A Study of Vigilantism in Nigeria. In Wilhelm Heitmeyer, Heinz-Gerhard Haupt, Stefan Malthaner, and Andrea Kirschner (eds), *Control of Violence: Historical and International Perspectives on Violence in Modern Societies*. New York: Springer, 536–69.

Koblentz, D.G. (2013). Regime Security: A New Theory for Understanding the Proliferation of Chemical and Biological Weapons. *Contemporary Security Policy*, 34(3): 501–25, doi: 10.1080/13523260.2013.842298.

Kuku, K. (2013). *Assessing the Dynamics and Sustainability of the Niger Delta Amnesty Programme*. A presentation made by Kingsley Kuku, Special Adviser to the President on Niger Delta to Nigeria's nationals in Diaspora. Publication of the Amnesty Office, Abuja: Nigeria.

Last, M. (2008). The Search for Security in Muslim Northern Nigeria. *Africa*, 78(1): 41–63, doi: 10.3366/E0001972008000041.

Leach, M. (2004). Introduction to Special Issue: Security, Socioecology, Polity: Mande Hunters, Civil Society, and Nation-States in Contemporary West Africa. *Africa Today*, 50(4): 7–16, doi: 10.1353/at.2004.0052 .

Loader, I. (2000). Plural Policing and Democratic Governance. *Social & Legal Studies*, 9(3): 323–45, doi: 10.1177/096466390000900301.

Mbembe, A. (2001). *On the Postcolony*. Berkeley CA: University of California Press.

McCall, J.C. (2004). Juju and Justice at the Movies: Vigilantes in Nigerian Popular Videos. *African Studies Review*, 47(3): 51–67.

Naanen, B. and Nyiayaana, K. (2013). State Failure and the Niger Delta crisis. In Mojubaohu O. Okome (ed.), *State Fragility in Nigeria*. London: Palgrave Macmillan, 111–46.

Naanen, B. and Tolani, T. (2014). *Private Gain Public Disaster: Social Context of Illegal Oil Bunkering and Artisanal Refining in the Niger Delta*. Report of the Niger Delta Environment and Relief Foundation (NIDEREF). Choba, Port Harcourt: NIDEREF.

Newby, B. (2012). *Watchful Guardian or Dark Knight? The Vigilante as a Social Actor*. International Foundation for Protection Officers, July, http://www.ifpo.org/wp-content/uploads/2013/08/Newby_Vigilante.pdf.

Nolte, I. (2007). Ethnic Vigilantes and the State: The Oodua People's Congress in South-western Nigeria. *International Relations*, 21(2): 217–35, doi: 10.1177/0047117807077005.

Nyiayaana, K. (2011). From University Campuses to Villages: A Study of Grassroots-Based Cult Violence in Ogoniland. *Eras*, 12(2): 1–35.

Obi, C. (1999). Resources, Population and Conflicts: Two African Case Studies. *Africa Development*, 24(3): 47–70.

Obi, C. (2006). *Youth and the Generational Dimensions to Resource Control Struggles in the Niger Delta*. Council for the Development of Social Research in Africa (CODESRIA) Monograph Series, Dakar: CODESRIA.

Odoemene, A. (2012). The Nigerian Armed Forces and Sexual Violence in Ogoniland of the Niger Delta Nigeria, 1990–1999. *Armed Forces & Society*, 38: 225–51, doi: 10.1177/0095327X11418319.

Okonta, I. (2006). *Behind the Mask: Explaining the Emergence of the MEND Militia in Nigeria's Oil-bearing Niger Delta.* Working Paper, No. 2 Institute of International Studies, University of California.

Okorobia, A. and Olali, S.T. (2013). Ethno-nationalism and Identity Conflicts in Nigerian History: The Niger Delta situation to 2012. *Mediterranean Journal of Social Sciences,* 4(4): 431–47, doi:10.5901/mjss.2013. v4n4p431.

Pratten, D. (2008a). The Politics of Protection: Perspectives on Vigilantism in Nigeria. *Africa,* 78(1): 1–16, doi: 10.3366/E0001972008000028.

Pratten, D. (2008b). The Thief Eats His Shame: Practice and Power in Nigerian Vigilantism. *Africa,* 78(1): 64–83, doi: 10.3366/E0001972008000053.

Raleigh, C. (2014). Pragmatic and Promiscuous: Explaining the rise of Competitive Political Militias across Africa. *Journal of Conflict Resolution,* July 3: 1–28, doi: 10.1177/0022002714540472.

Reno, W. (2002). The Politics of Insurgency in Collapsing States. *Development and Change,* 33(5): 837–58, doi: 10.1111/1467-7660.t01-1-00251.

Rogers, D. (2009). *Postinternationalism and Small Arms Control.* Farnham: Ashgate.

Ruteere, M. and Pommerolle, M. (2003). Democratizing Security or Decentralizing Repression? The Ambiguities of Community Policing in Kenya. *African Affairs,* 102(409): 587–604.

Saro-Wiwa, K. (1995). Nigeria in Crisis: Nigeria, Oil and the Ogoni. *Review of African Political Economy,* 22(64): 244–6.

Smith, R.S. (1989). *Warfare and Diplomacy in Precolonial Africa.* Madison: University of Wisconsin Press.

Tilly, C. (1992). *Coercion, Capital and European States: AD 990—1992.* Oxford: Blackwell.

Watts, M. (2008). *Petro-insurgency or Criminal Syndicate? Conflict, Violence and Political Disorder in the Niger Delta.* Niger Delta Economies of Violence Working Paper, No. 16, http://oldweb.geog.berkeley. edu/ProjectsResources/ND%20Website/NigerDelta/WP/16-Watts.pdf.

Young, C. (2004). The End of the Post-Colonial State in Africa? Reflections on Changing African Political Dynamics. *African Affairs,* 103(410): 23–49, doi: 10.1093/afraf/adh003.

Chapter 11
Neo-Liberal Peacebuilding in Libya: Sketching the Path to Reconciliation

Saira Bano Orakzai

Abstract

The post-2011 civil war and ongoing conflict in Libya has manifold spatial dimensions. The conflict has altered the social and spatial geography in the Middle East and Africa, and the involvement of external state and non-state actors has magnified the historical, social and transnational aspects of the conflict. This chapter examines the ongoing conflict between warring militias in Libya: a conflict over space, order and resources that follows in wake of Colonel Muammar al Gaddafi's 42-year rule, which was overthrown in October 2011. In order to understand the ongoing conflict in Libya, two factors are important to consider. First, it is a struggle for control over territorial space that has intensified pre-existing ethnic polarization. Second, it is a quest by the conflicting parties to establish a new order to their own advantage. This conflict has now been termed a civil war, driven by ethnic tensions and regional interferences. This chapter aims to examine the impact of post-conflict neo-liberal peacebuilding in Libya in order to sketch a path for long-term reconciliation.

Introduction

The Arab Spring, which started in Tunisia in 2010 and subsequently engulfed the Middle East and North African (MENA) region was by February 2011, the catalyst for enabling a mass popular uprising to erupt and engulf Libya (Dabashi 2012: 5; Laremont 2014). These protests-blooded by Gaddafi, the US and NATO-have resulted in civil war and ongoing conflict throughout Libya. The civil war in Libya is one conflict where the socio-political dynamics of local spaces have influenced the physical materiality of the conflict itself. This chapter will thus examine the spatial dimension of the conflict in Libya as a quest to pursue a certain form of order by different groups, within the paradigm of civil war and ethnic conflict. The chapter will also look at how the uprising influenced by the Arab Spring transformed into a civil war driven by ethno-political polarization. It will further examine the failure of neo-liberal peacebuilding approaches, used by the international community, to resolve the conflict and reconstruct Libya. More specifically, this chapter asks: a) what historical factors have contributed to the intensification of spatial cleavages that appear in Libya?; b) to what extent do spatial cleavages influence the ethnic conflict and impact on the civil war?; and c) how is the quest to control space influenced by external actors and the impact of the neo-liberal peacebuilding approach in Libya? The chapter also explores how the historical process of ethno-territorial polarization is visible in the social and physical geography of the region. Within the theory of conflict transformation, the chapter examines the integrated framework of peacebuilding as proposed by John P. Lederach (1997). This will help in sketching the path to reconciliation in Libya.

A Brief History of Libya

Historically, the territories comprising modern Libya were part of the Ottoman Empire, and for 20 years after the Italo-Turkish war of 1911–1912 these territories were occupied by an Italian colonial government. In 1934, Italy united these territories into the colony of Italian Libya, which was later seized from the Italians in 1942–1943 and divided among the allied French (Fezzan) and British (Tripolitania-Cyrenaica) forces. Libya also has a history of colonial resistance. Prominent among its anti-imperialist movements was the almost 20-year resistance movement led by Omar al Mukhtar, who commanded tribal troops from the eastern region against the Italians until his execution in 1931. This anti-colonial movement had a far-reaching impact, mainly for the revolution which was led by Gaddafi in 1969 against foreign powers and their control over Libya (Pargeter 2012). Later in 2009, when Gaddafi visited Italy, he wore a badge carrying a picture of the execution of Omar al Mukhtar. Nevertheless, during the uprising in 2011, Mukhtar was termed as the idol of rebels by Gaddafi in the eastern province (Khatib 2012: 192).

When Libya declared political independence in 1949, it was the first African state to do so through a resolution of United Nations General Assembly. Before the discovery of oil reserves in 1959, however, Libya, under the rule of King Idris al Sanusi (head of the Sanussiyyah Sufi Order of Islam), was one of the most impoverished nations in the world and relied heavily on foreign aid (Pargeter 2012: 36). In 1953, for example, Libya signed an agreement with Britain granting it access to ground military facilities and flight rights over Libyan airspace, in return for £2.27 million per year in budgetary aid and £1 million in economic development funds between 1953 and 1958. A similar agreement with the United States (US) government gave US armed forces the right to use Wheelus Air Base in return for economic aid, and the Libyan government also gave concessions to American oil companies for oil exploration (Pargeter 2012: 44). During this period, the foreign policies of western powers and their activities in Libya were determined by oil interests thus influencing Libya's policies in turn giving the image of imperialist control over Libya's national oil assets (Paoletti 2011: 316). However, its newly-tapped oil resources also meant that Libya was able to start exporting oil, which enabled the nation to thrive economically on its own.

Within a decade, the country's per capita income had grown from US$25–30 to US$2000 per annum (Pargeter 2012: 41). Alongside the oil boom, the Libyan government introduced a reform agenda which led to increased migration from rural areas to the capital cities, resulting in a new cosmopolitanism. The changes to Libya's economy also offered new economic and trade opportunities for its people. The oil-based economy also created a new class of bureaucrats and technocrats. With the introduction of a broad-based education system, new educational programs and ideologies were able to be disseminated. After the successful nationalization drive in neighboring Egypt under Gamal Abdul Nasser, Libyans also began to be influenced by revolutionary socialist ideas.

In 1969, Colonel Gaddafi deposed King Idris in a military coup led by a young officers' movement inspired by the Egyptian revolution under Nasser, and started the processes for the eventual nationalization of the country's oil industry. Like Egypt's, the Libyan revolution had anti-imperialist tendencies and was socialist in orientation. The coup was followed by multiple political and social reforms under a system of governance called *Jamahiriya* (a term coined by Gaddafi and typically translated as the "state of the masses") (Pargeter 2012: 42–4). With the change of regime, the center of political power shifted from eastern Cyrenaica to western Tripolitania. During the next 42 years of Gaddafi's rule, Libya experienced several periods of economic and military sanctions and diplomatic stand-offs with the West, on the issues of terror links and terrorist activities including the Berlin discotheque and Lockerbie bombings. Sanctions were eased briefly in 2003 when Libya suspended its program of enriching uranium for weapons of mass destruction (Pargeter 2012: 42–4).

There have been two central features in the development of modern Libya, according to Dirk Vandewalle (2012): oil and the revenues generated by it. Oil and gas reserves were in abundance compared to the country's small population of 6.5 million. In 2010, despite sanctions by the UN, Libya had gold and foreign exchange reserves of US$4 billion and an estimated annual income of US$6–US$8 billion (Metz 1987). Thus, despite ranking as one of the poorest nations in the world in the 1950s, Libya, at the time of the uprising in 2011, had the highest Human Development Index (HDI) in Africa at 0.784, ranking it 55th in the world (United Nations Development Program 2010). It had free health care, education and welfare systems, and an annual growth in GDP of five percent and per capita income of US$13319.1 (United Nations Data 2011). According to a World Bank (2010) report, Libya also had an improving record of women's rights, with more women receiving education and employment. The Libyan government also constructed the Great Man-Made River (GMR) providing fresh water and sanitation to its people. Illiteracy and homelessness were mostly eradicated under Gaddafi, thereby improving the quality of life of the average citizen in Libya (Hussein 2013). However, its oil dependency meant that the Libyan economy lacked economic diversification.

Despite economic development and the oil economy, however, the masses remained disempowered. Fluctuations in the oil market, the increasing globalization of the market economy, and the state's focus on nationalization led to public dissatisfaction and mismanagement and corruption enabled by lack of accountability and transparency. For its part, the regime mostly blamed sanctions and international security for its economic ills. These issues, and the people's concerns with the government, were raised in the National General People's Congresses (Sawani 2014: 85). Saif ul Islam Gaddafi, son and heir designate of Gaddafi, initiated reforms not only for economic and political liberalization, but also to ease international sanctions and improve relations with western powers. The issue of Lockerbie was resolved and economic restructuring commenced, but the absence of accompanying political and legal reforms limited what could be achieved. The establishment of the Gaddafi Development Foundation in 2003 did lead to some economic achievements, especially through the National Economic Strategy for Youth (young people constituted 65 percent of the total population), but structural issues arising from extensive nationalization and a lack of private ownership lay deep within the system and posed challenges to reform (Sawani 2014: 86–7). The state also partially ended the welfare system as part of its reform, and the private ownership that was allowed was marred by corruption on the part of the ruling elite and others in positions of influence.

Despite these efforts at economic reform, the state continued to pursue a policy of strict control, state repression and severe human rights violations against its opponents. Libyan society—organized along ethnic and tribal lines—faced political repression, multiple levels of reform processes, and human rights violations. Moreover, there was centralization of power at the top while diffusion of power at the lower level in political and military circles in order to avoid any political dissent to uproot Gaddafi's government. The Libyan economy was dependent on oil revenues with no development of economic infrastructure independent of the oil industry, and excessive centralization of political power. In particular, Gaddafi's regime was opposed to the Sanussiyya Sufi order that was linked to his predecessor King Idris, and state policies reflected a rejection of conventional Sufi Islam. Furthermore, Gaddafi pursued a strong policy of tribalism and supported tribal structures instead of allowing political parties or organizations to flourish, which made tribes an important part of Libyan state and society. Gaddafi also pursued a policy of "pan-Arabism" and a "mono-Arab" state (Harding 2012), disregarding the existing ethnic cleavages within the state. This was underpinned by his Third International Theory—published in a short treatise outlining Gaddafi's political philosophy known as the *Green Book*—which reconciled Nasserist nationalism, Bedouin desert egalitarianism and stateless ideology (Paoletti 2011: 315). The rejection of conventional Sufi Islam in state policy was followed by a strict repression of political dissidents, especially Islamists (the Muslim Brotherhood) in Libya. Similarly, ethnic discrimination against Berbers and non-Arabs resulted in cleavages within the state structure that also paved the way for the movement for change known as the Arab Spring.

Connecting Space with Conflict: Physical Materiality and the Socio-Political Dynamics Shaping the Conflict and Civil War in Libya

Space and conflict provide a very important theoretical prism through which to examine conflicts involving identity, territory and resources. However, space, when considered in terms of physical space, is too narrow a concept through which to understand conflict, especially when considering the dynamics that lead to interrelationships between socio-economic issues. As Chojnacki and Engels observe, one of the most interesting aspects when examining conflict is exploring the connection between material conditions and the socio-cultural and political factors that contribute to the conflict (2013: 5). Under spatial theory, space is considered to be socially produced, while conflict is a social action. This brings space and conflict into a very interesting dialogue when examining conflict dynamics, opening avenues to be explored for reconciliation. In this chapter, the focus is on the conflict research perspective, with an emphasis on the symbolic relevance of locations, resources and collective identity. Reuber states that, in postmodern research, spatial geography connects with conflict research through six sub-fields which are helpful in deconstructing the discourses and narratives in a conflict situation (2000: 39–40). These sub-fields, which will be used in this chapter in an interconnected fashion, include territorial conflicts, boundaries, ecological politics, resource conflicts, geo-politics, the politics of identity, globalization and new international relations, symbolic representations of political power and, lastly, regional politics and new social movements.

Ethnically, Libya is comprised of diverse groups which reflect conflict dynamics through different periods of history. The major ethnic groups in Libya include Arabs, Amazigh (also called Berbers), Tuareg (nomads) and Toubous (of African descent). The country has been divided into: the oil-rich eastern region of Cyrenaica, where the Sufi order of Sanussi flourished during Ottoman rule and which retains many Turkish cultural features; the western region of Tripolitania which is Arab-Berber dominated; and the desert region of Fezzan, the home of the Toubou majority (Paoletti 2011: 305). These three regions reflect "physical separation ... [they have] differing colonial experiences, and diverse cultural traditions" (Pargeter 2012: 36). The vast location and division of the territory, coupled with ethnic and tribal cleavages, give rise to a single population that is replete with differing political perspectives and historical experiences.

Gaddafi came from the western region and belonged to the Qaddadfa, an Arabized Berber tribe located in and around Sirte. The Arabization of Libyan society under Gaddafi led to the marginalization of several non-Arab ethnicities which were denied equal citizenship and suffered from a range of discriminatory policies restricting political participation and basic social welfare (Martin and Weber 2012). This primarily affected the Toubou black African ethnic groups located in the southern province of Fezzan. Well-connected with Toubous in the northern regions of Chad, Niger and Sudan, Libya's Toubous were mostly living in the southern towns of Sabha, Kufra, Murzuq and Qatrun and constituted 0.2 percent of the total population. The area has been the site of local insurgency and conflict since 2007 (Martin and Weber 2012), and is the major focal point of the post-2011 civil war in Libya.

In the eastern region of Cyrenaica, with its capital of Benghazi and towns of Derna, al Baida and Tobruq, there is a more primordial sense of tribalism and Islam as opposed to the cosmopolitanism and federalism more popular in the western region. The people in the eastern regions and Benghazi (the center of an Islamist uprising in the 1990s) played an important role in the 2011 uprising. Indeed, the violent uprisings started in Benghazi. Thus, it is no surprise that representatives from the eastern region constituted the majority in the National Transitional Council (NTC) formed during the uprising (Sawani 2012: 6–7), making up for their marginalization during Gaddafi's long rule.

In the western region of Tripolitania or Barqa, which includes Tripoli and the important towns of al-Zawia, Misratah and Tajoura, the question of Arab-Amazigh ethnic polarization is very critical. The western region remained mostly pro-Gaddafi and was the beneficiary of favorable state policies due to its large ethnic Arab population. Despite this, the Amazigh (Berber) community comprising just ten percent of the total 6.5 million population of Libya, and living in this western region and extending up to Morocco suffered continued persecution during the Gaddafi regime which, for example, passed a series of discriminatory socio-political policies including the banning of the Tifinagh language of the Amazigh/Berbers (Harding 2012). Having endured discrimination and state repression for many years, the regions dominated by non-Arab ethnicities were more than ready for rebellion. Gaddafi in his 42 years of rule deliberately tried to play with the tribal politics and affiliations, and established the "regions" as the important unit of analysis in Libyan politics. During the last few decades of the regime, oil and resources became important factors dividing the regions and the post-Gaddafi period has seen a strong re-emergence of eastern-western regional politics.

The 2011 Popular Uprising and Civil War in Libya

The uprising in Libya can be seen as part of the so-called Arab Spring, which started in Tunisia and spread to Egypt and other parts of the Middle East. Benghazi, the capital of the eastern region, became the center of Libya's uprising, which started after the arrest and killing of prominent human rights activist Fethi Tarbel on February 15, 2011. The protests focused on the regime's human rights abuses and social program mismanagement and called for an end to Gaddafi's 42-year rule (Bhardwaj 2012: 81). The riots and protests spread into Tripoli and were dealt with through severe crackdowns involving the use of helicopter gunships and regime snipers. The coastal city of Misratah was taken over by anti-government militias amid attempts by the regime to restore order through the use of violence and repression.

The international community reacted swiftly, with the UN Security Council (UNSC) imposing sanctions on the regime on February 26, 2011. Gaddafi's offshore assets, as well as those of his family, were frozen by different countries. The National Transitional Council (NTC), formed on February 27 in Benghazi, was recognized as the main body representing opposition forces. On March 17, the UNSC imposed a no-fly zone over Libya and authorized airstrikes to halt Gaddafi's crackdown on insurgents. In the meantime, the International Criminal Court issued warrants for the arrest of Gaddafi and his son Saif ul Islam for crimes against humanity. The September 1, 2011 Paris Conference on Libya discussed the country's future and gave further international legitimacy to the NTC leadership. NATO's intervention (under UNSC Resolution 1973, passed on March 17, 2011) included 15 NATO countries and proved to be crucial in providing air strikes, military training and weapons for rebel forces. Further, international intervention in the Libyan conflict gave a sense of identity, recognition and instrumental capacity to the NTC to act as an anti-regime pro-democracy movement (Bhardwaj 2012: 86).

On October 20, 2011, Gaddafi was captured and killed by rebel militia in Sirte, caught on the run after his fortified town of Bab al Aziziya was captured by rebels. Decades of regional and international isolation (although partially ameliorated in his last years) made Gaddafi's regime susceptible to condemnation by the Arab League and the Gulf States, especially Qatar which had already shifted its support to the NTC. The NTC celebrated victory on October 23, 2011 and formed an interim government with the aim of bringing security, stability and the restoration of normal life for Libyans, and was charged with organizing elections for parliament (International Coalition for the Responsibility to Protect, 2011).

The NATO mission ended on October 31, 2011. Since the toppling of Gaddafi's regime, the sole aim of the international community has been the formation of a stable government. However, the existence of large stockpiles of weapons, given to insurgents by foreign governments, as well as the proliferation of the weapons of the former regime, has contributed to the protraction of the civil war. This volatile situation is similar to that witnessed in Afghanistan. After the Soviets withdrew in 1989, a civil war erupted in 1991 (with brief lulls in 1994 and 1999) due to both the availability of large stockpiles of weapons and the failure of efforts to form a broad-based unity government.

Unlike the Arab uprising led by civil society and labor unions in Egypt and Tunisia, the Libyan uprising was led by rebel groups, mostly from the eastern province. Maya Bhardwaj observes that the Gaddafi regime's crackdown exacerbated the grievances of the people and acted as a "proximate cause" for the uprising, while the militarization of the NTC by the international community and the diffusion of political actors made the civil war evitable (2012: 82). The ongoing civil war since 2011 is also rooted in the territorial division of Libya into rebel-controlled and loyalist-controlled cities. In the western region, the Islamist stronghold of Misratah and liberal Zintan towns are playing an important role in fueling the civil war. The opposition has mostly centered on the rural-tribal base, while exploiting pre-existing tribal-ethnic divisions within the society. The marginalized Berber community in the western region, the Toubou in the southern Fezzan region, and the people of the eastern province exploited this conflict to gain political benefits. The loyalists (i.e. the pro-Gaddafi local militias) are still concentrated in Tripoli and Sirte, as these areas were previously state controlled and of personal significance to Gaddafi.

Following the ousting of the Gaddafi regime, elections were held in Libya in August 2012. These were the first elections to be held since 1977. The Muslim Brotherhood won a majority in the 2012 elections and the NTC transferred power to the General National Congress (GNC). However, the new government was unable to draft a constitution and, instead of holding elections promised by the end of 2013, extended its mandate to December 2014. The failure to orchestrate a smooth political transition, amid limited initiatives for the disarmament, demilitarization and reintegration of rebel groups and militias, led to the formation of the Libyan National Army (LNA) by General Khalifa Haftar (a former member of the Gaddafi military turned dissident who had been living in exile in the US since the 1980s). The LNA challenged the Islamists and launched Operation Libyan Dignity on May 16, 2014. The Libyan Army's Special Forces also pledged its support to the group. As a result of growing political pressure, the GNC held new elections on June 25, 2014, but a deepening political crisis followed the subsequent Islamist loss to liberals and federalists.

Refusing to accept the election results, a coalition of Islamists named Libyan Dawn formed. Both alliances, Libyan Dignity and Libyan Dawn, have very loose political and military factions. Libyan Dawn consists of Islamists, Muslim Brotherhood, tribes of Misratah, Zintan militia, Berbers, the GNC, Former Prime Minister in Gadaffi's regime Mahmood Jabril factions, and the Loyalty to the Martyrs group, representing different shades of Islamists, liberals and ethnic affiliation. Similarly, the Dignity group is mostly comprised of anti-Gaddafi people, pro-revolutionaries and people discriminated against on ethnic grounds and is showing growing atomization, and getting closer in the alliance. Both groups have questionable agendas. Libyan Dawn started fighting after the elections in 2014 by laying siege to the Tripoli International Airport. The siege was laid by the Zintan militia.

As a result of the siege, the House of Representatives had to relocate from Tripoli to Tobruk. In August 2014, rebel militias took control of the airport and announced the restoration of the GNC as the governing authority of Libya. Now Libya had two parallel governments existing simultaneously, one led by General Haftar and another by Islamists. The dividing line of the Libyan conflict was now drawn between two loosely-defined groups with differing ideologies. According to Mansour al-Hisadi, a member of the Muslim Brotherhood in Libya, Ansar al Sharia-a radical Islamist group led by Mohammad Zahawi-and General Haftar represent "two extremes that will block Libya's progress. What they have in common is they are both against the democratic process-one in the name of religion and the other in the name of the military" (Fitzgerald 2014).

Ansar al Sharia is a radical Islamist group formed after the revolution. It is composed of networks of Islamists and former inmates of the Abu Salim Prison, where Islamists were kept during the crackdown by the Gaddafi regime. On September 11, 2012, the group attacked the US diplomatic compound in Benghazi and was subsequently declared a terrorist group by the US government and the United Nations. The group also includes people associated with the Salafi-jihadist network of ISIS and al Qaeda, and is involved in socio-economic projects and charitable organizations. It has declared the Libyan civil war a war on Islam by the west, and is strongly opposed to the liberals and General Haftar.

Politically, the Muslim Brotherhood (formed in 1949 and brutally suppressed by the Gaddafi regime) is a significant challenge. The group's violent reaction to losing the elections in 2012 also stems from the repression of the like-minded Egyptian Muslim Brotherhood by the Egyptian military, which resulted in the arrest and execution of hundreds of Muslim Brotherhood members. General Haftar's forces are also particularly targeting Islamists in the eastern province due to the Islamist sympathies of the people in this area (Fitzgerald 2014). Currently there are over four million displaced people in Libya and some of the nation's most vital infrastructure has been destroyed in the years following Gaddafi's downfall in October 2011. As such, this crisis requires immediate peacebuilding efforts to be taken up alongside national reconstruction. The next section will detail some problems with the peacebuilding measures currently being undertaken by the international community in Libya and discuss reasons for the lack of positive outcomes.

Conflict and the Failure of the Neo-Liberal Peacebuilding Approach

This section examines the impact of the neo-liberal peacebuilding project and its effect on the ongoing civil war and reconfiguration of state power in Libya. Libyans are faced with a tough challenge to create a new political order and a new society, deliberately destroyed in the 42 years of Gaddafi's rule. The civil war in Libya is one attempt by different groups to create order in the state. At present, as discussed earlier, two divergent trends are apparent. One is led by the liberals and federalists and supported and aided by the west. On the other side are the Islamists, supported by transnational state and non-state actors, mostly with ties to the Middle East and South Asia. As far as peacebuilding is concerned, Richmond opines that it is torn between two forms of liberalism (2010: 15). The first is based on state security and territorial sovereignty, while the second emphasizes human emancipation based on justice and equity.

Post-conflict peacebuilding is mostly concerned with Johan Galtung's (1996) concept of positive peace, which follows a bottom-up approach based upon local consensus. Yet, in the post-Cold War era it has become a multidimensional activity aimed at the construction of liberal peace, connecting peacebuilding with state building with or without local consent (Richmond 2010: 22). This conception includes the establishment of a vibrant civil society, a human rights regime, democratic and participatory processes, a market economy and good governance-the basic pillars of liberal peace. According to Richmond, the critics of liberal peace focus on "issues with its universal claims, its cultural assumptions, its top down institutional, neo-liberal and neo-colonial overtones, and its secular and rationalist nature" and call it a "hegemonic peace" (2010: 26). The local post-war reactions to peacebuilding or state-building arising from the intervention and emancipation of Iraq and Afghanistan, illustrates the rejection of liberal peace by its supposed beneficiaries.

Since the collapse of Gaddafi's government, numerous capacity building programs have been initiated in Libya by western powers. The UK government is carrying out peacebuilding projects in Libya through the Arab Political Participation Fund, which supports the development of civil society and the local media to encourage public participation, peacebuilding and the democratization process (UK Government 2013a) while the Conflict Pool Projects look at reforming the security, justice and defense sectors of the newly-formed Libyan government (UK Government 2013a; 2013b). These projects, operating since May 2011, aim to improve the security sector and build the capacity of the people. The UK government has also assisted by allocating £2 million for different projects in Libya that promote women's rights for political, economic and social emancipation (UK Government 2013a; Foreign & Commonwealth Office 2013).

Neo-Liberal peacebuilding after the end of Cold War, has made Security Sector Reform (SSR) an important part of its process and its connection with development has led to the formation of a security-development nexus. This is in contrast to the previous human security-centered approach. SSR is mostly based on state-centric security concepts and reform (of the armed forces and police forces) dictated by the donor states. It is also focused on institutional capacity building in conflict-torn countries. SSR and broader neo-liberal peacebuilding activities are considered to be state-building strategies that benefit donor states. In Libya, NATO countries and the US have pledged to train around 19,500 Libyan soldiers while the US will train 5,000 to 8.000 soldiers for a general purpose military force (Wehrey and Cole 2013: 4). Lacher (2013) observes that the issue of NATO's intervention in the Libyan crisis is particularly sensitive and has raised suspicions over the long-term interests of western powers in the country. The Islamists, after their defeat in the election of 2012 also raised this issue (Lacher 2013).

The United Nations Peacebuilding Fund (UNPBF) also allocated US$19 million to Libya, mainly for the purpose of empowering women and youth to fully participate in the July 2012 elections. In March 2013, the UNPBF approved another project worth US$500,000 for peace and state building, as well as SSR, in Libya. The project's main stated aims were the pursuit of transitional justice, constitutional reform, and the empowerment of women and youth. The UN Peacebuilding Mission is headed by the UN Support Mission in Libya, and it is providing support for countering the proliferation of illicit arms, promoting human rights and the rule of law, international humanitarian assistance and coordination, security sector reform and a peaceful democratic transition (UNPBF 2013). For its part, the role of the US in Libya is low key, due to its image in the Middle East and also due to the attack and killing of its diplomatic staff in Benghazi in 2012. Nevertheless, the US is active in assisting various peacebuilding projects in the country, such as those focused on women and youth, reconciliation, forgiveness and unity, encouraging the democratic process and other peacebuilding measures.

The discourse of the western-led humanitarian-interventionist approach to peace in Iraq, Afghanistan, Libya and Syria is highly contested because it is framed along lines of the liberal peace project. In this regard, the projection of a specific concept of peace and transformation emanating from Western liberal ideals into Muslim societies through "peacebuilding" and "reconstruction" is producing negative political trends, not least by strengthening jihadists arguments that it constitutes a form of Western imperialism. Jabri argues that this dimension of intervention differs from traditional approaches, as it rests on liberal societies acting as agents for the transformation of target societies rather than working towards conflict resolution (2010: 41). The purpose of this kind of peacebuilding is to redesign the societies in order to transform them into liberal (and thereby peaceful) societies. Williams points out that this form of reconstruction and peacebuilding can "[tie] reconstruction to the historical experience of the West in dealing with the 'Rest' over a period that can easily be traced back a couple of hundred years, and in some cases further" (2010: 59).

This form of peacebuilding is considered a continuation of the League of Nation's Mandate System or the United Nations Trusteeship System. Williams further argues that negotiation as a form of conflict resolution has been completely rejected, and instead "reconstruction" through military intervention has been adopted as a policy tool for transforming these societies along the lines of the Marshall Plan policies pursued in post-Second World War Germany and Japan (Williams 2010: 68). This form of state-building is now redefined as "peacebuilding." The liberal peace project is also visible in An Agenda for Peace, propounded by the then-UN Secretary General Boutros-Ghali in 1991, which bases the limits of state sovereignty on human concerns, together with concerns for indicators of state failure due to societal breakdown, warlordism and/or lack of working state institutions. Jabri points out that to intervene in other societies is by definition colonial, suggestive of dispossession, radicalised domination, and subjugation. Clearly, the historical record of the forms of intervention [mentioned above] directly points to resource dispossession, as witnessed in Iraq. However, the primary form of dispossession relates to the dispossession of agency, the capacity to determine what constitutes political identity. (2010: 42)

This, according to Jabri, comes under the liberal peace project's view of human security and protection or rescue. "Far from being an emancipatory project, therefore, the liberal peace project might be seen as reinforcing a hierarchical conception of subjectivities premised on the primacy of the European liberal self as against others whose modes of articulation remain 'other'" (Jabri 2010: 48). Jabri further cites the example of state building in Afghanistan through the epistemological construction of the "civilizing mission" and "responsibility to protect" (2010: 48), by establishing structures of governance while viewing the social breakdown of the society as having emancipatory potential, the forces of reaction as insurgency, and oppositional forces as militants and culprits. All of these constructions were applied to Afghanistan: the purpose being to use the military to achieve peace and development goals .Furthermore, this aspect of the liberal peace project is seen as dispossessing the target societies of self-determination and following an epistemological and ontological universalism which is not only centered around military and carceral power but also pedagogical power (Jabri 2010: 50–51).

The Path to Reconciliation

The failure of the liberal peacebuilding project in Libya is evident from the fact that the political process which wals designed to achieve stability has in fact resulted in a brutal civil war and a prolonged crisis. The capacity building programs have failed, as they were unable to target the root cause of the problem. Moreover, the political process is still nascent. There are parties on the ground fighting to establish an order of their own choice. The Political Isolation Law (2013) passed by the Libyan parliament banned all Gaddafi-era officials from participating in the political process (except those who defected). This law was one of the main reasons for the failure of the political process for reconciliation, resulting as it did in human rights abuses and the displacement of tribes and ethnic groups close to Gaddafi or those who supported Gaddafi during the uprising (Anadolu Agency 2015). The challenge at present is how to transform the complexity of this conflict into an opportunity for future reconciliation.

On February 2, 2015, the Libyan parliament in Benghazi repealed the Political Isolation Law so that Gaddafi-era officials could be part of the new Libyan society and serve in the government (Anadolu Agency 2015). These steps were essential to transform what had become a zero-sum conflict. The poison of polarization in Libya on the ground, especially at the societal level, deeply divides the society. In Libya, dialogue means different things to different people with a range of divergent interests. In the six tracks of Geneva talks, which started on January 26, 2015, the future of Libya's ceasefire, the role of the unity government and the role of General Haftar were some of the contentious issues under discussion (Housman 2015). For future political reconciliation and the formation of a unity government, it is important to remove polarizing personalities such as Haftar from future arrangements. However, on the ground, he has strong local support and long-term political ambitions which will create problems in case of his removal.

In the Geneva talks, major parties are not directly included in the dialogue process especially leadership of Libyan Dawn and Libyan Popular National movement (LPNM) known as Green Resistance has not taken part, but only those politicians who do not have any stake in the conflict nor have ground presence are included. Libyan Dawn have taken control over the Benghazi Central Bank further creating problems for future peace (Stephen 2015). The critical issues which need to be seriously dealt with are: the future of the security apparatus; the selection of leadership; the role of Benghazi in the future political setup; the security of oil reserves; the existence of multiple levels of command and control; as well as questions of dependence on/ownership of oil revenues (as the political empowerment is directly related to economic empowerment) (Housman 2015).

Economic ownership has fragmented since the demise of Gaddafi's policy of centralized ownership that kept the population dependent on the state. Now there is private ownership by the rival factions that control the oil resources. Equal access to and ownership of the oil reserves and associated revenues should be an important pillar of the dialogue process. This could completely change the nature of the Libyan state and must be a part of a deeper discourse concerned with resolving structural problems. One pressing problem for the peace process is the draining of cash resources in Libya which is creating an humanitarian crisis in Libya and contributing to the rise of Islamic State (IS) and its attacks on Libya, thus jeopardizing an already fragile peace process (Stephen 2015).

As mentioned earlier, the conflict following the uprising has led to the existence of two independent governments operating simultaneously rather than a broad-based unity government. However, the problems faced by Libya are deeper than just the absence of a national unity government. In the period since Gaddafi's downfall there has been serious damage inflicted to infrastructure, and the withdrawal of foreign expertise in health care and water has meant limited sanitation. For the reconciliation process to evolve there is need for a national dialogue on: the formation of a unity government; a ceasefire agreement; wider security arrangements; and building confidence and momentum around talks. To this end, local capacity building is an important step and, as witnessed in the prisoner exchanges organized by local communities (Donovan 2014), encourages localized solutions and emphasizes the importance of local councils for pursuing reconciliation. Local tribes and councils can also support the Geneva process, by helping to facilitate a ceasefire and communication between factions.

The role of "spoilers" in undermining the peace and reconciliation process is also an important issue to address, with the main challenges coming from those sections of the population who feel a lack of inclusion, in particular, Blacks of African descent, Berbers, and other minorities. Other groups, such as Islamists including the Muslim Brotherhood and pro-Gaddafi groups also fear exclusion. The ongoing conflict in Benghazi raises particular problems, as it connects inter-tribal divisions with revenues from oil reserves (Zurutuza 2015). In this regard the use of local sources for reconciliation, especially tribal mediators, could be used to advantage. Indeed, utilizing the existing tribal structure for the pursuit of long-term peace could bring positive results. The sidelining of Gaddafi-era supporters and officials is also problematic in this respect, as these officials are extremely influential in certain tribal circles. An inclusive approach is therefore essential for reconciliation. Also critical to the reconciliation process is the role of external actors, particularly those in the Middle East and the Arab world. Regional players like the United Arab Emirates (UAE), Saudi Arabia, Egypt, Turkey, and Sudan are important, as they support different groups and thus impact conflict dynamics. For example, the military leadership in Egypt wants to sideline the Muslim Brotherhood in Libya, while Saudi Arabia and the UAE support anti-Islamist groups. Meanwhile, Turkey and Qatar are playing the Islamist card by supporting Libyan Dawn (Tharoor and Taylor 2014). In February 2015, Egypt launched airstrikes against Islamist groups in Derna and Sirte as a reaction to the killing of 21 Coptic Christians by Islamist particularly IS's members thus increasing the fear of regional interference in Libya (*The Guardian* 2015).

To achieve reconciliation in such a complex conflict is undoubtedly a difficult process. Nevertheless, achieving reconciliation within a society is an important part of the process of conflict transformation. In order to have a successful peacebuilding process in Libya it is essential to respect the democratic process, to handle the question of the distribution of economic and political opportunities carefully, and to build local support by considering local needs. Theoretically, the reconciliation and healing process rests on relational empathy, forgiveness and the provision of justice in society. The present division of Libyan society into liberals and Islamists and its accompanying violence demands more effective modes of interaction. The use of force by General Haftar, and the anti-western approach of the Islamists, requires that different actors be incorporated into, rather than eliminated from, the democratic process and respect for the democratic process firmly established.

Many peacebuilding theories assume that people in a given society should value diversity and be tolerant of difference, whether based on religion, ethnicity or race. Johan Galtung's (1996) concepts of "negative" and "positive" peace, as applied to peacebuilding, define the termination of conflict as "negative peace" and post-conflict peacebuilding ventures as "positive peace." Most peacebuilding strategies also stress the need to address the structural problems and long-term relationship dynamics that are at the root of the tensions between conflicting parties, as a way of overcoming structural, relational and cultural tensions. The case of Libya needs a long-term approach to peacebuilding as an integrated concept, due to the complicated nature of the civil war and Libya's history as a dysfunctional state.

Lederach (1997: 74–5) maintains that violent conflicts are mostly followed by negotiation, and that violence is a cyclical process with attendant humanitarian crises that obscure the long-term view of conflict by drawing attention solely to the need for complex disaster management processes. Lederach supports a framework that not only includes complex disaster management, but also incorporates a transformative peacebuilding model that focuses on building sustainable relationships. He suggests three levels of response to conflict structures: a short-term response for crisis prevention and complex disaster management; a long-range response for visioning the common future; and a middle-range response for connecting short-term and long-term responses when designing social change processes of intervention (1997: 76–7). Lederach observes the idea of

> "structures" suggests the need to think *comprehensively* about the affected population and *systematically* about the issues at hand. "Process" underscores the necessity of thinking creatively about the *progression* of conflict and the *sustainability* of its transformation by *linking* roles, functions and activities in an integrated manner. Together, the two sets of lenses suggest an integrated approach to peacebuilding ... (1997: 79 [emphasis in original])

Theoretically speaking, the traditional peacebuilding process uses the nation state as its basic unit of analysis and focuses on root causes and structural changes, while strategic peacebuilding in the post-Cold War era assumes the presence of multiple actors and the need for multiple intervention methods to build sustainable peace. Thus, a transformative process focused on realizing social justice, ending violent conflict, and creating cooperative relationships is a complex process. Lederach's approach to peacebuilding is based on integrating these multiple dimensions and timeframes for peacebuilding and transformation (1997: 26–7). Interestingly, Ury considers the role of the local population in the peacebuilding and transformation process as that of developing a "social immune system, preventing the spread of the virus of violence" (2000: 7).

Libya is a vast and diverse country, but its ethnic cleavages are not the basis of the conflict itself (although they have fed into the competing grievances of the people). It is the lack of economic and political diversification, as well as discrimination within the state structure, which has produced the present conflict dynamics. The majority of Libyans adhere to the Sunni sect of Islam (Malaki subsect) and Sanuyyiya Sufi order, which makes it a fairly religiously homogenous country. While marginalized, the Berber and Tuareg ethnic minorities have not expressed separatist sentiments. The state's discriminatory structure and the absence of citizenship equality, lack of political freedom and prevalent human rights abuses have been mostly responsible for uprisings and insurgencies over the decades. The marginalized eastern province of Cyrenaica has participated with the western Tripolitania in a joint struggle to remove the government of Gaddafi. The uprising of 2011 and subsequent civil war has depicted that the question that will be important is of resources, power structure and establishing order, between the conflict parties.

One of the important factors requiring attention is the building of a civil society structure in Libya at the grass root level which is locally developed and owned. Under Gaddafi, a deliberate attempt was made to keep different structures of affiliation intact (tribal, ethnic, regional) thereby restricting opportunities for the development of political and less cohesion in political sense was allowed. One of the contentious issues in this regard is the proliferation of militias, rebels and other groups with large stockpiles of arms, which hampers ongoing crisis prevention and disaster management. Here the African Union and the Arab League should play an important role in this conflict, particularly in relation to its connections with other regional conflicts in Chad, Nigeria, Mali and Algeria. A centralized army and demilitarization under UN auspices is also an important step in ameliorating the consequences of UN resolutions authorizing the use of force and supply of arms to opposition camps during the uprising.

In line with the foregoing, one of the most important challenges faced by the post-Gaddafi government in Libya is creating a state for all ethnic and regional minorities and avoiding the lack of political inclusion experienced under Gaddafi. The question of grievances is also three-layered: The pre-uprising; Gaddafi era; and long term. In February 2012, an agreement for a national reconciliation and transitional justice law was reached and a fact-finding and reconciliation committee was formed by the elected government of Libya. However the mechanism could not be utilized as these sensitive issues require an in-depth examination of local sensitivities, diverse experiences and pre-and post-war divisions (Peaceful Change Initiative 2012: 2).

In the civil war, people belonging to pro-Gaddafi territories have been subjected to revengeful attacks especially in Sirte, Twaurgha. The question of allocation of seats in the elections to different regions and communities, and allocation of resource is also one of the contentious issues. Similarly, people of Derna in eastern region have been subjected to heavy use of military and air force in order to target the Islamists in the area. The communal and ethnic conflict has also intensified with the black-Africa people of Toubou, Tuareg on the question ethnic discrimination and the pre-uprising role of the Tuareg people (with strong ethnic ties to and post-Gaddafi political connections to insurgent groups in the Malian region of Timbuktu) in the Gaddafi security setup and punitive measure taken against them by the Misratah community after the uprising. There is also conflict between tribes of Al Zuwarah and Al Jamel/Raqdalin over the question trade across Tunisia, job quotas and control of local councils. The local community of Sirte (the hometown of Gaddafi) also feel socially and politically isolated and subject of punitive measure by the rest of communities due to their support to Gaddafi during the uprising. Similarly, the presence of Gaddafi era officer in civil and military sectors is also one of the contentious issues.

Conclusion

The peacebuilding and reconciliation process in Libya is a resource-intensive project (Dobbins and Wehrey 2011) as it requires consideration of the spatial conditions, ethnic issues and conflict grievances emerging out of the present civil war. Libya is an oil-rich country, with oil reserves its main economic base for development. Even in the absence of economic diversification and with the imposition of sanctions, the pre-war per capita income in Libya remained US$13319.1 (United Nations Data 2011) per year. Based on Lederach's integrated model of peacebuilding, the Libyan state requires a model of peacebuilding which is rooted in local sources and locally driven and owned, instead of a peacebuilding project imported from abroad. Further, the model should focus on the social, economic and political structures of the society as the drivers of development (while working for the sustainability of the process as well as supporting actors and their functions).

To sum up, the civil war in Libya has local and international dimensions, which need to be addressed adequately. It is important to formulate an approach which is human-centered and locally driven (but aided by regional actors), in order to address the grievances of all communities. Libya has experienced four decades of a dysfunctional state that failed to diversify both political and economic resources throughout the larger community, despite economic stability. The struggle to control territorial space by actors in the conflict must be dealt with through fair and equal democratic and political participation that does not advantage any specific conflict actor. The role of the regional and international community is critical for coming to an understanding of the root causes of ethnic, regional and ideological problems; understanding that can then underpin a peacebuilding strategy for Libya. Three main areas of concern have emerged out of this chapter, each of which can play an important role in diffusing tensions: economic diversification, locally-owned national systems of government, and the centralization of oil resources and revenues and their equal distribution. Moreover, it must be accepted that any effort to restructure Libyan society based on liberal peacebuilding, as experimented with in Iraq and Afghanistan, will be met with local resistance, as is already evident in the form of the Islamist-Liberal divide. To create a peacebuilding process that can lead to sustainable peace and development, it is essential to utilize local and regional understandings of peace and reconciliation for the reconstruction of Libya, along with help from international bodies to assist with the disarming and demilitarization of militias and rebel forces.

References

Bhardwaj, M. (2012). Development of Conflict in Arab Spring Libya and Syria: From Revolution to Civil War. *Washington University in St. Louis International Review*: 76–97, https://pages.wustl.edu/wuir/development-conflict-arab-spring-libya-and-syria-revolution-civil-war.

Chojnacki, A. and Engels, B. (2013) Material Determinism and Beyond: Spatial Categories in the Study of Violent Conflict. *SFB- Governance Working Paper Series* No. 55.

Dabashi, H. (2012). *The Arab Spring: The End of Postcolonialism*. London: Zed Books.

Dobbins, J. and Wehrey, F. (2011) Libyan Nation Building after Gaddafi, *Foreign Affairs*, August 23, http://www.foreignaffairs.com/articles/68227/james-dobbins-and-frederic-wehrey/libyan-nation-building-after-qaddafi.

Donovan, B. (2014). Transforming a Culture of Revenge in Post-revolution Libya, *NIMATI: Innovations and Empowerment*, January 10, http://namati.org/transforming-a-culture-of-revenge-in-post-revolution-libya/.

Fitzgerald, M. (2014). Libya's Rogue "War on Terror." *Foreign Policy*, June 5, http://foreignpolicy.com/2014/06/05/libyas-rogue-war-on-terror/.

Foreign & Commonwealth Office (2013) *Human Rights and Democracy: The 2012 Foreign & Commonwealth Office—Libya*, http://www.hrdreport.fco.gov.uk/human-rights-in-countries-of-concern/libya/?showall=1.

Galtung, J. (1996) *Peace by Peaceful Means: Peace and Conflict, Development and Civilization*. London: Sage.

Guardian, The. (2015) The Guardian view on Libya: More Diplomacy, not bombs, required: Editorial. February 24, http://www.theguardian.com/commentisfree/2015/feb/24/guardian-view-libya-more-diplomatic-efforts-not-air-raids-required.

Harding, L. (2012). Libya beset by Ethnic Tensions as Elections Loom. *The Guardian*, July 4, http://www.theguardian.com/world/2012/jul/04/libya-ethnic-tension-elections-berbers.

Housman, L. (2015). Libya's Green Resistance: Big Absentee at Geneva Talks but not Silent, January 27, http://english.pravda.ru/hotspots/conflicts/27-01-2015/129621-green_resistance-0/.

Hussein, M. (2013) Libya Crisis: What Role do Tribal Loyalties Play? BBC Monitoring, February 21, http://www.bbc.co.uk/news/mobile/world-middle-east-12528996.

International Coalition for the Responsibility to Protect (2011). *Libya Post-Gaddafi*. http://www.responsibilitytoprotect.org/index.php/crises/190-crisis-in-libya/5646-crisis-in-libya-post-gaddafi.

Jabri, V. (2010). War, Government, Politics: A Critical Response to the Hegemony of the Liberal Peace. In O.P. Richmond (ed.), *Palgrave Advances in Peacebuilding: Critical Developments and Approaches*. New York: Palgrave Macmillan, 41–57.

Khatib, L. (2012). *Image Politics in the Middle East: The Role of the Visual in Political Struggle*. London: I.B. Tauris.

Lacher, W. (2013) The Fault Lines of the Conflict: Political Actors, Camps and Conflicts in the New Libya, *SWP Research Papers*. file:///D:/libya/2013_RP04_lac%20libya.pdf.

Laremont, R.R. (ed.) (2014). *Revolution, Revolt and Reform in North Africa: The Arab Spring and Beyond*. London: Routledge.

Lederach, J.P. (1997) *Building Peace: Sustainable Reconciliation in Divided Societies*. Washington DC: United States Institute of Peace.

Martin, P. and Weber, C. (2012). *Ethnic Conflict in Libya: Toubou*. http://www4.carleton.ca/cifp/app/serve.php/1394.pdf.

Metz, H.C. (ed.) (1987). Libya: The Economy. In *Libya: A Country Study*. Washington: GPO for the Library of Congress, http://countrystudies.us/libya/.

Paoletti, E. (2011). Libya: Roots of a Civil Conflict. *Mediterranean Politics*, 16(2): 313–19.

Pargeter, A. (2012). *Libya: The Rise and Fall of Gaddafi*. New Haven: Yale University Press.

Peaceful Change Initiative (2012). *A Peacebuilding Agenda for Libya, Peaceful Change Initiative*. October, http://www.peacefulchange.org/uploads/1/2/2/7/12276601/a_peacebuilding_agenda_for_libya_web.pdf.

Richmond, O.P. (2010). A Genealogy of Peace and Conflict Theory. In O.P. Richmond (ed.), *Palgrave Advances in Peacebuilding: Critical Developments and Approaches*. New York: Palgrave Macmillan, 14–38.

Reuber, P. (2000). Conflict Studies and Critical Geopolitics-theoretical Concepts and Recent Research in Political Geography. *Geo Journal*, 50: 30–43.

Sawani, Y.M. (2012) Post-Gaddafi Libya: Interactive Dynamics and the Political Future. *Contemporary Arab Affairs*, 5:1: 1–26, http://www.tandfonline.com/doi/pdf/10.1080/17550912.2012.650007.

Sawani, Y.M. (2014) The February 17 Intifada in Libya: Disposing of the Regime and Issues of State Building. In R.R. Laremont (ed.) (2014). *Revolution, Revolt and Reform in North Africa: The Arab Spring and Beyond*, London and New York: Routledge, 75–104.

Stephen, C. (2015). Libya Peace Talks Gain Urgency after ISIS Attack on Tripoli Hotel. *The Guardian*, January 29, http://www.theguardian.com/world/2015/jan/29/libya-peace-talks-urgency-after-isis-attack-tripoli-hotel.

Tharoor, I. and Taylor, A. (2014). Here are the Key Players Fighting the War for Libya, All Over Again. August 27, http://www.washingtonpost.com/blogs/worldviews/wp/2014/08/27/here-are-the-key-players-fighting-the-war-for-libya-all-over-again/.

UK Government (2013a) *Supporting Sustainable Change in Libya.* https://www.gov.uk/government/policies/working-for-peace-and-long-term-stability-in-the-middle-east-and-north-africa/supporting-pages/supporting-sustainable-change-in-libya.

United Nations Data (2011) *Libya.* https://data.un.org/CountryProfile.aspx?crName=Libya.

United Nations Peacebuilding Fund (UNPBF) (2013). *Libya.* http://www.unpbf.org/countries/libya/.

United Nations Development Program (2010). *Human Development Report: Libya.* http://hdr.undp.org/en/countries/profiles/LBY.

Ury, W.L. (2000). *The Third Side: How We Fight and How We Can Stop.* New York: Penguin.

Vandewalle, D. (2012). *A History of Modern Libya.* Cambridge: Cambridge University Press.

Williams, A.J. (2010). Reconstruction: The Missing Historical Link. In O.P. Richmond (ed.), *Palgrave Advances In Peacebuilding: Critical Developments and Approaches.* New York: Palgrave Macmillan, 58–73.

Wehrey, F. and Cole, P. (2013) Building Libya's Security Sector. *Policy Outlook.* Carnegie Endowment for International Peace, August, http://carnegieendowment.org/files/building_libya_security.pdf.

World Bank (2010). *Country profile Libya.* http://search.worldbank.org/all?qterm=Libya+2010&os=10.

Zurutuza, K. (2015). Libya's Berbers Fear Ethnic Conflict. *Aljazeera News*, January 6, http://www.aljazeera.com/news/middleeast/2014/12/libya-berbers-fear-ethnic-conflict-2014123065353199495.html.

Chapter 12
Building Peace with Warlords in South Sudan: A Gendered Structure

David John Duriesmith

Abstract

Since the official end of conflict between the Republic of the Sudan and the Sudan People's Liberation Army (SPLA) in 2005 efforts to build peace have proliferated in South Sudan. Although these programs have drawn on considerable resources and gained the rhetorical support of the southern administration they have had little success in demilitarizing the world's newest state. With the re-emergence of organized armed conflict between factions in South Sudan since December 2013 there is a new need to understand the failure of peacebuilding. This chapter will explore the gendered dynamics of peacebuilding programs in South Sudan, suggesting that they have primarily been focused on the reconstruction of patriarchal authority and the entrenchment of militarized masculinity. The chapter suggests that the peacebuilding agenda in South Sudan has a distinct gendered structure that has been ignored in much of the current analysis. Furthermore, that the peacebuilding efforts in South Sudan should be understood to be a failed attempt to establish order between groups of militarized men and that the failed process of peacebuilding has been structured to further marginalize groups of non-militarized men, women, and non-violent forms of conflict resolution.

Introduction

In the wake of widespread conflict breaking out across the Republic of South Sudan in November and December 2013, international commentators have begun to ask what went wrong with the world's newest state. After seceding from Sudan in 2011, South Sudan it was hoped would have a bright future. Since then the state has faced increasing difficulties with corruption, nepotism, instability and factional in-fighting within the government. Although progress until mid-2013 had been slow, official programs have been in place to begin a process of Disarmament, Demobilization and Reintegration (DDR) (Nichols 2011). As part of the Comprehensive Peace Agreement (2005) the southern Sudanese administration was required to carry out wide-ranging peacebuilding programs. These programs, in theory, were supposed to begin a process of building positive peace by destroying weapons and removing combatants from the control of armed organizations before integrating them into society. In line with the Sudan People's Liberation Army's (SPLA) obligations they were required to begin a extensive process of demilitarization, including reductions in the number of military personnel, destruction of civilian small arms and an increased role for civil society in the functioning of the state. Far from the achieving the goals of stabilizing and reconstructing the Southern Sudanese state these programs have done little in real terms in disrupting the power of the military.

Although much has been written about the role of corruption, ethnicity, opportunism and militarism in the current fighting (Amusan 2014; Sandu 2011), the gendered dynamics of peacebuilding have received little attention. Over the decades of conflict in South Sudan the armed men of the SPLA were able to obtain a dominant place in society, gaining key roles in state leadership and pushing many of the traditional civilian leaders to peripheral positions (Mampilly 2011: 138–41). This gradual process of power accumulation fits best with feminist understandings of militarization, where society is transformed to reflect military values, to venerate military service and to reward military personnel (Jok and Hutchinson 2002). Although the international community has largely welcomed the members of the SPLA as freedom fighters in the post-conflict period, their actions during the conflict often bear closer resemblance to warlords, accumulating personal power and influence over the general population (Stern and Bubenzer 2011). During the height of the secessionist war, the leaders of the SPLA gained significant political, economic and cultural power over civilian society in the South.

This chapter suggests that the current failure of peacebuilding in South Sudan can be, in part, attributed an inability to recognize and respond to the gendered dynamics of militarization. International peacebuilding attempts are working towards a strong state and to improve the weak infrastructure in South Sudan. Although these attempts have yielded some positive results they have so far not been successful in diffusing the central power of military men in South Sudan. The DDR programs in South Sudan have not significantly impacted on the material capacity of the SPLA and its splinter factions to engage in war. To understand the failures of peacebuilding in South Sudan this chapter asks, how did gender shape the DDR programs between 2005 and late 2013?

To answer this question the chapter aims to explore the design, implementation and impact of DDR programs in South Sudan with a particular focus on its gendered dimensions. The DDR programs include a wide range of policies and initiatives across the state with the aim of transitioning South Sudan back towards a "normalized civilian society" (Nichols 2011). These programs primarily included voluntary civilian disarmament, involuntary retirement of combatants, vocational training of ex-combatants and some funding for community integration programs. The core initiatives within these programs have been the demobilization of certain groups of soldiers (women, older men and boys) as well as targeted disarmament programs in some civilian areas. For a state that has experienced more wartime than peace since its independence from the British in the mid-twentieth century these programs were intended to establish normalization in a country that has not experienced a normal state of affairs in a lifetime.

In an attempt to construct this peace, programs have looked to other states successes and failures in peacebuilding. Learning from the experiences of programs including those in Sierra Leone, Liberia, and Burundi the UN-led programs in South Sudan aimed to decouple combatants from military organizations. These endeavors have historically focused on first removing the weaponry from combatants, in a desire to undermine their ability to continue fighting (Levely 2014). Secondly they aim to detach combatants from military organizations by disbanding units and physically removing fighters from the command structure (Stone 2011). Finally they have worked to reintegrate combatants into civilian society by providing vocational training, counselling and social services. Internationally, these programs have had considerable success with the first two goals, although the success of reintegration programmers has been mixed (Janzen 2014). Despite their successes, in many instances these programs have been structured along strict gendered lines, reinforcing male privilege and marginalizing female combatants (McKenzie 2009). This chapter aims to continue the research into gender and militarization by building on the scholarship of Lydia Stone (2011), by looking at the gender dynamics of peacebuilding in light of their recent failure, and with a direct examination of masculinities in this volatile state.

It focuses specifically on the role of gender in the failure of peacebuilding attempts, rather than broadly on gender and peacebuilding or on the many other significant components of the process. This is not to suggest that the other impacts of peacebuilding are insignificant or that there have not been some successes brought about by these programs. Rather, the aim of this chapter is to look at the specific ways in which gender, and particularly masculinity, impacted on the failure of peacebuilding between 2005 and 2013. This is intended to provide complimentary work to the existing scholarship of feminists such as Mckenzie (2009) on peacebuilding and female combatants, the work of Jok and Hutchinson (2002) on militarization and violence as well as the scholarship on peacebuilding more broadly.

This chapter suggests that the DDR process failed due to the continuing significance of militarized masculinity within Southern Sudanese society. If the peacebuilding process had succeeded in overthrowing the existing gender order, undermining the dominance of militarism in the post-war society, it would not have been possible for violent civil conflict to re-emerge.

The most recent stage of conflict in South Sudan broke out in December 2013 and has now claimed upwards of tens of thousands of lives. The two groups currently clashing in South Sudan have broadly been characterized as government forces and rebels. The government forces are led by the Dinka ethnic groups under Salva Kiir, South Sudan's President. The rebel forces are primarily constituted by the Nuer ethnic group and are led by the former Vice President, Riek Machar. The groups described as rebels have only just recently split from the main government forces, when fighting started last year. However the rebels are a continuation of Machar's splinter group, the SPLA-Nasir, who began fighting against the main SPLA forces more than 20 years ago (Mampilly 2011: 141). Far from being motivated by primordial ethnic differences, the original split between Machar and the SPLA—at the time led by former President Dr John Garang—was motivated by personal ambitions and ideological disputes about succession.

During the first period of fighting between SPLA and SPLA-Nasir, between 1991 and 2002, both groups aggressively preyed on civilian populations, engaging in systematic sexual violence, maiming civilians, looting, and other abuses (Jok 2006: 61). Although both groups targeted civilians of opposing ethnic groups, their attacks focused more on accumulating personal wealth, demonstrating power, and reprisals for perceived challenges to the authority of their leaders. Tensions between ethnic groups in South Sudan have a long history (Jok and Hutchinson 2002: 101–3) that extend to well before the beginning of the civil war in Sudan. Researchers Jok, a South Sudanese Dinka, and Hutchinson, an ethnographer with 30 years' experience working in Nuer communities, have explored the dynamics of conflict within South Sudan. They concluded that the escalation of armed conflict was primarily a struggle between armed men for positions of power. During the 1990s both groups justified predatory violence by claiming that they were simply protecting their own against the predations of other ethnic groups, or conducting reprisal attacks for previous acts of aggression. In practice the violence of both groups was devoted to establishing control over civilian populations, extracting resources, and challenging the authority of other armed men.

Historically, when Nuer and Dinka ethnic groups fought, the struggles tended to be small in scale and led to very few casualties due to strict norms surrounding the practice of combatants. In contrast the current fighting—like the conflicts from the 1990s—differs profoundly from traditional ethnic wars because it involves prolonged fighting, few restrictions on who is targeted, and widespread indiscriminate killing. Both Machar and Kiir did not gain their positions of power in South Sudan on the basis of political skills, but because of their long-established military dominance. Despite commanding militias implicated in brutal attacks on civilians (Human Rights Watch 1994) both were rewarded with positions of power, influence and wealth when South Sudan was established as a new nation after the war with the North ended. The reality is that the military men who now lead South Sudan took few significant steps to disarm, demobilize or reintegrate their soldiers into society. This meant that their forces have remained armed and ready to go war, and they have simply picked up where they left off when the struggle between Machar and Kiir restarted. This continues the longstanding trend towards a pattern of leadership that most closely resembles warlordism in South Sudan. In line with the scholarship on the concept of warlords, the patterns of Kiir Machar, and many other SPLA leaders, has resembled a process of privatization of power and force (Vinci 2008: 1–3) since the early 1990s.

Militarism and Gender Order

Every society is structured by a distinct gender order. Though all societies are defined by the gender relationships between men and women each will involve different power relationships between groups of men and women. To understand the dynamics of post-conflict reconstruction, the construction of the gender order (Cockburn 2010) can be explored by looking at the relationships between groups of men and women on the basis of class, ethnicity, age, location, sexuality, gender, religion and community (Caprioli, Gendered Conflict 2000: 53). In South Sudan these factors define relationships in nuanced and intersecting ways, one group of men may define their relationship with other groups of men on the basis of profession, for example military men in relation to agrarian farmers. For the same group, but in relationship to another section of society their ethnicity may be more significant. The gender order is defined by the gendered dynamics of these relationships and the dynamics of power that construct hierarchies between groups in society.

In utilizing the concept of the gender order this chapter draws on the scholarship of sociologist Connell (2005: 98–101). Connell introduces the concept of the gender order to emphasize the hierarchies that exist between the range of masculinities and femininities in society. Key to Connell's concept is that society should not just be understood as a range of power relationships between men and women on the basis of class differentials. Instead, he suggests that in any given society a range of competing gendered constructions define different groups' positions of dominance and subordination.[1] By looking at the relationships as establishing a gendered hierarchy it is possible to explore how peacebuilding programs work to reinforce or destabilize the relationships between groups in society. To understand the gender order in South Sudan it is necessary to view this in light of the militarization of gender that has occurred during the 1990s.

Prior to the development of the Second Civil War in South Sudan, the men who were engaged in formal military service occupied a secondary position within society. Although a substantial number of men, particularly a body of well-educated high ranking officers held significant positions, their authority was secondary to the dominating government in Khartoum and to the traditional tribal and religious leaders in southern communities. As the conflict progressed, the power relationships between groups within southern society changed and military men began to take on a more dominant role (Hutchinson 2000: 10). This process fits well with feminists' understandings of the militarization of masculinity. The shift of the most privileged and dominant group within Southern Sudanese society from civilian elders, who defined their status on the basis of age, genealogy or religious claim to military men whose status was defined by military prowess, heroic exploits or rank signifies a shift in the gender order. Jok and Hutchinson record the process of militarization within Nuer and Dinka communities as having occurred directly during the 1990s, when the two main factions of the SPLA split and began the original campaign of violence (Jok and Hutchinson 2002).

In 1993 when Kiir and Machar originally split both of their factions worked to recruit substantial numbers of young males from refugee camps and displaced communities. Within these camps, military leaders exercised authoritarian control over recruits, using brutal violence to punish and control soldiers (Hutchinson 2000). During the final decade of conflict with Khartoum this led to the accumulation of considerable power and resources into the hands of a limited number of commanders, undermining the authority and strength of civilian leadership and authority structures. This has had a pervasive impact on South Sudanese society, destabilizing the existing social hierarchies based on religious authority age or tribal authority (Jok 2007: 232–3). During the post-conflict era, the impact of militarization has continued. Despite the creation of an official civilian government, the leadership of the Sudan People's Liberation Movement (SPLM)—the political wing of the SPLA—and the government they have formed, remained dominated by military men. The process of militarization shook the southern Sudanese gender order, repositioning military men to a place of significant power and influence. Post-conflict reconstruction and DDR programs have not addressed the impact of militarization on the gender order, or challenged the dominance of military men.[2]

Rebuilding society after prolonged conflicts poses considerable difficulties for policy makers. Entrenched military culture, longstanding grievances developed over decades of war, degraded infrastructure and weak civic institutions all ensure that this task is difficult and requires the cooperation of many segments in society. In South Sudan these efforts have been complicated by the post-conflict dominance of the SPLA. Although these programs had some limited success in the rebuilding effort until 2013 the attempts to demilitarize society largely failed. This failure could be analyzed in a number of lights and has been explored extensively by non-governmental organizations (NGOs) (Young 2007; Nichols 2011; Internally Displaced Monitoring Group 2010; Ali 2011).

Peacebuilding programs in South Sudan have not successfully addressed the importance of masculinity in constructing the willingness of combatants to reintegrate into society. The aims of such programs were to undermine armed conflict and organized atrocities by integrating combatants back into civil society (Gross, Kudelko and Purvis 2011). Within South Sudan these programs reinforced the power of militant men, further marginalizing female combatants and civilians. Since 2005 women have been marginalized and ignored in

---

1   In the case of Australia, Connell (2005) suggests that this can be seen in the tension between traditional working class masculinity that defined the national ideology for decades and a new corporate white collar masculinity that has begun to dominate society in terms of material power.

2   Since independence women have made significant steps to gain recognition and positions of authority in South Sudan (Ali 2011). Despite these efforts, and guarantees of 25 percent female representation within the CPA the inter-conflict period has not been characterized by women gaining substantial power within the state. Research from Jane Kani Edwards (2014) on women's participation has suggested that there are systematic cultural, informal and formal barriers to women's involvement. The marginalization of women within Southern Sudanese politics is a much larger subject than the scope of this chapter and combines both factors that relate to militarization, such as the veneration of militarized masculinity, and those that don't, such as very low literacy rates in women and girls.

peace-building efforts. Studies on peace-building suggests that empowering women has many positive impacts on social stability and development (USAID 2012). Inequality in South Sudan has had a significant negative impact on economic development. After the conflict ended, women were quickly returned to "traditional" female roles and often excluded from independent involvement in society (Jok 2006: 61). Female populations who had been subjected to widespread rape and abuse have received scant attention and treatment (D'Awol 2011: 54). The focus on social reconstruction often prioritizes the "high politics" of armed men rather than addressing the pervasive impact of conflict on the majority of society (McKenzie 2009: 243). Prioritizing the high politics of state reconstruction has not only marginalized women and civilian men in South Sudan, it has reinforced the dynamics of warlordism that fueled the conflict. By monopolizing reconstruction efforts military leaders have been able to further entrench client relationships, using public funded programs to reward loyal followers. The resulting privatization of violence has substantially enhanced the factions' ability to fight, shackling combatants to their commanders rather than to a civil duty within the state (Jok 2011: 3).

To understand the gendered dynamics of international politics, Cynthia Enloe (2000: 1–3) reminds us that we must begin by asking where are the women. The decades of conflict in South Sudan have had a brutal effect on women who have been targeted by all armed groups. Many thousands of women are believed to have been subjected to rape (D'Awol 2011), however, the lingering effects of violence against women in South Sudan has not yet been fully measured. Though the social conditions for both men and women improved during the inter-war period, women still experience disproportionate exploitation and oppression including widespread gender based violence in the post-war context (Ali 2011: 11). This has been compounded by programs structured to reconstruct a patriarchal envisioning of pre-war Southern Sudanese society.

Programs in South Sudan have been constrained by limited vision and aims. Most existing DDR programs outside of South Sudan have first aimed to remove weapons from society, remove combatants from the control of military leaders, and give male combatants formal employment. In states such as Sierra Leone (Women's Commission for Refugee Women and Children 2002) and Mozambique (Bouta 2005: 8) women were either excluded from DDR programs, having been classified as non-combatants on the basis of their gender, or pushed towards feminized roles in the post-conflict periods. For many women this meant that they were directed to draw upon their "feminine" skills by directing them towards employment in tailoring, cookery, crafts and other traditionally feminized roles (Ortega 2010). Furthermore, women who have been associated with armed groups often are subjected to disproportionate stigma compared to their male counterparts, meaning that meaningful reintegration has been difficult to achieve. This has meant that women are often excluded from DDR programs, and when they have been included their involvement has often been structured to further marginalize them by placing them back into strictly feminized roles.

The inter-conflict path to reconstruction in South Sudan has been more successful in integrating female combatants, child soldiers and older soldiers than it has been in demobilizing the young male combatants that constitute the majority of SPLA fighters (Stone 2011: 43). DDR programs have focused on three key projects. The first of these has been demobilizing SPLA combatants, this component primarily carried out on the state military has focused on removing older combatants, young boys and female combatants from the SPLA. Although the SPLA had committed to quite a wide-reaching demobilization program (Stone 2011) by 2011 only 13 percent of the 90,000 combatants which the SPLA had agreed to demobilize had begun the process. Within this percent a disproportionate number of women, older combatants and young boys have been demobilized. The second key objective of the process had been civilian disarmament, similar to the demobilization program the SPLA had agreed to participate in widespread destruction of civilian small arms. Finally the programs were intended to successfully reintegrate combatants into civilian society by providing vocational training and other community-based programs. The DDR program in South Sudan successfully included thousands of women associated with armed groups, providing them with vocational training and some economic support (Stone 2011: 1). The active focus on including female combatants in South Sudan may appear to be an attempt to avoid the failings of other DDR programs earlier in the decade. Though the peacebuilding efforts actively worked to include women, they failed to address some of the most basic problems caused by militarized masculinity, such as the marginalization of civilian youth, the spread of military corruption and the epidemic of sexual violence in South Sudan.

Unfortunately the success of DDR programs in South Sudan at including women should not be interpreted as a successful adoption of feminist concerns. Rather, their focus on female combatants without attempting to disarm and demobilize male soldiers is part of the broader peace-building programs that reinforce the power of militarized men. South Sudanese DDR programs failed to successfully demobilize male combatants, who have largely remained within the SPLA and have been merged into state militaries or local militias (Gross, Kudelko and Purvis 2011: 12). Since independence, the SPLA has remained a powerful organization in the South with significant influence over the practices of the state. The "peacetime" power of the SPLA within the South Sudanese government has meant that they have been able to largely avoid wide-spread demobilization and disarmament (Stone 2011: 1). Rather than seriously attempting disarmament, the SPLA have used the DDR programs as a mechanism to retire combatants who are too old, injured or no longer useful to the SPLA without needing to provide them with financial support. This has allowed a program originally designed to reduce the size and impact of the SPLA to transform into an internationally funded form of social security for ex-combatants without substantially impacting the influence or capabilities of SPLA associated armed groups (Stone 2011: 1–8).

The failure to successfully unsettle the SPLA's social power in the post-secessionist conflict period has been disastrous for non-combatants in the South. Predatory forms of violence against women have persisted among many armed groups (Gross, Kudelko and Purvis 2011: 13), and brutal sexual violence against female civilians remains largely unpunished when the perpetrator is a member of an armed group (D'Awol 2011: 53). In contrast to many other forms of sexual violence already present within South Sudanese society, the use of sexual violence by armed forces is often directed towards relative strangers. Even though detailed large scale surveys of sexual violence do not yet exist, qualitative evidence supports the notion that the end of conflict has not put an end to the abduction and gang rape of women by soldiers (Gross, Kudelko and Purvis 2011: 12). The continuation of this practice, which was used as a weapon of war during the years of conflict, has also impacted on the large international migrant workforce of women in South Sudan. The wide-spread incidence of "stranger rape" has further contributed to a burgeoning prostitution industry in the southern capital of Juba that is largely structured to serve male soldiers (D'Awol 2011: 66).

The continuing crisis of sexual violence across South Sudan has been compounded by the prominence of spousal abuse. Patterns of spousal rape and sexual coercion that have developed as a result of militarization and war have continued since the end of formal hostilities. During the first decade of conflict, Jok Madut Jok (1999: 432) recorded the erosion of women's rights within marriages. As war progressed, marital sexual relationships within South Sudan were reorganized as a reproductive duty for women—a necessary national service. As conflict progressed the existing norms that protected women's reproductive rights and agency within marriage were eroded Jok (1999: 432). Since the end of conflict, women's agency has been further constrained by the rapid increases in "bride price" (Ali 2011: 9). This price has been driven up by the wealth from ex-patriot families, but has also been fueled by soldiers with increased incomes since the end of conflict. One of the impacts of the increased bride price is that men have come to expect unrestricted sexual access to their wives as a greater emphasis has been placed on the marriage contract as purchasing the rights to sexual service (Stern and Bubenzer 2011: 17).

Though martial rape is not recognized as criminal, or even a problem in most instances, the pressure to be sexually available has dramatically increased. In this way the impact of militarization and war is not contained by the boundaries of official war and peace. The creation of norms around wartime responsibility to produce the next generation of soldiers has fundamentally altered the reproductive norms that had previously restrained men's coital entitlements (Sten 2011). Exceptions made for wartime conditions, such as men demanding sexual access prior to weaning an earlier child, were justified due to soldiers' long stints at the front. With then end of official hostilities these exception concessions to national duty were not wound back, instead in many instances men's demands for sexual access were increased. For the wives whose lives remain militarized through their husbands continuing involvement in the new state military, their existence is still controlled by a culture dominated by militarization and male entitlement. This has created a continuum of violence (Caprioli 2004) between the secessionist war, where norms of male entitlement to sexual services from women were entrenched, to the inter-conflict period, where these norms became part of civilian culture through the inflation of bride price and during the current conflict as sexual violence proliferates.

Importantly, for understanding the implementation of peacebuilding programs in South Sudan the focus on removing women and older combatants from the armed services illuminates the gendered dynamics behind peacebuilding programs. The failures of peace building programs in South Sudan are examples of what happens when programs try to address the most visible symptoms of war (organized violence) without addressing the root cause. The peace-building programs have focused their attention on making sure that, particularly young men are lifted from the lowest position in society by providing them with employment, income and social status. This approach has been successful in lessening violent conflict between groups of men, but without challenging the abuse of women and children that was normalized during the years of war. This is another instance of a patriarchal bargain being struck between state leaders and young male militants rather than a coherent effort to unmake war or unsettle its core causes. Not only does this approach tend to exclude women at each stage, due to a variety of factors, it also aims to serve the oppressive power structures that existing prior to conflict, albeit in a more inclusive form. At the most basic level these programs have worked to re-establish patriarchal bargains that placate young armed men in society. Megan MacKenzie (2009: 261) has critiqued this approach to peacebuilding as being insufficient and short sighted. She has argued for "a truly progressive developmental post-conflict reconstruction program" that would "include more radical change in the area of women's status in society." This has not happened. Instead, the treatment of combatants since 2005 has entrenched male power, encouraged warlordism and militarism.

As part of the Comprehensive Peace Agreement (2005) with the Sudanese state South Sudan agreed to a wide-ranging program of DDR to encourage stability and long-term peace in the region. Taking a soft approach, it was decided that the DDR program would encourage around 45,000 combatants to voluntarily demobilize, rather than requiring mandatory demobilization or strong quotas for SPLA disarmament (Nichols 2011: 10–11). The original intent of this program was to begin the path towards reconstruction, stabilization and demilitarization in the region. In practice, these program strategically disarmed groups that threatened the power of the SPLA elite without significantly impacting on the martial capacity of the main SPLA factions. This can be seen in the success of the civilian disarmament program in northern Jonglei State targeting the Lou Nuer ethnic group. In comparison to the meagre success of other programs the disarmament efforts focusing on the Lou Nuer has been able to remove around 3,000 weapons from civilians (O'Brien 2009: 10–11). This successful program primarily targeted civilians affiliated with the White Army, a decentralized ethnic militia that previously backed Riek Machar's breakaway faction during the 1990s (O'Brien 2009: 21). This successful disarmament program did not substantially contribute to increased stability across the state, or reflect the extent of the state's capacity to disarm militias broadly. It does however indicate the SPLA's capacity to implement meaningful disarmament when it suited their interests, such as disarming a volatile opposing militia. In light of the SPLA's successful disarmament campaign targeting the White Army, their demobilization of female combatants and the lack of concerted effort to demilitarize state militaries, how should the peacebuilding programs in South Sudan be understood?

Ungendered analysis has tended to emphasize state incompetence, corruption, and the competition between Riek Machar and Salva Kiir's offices (O'Brien 2009: 49). Although all of these factors are significant the gendered impact DDR has remained hidden. The structure and implementation of DDR programs in South Sudan has reinforced warlordism and militarized masculinity, both forces of which have contributed to the re-emergence of conflict since 2013. Warlordism, in the form of privatizing violence and military resources (Marten 2006–7), has allowed state officials to treat DDR initiatives as a mechanism to manage their own and their opponents' personal armed groups. One of the core aims set out in the DDR program was to remove military power from the hands of the small number of commanders who had gained control of the various armed groups between the early 1990s and the end of conflict with the North (O'Brien 2009). Despite this stated aim the implementation of the DDR program reinforced the authority of military men over combatants. Due to the influence of military men in the SPLA over the South Sudanese government since the end of the secessionist war DDR was used as a way to privatize power further, providing a state funded retirement program for older soldiers and as a means of weakening opponents' military capabilities.

The use of DDR to retire older soldiers from armed service encouraged the privatization of violence by allowing commanders to reward good service with vocational training and support that is organized by DDR programs without substantially damaging their military capacity. This has contributed to the trend towards warlordism within South Sudan since the early 1990s by entrenching relationships of patronage from commander to combatant. Rather than undermining the martial capacity of armed men it has helped to protect their dominant position at the top of the gender order. Rewarding older combatants in this way has protected the loyalty of current combatants, demonstrating that they will be looked after beyond their current service.

The partisan use of these programs as a reward further tied the loyalty of combatants to their commanders, further strengthening the privatization of violence that has contributed to the current conflict so destructively.

This accumulation of power also includes a gendered dimension. Reinforcing the authority and power of military men has had a wide ranging impact on southern Sudanese life, from marriage, to justice and economics. Since the end of conflict in South Sudan, Marc Sommers and Stephanie Schwartz have recorded the increased privileging of military men within marriage relations and society more broadly (Sommers and Schwartz 2011). The increased political control of military men has enabled them to dominate the marriage market in South Sudan, making it difficult or impossible for young civilian men to afford bride price. This further entrenched the dominance of military men within the gender order, making it difficult for civilian males to fulfil the social expectations of marriage and reproduction (Sommers and Schwartz 2011: 10). The privileging of militarized masculinity and the centralization of power within armed organizations has had the pervasive effect of protecting the hegemony of militarized masculinity within the existing gender order. This social impact of militarization and the dominance of militarized masculinity within the southern Sudanese gender order has facilitated warlordism, making combatants further dependent on military leaders, not only for subsistence but also for social status.

Conclusion

The implementation of DDR programs in South Sudan has a distinct gender structure. This can be seen in its failure to substantively challenge the authority and power of SPLA elites, the removal of undesirable elements such as female combatants from the state armed forces and the use of disarmament programs as a proxy method of undermining the power of rivals. The design and implementation of the DDR programs in South Sudan entrenched militarized masculinity as dominant within the gender order. By fostering dependent relationships between combatants and commanders, while marginalizing civilian men, the SPLA were brutally successful in fostering the trend of warlordism and privatized violence. When leadership tensions flared between the Riek Machar and Salva Kiir in 2013 they flourished in an environment with a strong military culture and a body of male combatants deeply dependent on their commanders who provided them with economic security, cultural legitimacy and social status as men. If DDR programs had succeeded in challenging militarism in South Sudan, not only by implementing meaningful disarmament, but by also challenging the social status of soldiers and the patterns of privilege and patronage that ensured loyalty to SPLA leaders, then it seems unlikely that Machar and Kiir would have had their current successes in mobilizing young men to participate in their respective leadership struggles.

References

Ali, N.M. (2011). *Gender and Statebuilding in South Sudan.* Washington DC: United States Institute of Peace.

Amusan, L. (2014). Germinating Seeds of Future Conflicts in South Sudan. *African Conflict & Peacebuilding Review*, 4(1): 120–33.

Anning, C. (2014). South Sudan's Civil War puts 5 million at Risk of Ethnic Violence and Famine. *The Independent*, May 18, http://www.independent.co.uk/news/world/africa/south-sudans-civil-war-puts-5-million-at-risk-of-ethnic-violence-and-famine-9391340.html.

Bouta, T. (2005). *Gender and Disarmament, Demobilization and Reintegration: Building Blocks for Dutch Policy.* The Hague: Netherlands Institute of International Relations.

Caprioli, M. (2000). Gendered Conflict. *Journal of Peace Research*, 37(1): 51–68.

Caprioli, M. (2004). The Continuum of Violence: A Gender Perspective on War and Peace. In W. Giles, and J. Hyndman (eds), *Sites of Violence: Gender and Conflict Zones.* Berkeley, CA: University of California Press, 24–44.

Cockburn, C. (2010). Gender Relations as Causal in Militarization and War: a Feminist Standpoint. *International Feminist Journal of Politics*, 12(2): 139–57.

Connell, R. (2005). *Masculinities.* Cambridge: Polity Press.

D'Awol, A.M. (2011). *Sibu ana, sibu ana* (leave me, leave me): Survivors of Sexual Violence in South Sudan. In F. Bubenzer, and O. Stern (eds), *Hope, Pain & Patience: The Lives of Women in South Sudan.* South Africa: Sunnyside.

Edwards, J.K. (2014). *A Strategy for Achieving Gender Equality in South Sudan.* Juba: The Sudd Institute.

Enloe, C. (2000). *Bananas, Beaches and Bases: Making Feminist Sense of International Politics.* Berkeley: University of California Press.

Gearan, A., and Raghavan, S. (2014). U.S. Appears Unable to Pull South Sudan Back from the Brink of Civil War. *The Washington Post*, May 14, www.washingtonpost.com/world/us-appears-unable-to-pull-south-sudan-back-from-the-brink-of-civil-war/2014/05/03/d9280bda-386b-4249-94e0-b5292610e5bb_story.html.

Gross, C., Kudelko, K., and Purvis, C. (2011). *Gender-based Violence in Southern Sudan: Justice for Women Long Overdue.* New Haven: Allard K. Lowenstein International Human Rights Clinic at Yale Law School.

Human Rights Watch (1994). *Civilian Devastation: Abuses by all Parties in the War in South Sudan.* New York: Human Rights Watch.

Hutchinson, S.E. (2000). Nuer Ethnicity Militarized. *Anthropology Today*, 16(3): 6–13.

Internally Displaced Monitoring Group (2010). *Southern Sudan: Overcoming Obstacles to Durable Solutions Now—Building Stability for the Future.* Oslo: Norwegian Refugee Council.

Janzen, R. (2014). Guatemalan Ex-Combatant Perspectives on Reintegration: A Grounded Theory. *The Quantitative Report*, 19(1): 1–24.

Jok, J. (1999). Militarisation and Gender Violence in South Sudan. *Journal of Asian and African Studies*, 34(4): 427–42.

Jok, J. (2006). Violence and Resilience: Women, War and the Realities of Everyday Life in Sudan. *The Ahfad Journal*, 23(2): 58–80.

Jok, J. (2007). *Sudan: Race, Religion, and Violence.* Oxford: Oneworld Publications.

Jok, J. (2011). *Diversity, Unity, and Nation Building in South Sudan.* Washington DC: United States Institute of Peace.

Jok, J., and Hutchinson, S. (2002). Gender Violence and the Militarisation of Ethnicity: A Case Study from South Sudan. In R. Werbner (ed.), *Postcolonial Subjectivities in Africa.* London: Zed Books, 84–108.

Lively, I. (2014). Measuring Intermediate Outcomes of Liberia's Disarmament, Demobilization, Rehabilitation and Reintegration Program. *Defence and Peace Economics*, 25(2): 139–62.

Mampilly, Z.C. (2011). *Rebel Rulers: Insurgent Governance and Civilian Life During War.* New York: Cornell University Press.

Marten, K. (2006–7). Warlordism in Comparative Perspective. *International Security*, 31(3): 41–73.

McKenzie, M. (2009). Securitization and Desecuritization: Female Soldiers and Reconstruction of Women in Post-conflict Sierra Leone. *Security Studies*, 18(1): 241–61.

Nichols, R. (2011). *DDR in South Sudan: Too Little, Too Late?* Geneva: The Small Arms Survey, Graduate Institute of International and Development Studies.

O'Brien, A. (2009). *Shots in the Dark: the 2008 South Sudan Civilian Disarmament Campaign.* Geneva: The Small Arms Survey, Graduate Institute of International and Development Studies.

Ortega, L.M. (2010). *Transitional Justice and Female Ex-Combatants: Lessons Learned from International Experience.* New York: International Centre for Transnational Justice.

Sandu, C. (2011). The South Sudan Coup: A Political Rivalry that Turned Ethnic. *Conflict Studies Quarterly*, 7(1): 49–65.

Sommers, M., and Schwartz, S. (2011). *Dowry and Division: Youth and State Building in South Sudan.* Washington DC: United States Institute of Peace.

Sten, O. (2011). This is how Marriage Happens Sometimes: Women and Marriage in South Sudan. In F. Bubenzer and S. Orly (eds), *Hope, Pain & Patience: The Lives of Women in South Sudan.* Cape Town: Sunnyside, 1–24.

Stern, O., and Bubenzer, F. (2011). Introduction. In O. Stern, and F. Bubenzer (eds), *Hope, Pain & Patience: The Lives of Women in South Sudan.* Cape Town: Sunnyside, i–xix.

Stone, L. (2011). *Failures and Opportunities: Rethinking DDR in South Sudan.* Geneva: The Small Arms Survey, Graduate Institute of International and Development Studies.

Stone, L. (2011). "We Were All Soldiers": Female Combatants in South Sudan's Civil War. In O. Stern, and F. Bubenzer (eds), *Hope, Pain & Patience: The Lives of Women in South Sudan.* Cape Town: Sunyside, 25–52.

USAID. (2012). *Gender Equality and Female Empowerment.* Washington DC: USAID.

Vinci, A. (2008). *Armed Groups and the Balance of Power.* Oxon: Routledge.

Women's Commission for Refugee Women and Children (2002). *Disarmament, Demobilization and Reintegration, and Gender-Based Violence in Sierra Leone.* New York: Women's Commission for Refugee Women and Children.

Young, J. (2007). *Sudan People's Liberation Army Disarmament in Jonglei and its Implications.* Pretoria: Institute for Security Studies

Chapter 13

Peacebuilding in the Democratic Republic of Congo

Mbekezeli Comfort Mkhize

Abstract

The ongoing conflict in the Democratic Republic of Congo (DRC) has proven to be its biggest challenge since independence in 1961. Millions of civilians have been left internally displaced, particularly in Eastern DRC. The surge of violence continues, regardless of interventions from all levels. The involvement of neighboring countries has created an unfavorable climate for a sustainable peace, and has arguably contributed to a deterioration of the situation. Peace has therefore remained elusive. This chapter will argue that the repeated failures of various peace agreements demonstrate that only a context-specific response in the DRC—driven by local communities—will result in a favorable peace process that can address and ultimately end the conflict. In the midst of growing security concerns, it is necessary to explore the appropriateness and sustainability of such responses in these protracted conflicts. Indeed, despite the considerable proliferation of research projects focusing on the peace process in the DRC, few studies have dealt specifically with the viability of this response at any length.

Introduction

The Democratic Republic of Congo (DRC), formerly known as Zaire, has endured recurring episodes of relentless violence and conflict, in particular violence against women, such as rape, resulting in high rates of casualties, deaths and internally displaced peoples, since the 1990s (Human Rights Watch 2010: 98). The most turbulent and volatile epoch resulting in humanitarian disaster was between 1996 and 1997. This epoch saw the outbreak of the First Congo War in November 1996. Widely referred to as Africa's First World War (Shekhawat 2009), or alternatively Africa's World War (Williams 2013; Kjerksrud and Ravndal 2011) in scholarly debates, the war ended with the toppling of President Mobutu Sese Seko in May 1997 (Ahere 2012). Africa's First World War epitomized "the end of the principle of non-interference in the internal affairs of member states" (Daley 2006: 303). This demonstration of yet another failed state in Africa is a serious security predicament (Ahere 2012; Aning and Salihu 2014; Nibishaka 2011; Williams 2013), despite the peacekeeping efforts of the United Nations, the costs of which are estimated at US$8.73 billion since 1999 (United Nations 2012 cited in Ahere 2012). Regardless of the myriad peace agreements that have been signed, and the massive financial inputs spent for the sole purpose of facilitating peace, no significant breakthrough (which translates to peace on the ground) in ending the conflict has been attained, and a strong state has not evolved. To date, the peace process has essentially failed and peace remains elusive. Therefore, understanding the rationale behind the failure of peacebuilding in the Congo is critical for any person interested in current African affairs and in international politics and international security (Autesserre 2011).

The causes of the conflict have included the existence of discernible competing networks of local rebel groups, militias and insurgents, and regular forces from neighboring countries who have clashed over access to land and resources "and contributed to a flourishing war economy" (Gilpin, Morris and Funai 2009: 1; also see Williams 2013). Despite abundant natural resources, vast numbers of the population in the DRC continue to be economically and politically marginalized (Ahere 2012). The so-called "resource-curse" has thus been central to the conflict in terms of both the cause and source of the continuation of conflict (see Stabrawa 2003). Illegal mining has proliferated in eastern DRC, and the proceeds of these conflict minerals have often been used to fund the purchase of weapons, thus fueling conflict and contributing to human rights abuses in the DRC (Cook 2012; Mbubi 2014). Also fueling the conflict has been the spill-over effects of regional conflicts, such as the Rwandan genocide and civil war in 1994–1995, which lead to thousands fleeing across the border into the DRC seeking refuge, often complicating any interventions (Cook 2012: 2). Furthermore, between 1998 and 2003 the country's security predicament was characterized by this significant shift from a local to a regional conflict, which saw Angola, Chad, Sudan, Namibia and Zimbabwe, supporting the Congolese government, while Burundi, Rwanda and Uganda supported the rebels (Shekhawat 2009). According to Shekhawat, "[m]any other militia groups that claimed to be defender groups for their community also became active participants in the conflict" (2009: 8). The proliferation of small arms and light weapons, and the increase in a militaristic ideology has also had an impact on communities in the DRC, and elsewhere across Africa since the end of the Cold War (Daley 2006).

Part of the problem, as will be discussed below, is that the peace process has not been inclusive of women or other groups within civil society that have a stake-hold in peace. Furthermore, in the midst of the myriad of these ill-conceived interventions, there has been a continuous fragility of the state in the DRC which has complicated the realization of the peace process (Aning and Salihu 2014). Against this backdrop, the principal purpose of this chapter is to explore the enabling environment for a peace process through employing a context-specific response in the DRC to give impetus to the revitalization of the peace process in the country. The weaknesses of previous peace agreements will be examined in an attempt to determine the challenges inhibiting a successful peace process.

Background to the DRC Conflict

The DRC has been plagued by chaos, violence and disorder since gaining independence on June 30, 1960 (Swart 2011). The DRC's tumultuous and deplorable history has been considerably influenced by a plethora of epochs, namely, the Congo Free State (1885–1908); the Belgian Congo (1908–1960); the Congo Republic (1960–1971); Zaire (1971–1997); and subsequently, the Democratic Republic of the Congo (since 1997) (Swart 2011). Common among these epochs has been the brutal and violent forms of leadership. Upon gaining independence in 1960, the country was devastated by ubiquitous mutiny and secessionists movements (Shekhawat 2009), which could be attributed to the lack of a smooth transition from the colonial powers (Belgians) to the independent state of Zaire. The first democratically elected Prime Minister, Patrice Lumumba, appeared to be highly fallible, and came under attack from within, with support from outside. Under these circumstances, the country began to implode (Shekhawat 2009). The politics of the Cold War also created and perpetuated further divisions within the country. The Soviet Union declared its support for Patrice Lumumba's administration, while the United States (US) strongly opposed this independent administration (Shekhawat 2009). The US was of the view that the embattled Lumumba and his supporters would allow the break-up of the Congo and create a vacuum ready for Soviet domination and control over central Africa. Patrice Lumumba was subsequently ousted and soon after assassinated in 1961, during a coup led by army general Mobutu Sese Seko.

With the direct support of the US and Belgium, Mobuto assumed the office of President himself. In 1971, after successfully quelling all new rebellions, Mobutu changed the name of the country to Zaire. Mobuto remains infamous for his violent period of dictatorship, which saw his personal wealth amass, while the masses remained impoverished. It was also a period of misguided and corrupt officials (Solomon and Swart 2004). The dismantling of Mobutu Sese Seko's autocratic rule was only made possible by the end of the Cold War which added more impetus to internal resistance to his regime (Lotze et al. 2008). The economy which had nearly collapsed owing to unprecedented mismanagement, corruption, and authoritarianism (Shekhawat 2009) created a fertile ground for conflict and bad governance. By the mid-1990s when his rule came to an end.

Subsequent to Mobutu's inept and autocratic rule, Angola, Uganda, Burundi and Rwanda began to share a collective voice over the elimination of Mobutu (Williams 2013). Not only did they express visible discontent with his autocratic leadership, these countries went as far as eliminating the base he provided to their enemies. In 1997, fierce political turmoil began when the Alliance of Democratic Forces for the Liberation of Congo (*Alliance des Forces Démocratiques pour la Libération du Congo*—AFDL), a group of exiled Congolese revolutionary parties led by Laurent Desire Kabila, marched into Kinshasa and ousted Mobutu (Williams 2013). This group was able to galvanize massive support from many parts of the African continent. The weakened support for Mobutu and the existence of a power vacuum in Kinshasa served as the fertile ground for his ousting to succeed (Miti 2012).

Despite the initial euphoria regarding this sudden power change, President Laurent Kabila continued where his predecessor had left off. His autocratic administration coincided with the Second Congo Conflict—widely referred to as the world's deadliest conflict since World War II (Shekhawat 2009). Upon coming to power, Kabila neglected the internal opposition to Mobutu. From the outset, Kabila's inability and lack of political base fueled growing frustrations, not only within Congolese borders, but also in Rwanda and Uganda. There were typically mixed feelings in the country concerning Kabila's leadership. According to Turner (2001 cited in Williams 2013), the dominant presence of Rwandan troops in Kinshasa fueled growing frustrations among Congolese civilians. A long-time Congo expert, Herbert Weiss, explains Kabila's dilemma painstakingly:

> On the one hand, the Congolese public quite widely resented the Rwandan/Tutsi presence and wanted Kabila to free himself from their control or influence. On the other hand, the Congolese Tutsi wanted Kabila to reward them for having played a large part in putting him in power. (Weiss 2008: 8, cited in Williams 2013: 88)

In the Eastern DRC, politicization along ethnic lines re-emerged, especially in Kivu provinces (Lotze et al. 2008). In 1998, an open conflict began between Laurent Kabila and the Congolese forces supported by Rwanda. In December 1998, the then-vice-president of Rwanda, Paul Kagame, finally admitted that Rwandan troops were aiding the DRC rebels (Solomon and Swart 2004).

On the other hand, Angola, Namibia, and Zimbabwe joined the fray in support of Kabila (Lotze et al. 2008; Solomon and Swart 2004). The support for Kabila was inspired by Mobutu Sese Seko's refusal to grant Zairean nationality to ethnic Tutsis (Solomon and Swart 2004). In the end, the conflict claimed the lives of approximately four million people. However, the ferocious crisis in the DRC remains an intractable barrier facing not only the African continent, but also the world at large.

According to Carayannis (2009), the DRC crisis is a concern that continues to dominate international discussions in terms of conflict resolution and management:

> The conflict in the Congo has involved at least nine African states and a number of proxy movements with varying degrees of local mobilisation and support. The first war began in September 1996 as an invasion by a coalition of neighbouring states of what was then Zaire, and succeeded in replacing president Mobutu with Laurent Kabila in May 1997. International action during the first war took the form of weak declaratory UN resolutions on the war, and intense international and regional diplomatic efforts to negotiate Mobutu's exit. (Carayannis 2009: 6)

The second conflict was highly foreseeable and evident during Kabila's regime, partly because during the ousting of Mobutu Sese Seko, no pertinent compromises were reached. On the one hand, bad governance and the surge of corruption continued to undermine Kabila's leadership relentlessly, creating an environment conducive to conflict. According to Shekhawat (2009), Kabila also undoubtedly encouraged favoritism and nepotism, just as Mobutu Sese Seko had done. On the other hand, these unfavorable conditions, including the plummeting economy, have pushed the country towards the world's most deadly conflict since World War II. As a consequence, the DRC has been characterized by continuous chaos, turmoil, instability, violence, and brutal conflict (Swart 2011).

In the midst of myriad challenges, Laurent Kabila began to view Rwandan and Congolese Tutsis differently, although they actively supported his rebellion (French 2006 cited in Williams 2013). In January 2001, Laurent Kabila was assassinated and his son, Joseph Kabila, took over the Presidency of DRC. In 2001, the Inter-Congolese dialogue was initiated to provide the enabling environment for peace and democracy (Shekhawat 2009). In April 2003, the Pretoria Peace agreement paved the way for the installation of a transitional government with the aim of reunification, pacification, and reconstruction of the country (Shekhawat 2009). On July 18, 2003, the Transitional Government came into being. A new Constitution was adopted in 2005. The elections were held in 2006. The newly-elected Joseph Kabila became the elected President of the country.

Indeed, despite these sterling events, the violent activities did not come to an end. The eastern provinces, in particular, became more deplorable and unstable while the rebel groups continued to fight among themselves and with the government. Although in 2009 Carayannis (2009) predicted that the situation could get worse as many regional actors were considering disengaging from the conflict in the east, by 2014 a slight improvement was noted in terms of collaborations and concerted efforts destined to bring about peace. Regional and international partners were now more engaged and relatively coordinated, and the threat to the government from rebels had been reduced, since the late 2013 defeat of the March 23 Movement (to be discussed below) (Shepherd 2014; see Neethling 2011). However, in 2015 civil society in the DRC remains tumultuous. Although, the DRC is not immersed in a large-scale civil conflict, the scale of displacement within and outside the DRC remains serious (United Nations High Commissioner for Refugees [UNHCR] 2015). By 2014 there were approximately 2.7 million internally displaced people (IDPs) (UNHCR 2015). Exacerbating this in 2015, the DRC is now home to millions of refugees from the Central African Republic (CAR) who fled insecurity and violence in their own country. This has created more problems for the already embattled DRC (UNHCR 2015).

Therefore, Muyingi (2013) asserts that the DRC has been the scene of multiple conflicts at local, national, and regional levels. These conflicts have inexorably caused the country to become a site of decimated natural environments and infrastructure. Nevertheless, various efforts in the form of peace agreements and protocols have been signed since the start of the conflict in the 1990s in an attempt to revitalize and restore stability and order in the country. On the whole, however, the peace agreements did not bring about effective and sudden changes in the country. Extrapolating from previous peace agreements and peacebuilding initiatives in the country, it becomes apparent that there are many factors that contributed to this repeated failure. The factors are thus worth interrogating.

Previous Peace Agreements and Peacebuilding Initiatives

Generally, it is understood that peace is a "process as opposed to just an abrupt end to conflict" (Daley 2006: 310). It is common knowledge that for a peace process to end war, as Daley (2006) further contends, it should be founded upon certain principles such as broad-based transitional government, demobilization and reform of the national security apparatus. By 2004, there had been approximately 23 recorded peace initiatives since 1997 in the DRC (Solomon and Swart 2004), but these have been plagued by a series of crises that have nearly brought the country to the brink of full-scale war on many occasions (see Table 13.1, p.175). In 2015, 11 years later, the DRC continues to be surrounded by a continuous failure of peace agreements. As a result, millions of people are still internally displaced. The situation is clearly "fragile" and peacekeepers from the United Nations (UN) have been deployed in the country since 1999 to facilitate and ameliorate the implementation of these peace agreements (Neethling 2011). Yet, despite their deployment peace has proved to be elusive because "[t]he peace negotiations have followed contemporary conflict resolution models that have a standard formula of peace negotiations, with a trajectory of ceasefire agreements, transitional governments, demilitarization, constitutional reform and ending with democratic elections." (Daley 2006: 303). However, acting in accordance with these contemporary conflict resolution models has actually led to failure, mainly because local dynamics have not been considered and the historical and multifaceted nature of the conflicts have not been adequately addressed (Daley 2006). It has thus become apparent that reaching a peace agreement in the DRC is fraught with difficulties and challenges.

The United Nations (UN) peacekeeping mission known as MONUC (the United Nations Mission in the Democratic Republic of Congo—Mission de l'Organisation des Nations Unies en Republique Democratique du Congo), became operational in 1999, and was mandated to protect civilians. MONUC's presence in the DRC created a favorable environment for the 2006 first-ever multiparty elections, and was the world's largest and most expensive UN peacekeeping mission (Neethling 2011). According to Tull, UN Peacekeeping, through MONUC, had four fundamental phases when executing the peacekeeping operation:

> The first phase began with the creation of MONUC in 1999 and ended with the Pretoria accord on the formation of a government of national unity in late 2002. The second phase of MONUC's deployment (2003—2004) began in the wake of Pretoria accord in 2002. The third phase, from October 2004 to December 2006, mainly

revolved around the organization of presidential, parliamentary and provincial elections. The fourth phase began in the wake of the 2006 elections. (Tull 2009: 217–18)

Furthermore, MONUC struggled with the inconsistent approach to the vague concept of "robust peacekeeping" (Tull 2009: 15). This inconsistency was evident during the critical stages of the peace process whereby "the concept tried to wage peace when it should have used force" (Tull 2009: 15). According to Tardy (2011:152), "the concept of robust peacekeeping emerged in response to the failures of the UN in Rwanda and Bosnia and Herzegovina, where peacekeepers were passive witnesses to massive violations of human rights." The concept of robust peacekeeping thus sought to rekindle and revitalize the active role of peacekeepers in quelling grave human rights violations. The critics further contend that "MONUC also failed to adapt to a dynamic conflict environment" (Tull 2009: 215).

Therefore, given the growing difficulties on the ground, in negotiations between the DRC government and the UN Security Council, on May 28, 2010, MONUC was transformed from a limited observer force to a multi-dimensional and integrated stabilization operation, known as MONUSCO (the United Nations Stabilization Mission in the Democratic Republic of the Congo—Mission de l'Organisation des Nations unies pour la stabilisation en République démocratique du Congo) (MONUSCO cited in Kjerksrud and Ravndal 2011). This change only came into effect on July 1, 2010. Following the replacement of MONUC by MONUSCO, the mandate for the peacekeepers was also drastically revised. According to Neethling (2011: 27) "the long-term plan was to work towards a gradual shift away from military peacekeepers to civilian functionaries focusing their efforts on peacebuilding through institutional reconstruction and Security Sector Reform (SSR)."

Prior to 2010, transforming the MONUC was necessary in response to the growing need for civil-military cooperation to protect the civilians. The post-2010 MONUSCO had to widen its scope by dealing strategically with a wide spectrum of operations through establishing co-operations and partnerships. Indeed, transformative changes were done because despite MONUC's efforts to ensure disarmament, local militias and foreign rebel groups continued to operate in the Eastern Congo (Daley 2006). Transformed strategic operations thus became inevitable in the country. Addressing the challenges faced by MONUC did not only require the widening of MONUSCO's scope, but it also required actively rebuilding the state's security sector by developing a secure environment based on development, rule of law, good governance and local ownership of security sectors (Neethling 2011).

Similarly, the Lusaka Ceasefire Agreement was signed by Angola, the DRC, Namibia, Uganda, Rwanda, and Zimbabwe in an attempt to bring an end to the hostilities within the territory of the DRC. However, the agreement did not do much in terms of remedying the situation. Signed on July 10, 1999, the agreement had as its main objective the addressing of several issues, including the cessation of hostilities. Indeed, the agreement:

> seeks to bring an end to the hostilities within the territory of the DRC. It addresses several issues including the cessation of hostilities, establishment of a joint military commission (JMC) comprising representatives of the belligerents, withdrawal of foreign groups, disarming, demobilizing and reintegrating of combatants, release of prisoners and hostages, re-establishment of government administration and the selection of a mediator to facilitate an all-inclusive inter-Congolese dialogue. The agreement also calls for the deployment of a UN peacekeeping force to monitor the ceasefire, investigate violations with the JMC and disarm, demobilize and reintegrate armed groups. (United Nations Peacemaker 1999: 1).

The Lusaka Ceasefire Agreement sought mainly to see the DRC embarking on the process of Disarmament, Demobilization and Reintegration (DDR) (Lilly 2005). While the UN had reported that approximately 11,500 combatants had handed in their weapons by March 2005 (17th Report of the UN Secretary General on the MONUC, cited in Lilly 2005), early developments indicated that there were difficulties in the implementation of the DDR program, which ultimately proved to be totally ineffectual on the ground. Lilly (2005) cites a lack of political will as the major challenge that led to the elusiveness and failure of DDR. Although the agreement sought to sensitize the warring parties about the urgent need to disarm, demobilize, and reintegrate, "the former warring parties were unwilling and/or lacked the confidence in the peace process to downsize their military forces" (Lilly 2005: 375). Consequently, the reintegration process was badly derailed. Boshoff and Rupiya (2003) concur that the Lusaka Ceasefire Agreement did not fully deliver on its mandate. According to Daley (2006), the Lusaka Peace Accord was a ceasefire agreement without a peace agreement. This, then, led to neither a ceasefire nor peace (Daley 2006:312).

While the success of the DDR depended entirely on military integration, the latter was delayed. The other weakness of the DDR was that the promises of demobilization payments were not met (Daley 2006), and the retired ex-combatants had to grapple with unemployment (Daley 2006). The only positive outcome of the agreement was the Inter-Congolese Dialogue (ICD). According to Boshoff and Rupiya (2003), the ICD was the only entry point for civil society and unarmed political groups in the Congo to become part of the peace process. The inclusion was also motivated by the role these groups played in the struggle against the Mobutu regime during the early 1990s.

On September 17, 2002, troops were withdrawn from the eastern part of the DRC. Even though this move signaled the end of the war, various agreements that facilitated troop withdrawals were often imprecise, confused, and problematic (International Institute for Strategic Studies (IISS) 2002). There was also a Luanda Agreement made between Kinshasa and Kampala in September 2002. In the same breath, the Pretoria Agreement was signed a few months later on December 17, 2002. This agreement sought to facilitate the transition of a militaristic country into a democracy and to guarantee the end of conflict (International Federation for Human Rights 2008 cited in Nibishaka 2011). However, the agreement did not yield positive results, and conflict continued for another eight years after the signing of the agreement. The ceasefire attempts included the 2002 Pretoria Agreement between Kinshasa and Kigali which provided the basis for the Ituri Pacification Agreement (Nezan 1998 cited in Boshoff and Rupiya 2003). The lack of political will (Tardy 2011) is made clear here by the failures of the Pretoria and Luanda Agreements to bring about peace and reconstruction. They depended on a number of signatories (International Institute for Strategic Studies (IISS) 2002). However, invariably these signatories often consciously or unconsciously derailed the process, motivated by "those who find wars more profitable politically and economically than peace" (Daley 2006: 312). In this regard, some countries may only participate in ending the fighting when it is in their interest to do so. For example, Uganda and Rwanda only withdrew their troops once they were happy with the outcome of the conflict, yet when they did so, it created a power vacuum, which became a further source of instability (International Institute for Strategic Studies (IISS) 2002).

A further peace agreement, known as the Global and All Inclusive Peace Agreement, was signed by the Congolese warring parties in December 2002. This agreement was considered to be a transitional power-sharing peace agreement (Daley 2006). The signing of this agreement was attributed to international pressure which was mounting at the time (Boshoff and Rupiya 2003). According to Lilly (2005: 371), this peace agreement was based on a 4+1 formula whereby Joseph Kabila instinctively became the President after the assassination of his father, Laurent Kabila, and prior to the 2006 elections. After the elections, he retained his position. Since this period, Joseph Kabila continues to hold the office of President of the DRC. The agreement also led to the withdrawal of foreign troops from the Congolese territory (Daley 2006). Indeed, this arrangement was aimed at securing a successful transitional government. To achieve this arrangement, four vice-presidents representing the various armed groups during the war, the opposition, and civil society came together (Lilly 2005). Not surprisingly, this led to the creation of political fiefdoms with each group striving to retain control and not being prepared to make the necessary compromises to move the peace process forward. Furthermore, the difficulty was that "the armed groups in the north-eastern district of Ituri were never part of the Global and All Inclusive Peace Agreement" (Lilly 2005: 375).

Moreover, the 2008 Goma Peace Conference was typical of a top-down process whereby the local actors were involved in national and regional strategies and alliances (Matagne 2011). As such, the Goma Peace Agreement was linked to a comprehensive development and peacebuilding program which did not prioritize local matters (Matagne 2011). Invariably, in these cases, the possibility of fallibility and impossibility of a successful agreement is always extremely high. Owing to such a poorly organized plan, the agreement did not therefore bring about the desired end.

The Early Warning and Rapid Response Cell (EWRRC) was created in May 2009 to represent a new civil-military initiative (See United Nations, *Concept note on the Establishment of a Rapid Response Mechanism in the context of Joint Operations* MONUC/FARDC, Kinshasa, 2010 cited in Kjerksrud and Ravndal 2011).

According to Kjerksrud and Ravndal (2011: 7), "the EWRRC was a multi-disciplinary working group composed of senior representatives from human rights, child protection and civil affairs organizations, the UN police and the UN military forces." Like MONUC, the EWRRC's main aim was to ensure protection of civilians, and yet large numbers of people continued to be internally displaced.

Therefore, despite several attempts to bring about peace, it is unanimous that most (if not all) of the peace agreements have failed. The biggest setback in the peacebuilding initiatives took place when there was an announcement by the DRC government in September 2009 that MONUC would be withdrawn in 2011. The announcement came as a result of MONUC's inability to protect everyone (particularly civilians) at risk (Neethling 2011). Indeed, despite MONUC being a costly exercise, the announcement proved to be inevitable, precisely because there was no arrangement for tracking down and handing over "war criminals" or for disarming the warring factions (International Institute for Strategic Studies (IISS) 2002). Many observers and stakeholders in the DRC conflict were caught off guard (Neethling 2011). MONUC had visible difficulties in carrying out its fundamental peacekeeping operations. In looking closer at the withdrawal and the rationale behind, it is argued that "the DRC government's announcement coincided with pressure on the UN and its Security Council (SC) ahead of the country's 50th anniversary of independence in June 2010 to produce a plan for ending MONUC's work in the DRC" (Neethling 2011: 24). The radical changes in peacekeeping operations took place regardless of the looming election, and on June 30, 2010 the UN withdrew approximately 2000 military personnel. Furthermore, the rationale behind President Joseph Kabila's insistence on the departure of the UN from the DRC was arguably because the presence of a UN peacekeeping operation made him look weak (Neethling 2011).

Nonetheless, as Daley (2006) maintains, there is a poor understanding of what the peace process means, and peace agreements only mark the start of the process. This is clearly seen by the fact that despite all these attempts at peace in the DRC fighting still lingers on in the country (Boshoff and Rupiya 2003). For example, in 2009, the Mai-Mai Sheka (a group which was formed in 2009 by mineral resources business people) contributed greatly to violence in DRC by launching a series of attacks on civilians and also UN peacekeepers (International Coalition for The Responsibility to Protect [ICTRP] 2015). Meanwhile, in 2010, the mass rape of more than 240 women was carried out in eastern Congo by members of the Rwandan Democratic Forces for the Liberation of Rwanda (FDLR) and the Mai-Mai Sheka rebels (ICTRP 2015). Between 2009—2015, the Lord's Resistance Army (LRA) had killed over 300 civilians in the DRC. In the same breath in 2012 the M23 (widely known as the March 23 Movement or Mouvement du 23 Mars, which came into existence in April 2012 when hundreds of Tutsi soldiers of the national army, the Armed Forces of the Democratic Republic of Congo—Forces armies de la Republique democratique du Congo [FARDC], mutinied over poor standards of living conditions as well as poor pay, and thus named after the March 23, 2009 Peace Agreement), fought the FARDC and eventually took the city of Goma, located in the North Kivu province, thus forcing civilians to flee the area. During the fight, the M23 and the FARDC committed many human rights abuses such as mass rape and arbitrary executions (ICTRP 2015).

In 2013, 39 Congolese officers were tried for rape and acts of sexual violence (ICTRP 2015). Furthermore, in March 2013,

> the United Nations Security Council (UNSC) approved a first-ever Force Intervention Brigade (FIB—a group approved by the UNSC to deal with M23 and other rebel groups), to use *all necessary means* such as force against the M23 and other rebel groups in order to enforce, among others, civilian protection, neutralization of armed groups, arms embargo implementation, and provision of judicial processes in the country. (ICTRP 2015: 3)

The M23 was thus defeated. The defeat of M23 in November 2013 provided a strong testimony about the effectiveness of FIB. Because of escalating violence, and the degenerating situation in the eastern DRC, the urgent corrective measure needed to be taken. As a result, President Joseph Kabila used the International Conference on the Great Lakes Region (ICLGR) as a platform for discussion by convening a series of meetings that resulted in the Kampala peace talks (ICTRP 2015). Furthermore, on February 2013, a UNSC-brokered peace agreement between the ICLGR Heads of State was signed by Angola, Burundi, the Central African Republic, Congo-Brazzaville, the DRC, Rwanda, South Africa, South Sudan, Tanzania, Uganda, and

Zimbabwe. The agreement was formally called the Peace, Security, and Cooperation Framework for DRC and the Region (ICTRP 2015:4). The agreement sought to encourage the FDLR to disarm. However, in October 2014 a UN Group of Experts and MONUSCO confirmed that the FDLR continues to recruit and organize troops, suggesting that the group was not prepared to demobilize.

Indeed, despite a plethora of failed peace agreements and initiatives mentioned above, recent developments from 2013–2015 indicate that widespread insecurity in the country is still prevalent. Despite the prevalence of insecurity, the latest landmarks culminating from collective efforts made between the FARDC and the FIB is yielding results in dismantling the M23 (ICTRP 2015). The complete removal of the Rwandan rebel group from the DRC's home soil rightfully attests to the recent landmarks. The removal further attests to a "close collaboration between MONUSCO's FIB and the FARDC in an effort to curtail and ultimately eradicate the remaining rebel factions in the region" (ICTRP 2015: 4). Although there has been a successful removal of a Rwandan rebel group and improved relations between MONUSCO's FIB and the FARDC, the FDLR remains the region's largest security concern, according to a December 2014 UN-Secretary-General report on the DRC. Such growing security concerns in the region are attributed to Rwanda's efforts to stifle FIB efforts in dealing with the FDLR. This is precisely so because the FDLR is composed of ex-*genocidaires* from the 1994 Rwandan genocide (ICTRP 2015).

Finally, in response to the growing security concerns caused by the FDLR, on January 29, 2015 the army of the DRC, supported by MONUSCO and the FIB, launched a military campaign against the FDLR. This close cooperation seeks to end continuous human rights abuses such as mass rape of women, and the repeated killings of civilians in the country. Despite the region-wide security crisis, internally, "there is currently a major security threat that arose in DRC over alleged attempts by the current government to delay the 2016 national elections, in which current President Joseph Kabila would be unable to participate due to a two-term limit" (ICTRP 2015: 4). The delay, by the current government, simply creates instability, discontinuity and unpredictability about the political future of the country.

Why has Peace been Elusive?

The DRC has been a site whereby agreements that are reached by one group of individuals are often not accepted by another, leading to disagreements and crisis (Daley 2006). This has been a trend for the DRC peace process. Although a long list of peace agreements have been devised for the DRC, as shown in Table 13.1, these agreements have just continued to create more secessionist (breakaway) organizations in the country. Indeed, therefore despite the signing of peace agreements, the discernible limited peacekeeping experience and lack of financial resources, in conjunction with primarily reactive rather than preventive and proactive initiatives have made the peace process elusive (Dzinesa and Laker 2010). The efforts earmarked for bringing about peace and stability, have thus been tenuous and ineffectual in terms of creating a fertile environment for a lasting peace.

A number of critics (Autesserre 2011; Koko 2011; Lilly 2005) have argued that the peace processes have not considered the local dynamics, partly because they have been fashioned by universalistic conflict resolution models (Daley 2006; Koko 2011). While it may be the case that the DRC is among the most challenging post-Cold War peacekeeping undertakings of the international community (Neethling 2011), it has not helped that the conflict resolution models do not reflect the realities on the ground, and have often followed a Eurocentric approach. The peace agreements have been plagued by miscalculations, misinterpretations, and misconceptions. The local dimensions that have not been factored in include, among others, local conflicts over land, food and mineral resources, particularly in the eastern parts of the country (Matagne 2011). While local dimensions might have a potential in steering peace negotiations in the right direction, the interventions and attempts have focused on macro-level issues (large-scale processes) such as economic decline, unemployment, housing, and the general state of the economy.

Furthermore, the conflict resolution models in play have typically assumed that the implementation of liberal democracy and neo-liberal economic reforms offer the best chances for peace (Daley 2006). This predominantly international peacebuilding culture often inadvertently forces interveners to ignore the micro-level tensions (in the form of small-scale, individual and/or group interactions) that often ravage macro-level

Table 13.1   A historical trajectory of peace agreements and initiatives in the DRC, 1999–2015

Peace Agreement(s)	Year	Challenge(s)	Outcome(s)
Lusaka Peace Agreement	July 10, 1999	The lack of political will inhibited progress	Did not remedy the deplorable situation
Lusaka Peace Accord	July 10, 1999	There were delays in military integration	Succeeded in paving the way for Inter-Congolese Dialogue
MONUC	First phase: 1999	MONUC's role was very limited	There was a withdrawal of foreign armies in the DRC
The Luanda Agreement	September 6, 2002	It was difficult to execute the resolutions, for example, Uganda did not want to withdraw its troops	Difficult to formalize peace between DRC and Uganda
Pretoria Agreement	December 17, 2002	Did not guarantee the end of conflict	Did not make a vast difference. The conflict continued
The Global and All-Inclusive Peace Agreement	December 16, 2002	Armed groups were excluded	Led to the creation of political fiefdoms
MONUC	Second phase: 2003–2004	There were disruptions from the eastern parts of DRC, ethnic militias fought over control of the city	Transitional government managed to move to the center of political attention
MONUC	Third phase: 2004–2006	MONUC was backed by an EU interim force (EUFOR DRC)	Organized a large logistical operation to prepare the registration of voters. Trained Congolese police officers to provide security for the elections
MONUC	Fourth phase: 2006	Coincided with 2006 elections. It was planned for security sector reform, but it had limited capacity.	Insecurity was widespread. Protecting civilians proved to be a mammoth task.
Goma Peace Conference	January 23, 2008	Was not inclusive and it followed a top-down approach	Did not achieve the desired outcome
MONUSCO	July 1, 2010	It sought to transform the state from poor governance to the respect for human rights and the upholding of the rule of law. However, there were difficulties on the ground.	Widespread insecurity nevertheless continued in the country
MONUSCO	January 29, 2015	The army of DRC, supported by MUNOSCO, officially declared the start of operations and military campaign	Still too early to determine the effectiveness of the initiative

settlements (Autesserre 2011). This globalized culture unwittingly influences the interveners' understanding of the causes of violence in two ways. First, the culture haphazardly concludes that because the DRC is seen to be violent, elections are the best mechanism for building peace (Autesserre 2011). Second, the international peacebuilding culture only incorporates the understandings shared by the international peacebuilding stakeholders (Autesserre 2011). Strictly conforming to this international peacebuilding culture has often led to a total disregard of the local dimensions pertinent within a community, region or country. This conflict resolution trap becomes inevitable when the models put forward are mostly funded by Western governments (Daley 2006), and are thus donor driven, thereby steering the negotiations to suit their needs (Daley 2006; Tardy 2011). Furthermore, other developing countries which typically contribute troops to international peace keeping operations, are also able to shape the politics of peacekeeping in the field (Tardy 2011).

Indeed, the peacebuilding efforts in the DRC are typically a mammoth task (Carayannis 2009). Since the Great Lakes region is increasingly divided, insecurity fueled by instability and chaos remains high (Aning and Salihu 2014). Koko (2011) argues that the interventions and peace agreements for the DRC have also been unsuccessful due to the lack of a regional perspective on post-conflict peacebuilding for the Great Lakes region. In essence, the most common challenges inhibiting the creation of a durable peace process in the DRC have been the following:

> The non-completion of the security sector reform; the continued weakness of the state (unable to monopolize instruments of violence and project its might on the entire national territory); the neglect of local dimensions of the conflict; a crumbled economic sector; an unfriendly regional environment; the absence of a long-term post-conflict peacebuilding strategy for both the DRC and the Great Lakes region, the continued presence of foreign armed groups operating on the DRC territory. (Koko 2011: 140–41)

Furthermore, as Simons, Zanker, Mehler and Tull (2013) determined, there was very little or no local content in the actual peace agreements made in the DRC. The local content often exhibited crucial differences in the conflict history and dynamics and perceptions of peace (Simons et al. 2013). Autesserre (2011) concludes that the peace process in the DRC has largely followed a top-down approach (by international actors), despite the strong propositions that bottom-up approaches driven by local grassroots actors are necessary (Matagne 2011).

Finally, the peace processes have also excluded significant groups which should play a leading role, namely women and some civil society organizations. Women have in particular suffered and endured repeated cases of sexual violence, mutilation and death during this conflict, with for example over 7000 reports of women or girls being raped (Human Rights Watch 2010: 98). Yet, women have been excluded from formal peace negotiations. Furthermore, civil society groups were also not invited to the peace negotiating tables, which were reserved for the armed groups and militias, and government representatives. Therefore, the peace process actually reinforced a patriarchal and ethicized politics of the state, and failed dismally to ensure a more inclusive politics (Daley 2006).

Employing a Context-Specific Response

In view of the formidable elusiveness of peace, the conflict needs to be resolved through the use of a context-specific response which has the potential to respond squarely to the challenges facing the DRC, unlike previous peace agreements which consistently applied a one-size-fits-all approach. Therefore, in order to succeed as Autesserre (2011) argues, the implementation of peace agreements must also be driven by local agendas which includes the individual, the family, the clan, the municipality, the community, and the district, involved in all stages of the peace process. According to Daley (2006), the concept of peace requires more fundamental transformations than those envisaged in contemporary conflict resolution models.

Importantly, local content needs to be taken seriously because peace can mean very different things to different people. Local-level intervention or a bottom-up process can potentially end a civil war. This form of intervention is driven by grassroots organizations as well as local authorities and civil society representatives (Autesserre 2011). It should also be reiterated that the realization of a settlement or a peace process or both depends entirely on public trust and participation. In other words, because the peace process that is imposed from above is most likely to experience problems during the implementation phase, a bottom-up approach, and context-specific response is more able to respond to the root causes of the conflict.

In view of the rapidly growing nature of human insecurity and recalcitrance by the militias in the Great Lakes region, Matagne (2011) recommends a multi-level peacebuilding initiative combining top-down and bottom-up strategies, including local content and dynamics, in order to restore order in the DRC. Nibishaka (2011) also argues that a multi-level approach is crucial, precisely because the extent and nature of the DRC conflict has changed so drastically over time involving a convergence and/or interplay of internal and external factors. A multi-level approach, or "a sustained intervention from a multiplicity of stakeholders in order to address aspects of the regional political economy that perpetuate cross-border abuse of the country's abundant resources" (Gilpin, Morris and Funai 2009: 1) could curtail the growing security concerns in the country by attending to the influence of resources in the conflict and by incorporating all the affected groups including women and civil society.

Conclusion

Despite a plethora of peace agreements that have been ratified, the conflict in DRC continues to be most intractable owing to a wide array of causes. The responses have not sufficiently addressed the multiplicity of these causes. However, given the fact that the conflict has entirely engulfed the region, the responses need to be able to deal with the negative influence of the neighboring states whose interventions have had spill-over effects for the DRC conflict. The peace agreements aimed particularly at achieving a sustainable peace process have mostly failed to achieve the desired end. This is particularly so because most of the peace agreements are driven largely by the international peacebuilding culture. The international peacebuilding culture (mostly dominated by a "one-size-fits-all" approach) has not seriously considered the environment in which it is introduced. In addition, the political dialogue processes have often been condemned due to lack of trust, inclusiveness, and leadership. There has also been a lack of political will in implementing the peace agreements. Despite these concerted efforts conflicts continue to ravage the country.

In view of the failure of previous agreements, this chapter has recommended that the DRC conflict should be resolved through the use of a context-specific response, more appropriate owing to its insistence on a multidimensional approach, which embraces a convergence of the local-level or bottom-up, and a regional approach. Such an integrated approach can help address the interlocking local and regional challenges. Furthermore, the multidimensional approach can also better address the many causes of the conflict, with the potential to end the ongoing violence in the DRC. The success of such a response will however depend largely on the degree of commitment by the relevant actors.

References

Ahere, J. (2012). The Peace Process in the DRC: A Transformation Quagmire. *Policy and Practice Brief*, 20: 1–7.

Aning, K. and Salihu, N. (2014). The African Security Predicament. In J.J. Hentz (ed.), *Routledge Handbook of African Security*. London: Routledge, 9–20.

Autesserre, S. (2011). The Trouble with the Congo: A Precis. *African Security Review*, 20(2): 56–65.

Boshoff, H. and Rupiya, M. (2003). Delegates, Dialogue, and Desperadoes: The ICD and the DRC Peace Process. *African Security Review*, 12(3): 29–37.

Carayannis, T. (2009). *The Challenge of Building Sustainable Peace in the DRC*. A background paper, Geneva: The Centre for Humanitarian Dialogue.

Daley, P. (2006). Challenges to Peace: Conflict Resolution in the Great Lakes Region of Africa. *Third World Quarterly*, 27(2): 303–19.

Dzinesa, G. and Laker, J. (2010). *Post-conflict Reconstruction in the Democratic Republic of the Congo (DRC)*. Cape Town: Centre for Conflict Resolution.

Gilpin, R., Morris, C., and Funai, G. (2009). *Beyond Emergency Responses in the Democratic Republic of Congo: Regional Solutions for a Regional Conflict*. Washington DC: United States Institute of Peace.

Human Rights Watch. (2010). *World Report 2010: Events of 2009*. http://www.hrw.org/sites/default/files/reports/wr2010.pdf.

International Coalition for The Responsibility to Protect (ICTRP) (2015). *Crisis in the Democratic Republic of Congo*. http:www.responsibilitytoprotect.org/index.php/crises-in-drc.

International Institute for Strategic Studies (IISS) (2002). Peace in the Democratic Republic of Congo? *Strategic Comments*, 8(8): 1–2.

Kjerksrud, S. and Ravndal, J.A. (2011). Emerging Lessons from the United Nations Mission in the Democratic Republic of Congo: Military Contributions to the Protection of Civilians. *African Security Review*, 20(2): 3–16.

Koko, S. (2011). From Conflict to Ever-eluding Peace. *A Journal of Social Justice*, 23(2): 139–43.

Lilly, D. (2005). Faltering Reform of the Security Sector Impedes the DRC Peace Process. *Conflict, Security & Development*, 5(3): 371–9.

Lotze, W., Barros de Carvalho, G., and Kasumba, Y. (2008). *Peacebuilding Coordination in African Countries: Transitioning from Conflict*. Durban, African Centre for the Constructive Resolution of Disputes (ACCORD).

Matagne, G. (2011). The Trouble with the Local in the Congo: The Challenges of Multi-level Peacebuilding Initiatives. *African Security Review*, 20(2): 80–85.

Mbubi, B. (2014). The Role of Conflict Minerals in the Peace Process in the DRC. *Peacebuilding*, 2(2): 224–6.

Muyingi, M.A. (2013). African Ethics and the Moral Possibilities of Ubuntu towards Conflict Resolution in the Democratic Republic of Congo (DRC). *Mediterranean Journal of Social Sciences*, 4(3): 561–8.

Neethling, T. (2011). From MONUC to MONUSCO and Beyond: Prospects for Reconstruction, State-building and Security Governance in the DRC. *South African Journal of International Affairs*, 18(1): 23–41.

Nibishaka, E. (2011). Natural Resources and Conflict in the Democratic Republic of Congo (DRC): The Failure of Post-conflict Reconstruction Strategies. *Southern Africa*, March. Johannesburg: Rosa Luxemburg Stiftung.

Shekhawat, S. (2009). *Governance Crisis and Conflict in the Democratic Republic of Congo*, Working Paper No.6. Mumbai: Centre for African Studies, University of Mumbai.

Shepherd, B. (2014). *Beyond Crisis in the DRC: The Dilemmas of International Engagement and Sustainable Change*. Chatham House, Research Paper, Africa Programme. http://www.chathamhouse.org/sites/files/chathamhouse/field/field_document/20141222DRC_Research_Paper.pdf.

Simons, C., Zanker, F., Mehler, A., and Tull, D.M. (2013). Power-sharing in Africa's War Zones: How Important is the Local Level? *The Journal of Modern African Studies*, 51(4): 681–706.

Solomon, H. and Swart, G. (2004). *Conflict in the DRC: A Critical Assessment of the Lusaka Ceasefire Agreement*. Pretoria: South African Institute of International Affairs.

Swart, G. (2011). A Vanquished Peace? The Success and Failure of Conflict Mediation in the Democratic Republic of the Congo. *Southern African Peace and Security Studies*, 1(1): 43–63.

Tardy, T. (2011). A Critique of Robust Peacekeeping in Contemporary Peace Operations. *International Peacekeeping*, 18(2): 152–67.

Tull, D.M. (2009). Peacekeeping in the Democratic Republic of Congo: Waging Peace and Fighting War. *International Peacekeeping*, 16(2): 215–30.

United Nations High Commissioner for Refugees (UNHCR) (2015). *2015 UNHCR Country Operations Profile: Democratic Republic of the Congo*, http://www.unhcr.org/pages/49e45c366.html.

United Nations Peacemaker (1999). *Ceasefire Agreement (Lusaka Agreement)*, July 10, http://peacemaker.un.org/drc-lusaka-agreement99.

Williams, C. (2013). Explaining the Great War in Africa: How Conflict in the Congo became a Continental Crisis. *The Fletcher Forum of World Affairs*, 37(2): 81–100.

Chapter 14

From Insurgency to Governance and Peacebuilding: Africa's Future

John Idriss Lahai and Tanya Lyons

In cognizance to some of the pertinent literature, after the 1960s the political trends in contemporary Africa have been very precarious. For instance, the end of colonial rule only brought an end to one form of conflict (i.e. imperialist wars), but others remain. Through what he referred to as the "new paradigm of war," Smith (2006) correctly concludes that armed conflicts, irrespective of the typology,

> are no longer a single massive event of military decision that delivers a conclusive political result, rather ...
> conflicts tend to be timeless, since we are seeking a condition, which then must be maintained until an agreement
> on a definitive outcome, which may take years or decades [to materialise]. (Smith 2006: 17)

For Berdal and Malone (2000: 2), what makes the contemporary conflicts in Africa hard to resolve—amid what makes most of them also "senseless conflicts"—is the inability of combatants to prioritize the defeat of the enemy over the competing individual interests of some participants in the conflict (and the irrational attempts to institutionalize violence as a means of achieving their aims).

Through a pluridisciplinary lens this volume has discussed the major political, economic and socio-cultural changes that have taken place within the postcolonial states of Africa since the 1960s. The various typologies of armed conflict, violence and fragility, and the processes of peacebuilding and democratic governance, and their impacts on the very discourse of postcoloniality in the continent, have been analyzed. Some of the key issues of insurgency, governance and peacebuilding have been addressed. This volume has drawn upon the strengths and limitations of the multi-disciplines of political science, international relations, security studies, African studies, gender and feminist studies, and anthropology, and the contributing authors have demonstrated that the forms and formulations of policies, the trends of conflict and the prospects for peace in the continent have a direct relationship to the very historiographies of the people. The processes involved in the creation of warring factions, such as the Revolutionary United Front (RUF), National Patriotic Front of Liberia (NPFL), Boko Haram and al-Shabaab, among others; the political representations of warlords (and politicians) across the Africa continent; the violent, and sometimes subtle transformation of the continent into a political market place; and the creation of the platform for terrorism wars, secessionist wars, resource-driven wars; and by necessity, grassroots peacebuilding activities, and the engendered processes of peace negotiations; and their neo-liberal outcomes to compete, gives us a synoptic overview of the very origins and character of the African Frontier.

Collectively, the contributors, through competing perspectives on the external and internal issues that are of importance to our understanding of Africa, have traced the origins and character of wars, the nature of wars, and the prospect for peace. In Chapter 1 for example, Lahai and Lyons explained, through an anthropocentric lens, the history and theories that have been used to understand conflicts and peacebuilding in the continent. Unlike other existing literatures, they have positioned the discourse of "place" and "self" to understand not just the place of the continent in the international system, but how the people have framed an understanding of what Africa is (and/or what it should be). They have shown how, by emphasizing the very idea of a "colonial past" in the theorization of the continent and its people, both the Eurocentric and Afrocentric scholars have created a marginal space on which the continent is being understood and imagined. For them, as was buttressed in the other chapters in this volume, though the past has played a role in the making of protracted wars, the future of the continent should be about grafting a path that draws a balance between the interests of the African political persons and the desires for peace and progress held by the marginalized. Highlighting this balance between individual opportunism and the ability of a state to find peace, in Chapter 2, John Idriss Lahai and Tanya Lyons examined the character of insurgent opportunism, rebel governance and the political constructions of peace in Liberia and Sierra Leone. They argued that despite peace being elusive, being able to understand the opportunistic nature of these resource driven wars, should be the first step to resolving instability and conflict. Then, prioritizing the people's desire for justice on their own terms, and not settling on the interests of the international community, will also enable a clearer peace process to occur.

However, as Lahai contends in Chapter 5 in his study of the politics of the Responsibility to Protect in the Darfur conflict, until the external processes, which are aimed at the promotion of peace, are framed with the intentions and purposes to building peace (that promotes the desires of the African people in the warscapes and peacescapes of the continent), the probability that wars will become a thing of the past diminishes.

From Oscar Gakuo Mwangi's analysis in Chapter 6, as in the other chapters, we notice that the conditions that perpetuate conflicts and eventually, state collapse, also have a direct relationship to the human condition. Thus whether greed and grievance, or the inability of African politicians (and their crop of "bad followers") to reject bad governance and promote good governance, has a direct relationship to how the human condition has, vis-à-vis situated (a) the continent (within the international political economy); (b) the question of marginality; and (c) the environment on which war or peace are made. Through the chapters presented here, we have come to the realization (if not, a reaffirmation of the facts) that what Africa is, and, what it is expected to be, requires us to re-assess the fundamental questions beyond the theoretical nuances and the intersubjective understanding of Africa as a burden. What is needed is a multipronged approach that neither trivializes the less important issues of, say, the gendered representations or theocratic under-currents that are shaping state governance, or the cultural understanding of the people. A multipronged approach that would, as Duyvesteyn et al. argued in Chapter 3 above, shed light on the policy debate on insurgency, governance and peacebuilding in contexts of state fragility. Of course, the policy debate is not without its corresponding geo-political implications. From South Sudan to Libya, and from Somalia to Sierra Leone, the African borderland cannot just be positioned as a unit for the experimentation of policies, but it is, in itself, an anthropomorphic history, a theory, a policy and a practice.

Thus, as we shall see, the African Frontier (its future and the prospect for peace) can best be understood through the re-imagination of "place" within the discursive representation of incidences of insurgency, governance and peacebuilding on one hand, and the acceptance of African countries as equal partners in the (re-)shaping of human history in an ever-changing world, on the other.

African Futures

Is the idea of an African future that is built on peace, stability, human development and human security possible? Or is this future a mere expression of possibilities for change in an uncertain world? Irrespective of the contending views around these pertinent and interrelated questions, there is one major problem that can be identified with this bold idea of a progressive Africa. This problem is found within the nuances of what can be referred to as a theoretical obsession with the politics of apportioning blame within the historical narratives about the ills of colonialism and postcolonialism. For the most part, however, this obsession is not a by-product of a belated expression of grief about the place of the continent in the (post)colonial libraries, but a subtle act provoking an awareness on the contentions and contradictions; certainties and uncertainties in the management of the historiographies of the continent (see Okunoye 2010; Wai 2012a).

This theoretical challenge it should be noted, shows that there has been a deliberate effort to refute the textual attitude in the postcolonial writings about the continent's past, present and future (see Englebert 2000; Goldsmith 2000). In recent decades, however, there have been calls for the creation of an Africanist project that reflects an imaginative historical narrative that would rewrite the decolonized geographies of Africa and eliminate its corresponding artificial identities and intersubjective political and civilizational stereotypes (see Desai 2001; Dolek 2008). In their attempt to understand this artificiality, and attached discourse of marginality of the postcolonial states in Africa, Africanist scholars have used a postcolonial imagination in an attempt to reinvent the continent.

For their part, through their sub-regional organizations, African politicians at all levels of the political landscape, have tried (with mixed results) to use political and economic solidarity to authenticate their claims to international legitimacy, for example Rwanda's Kagame and Uganda's Musevini, as argued in Chapter 4 by Twagiramungu. Yet their inability to find a future that is not affected by the dirges of bad governance and wars at the national levels, and at the international level, to promote policies that are not affected by the global power imbalances, reveals an incredible power behind the politics of representation. Beyond its crude and nuanced constructions, the dialectic imaginative context within which the postcolonial histories of Africa have been written on one hand; and, on the other, the way how national and international actors have conducted themselves in the continent, cannot be understood in isolation to the cultural utility and symbolism of "place" in the historical processes of political resistance, state failure and recuperation.

From this, we know that what is known about the future of Africa, and how we come to know it, is intrinsically linked to the question of whether the externally framed neo-liberal solutions to the problems affecting the continent will achieve their intended outcomes. Though with nuanced variations in their understanding of what role the European Union, for example, should play in this future—beyond what is and towards what it should be—for African countries, as Adebajo and Whiteman (2012) have argued, the prospect to deconstruct the political framing of peace and development priorities in the continent also hinges on the possibilities of an altruistic theoretical re-imagination about the peoples of Africa. It is self-evident that as a result of the fluid nature of power asymmetry in international and national politics (see Bishai 2004; Waltz 2001), it becomes difficult to gauge progress on human security, development and good governance through the mere theoretical repositioning of the continent within a frontier created for and regulated by western liberal states (see for example Duffield 2001). Moreover, since it is still not possible to totally rely on the idea or prospects of an African solution to Africa's problems, and indeed its other development challenges, the pre-colonial African political institutions and individual sub-cultures (which have long since been rendered unproductive and, therefore, incompetent to challenge the dominant neo-liberal discursive empiricism and epistemologies about Africa's future), it simply means that whatever the tendencies are, the local realities in the postcolonial states should be analyzed in ways that do not distort the established principles of liberalism and its framing of the place of Africa in international politics.

Against this backdrop, the uneasiness that has developed out of the claim of an international responsibility towards peace, security and development in Africa (see Kaplan 2001), suggests that the overarching agenda goes beyond attempts to proffer solutions to the crises affecting the continent. It is about making a case for a discursive truth about a future that is built on an externally conditioned, albeit fragile, political and economic foundations. With this being the case, many scholars have tried to interpret the reasons behind the external framing of solutions to the problem of political fragility in the continent. To understand the matrix (which goes beyond the margins of an Africanized theoretical foundation) behind the political sensitivities surrounding fragility, van de Walle (2001) contends that within the externally framed internal working of the African economies and the politics of permanent crisis, is the problem of how we have come to understand the epistemological structures within which knowledge about the socio-economic and political future of the continent is produced. What is the nature of these structures that makes knowledge production and the interpretative dispositions that they promote possible? What are the modalities of the dominant and dominating perspectives? And, what is the role of theories in defining Africa's postcolonial position in the world, and its relationships with the international community (of states, multilateral organizations and the international financial/development institutions)? What is the nature of the involvement of the people of Africa in the articulation of the future of their continent?

Through a somewhat controversial theoretical narrative, which also draws on his experiences of the war in his native country Sierra Leone, Zubairu Wai (2012a) contends that as a result of the western empiricist ways in which the knowledge about the future of Africa (and the discursive representation of the local realities in individual African countries) have been framed, is a pointer that the continent's futures have already been discussed, and solutions reached, even before the present trends of both political and economic fragility emerges. He argues that the "will to the truth" about Africa's past, present and future is largely determined by the inter-subjectivities surrounding the possibilities of western neo-liberal solutions for African's problems. Citing the works of other Sierra Leonean scholars such as Ibrahim Abdullah, Ismael Rashid, and Lansana Gberie, who had written extensively on the conflict in Sierra Leone, Wai contends that their inability to critique the dominant existing research that leans towards the categorization of African conflicts as contests between "savages," as well as their failure to discuss the ways how the interventionist liberal peace processes of the west have created the structures for fragility to thrive in the continent, exposes the theoretical powerlessness of most Africanist scholars to re-write the postcolonial political histories of the continent (Wai 2012a).

Central to his analysis is the attempt to make a case for how the theoretical and methodological formulations of knowledge, in its truer post-structuralist interpretations, have created entrenched neo-liberal thought processes over the objective truth about Africa's future. He sees the conditions under which knowledge about Africa and its futures is produced (i.e. *what people know*, and the *processes involved in knowing what they already know*, or *are interested in knowing about Africa*) as theoretically immersed, and practically bound to the epistemological regions of possibilities allowed by the western economic, socio-cultural and political discourses (see also Mudimbe 2009). To this, Wai concludes that the so-called differences between western scholarship and what is Africanist in character is in fact a restatement of the same thing (Wai 2012a: 126).

A critical reading of Wai's lucid analysis reveals how, in an attempt to counter western theoretical empiricism, Africanist scholars have ended up viewing and understanding the future of the continent as a victim of the elaborate neo-colonial political and cultural agenda of the core capitalist states of the free societies in the west. Thus, inasmuch as there is an inclination to break-free from the dominant praxes and power structures, it is apparent that the theoretical nuances surrounding insurgent wars, governance and peacebuilding will remain trapped under the sagas of the postcolonial neo-liberal historical narratives that have made it nearly impossible for the people, for whom and by whom these ideas are produced, to find a space for the generation of a deconstructive discourse about the problems affecting their continent (Wai 2012a; see also Wai 2012b).

In an attempt to show that there are boundaries when one attempts to rewrite Africa, the doyen of Africanist literary thought, Valentin Y. Mudimbe (1988, 1994, 2013), writes that even if Africa changes for the better, and with it a new crop of scholars who are able to reconfigure a new Africa emerge, they will still be faced with the problem of application. Drawing on the intertextuality of the colonial African foundations (including the foundational western thoughts around modernism and westernization), and the postcolonial discursive representation of Africa, Mudimbe (2009) also questions the relevance of knowledge about Africa's postcolonial future. However, not all will accept his shrewdness about the true nature of the politics surrounding the order of knowledge about Africa, as many would criticize him for being opaque and very difficult to understand. No matter the criticism, these renowned Africanist scholars have helped us to understand how, in an attempt to explain Africa's futures, there has been a deliberate alteration of the epistemological foundations of the emergent idea of an African solution to Africa's problems. The spatial weight that western political narratives have over African philosophical discourses—on what the future holds for the continent—can be said to have made it very difficult for these African scholars to find a space for their theoretical positioning of conflicts and peacebuilding within the generalist ideas of what should or should not be included in the framing of South-South international relationships.

Despite the fact that some of these scholars are limited by their own bold intentions, the way in which they expressively present their frustrations has given credence to the conclusions of Franz Fanon whom, drawing from the European humanists and classical Marxist scholars such as Karl Marx himself, and Georg Wilhelm Friedrich Hegel, he had, in most of his writings, contended that Africa will, in practical political terms, remain the *Wretched of the Earth* (Fanon 1963). He, like his contemporaries such as Andre Gunder Frank, who had sought to understand the processes of underdevelopment in Latin America, understood the difficulty of finding a pure space from which he could have proposed an epistemological idea of a regenerated continent. This is the central theme in his seminal work, *Black Skin, White Mask* (Fanon 1952). Here Fanon argued that scholarship about the local realities of the postcolonial state can only break free from empiricist servitude if efforts are made to understand the continent beyond the boundaries of western empiricism, and to find alternative spaces whereby a "new" Africa can be theorized. However, he was unable to show how, by imagining a future for Africa that is free from wars, and totally committed to peace and security, the people, whose histories have been revealed were held captive by both the colonial and postcolonial forms of government, can be liberated. To this, no matter what is said about the future of the continent, it is hard to understand the past and present, or even predict the future, outside of the vestiges and regions of neo-liberalism, westernization and western modernity, which are the blueprints for the universalization of neo-liberal political thoughts, economic policies and cultural practices (see Fukuyama 1992), and trust among states and non-state actors in postcolonial Africa, and between Africa and the wider world (Booth and Wheeler 2008; Keating and Ruzicka 2014; Herz 2003).

The Role of Research and Practice in Creating the Way Forward for Africa

From the aforementioned analysis of what the future of Africa is or supposed to be, one can see that there is a real challenge in trying to create a space for a generation of new perspectives about the present realities and the future of Africa. Therefore, if delinking from western empiricism is a possibility, taking into consideration the asymmetrical knowledge differentials, scholarship about the importance of Africa (irrespective of the failure of state building and the promise of state failure, within the broader discursive reinterpretation of the security-development nexus in international economic and political relations) will still be confronted with questions and dilemmas of when and where to start the process of framing the prospective role that research will have in helping develop a new continent. In tandem, what should or should not be included as a way forward?

In drawing a connection between the rhetorical discourses surrounding the textual representation and the normativity of knowledge-framing about the way forward for the continent (and the impact that an Africanist model of governance would have on the people), Blake (2009), argues that the fundamental factor for the levels of political instability and economic fragility that many African countries have experienced reflects a crisis in value-orientations. This crisis, Blake contends,

> is brought about by the displacement of the core African moral principles and their replacement with alien values notably from the West, during the colonial era and unfortunately even after decolonization, resulting in a protracted state of anomie (i.e., *a breakdown emanating from a breakdown of standards due, in part, to the lack of purpose or ideals*) within African normative contexts. (Blake 2009: 9; emphasis added)

For Blake, the best way out is to transform these dysfunctional values (in a postmodern era) into platforms for the reconfiguration of the discourses of self, place and identity. Instead of displacing the *Eurafrique* sentiments on which the neo-liberal agenda for peace is located, Blake used his analyses of knowledge-framing of the continent in archaeology and politics. Using this framework, he explains why it is important to re-conceptualize the postcolonial states of Africa through the cryptic intertextual narratives found in the material, structural and constitutive knowledge about the continent's past. Though it remains a controversial conclusion, his suggestion that this should be the new standpoint of how to reimagine the interpretative solution for the mirage of political and security challenges affecting postcolonial Africa, is nonetheless interesting. Through a series of lucid dialogical analyses of what he refers to as a "geosemiotics interpretation" (or the study of the social meaning of the material placement of discourses and the actions of people in their materialistic-conditioned world) (Blake 2009: 3), of the vertical and horizontal intertextuality of the ancient African texts (mostly of Pharaohnic Egyptian origins), Blake shows how the linguistic structures of intertextuality affects the theoretical interpretation of the available knowledge about the role of research on Africa's past and present challenges, and future possibilities for progress.

However, even if Blake's suggestions of a return to textual normativity (which he believes offers a more pragmatic research-based theoretical approach that takes into account the applied, categorical and etymological possibilities for a re-conceptualization of the place of Africa within the dominant historical and philosophical discourses of peace and change) could achieve the intended impact of pacifying the hostile attitude and behaviors towards an Africanized explanation of the origins and characters of wars, it cannot be used as a compass to chart the way forward for the continent. Whatever the case maybe, without an Africanized way forward, what should be seen as the tenets of governance and peacebuilding for the postcolonial states will remain an illusion for much of the continent.

Of importance to the role of research in framing a sustainable policy practice for progress is the question of whether the intensification of the quest for a liberal peace and development project would also mean the perfection of western political thought processes and economic ideas that do not necessarily reflect the anthropological, cosmological and axiological worldviews of the peoples of Africa, in explaining the way forward for the continent in a globalized world.

It is against this backdrop that we conclude that a hybrid approach to peace, security, governance and development in the continent is the surest means to achieve a future that is based on human security. By hybrid approach, we mean policy directives that neither rely on the framing of the continent's future along the lines of Kaplan's (2001) *Eurocentricism*, nor on alternative thought processes that seek to play the victim only to end up co-opting and/or stage-managing an essentialist criticism of neo-liberalism in the continent. Rather, the adoption of a policy approach that is practically possible, for example policies that proffer solutions that will enable the ordinary masses to transform their marginal spaces into platforms on which they will frame for themselves a progressive continent.

Through this, Zartman (1995) has argued that the possibilities of moving on from the politics of "blame-gaming," towards reinvented nuances in the theorization of the continent, will be enhanced. Besides him, other scholars (see Hill 2005; Mamdani 1996; Desai 2001; Jackson 2000) have called for the reconceptualization of the notions of "self" and "identity" within the broader anthropological and structuralist representations of Africa in the political sciences and international relations' research and praxes. A major associated problem with this suggestion has to do with the question of whether the positioning of Africa's "otherness" within the discourses of self and place would lead to the reinforcement of class differences and their engendered consequences on people's subjectivities and marginalities. It can be observed that in African politics, identity (as an outcome of an aesthetic embodiment of "otherness") is both a tool for the collectivization of competing individual desires for change and progress (or backwardness, thereof) (see Mazrui 1995), and a key instrument in the factorization of an Africanist agenda for peacebuilding and good governance (see Mbembe 2001; Migdal 1988; Mkandawire 2001). Moreover, as Sa'ar (2005; see also Turshen 1998; 2001; Schroven 2006; Ojukutu-Macauley 2013) argues, situating place is no guarantee that it will not reinforce the silencing of marginal groups, including women and children, whose "otherness" is largely understood and interpreted along the constructs that perceive them as the violated.

Beyond the social issues lies the political impact. In that, the lack of a hybrid postcolonial people-centric governance model has predisposed the continent to war. Bad governance has always been a driving force perpetrating war. It is among the causes of war. Of course, this is not to say that bad governance is the only cause of wars.

Throughout this volume, we have shown how social inequalities and fragilities caused by cultural contentions and contradictions are a recipe for conflict and a consistent problem for peacebuilding. In Chapter 7 Agbiboa has provided ample warning to the international community how this would play out if insurgent groups such as Boko Haram are not contained. It is unclear at the time of writing if the March 2015 Nigerian elections which saw President Goodluck Jonathan being replaced by Muhammadu Buhari (whose election promises included defeating Boko Haram), will affect any significant change in the conditions pertaining to the rise of violent extremism in this country. In Chapter 8 however, Bah's analysis explicitly argued that the Guinean state was able to avoid conflict and civil war to the extent of many other countries, such as the DRC, and the encroaching "bad neighborhood" effect through its internal strengths to mitigate the security threats and write its own future narrative. In Chapter 13 Mkhize demonstrated how the DRC failed to avoid this same effect and continues to endure conflict, despite a plethora of peace agreements and international initiatives. There clearly is no one-size-fits-all approach to building peace. In Chapter 9 above, Munro and van der Horst provided an account of the potential for effective peacebuilding in Sierra Leone for example, based on the acknowledgement and compromise required between formal sector and informal sector reforms and developments, with a focus on youth employment as an obvious precursor for stability. In Chapter 10, Nyiayaana's insightful account of the arming of vigilante groups in local communities in the Niger Delta provides some account of the quest for African solutions to find peace, but through its very conception, these vigilantes have only contributed to the spread of small arms in the region, and highlighted the policy gaps which have prevent the sustainability of any attempts at peacekeeping. Furthermore, as Orakzai in Chapter 11 has argued, no amount of external intervention will bring an end to civil conflict, in this case in Libya, without due attention to localized and regional understandings of reconciliation, peace-building and reconstruction. In the case of the attempts at Disarmament, Demobilization, and Reintegration (DDR), Duriesmith has in Chapter 12 in this volume provided a pertinent account of the gendered dimensions of such programs in the case of South Sudan, and argued that they were not successful because the traditional male elites, or "African Big Men" of the leading political parties, were not adequately challenged, and their masculinized authority enabled the rise of warlordism and thus the continuation of violence, rather than the establishment of peace.

This volume has not trivialized the commonly understood importance of the geo-political framing of a neo-liberal path to the resolution of African conflicts. After all, the attempts by pan-Africanist scholars to counter the neo-colonial narratives, as we established above, had only ended up reinforcing the will to frame a non-liberal model of governance, through which many wars have been fought and many peace processes have failed, and most efforts to use the third narrative (of "self" and "place") as alternatives for the development of a people-centric governance trajectory, have only led to the entrenchment of inescapable uncertainties.

That notwithstanding, within the African Frontiers there have always been intersubjective claims of an epistemological and etymological obligation to talk for the vulnerable populations of Africa. Unfortunately, there have also been instances where researchers tend to forget that their research subjects, the vulnerable people, depended on them to make their opinions heard. But as a result of the emergence of a nuanced power-induced clash of competing theories, these people have been objectified for the sake of a knowledge that celebrates the competing perspectives of say, feminism, liberalism, structuralism, postcolonialism, and Marxist empiricism, among others. Within these competing perspectives, there is seldom a space for other scholars, especially those with neutral narratives, whose intentions are neither to compromise nor accept, as sacrosanct, the existing competing theoretical perspectives. Scholars of the main sub-fields of the social sciences such as economics, political science, gender and feminist studies, and international relations, due to self-imposed methodological limitations, would always have to find a position between the main competing standpoints. The political theorization of Africa's place in the global system is one area where there seems to be no room for neutrality.

As such, what we have succeeded in doing in this volume has been to present the etymological problems of insurgencies, governance and peacebuilding. Through their analyses of the formulation and application of the incidences of wars and peacebuilding on the people, the contributing authors have been able to use present anthropocentric perspectives on the challenges posed by armed insurgencies, violence and fragility, and the prospects for peace and good governance.

References

Adebajo, A. and Whiteman, K. (eds) (2012). *The EU and Africa: From Eurafrique to Afro-Europa*. New York: Columbia University Press.

Berdal, M. and Malone, D.M. (eds) (2000). *Greed and Grievance: Economic Agendas in Civil Wars*. Boulder and London: Lynne Rienner Publishers.

Bishai, L. (2004). Liberal Empire. *Journal of International Relations and Development*, 7(2): 48–72.

Blake, C. (2009). *The African Origins of Rhetoric*. New York: Routledge.

Booth, K. and Wheeler, N.J. (2008). *The Security Dilemma: Fear, Cooperation and Trust in World Politics*. New York: Palgrave Macmillan.

Desai, G. (2001). *Subject to Colonialism: African Self-Fashioning and the Colonial Library*. Durham, NC: Duke University Press.

Dolek, C. (2008). The Myth of "Failed State" in Africa: A Question on Atomistic Social Ontology? *Journal of Turkish Weekly*, April 29, http://www.turkishweekly.net/op.-ed/2360/the-myth-of-failed-state-8217-in-africa-a-question-on-atomistic-social-ontology.html.

Duffield, M. (2001). *Global Governance and New Wars: The Merging of Security and Development*. London: Zed Books.

Englebert, P. (2000). *State Legitimacy and Development in Africa*. Boulder, CO: Lynne Rienner.

Fanon, F. (1952). *Black Skin White Mask*. New York: Grove Press.

Fanon, F. (1963). *The Wretched of the Earth*. New York: Grove Press.

Fukuyama, F. (1992). *The End of History and the Last Man*. New York: Free Press, Simon and Schuster.

Goldsmith, A.A. (2000). Sizing up the African State. *The Journal of Modern African Studies*, 38(1): 1–20.

Herz, J. (2003). The Security Dilemma in International Relations: Background and Present Problems. *International Relation*, 17(4): 411–16.

Hill, J. (2005). Beyond the Other? A Postcolonial Critique of the Failed State Thesis. *African Identities*, 3(2): 139–54.

Jackson, R.H. (2000). *The Global Covenant: Human Conduct in a World of States*. Oxford: Oxford University Press.

Kaplan, R. (2001). *The Coming Anarchy: Shattering the Dreams of the Post Cold War*. New York: Random House.

Keating, V.C. and Ruzicka, J. (2014). Trusting Relationships in International Politics: No Need to Hedge. *Review of International Studies*, 40(4): 753–70.

Mamdani, M. (1996). *Citizen and Subject: Contemporary Africa and the Legacy of Late Colonialism*. Princeton, NJ: Princeton University Press.

Mazrui, A. (1995). Blood of Experience: The Failed State and Political Collapse in Africa. *World Policy Journal*, 12(1): 28–34.

Mbembe, A. (2001). *On the Postcolony*. Berkeley: University of California Press.

Migdal, J.S. (1988). *Strong States and Weak States: State-Society Relations and State Capabilities in the Third World*. Princeton, NJ: Princeton University Press.

Mkandawire, T. (2001). Thinking About Developmental States in Africa. *Cambridge Journal of Economics*, 25(3): 289–313.

Mudimbe V.Y. (2013). *On African Fault Lines: Meditations on Alterity Politics*. South Africa: University of Kwa-Zulu Natal Press.

Mudimbe, V.Y. (1988). *The Invention of Africa: Gnosis, Philosophy, and the Order of Knowledge*. Bloomington:Indiana University Press; London: James Currey.

Mudimbe, V.Y. (1994). *The Idea of Africa*, Bloomington, Indiana University Press.

Mudimbe, V.Y. (2009). About a Will to Truth: A Meditation on Terror. In P. Nkashama Ngandu (ed.), *Itinéraires et trajectoires: mélanges offerts à Clémentine Faïk-Nzuji-Madiya*. Paris: L'Harmattan, 227–36.

Ojukutu-Macauley, S. (2013). Clapping With One Hand: The Search for a Gendered "Province of Freedom" in the Historiography of Sierra Leone. In S. Ojukutu-Macauley and I. Rashid (eds), *Paradoxes of History and Memory in Post-Colonial Sierra Leone*. Lanham: Lexington Books, 37–58.

Okunoye, O. (2010). Half a Century of Reading Chinua Achebe's Things Fall Apart. *English Studies*, 91(1): 42–57.

Sa'ar, A. (2005). Postcolonial Feminism, the Politics of Identification, and the Liberal Bargain. *Gender and Society*, 19(5): 680–700.

Schroven, A. (2006). *Women after War: Gender Mainstreaming and the Social Construction of Identity in Contemporary Sierra Leone*. Berlin, Germany: Lit Verlag/Spektrum 94.

Smith, R. (2006). *The Utility of Force: The Art of War in the Modern World*. Harmondsworth: Penguin.

Turshen, M. (1998). Women's War Stories. In M. Turshen and C. Twagiramariya (eds), *What Women Do In Wartime: Gender And Conflict in Africa*. London: Zed Books, 1–26.

Turshen, M. (2001). Engendering Relations of State to Society in the Aftermath. In S. Meintjes, A. Pillay, and M. Turshen (eds), *The Aftermath: Women in Post-conflict Transformation*. London: Zed Books, 78–98.

van de Walle, Nicolas (2001) *African Economies and the Politics of Permanent Crisis, 1979–1999*, Cambridge: Cambridge University Press.

Wai, Z. (2012a). *Epistemologies of African Conflicts: Violence, Evolutionism and the War in Sierra Leone*. London: Palgrave Macmillan.

Wai, Z. (2012b). Neo-patrimonialism and the Discourse of State Failure in Africa. *Review of African Political Economy*, 39(131): 27–43.

Waltz, K.N. (2001). *Man, the State, and War: A Theoretical Analysis*. New York: Columbia University Press.

Zartman, I.W. (1995). Introduction: Posing the Question of State Collapse. In W. Zartman (ed.), *Collapsed States: The Disintegration and Restoration of Legitimate Authority*. Boulder, CO: Lynne Rienner, 1–14.

Index